THE ENCYCLOPEDIA OF UNITED STATES
SILVER & GOLD COMMEMORATIVE COINS
1892–1954

ANTHONY SWIATEK AND WALTER BREEN

F.C.I. PRESS, INC./
ARCO PUBLISHING, INC.
NEW YORK

Second Printing, 1981

Published by Arco Publishing, Inc.
219 Park Avenue South, New York, NY 10003

Copyright © 1981 by FCI Press, Inc.

Library of Congress Cataloging in Publication Data

Swiatek, Anthony.
  Encyclopedia of U.S. silver & gold commemorative
    coins, 1892–1954.
  Bibliography: p. 355
  Includes index.
  1. Commemorative coins—United States—Dictionaries.
I. Breen, Walter H., joint author. II. Title.
CJ1839.S9   737.4973   80-14074
ISBN 0-668-04765-8 (Cloth Edition)

Printed in the United States of America

DEDICATION

This book is dedicated to Gloria Rubio Swiatek and Marion Zimmer Bradley Breen for their patience, understanding and assistance in its preparation.

We also dedicate it to the betterment of knowledge about United States commemorative coinage.

CONTENTS

FOREWORD

The inspiration for this book was Anthony Swiatek's *Coin World* articles on commemorative half dollars, his exhibits of these coins with original holders at major conventions, and the great storehouse of knowledge that is Walter Breen's. For some years, commemorative series have been in the doldrums. Even the Bicentennial promotions and the re-publication of Slabaugh's excellent monograph couldn't rescue them. It occurred to us that the Swiatek serial could be greatly improved by tying in the original history of these coins—an amusing and often scandalous tale—with the current public interest in nostalgic American collectibles of all kinds. Since nothing has ever been published in detail about the series outside of the magazines aimed at coin collectors (and so far as we know nothing has ever been published about the original holders even there), this book is an altogether new venture. The research, editing, and love for numismatic knowledge is displayed here in the multifold genius of Walter Breen, and the ability of Anthony Swiatek to spread the ''word'' about these beautiful coins.

We've found that there is a great deal more to collecting commemoratives than anyone had ever previously suspected. So, far from being a dead series, these are just a beginning, and collecting them is a whole new game. Here, then is what we've found out about the game, its origins, its history, its rules, objects and makers. Your coin shops and coin conventions have the counters. Have fun!

ACKNOWLEDGMENTS

Credit is due to the following individuals whose contributions made this work possible.

Stanley Apfelbaum
David T. Alexander
Gerald Bauman
Aubrey E. Bebee
David L. Benway
Bill Brown
Q. David Bowers
Hy Brown
Catherine E. Bullowa
Frances D. Campbell, Jr.
Tom DeLorey
Ed Fleischmann
Joe Flynn, Jr.
Harry Forman
Les Fox
William Gay
Ron Gillio
Henry Grunthal
Gene Hessler
John Hunter
Arthur M. Kagin
Donald Kagin
John Kamin
Sol Kaplan
Abe Kosoff
Julian Leidman

Joe R. Long
Lester Merkin
James L. Miller
Joe Muraca
Paul Nuggett
John Pasciuti
William A. Pettit
Joel Rettew
Maurice Rosen
Gloria D. Rubio
James F. Ruddy
Margo Russell
Dr. Harold K. Skramstad, Jr.
Benjamin Stack
Harvey G. Stack
Norman Stack
Dr. Charles R. Stearns
Joseph F. Swiatek
Herbert Tobias
Douglas Weaver
Harold Whiteneck
Charles Wormser
Joseph B. Zywicki

Credit is also due the following institutions, societies and publications for data and service: The American Numismatic Association; the A.N.A. Certification Service; the American Numismatic Society; the Chicago Historical Society; the Field Museum of Natural History; *Coin World;* the F.C.I. Advisory; and The Institute of Numismatic and Philatelic Studies.

INTRODUCTION TO THE COMMEMORATIVE CONCEPT

The commemorative concept, the practice of making coin devices alluding to some locality, event, or important personage (not limited to the ruler who ordered the issue of the coin), is nearly as old as coinage itself. Allusions of this kind are virtually world-wide and fall into a number of easily recognized classes. In the early centuries of coinage, commemorative issues were not always clearly distinguished from any other kind of coinage, whereas in more recent epochs there has been an increasing effort to segregate commemoratives from the ordinary workaday coins. Commemorative issues of the United States acquire a new perspective when studied in this larger context. In what follows we propose to analyze these trends and offer some hypotheses about their purposes and consequences.

Among the very earliest devices found on archaic Greek coins are some identified as city badges. Some of these allude to local religious cults, others to local industry or pastimes, still others to the name of the city-state issuing the coins. Remarkably, modern commemoratives still bear similar devices.

On tetradrachms of Athens we find not only the head of the patron goddess Athena after whom the city was named, but the owl, her sacred bird, and hence the coins came to be known as "owls." On electrum staters of Ephesus is a grazing stag, alluding to Diana "of the Ephesians," the Huntress, to whom the beast was sacred. Similarly, coins of the island of Rhodes (sacred to Apollo Helios) portrayed this god. One could argue that the very effigy of Ms. Liberty formerly found on United States coins perpetuated this tradition; nor is it a good refutation to say that nobody worships any such goddess, for even in Athens the goddess Athena was portrayed long after the intelligentsia had become skeptical. Even such scandalous devices as the ithyphallic satyr carrying off

a nymph on staters of Thasos in Thrace reflect local religious observance, here that of Dionysos.

The anchor on Apollonian coins clearly alluded to that seaport's primary industry, even as did the grapevine on those of Maroneia (then famous for its wines), or the ship's prow on those of Samos, then the chief maritime port in the Aegean Sea.

Sometimes a device's meaning is less clear, as on the Aeginetic coins depicting a sea-turtle. We don't know if the turtle was sacred to the local god (perhaps Poseidon?), a primary foodstuff or an export delicacy, but we can be absolutely sure that at the time of issue, the people who spent the coins must have known why this device marked them. Nor is it clear if the bullfight depicted on coins of Larissa and other nearby areas in Thessaly was religious as in Crete, or merely their local counterpart of the Olympic Games—much as when the Norse coins depicted skiers. (The bullfight in question consisted of a youth subduing a bull by grasping its horns and was nothing like today's barbaric Spanish ritual.)

The city-badge notion is echoed in the United States as late as 1936 when the village of Hudson, New York, had its own quaint city seal placed on a commemorative half dollar, complete with King Neptune riding backwards on a spouting whale—odd for a town over 80 miles from the ocean as the 747 flies.

Canting or punning devices are numerous, most often as reminders of the name of the issuing city. Ancient examples include, among many others, the seal (phoca) for Phocaea, the celery leaf (selinos) for the city of Selinos, the lion-headed waterspout (leontis) for Leontini, or the rose (rhodos) for the island of Rhodes—oddly echoed in the rose halfpence of Southern Rhodesia, itself named for Cecil Rhodes. This concept is repeated on modern commemorative coins. Two of the most famous American instances are the half moon representing Henry Hudson's flagship of the same name on the Hudson half dollar, and the cow's head (*cabeza de vaca*) referring to explorer Alvar Núñez Cabeza de Vaca on the Spanish Trail half dollar.

Battles were events frequently commemorated, then as now. After King Gelon of Syracuse defeated the Carthaginians at Himera, in B.C. 480, many Syracusan coins commemorated the victory by showing the Carthaginian lion (a city badge found on many coins of Carthage) beneath the horses' feet in the victory chariot. Similarly, the commemorative half dollars for the Battle of Antietam show the bridge at the battle site—here, though, the Antietam coins were issued not to celebrate the victory itself but to raise funds for a local exposition honoring its 75th anniversary. More famous instances, perhaps, are the Roman coins of Vespasian and Titus with IVDAEA CAPTA (Judea captured) commemorating the fall of Jerusalem, in 70 A.D. (or C.E. if you prefer); but then, the Romans were given to commemorating almost anything on their coins from assassinations (e.g. on Brutus's EID MAR or Ides of March denarii) to religious observances, and the coins themselves served as imperial propaganda.

However, not even the sports-loving Americans ever created a commemorative coin celebrating athletic victories, whereas one of Euainetos's finest chariot dies (on a Syracusan dekadrachm) does exactly that even as (on a much lower level) do Finnish and Japanese coins commemorating the modern Olympic Games.

In much the same way for almost every modern class of commemorative coin issued anywhere in the world there are ancient, medieval, Renaissance and later parallels by the hundreds, many very famous.

This process goes far enough that in many instances the distinction between commemoratives intended for some kind of special distribution, and those intended as normal circulating currency, either has become obscure, or was deliberately blurred at the time of issue. Instances of either type are numerous. Charlemagne had coins struck to celebrate his coronation as Holy Roman Emperor on Christmas Day, A.D. 800: the obverse portrays him in the Roman imperial style with a temple and XPIC-TIANA RELIGIO (Christian Religion) on the reverse. The numerous Byzantine gold pieces struck to celebrate the award of the title of "Caesar" to this or that imperial son may be viewed in much the same light. More recent examples are the special crowns issued for the coronation of Elizabeth II. More uncertain now, perhaps, are such items as the gold nobles of Edward III, on which the device of the king standing on shipboard supposedly refers to the Battle of Sluys, or the series of ducats of Johann Georg of Upper Saxony (1611–56) portraying on the reverse his ancestor Friedrich III, Martin Luther's patron. Sometimes only a single word added to coinage of regular design places it into commemorative class: here the most famous instances are the silver coins of Queen Anne with the word VIGO below her bust, which were made from precious metal captured from Spanish ships at the battle of Vigo Bay (1702), or the 1746 British coins with LIMA, struck from the bullion Anson brought back from his round-the-world expedition. In this exact category, too, are the American quarter eagles of 1848 with the word CAL., designating those struck from the first shipment of gold from California to reach the mint, ten months after James Marshall had discovered it at Sutter's Mill. This is (arguably) America's first commemorative coin.

One could similarly argue that certain portraits on coins are of commemorative character: notably, the "Jubilee" effigy on Queen Victoria's coins (1887–92), especially as this new portrait was specially commissioned for the celebration. American parallels are familiar enough: the Lincoln cent of 1909 and the Washington quarter of 1932 for a centennial and a bicentennial respectively, though neither one mentions the fact. More recently one could argue that the practice of placing the heads of lately deceased presidents on coins commemorates their deaths: the Roosevelt dime began it in 1946 (though there were abortive attempts to portray Lincoln in 1866 on the 5¢ piece), with the Kennedy half dollar and Eisenhower dollar continuing the trend. In all these commemorative portrayals the distinction between normal and commemorative coinage was deliberately blurred (to the advantage of the former), as the designs were continued in later years; and the same remark, on a briefer basis, has to be made for the U.S. bicentennial coinage reverses.

Actually, centennials and their multiples are frequent occasions worldwide for commemorative coins, not merely in the United States. Among the most famous examples of these are the Brazilian silver coins made for the 400th anniversary of the discovery of that territory, and the Icelandic 1930 set honoring the millennium of the Althing or statewide parliament.

Even before the recent proliferation of collectors, a brief survey of the known types of world commemoratives demonstrates not that other countries have been extravagant or even silly in the number or nature of commemorative designs, but instead that the United States has been singularly timorous and niggardly—and unimaginative—in its own issues. The ostensible reason alleged here for this fact has been fear of counterfeiting, which is absurd on the face of it: counterfeiters have, over the last 3,000 years, tended to favor designs so familiar as to be passed without special notice, rather than special designs so unfamiliar that everyone looks twice before accepting them as currency. (We are aware of numismatic counterfeits beginning with the Paduans of Renaissance Italy and proceeding through the Beckers to yesterday's Russian and today's Milanese, Lebanese, and other Middle Eastern frauds aimed at coin collectors; but that is another issue altogether.) The actual motive on the part of the Bureau of the Mint is quite different from the counterfeiting rationalization and even more irrelevant to the present day.

Though commemoratives in previous centuries tended by and large to be part of the normal coinage system, that was in many instances because the coins consisted of precious metal matching in weight and size and fineness one or another of the regular denominations (the very name commemorative half dollar reflects this fact). With the gradual proliferation of coin collectors worldwide, the trend has been to make commemoratives NCLTs (non-circulating legal tender coins with fixed nominal values at which they could theoretically circulate, but in practice do not), and aim them specifically at collectors. Some countries have become notorious for this practice which is parallel to that in what used to be known as "postage stamp countries." Because of certain abuses, the standard reference books have made a practice of relegating such NCLT issues to an appendix, as a kind of numismatic ghetto.

This practice is, to put it in the most charitable terms, irrational and short-sighted. Proof coins in the regular British designs, dating back to the Restoration of Charles II, were NCLTs in the strict sense. Prototypes and samples of proposed design (patterns and experimental pieces) were borderline cases; earlier ones could have circulated because of their weight and fineness, especially where the designs were either discretionary with the king's advisors or with the local mintmaster, rather than described by statute law. United States proof coins in the regular sets have always been NCLTs, even though here too (as with their British ancestors) occasional specimens slipped into the circulation contrary to the intent of makers or original buyers.

There has long been a feeling—rarely articulated—that if this or that person, event, or occasion deserves the ennoblement of portrayal on a commemorative coin, why not these others too? "The bust outlasts the throne;/ The coin, Tiberius." In other countries this has been less often a problem than in the United States, where each commemorative issue has required an Act of Congress, and has therefore been subject to a peculiar kind of competitive scrutiny based less on national interest than on compromise among competing local interests. During 1934–36, when President Franklin D. Roosevelt and the House Banking and Currency Committee were more tolerant of commemorative issues than ever before or since, almost every state and many cities and villages had their congressmen pushing commemorative bills into the committee hoppers, where compromises at times decided which bills emerged for debate. If this was the case, this process would insure that a few bills would pass or fail independent of any merit they might have, which possibly explains the inclusion in the United States' commemorative roster of such choices as the Huguenot-Walloon (which was unconstitutional because of its sectarian character), the Pioneer Memorial statue in Elgin, Illinois, the Village of Hudson, New York, or the fictitious "Cincinnati Musical Center" (unknown then or later to any of the Friends of Music groups supporting the local symphony and choral societies). It also possibly explains the omission of equally important centenaries and sesquicentennials such as those of the Continental Congress, the Articles of Confederation, the Bill of Rights, or the end of the Civil War—let alone any number of statehood centennials that didn't make it because of growing reaction against marketing abuses attending the issues for Texas, Arkansas, the Oregon Trail and the Boone Bicentennial.

This last remark requires a little explanation. When a commemorative coin is approved by both houses of Congress and becomes law (either by being signed, passed over a veto, or allowed to become law minus a presidential signature), the next step is for the commission sponsoring the local celebration—the same whose pressure on congressional friends had originally induced consideration of the bill—to make recommendations to the Bureau of the Mint for designs. After the designs have been worked out, arrangements have to be made for delivery of the coins by the Mint to the commission. Once in hand, the coins are the property of the commission, which markets them at a figure generally dependent on the quantity authorized to be minted, but always well above face value. The profits accruing to the commission count as fund-raising for the benefit of their local celebration. Usually particular coin dealers have either been chosen by the commissions, or have offered to buy up unsold residues (at lower figures) after the celebration is over.

The above-mentioned abuses (Boone, Arkansas, Oregon and Texas, described in detail in the main text) quickly exhausted FDR's patience, and in 1937 (following the Congressional election), the new members of the House Banking and Currency Committee in charge of such bills became far more critical. As a result, fewer bills emerged from committee, and on August 5, 1939, an act was passed that prohibited further production or issue of commemorative coins authorized prior to March 1, 1939. This bill was clearly aimed at the promoters of those same four abused issues.

For unknown reasons, President Truman decided to override objections to commemorative issues, indicating that he would approve at least the Iowa Statehood and Booker T. Washington issues, which became law as of August 7, 1946. Several other proposals for commemorative coins went to committee, but they did not pass.

However, on September 21, 1951, Congress passed a second act on behalf of S.J. Phillips, the promoter of the Booker T. Washington coins, enabling him to obtain the balance of his authorized coins (and those already made for him but not yet released from the mint's vaults) as the Washington/Carver half dollars.

Due to the aforementioned abuses of 1936–39, it is small wonder that all subsequent attempts to restore commemorative coinage in the United States have met with monolithic opposition. However, we hold out real hope that this state of affairs will change. Let's have the GSA act as exclusive distributor (thus avoiding the kind of abuses which led to the suppression of commemoratives in the past), and limit the subjects of commemorative coins to events of national (not merely local) importance. This procedure would neatly bypass every objection yet made by the authorities against resumption of such coinage, and the only ones to lose by it would be the very ones who have most to gain by a resumption of the freewheeling practices of 1936.

EXPLANATION OF CONTENTS

Choice of an order of presentation of the coins herein pictured and discussed has proved to be an exceptionally complicated and difficult problem; and the more we have learned about the circumstances of issue, the more difficult the compromise has become.

Simple alphabetical order, as adopted by the *Yeoman Guidebook* in recent editions, certainly is conducive to ease of locating any given issue—except that the coins are known by varying popular names rather than by their official titles: "Old Spanish Trail" vs. "Spanish Trail"; "Antietam" vs. "Battle of Antietam"; "Columbian" vs. "World's Columbian"; "San Diego" vs. "California-Pacific International Exposition"; "Rhode Island" vs. "Providence, Rhode Island, Tercentenary." In some instances the official titles have remained all but unknown and the popular names could appear in widely varying places in the alphabet.

Chronological order of appearance, or of authorization, is a logical alternative, with the virtue of illustrating shifts and developments of style, parallel to the history of art in coinage, and even to the history of art in the larger sense, from the Victorian rigidity of Barber and Morgan through the Frasers' bold nationalism and the Art Deco stylization of others to more frankly modern conceptions.

Yet even the phrase "chronological order of appearance" makes for problems in practice. In some instances even the month of release—either of the first piece of an issue or of bulk distribution—has obdurately refused to turn up despite extensive research. In other instances, the coins were released many years after striking (e.g., the 1928 Oregons were not released until 1933!). In still others, the branch mint coins of a 3-piece set were struck in different months from the Philadelphia coins of the same set (e.g., 1937 Boone: Philadelphia coins, January 1937; Denver, June; San Francisco, October), with coins of other issues coming out in the meantime.

And then we have anomalies like the Texas, authorized June 15, 1933, before the Boone or Maryland, but not struck until the late fall of 1934, after the Boone and Maryland issues; the Bennington/Vermont coins, authorized in February 1925, long before the Oregon or Sesquicentennial issues, but not struck until 1927; and the New Rochelle, authorized May 5, 1936, but not issued until April, 1937, and even then dated 1938!

This leaves chronological order of authorization, as dictated by the dates when Acts of Congress describing these issues were signed into law. But even here we run into conflicts with the dates on the coins, such as the above-mentioned New Rochelle. Plus, there are the eight instances where several different issues were authorized on a single day:

May 10, 1920.	Maine; Alabama (both types).
February 14, 1925.	Ft. Vancouver; Cal. Diamond Jubilee.
May 2, 1935.	Hudson; Providence, R.I.
May 5, 1936.	Cleveland; New Rochelle.
May 15, 1936.	Wisconsin; Bridgeport; Delaware.
June 16, 1936.	Elgin; Albany; Gettysburg.
June 26, 1936.	Robinson; York; Bay Bridge.
August 7, 1946.	Iowa; Booker T. Washington.

The Congressional Record specifies in what order these authorization bills were passed, but not necessarily in what order they reached the White House for signing, and certainly not in what order the President signed them into law. Newspaper research may provide answers to some few of these, but certainly not all.

Previous texts using one or another of the various attempts at a chronological order (Raymond (1957), earlier editions of the *Yeoman's Guidebook*, Taxay (1966), Slabaugh (1962 and 1976) thus, have been forced to adopt compromises.

Therefore, in this book we are using alphabetical order—though it is not without problems—as well as attempting to ease the student's task by providing cross-indexes not only to date of authorization, but also to dates of coinage and release (where known), and to both official titles and popular names—as many of the latter as we have found in numismatic publications including dealer pricelists.

DATES OF AUTHORIZING ACTS

August 5, 1892	Columbian Exposition
March 3, 1893	Isabella Quarter
March 3, 1899	Lafayette Dollar
June 28, 1902	Louisiana Purchase Dollars (all kinds)
April 13, 1904	Lewis & Clark Dollars (both dates)
January 16, 1915	Pan–Pacific (all denominations)
February 23, 1916	McKinley Dollars (both dates)
June 1, 1918	Illinois
May 10, 1920	Maine; Alabama (both types)
May 12, 1920	Pilgrim (both dates)
March 4, 1921	Missouri (both types)
February 2, 1922	Grant (both halves, both dollars)
January 24, 1923	Monroe Doctrine
February 26, 1923	Huguenot
May 9, 1923	Maryland
March 17, 1924	Stone Mountain
January 14, 1925	Lexington
February 14, 1925	Ft. Vancouver; Cal. Diamond Jubilee
February 24, 1925	Vermont
March 3, 1925	Sesquicentennial (both denominations)
May 17, 1926	Oregon (all dates)
March 7, 1928	Hawaii
June 15, 1933	Texas
May 14, 1934	Arkansas
May 26, 1934	Boone
June 21, 1934	Connecticut
May 2, 1935	Hudson; Providence, R.I.
May 3, 1935	San Diego 1935
June 5, 1935	Old Spanish Trail
March 18, 1936	Columbia, South Carolina
March 31, 1936	Cincinnati Musical Center
April 13, 1936	Long Island
May 5, 1936	Cleveland; New Rochelle
May 6, 1936	San Diego 1936
May 15, 1936	Wisconsin; Bridgeport; Delaware
May 28, 1936	Lynchburg
June 16, 1936	Elgin; Albany; Gettysburg
June 24, 1936	Roanoke
June 26, 1936	Robinson; York County; Bay Bridge
June 24, 1937	Antietam
June 28, 1937	Norfolk
August 7, 1946	Iowa; Booker T. Washington
September 21, 1951	Washington/Carver

RELEASE DATES

Note: Where an exact date is specified, it is normally that of manufacture of the first piece. Bulk strikings for public sale often had begun some months earlier, or continued for some months afterwards.

I. 1892–1924.
(Philadelphia Mint unless noted)

November 19, 1892	Columbian 1892. First 104 proofs, others.
January 3, 1893	Columbian 1893. First piece (a proof).
June 13, 1893	Isabella Quarter. First piece (a proof).
December 14, 1899	Lafayette Dollar. Entire issue on same day.
January ?, 1903	Louisiana Purchase Dollars (both types). Striking period, December 1902–January 1903.
September ?, 1904	Lewis & Clark 1904.
March ?, 1905	Lewis & Clark 1905. Some coined March, others June 1905.
June 29, 1915	Pan-Pacific Half Dollars. First piece. *S mint.*
June 29, 1915	Pan-Pacific Dollars. First piece. *S mint.*
June 29, 1915	Pan-Pacific Quarter Eagles. First piece. *S mint.*
June 29, 1915	Pan-Pacific Fifties. First piece. *S mint.*. Others of all denominations coined at intervals through August.
August ?, 1916	McKinley Dollars. First piece. Others coined in October.
February ?, 1917	McKinley 1917 Dollars. Entire issue.
August ?, 1918	Illinois.
September ?, 1920	Maine. Late summer for entire striking.
October ?, 1920	Pilgrim 1920.
July ?, 1921	Pilgrim 1921.
August ?, 1921	Missouri both types, first pieces. Bulk strikings in July.
October 21, 1921	Alabama 2 × 2.
December ?, 1921	Alabama plain.
April 27?, 1922	Grant Half Dollars, both types. Bulk strikings in March.
April 27?, 1922	Grant Dollars, both types. Bulk strikings in March.
June ?, 1923	Monroe. *S mint.* Bulk strikings May–June.
February ?, 1924	Huguenot. First piece. Bulk strikings February and April.

II. 1925–1935

Date	Philadelphia	Denver	San Francisco
January 21, 1925	Stone Mountain. Bulk strikings through March.		
April 19?, 1925	Lexington		

Date	Philadelphia	Denver	San Francisco
August 1, 1925			Ft. Vancouver. Airfreighted same day to exposition site.
August ?, 1925			Cal. Diamond Jubilee. Before August 26.
July 4, 1926	Sesquicentennial. Both denominations Bulk strikings, May–June.		
September ?, 1926	Oregon		
October–November, 1926			Oregon
January ?, 1927	Vermont		
(June 1928)	(Oregon. Released 1933)		
October ?, 1928	Hawaii Bulk strikings, June.		
July ?, 1933	1928 Oregon!	1933 Oregon	
July ?, 1934	Maryland	1934 Oregon	
October ?, 1934	Boone		
October ?, 1934	Texas Bulk strikings, Oct.–Nov.		
January ?, 1935	1935 Boone plain. Bulk strikings in March.		
April ?, 1935	Connecticut Bulk strikings, April–May.		
May ?, 1935		1935 Boone plain.	1935 Boone plain.
June 28, 1935	Hudson		
August ?, 1935			San Diego
September ?, 1935	Arkansas Bulk strikings in August.		
September ?, 1935	Spanish Trail		
October ?, 1935	Boone small 34.		
November ?, 1935		Boone small 34.	Boone small 34.
November ?, 1935	Texas	Texas	Texas
November ?, 1935		Arkansas	Arkansas

III. 1936

Date	Philadelphia	Denver	San Francisco
January ?	Texas		
January ?	Rhode Island		
February ?		Rhode Island	Rhode Island
May ?	Oregon		Oregon
July ?	Wisconsin		
July ?	Cleveland First bulk strikings (Remainder Feb. 1937)		
August ?	Cincinnati (Coined July)	Cincinnati (Coined July)	Cincinnati (Coined July)
August ?	Long Island		
August ?	York County		
September ?	Columbia, South Carolina	Columbia, South Carolina	Columbia, South Carolina

Date	Philadelphia	Denver	San Francisco
September ?	Bridgeport		
September ?	Lynchburg		
October ?	Elgin		
Oct.–Nov.	Albany		
Nov. 20?	Bay Bridge Other accounts say November 14–17		
? ?	Albany	San Diego	
? ?	Arkansas	Arkansas	Arkansas
? ?	Boone	Boone	Boone
? ?		Texas	Texas

IV. 1937–1939

Date	Philadelphia	Denver	San Francisco
January ?, 1937	1936 Robinson		
January ?, 1937	Roanoke		
January ?, 1937	Boone		
February ?, 1937	Extra Clevelands	Oregon	
March ?, 1937	Delaware		
April ?, 1937	1938 New Rochelle		
April ?, 1937	Texas		
May ?, 1937		Texas	Texas
June ?, 1937	Gettysburg	Boone	
June ?, 1937	Roanoke. Last few days of June only.		
August ?, 1937	Antietam Before Aug. 12		
September ?, 1937	Norfolk		
October ?, 1937			Boone
? ?, 1937	Arkansas	Arkansas	Arkansas
January ?, 1938	Texas	Texas	Texas
? ?, 1938	Arkansas	Arkansas	Arkansas
? ?, 1938	Boone	Boone	Boone
? ?, 1938	Oregon	Oregon	Oregon
? ?, 1939	Arkansas	Arkansas	Arkansas
? ?, 1939	Oregon	Oregon	Oregon

V. 1946–1954

Date	Philadelphia	Denver	San Francisco
November ?, 1946	Iowa		
December ?, 1946	B.T. Washington	B.T. Washington	B.T. Washington
November ?, 1946	B.T. Washington		
December ?, 1947		B.T. Washington	B.T. Washington
May ?, 1948	B.T. Washington	B.T. Washington	B.T. Washington
January ?, 1949	B.T. Washington	B.T. Washington	B.T. Washington
January ?, 1950	B.T. Washington	B.T. Washington	B.T. Washington Bulk strikings February.
January ?, 1951	B.T. Washington	B.T. Washington	B.T. Washington
August 1–6, 1951	Bulk strikings (final)		

Date	Philadelphia	Denver	San Francisco
December ?, 1951	Washington/Carver	Washington/Carver	Washington/Carver
March ?, 1952	Washington/Carver	Washington/Carver	Washington/Carver
December ?, 1952		Washington/Carver	Washington/Carver
January ?, 1953	Washington/Carver	Washington/Carver	Washington/Carver
December ?, 1953			Bulk strikings
January ?, 1954	Washington/Carver	Washington/Carver	Washington/Carver
February ?, 1954	Washington/Carver	Washington/Carver	Washington/Carver
August 1–6, 1954			Bulk strikings

THE ALABAMA CENTENNIAL HALF DOLLARS

Obverse

Reverse

Obverse of the 2 × 2 issue. The reverse is identical to that of the plain variety.

The Corpus Delicti: Alias *Alabama 2 × 2* or *Alabama 2–by–2* and *Alabama plain,* respectively.

Clues: Of the two people portrayed on obverse, the one identified as BIBB is William Wyatt Bibb (1780–1820), Alabama's first governor (1816–20). KILBY is Thomas E. Kilby, governor of Alabama when the coins were minted. The 22 stars flanking these portraits refer to Alabama's being the 22nd state to enter the Union, December 14, 1819. This same message is repeated by the numerals in the cryptic 2 × 2 in right field; the X (though commonly misread as times or by) refers to the red St. Andrew's Cross found on the Alabama state flag. (This cross also appeared in the Union Jack and the Confederate flag.) The date 1921 refers not to the celebration—which was already long over with—but solely to the year of mintage. The 1921 date was added to conform to the Mint Act of 1873 which requires the actual date of striking to appear on all United States coins. On reverse, the 1819–1919 dates are the actual ones of the centennial, and the warlike eagle (with shield and arrows, but no olive branch for peace) is that of the Alabama state seal, which also yielded the motto HERE WE REST (no pun intended about the sleepy Deep South). The initials LGF behind the eagle are those of Laura Gardin Fraser, designer and illustrious sculptor.

Opportunity: The Alabama Centennial Commission, under Mrs. Marie Bankhead Owen, had been sponsoring local events statewide during 1919 and 1920. Eventually these people realized that other celebration commissions had been raising funds by having Congress authorize commemorative coins. They instructed their friendly neighborhood Congressman, Rep. Lilius Rainey (D.-Ala.), to sponsor such a bill; he was successful and that became the Act of May 10, 1920.

Motive: Local pride, mostly. The Committee was a lame duck by the time the commemorative coin project began. Profits, if any, accruing from sales of the coins had to go somewhere relevant; Slabaugh says they were earmarked for "historical and monumental" projects, whatever those might have been.

Suspects: The Alabama Centennial Committee, consisting of Mrs. Marie Bankhead Owen (chair), Dr. Charles Stakely, Capt. William T. Sheehan; Congressman Rainey; Frank Spangler, cartoonist with the Montgomery (Ala.) *Advertiser,* who furnished the sketches approved by the Committee (below); and Laura Gardin Fraser.

Accessories: James Earle Fraser (husband of Laura Gardin Fraser), sculptor and member of the Federal Commission of Fine Arts. (By Executive Order of July 28, 1921, all proposed designs for new coins were to be ruled on by the Commission, though they may be, and in some cases have been, overruled. The Commission had been making recommendations in an advisory capacity since 1915.) Fraser recommended to H.R. Caemmerer, secretary of the Commission, that the Alabama Committee should be informed of the successful Missouri "special marking" and attempt something of the kind for their own coin. A number of the Missouri commemoratives had been marked with a 2*4 and that had resulted in an additional 5,000 sales: the Alabama Committee tried the same thing with their 2 × 2s, and sold 6,000 extra Alabama commemoratives.

Modus Operandi: Originally the coin was to be of quarter dollar denomination, but by an amendment passed April 21, 1920, this was changed to read HALF DOLLAR. After the authorizing act became law on May 10, 1920, the Alabama Centennial Committee solicited and judged proposed designs, rejected them all, and came up with its own impossibly bad concept, represented by Frank Spangler's sketch. On one side were portrayed jugate busts of James Monroe (president at Alabama's admission) and Woodrow Wilson (president at the time of the Centennial), with their names below, date 1920, statutory inscriptions and mottoes around. The other side—which they considered the obverse—was to display the State Capitol on Capitol Hill, complete with flag on dome and with steps leading up from Dexter Avenue in right foreground; * STATE OF ALABAMA * (the word OF atop the dome), CENTENNIAL 1819–1919 below. Mint Director Banker sent these recommendations to Charles Moore, chairman of the Fine Arts Commission, who sent them to James Earle Fraser. Fraser, understandably, objected on the perfectly good grounds that buildings do not make good coins designs (our current cent and 5¢ pieces are dismal testimony to the fact!). From the Commission this objection went successively to Rep. Rainey, Governor Kilby, and Mrs. Owen, who on June 24, 1920, proposed that the building be replaced by the Alabama State Seal design, more or less as it finally was to appear on the coins. For unknown reasons, no action followed; everyone was apparently waiting for the presidential election, because (among other things) that might make a difference as to the notion of portraying Woodrow Wilson.

The 1920 election inflicted Warren G. Harding on the country. From the Alabama point of view, it was unthinkable to put this president on *their* coin since he was a Republican. And so—a year later, on June 29, 1921—Mrs. Owen submitted new proposals for the design, featuring the jugate portraits of Bibb and Kilby rather than any presidents, and asked if bids could be taken for making the models and original dies. Nobody thought to remonstrate that portraying Kilby would be in violation of federal law (the Act of April 7, 1866) forbidding portrayal of any living individual on U.S. coins or currency. The Commission allowed the proposed designs to go through, but ignored the matter of submitting the proposal to bids. James Earle Fraser, as sculptor member of the Fine Arts Commission, assigned the project of making the models to his wife. This was a happy choice, as the overall design is excellent, the portraits successful, the eagle one of the finest ever to appear on a U.S. coin.

Following Fraser's recommendation, the first "silver souvenirs" had the 2 × 2 "special mark," some 6,000 being struck at the Philadelphia Mint during October, 1921. They were first offered for sale at $1 apiece in Birmingham, Alabama, during the morning of October 21, on the occasion of President Harding's visit to that city; later, they were distributed (still at $1 each) by various banks throughout the "Cotton State." Afterwards, the 2 × 2 mark was ground off the original hub, and the new variety (later known as the "Alabama plain") followed, some 64,000 being coined at Philadelphia during December, 1921. These were marketed the same way at $1 apiece for many months to follow. Most of the coins went to the general public; many were kept as pocket pieces, but during the 1926–36 Great Depression, many were spent, so that the vast majority of survivors of both types fall short of mint state.

No original envelopes or holders are known.

Sales dwindled, and eventually the Commission authorized the last remnant of the "plain" variety to be melted, resulting in the following tabular totals:

Authorized:	100,000 maximum (both types)
Coined, 2 × 2:	6,000 + 6 for assay. All sold.
Coined, plain:	64,000 + 38 for assay
Melted, plain:	5,000
Net mintage, plain:	59,000

Blow-up of the coin's flatly struck eagle claws. This was a common occurrence on the plain variety.

Note the visible clash mark in back of Kilby's head.

These figures are correct, though many old time collectors claimed that some 10,008 pieces of the December, 1921, delivery were 2 × 2 coins. That report derives from two delivery figures furnished by the mint: 10,000 (plus 8 for assay), and 54,000 (plus 30 for assay), a total of 64,000; but all were of the "plain" variety.

Collateral Evidence: Unconfirmed rumors persist of a matte proof of the 2 × 2 variety. Normal specimens are weak on eagle's feet as in the illustrations of both varieties as shown on page 3 (it is almost unheard-of to find an uncirculated example with full feet!), so that any matte proof should be considerably sharper in that area as well as on most feathers. Weakness on feet is not to be taken as evidence of wear: note the enlarged illustration.

Some early strikings of the "plain" variety show that the dies clashed, most plainly behind Kilby's head, where the clash marks correspond to parts of the outline of shield. These clashed die coins are very scarce.

THE ALBANY CHARTER HALF DOLLAR

Obverse

Reverse

The Corpus Delicti: Alias *The Albany.*

Clues: There has been dispute as to which side of this coin was intended for obverse. Fortunately, we have the testimony of Gertrude K. Lathrop, the designer, in *The Numismatist* 11/1936:909, who referred to the side with the beaver as obverse. This is an American beaver (*Castor canadensis*), common enough in the Albany area in the 17th century that trapping them for their pelts was the main industry of the settlers; a fact indicated by the beaver's appearance on the city seal. Use of maple keys for punctuation, and a maple branch in the beaver's mouth and paws, alludes to the maple being the New York state tree. Ms. Lathrop intended a symbolic reference to the growth and fertility of the community.

On reverse, Governor Thomas Dongan bids farewell to Robert Livingston and Peter Schuyler (later Albany's first mayor), the latter holding the newly acquired Albany city charter of July 22, 1686. (This charter is in the Manuscript Room of the New York State Library in Albany.) All are dressed in garments of the period and near Governor Dongan's foot are the designer's minute initials, GKL. Behind Dongan is a pine tree, echoed in the twin pine cones used for punctuation. These also were intended as

symbolic of growth and fertility. They also commemorate the plentiful pine trees in the Albany area. Airborne above the three gentlemen is an eagle, with the minute letters LIBERTY, balancing the plaque underfoot with 1936.

Opportunity: Local celebrations in Albany, under the Albany Dongan Charter Committee, 60 State Street; Act of Congress, June 16, 1936.

Motive: Local pride, and presumably also to help finance the celebrations. At a $2 issue price, That Five Finger Word may have been at least a minor element.

Suspects: Gertrude K. Lathrop, of Albany, was the designer and sculptor. She spent time at the Metropolitan Museum of Art, the Smithsonian Institution, the Museum of the City of New York, and the New York Historical Society, researching the costumes, and obtaining access to authentic portraits of Livingston and Schuyler. As no authentic portrait of Governor Dongan is known, she had to rely on contemporaneous descriptions.

Accessories: The Conservation Department of the State of New York, which graciously furnished a live beaver (earlier in this century an endangered species, but increasing in numbers thanks to the Department's efforts) as Ms. Lathrop's life model. The Albany Dongan Charter Committee appears to have suggested the motifs, but allowed her great latitude in developing her designs.

Modus Operandi: After a mild objection by Lee Lawrie, of the Federal Commission of Fine Arts, who feared that the minuscule word LIBERTY would not be legible when plaster models were reduced to half dollar size, Ms. Lathrop took the models to the Philadelphia Mint, where Engraver John R. Sinnock said that this would be no problem. (Ms. Lathrop had been unwilling to enlarge the word LIBERTY as this would have forced her to remove the eagle, to the definite detriment of the composition.) Now that this problem was disposed of, the Commission, on September 9, 1936, enthusiastically approved the models, which went to the Philadelphia Mint for reduction. We do not have the exact dates, but it is clear enough that the dies must have been completed in late September or October, and the 25,000 coins struck probably in October or November, with 13 reserved for assay. The Committee continued selling them for almost seven years, refusing to go below the original issue price. In 1943, after sales had come to a standstill, rather than lower the price, the Committee returned its remaining stock of 7,342 specimens to the Mint for remelting, leaving a low net mintage of 17,658.

Collateral Evidence: No proofs are reported, but several may have been made for John R. Sinnock. One blatantly phony proof recently seen (by A.S.) was not double struck.

The Albany Dongan Charter Committee distributed the coins by mail order in holders large enough to hold five pieces. One of them is illustrated; the verso of the front page has a brief historical sketch of Albany. About 85 of these original holders are now traced.

This low mintage issue is an excellent investment, especially since it is not as available as many believe. In the past, the demand for this coin was never great. It would always appear at coin shows—sometimes in roll quantity. However, with more and more collectors and investors buying up commemorative coins, the existing present day supply is rapidly drying up. There exists a combined hoard of 720 pieces. Even were all these coins dumped, present price levels would probably remain unaffected.

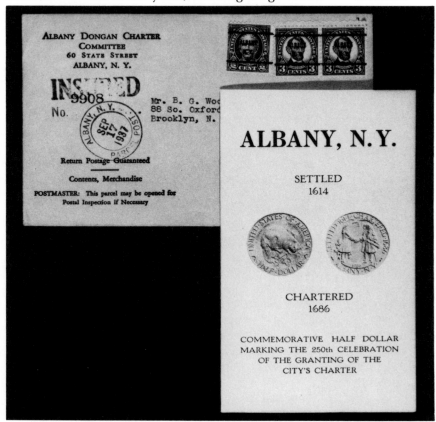

Original mailing envelope and holder used by the Albany Dongan Charter Committee to distribute the Albany Commemorative to its subscribers.

THE BATTLE OF ANTIETAM HALF DOLLAR

Obverse

Reverse

The Corpus Delicti: Alias *The Antietam*.

Clues: Generals George B. McClellan and Robert E. Lee were opposing commanders in the Battle of Antietam, the bloodiest single day in the Civil War, September 17, 1862. Three stars behind Lee represent his rank as General in the Confederate Army; two stars left of McClellan represent his rank as Major General in the Union Army. On reverse, Burnside Bridge was the major focus in the battle. Spanning Antietam Creek, near Sharpsburg, Maryland, this bridge was the key to strategic high ground overlooking Sharpsburg. It only later was named after General Ambrose E. Burnside (the hair into whiskers style known as sideburns had the same origin). Slabaugh (pp. 144–47) gives an account of the battle, as does every history book covering the war between the states, detailing how it ended in a draw though it halted Lee's invasion of the North, and how the smaller Confederate army could afford 2,700 deaths and 9,029 wounded far less than the much larger Union forces could afford their 2,108 corpses and 9,549 wounded. Monogram WMS behind Lee's shoulder is for William Marks Simpson, designer and sculptor, of Baltimore.

Opportunity: The Washington County Historical Society of Hagerstown, Maryland, worked with the United States Antietam Celebration Commission (of 45 E. Washington St., Hagerstown)—appropriately, since Park W.T. Loy was simultaneously chairman of the Historical Society and Secretary of the Commission—to set up a celebration in the area, September 4–17, 1937, known as the National Antietam Commemoration. This was to include a wide variety of what would later be called family entertainment, detailed in the brochure reproduced on pages 10–11. Political pressure exerted by Senator Millard Tydings (D.-Md.) resulted in passage of the Act of June 24, 1937, authorizing a maximum of 50,000 pieces.

Motive: Local pride, and to help finance the celebration. For once, the promoters deliberately tried to exclude speculators, and offered to furnish any quantity at $1.65 each. (Not that it helped: by the time these came out, people had begun turning away from commemoratives.)

Suspects: William Marks Simpson, of Baltimore, sculptor, designer.

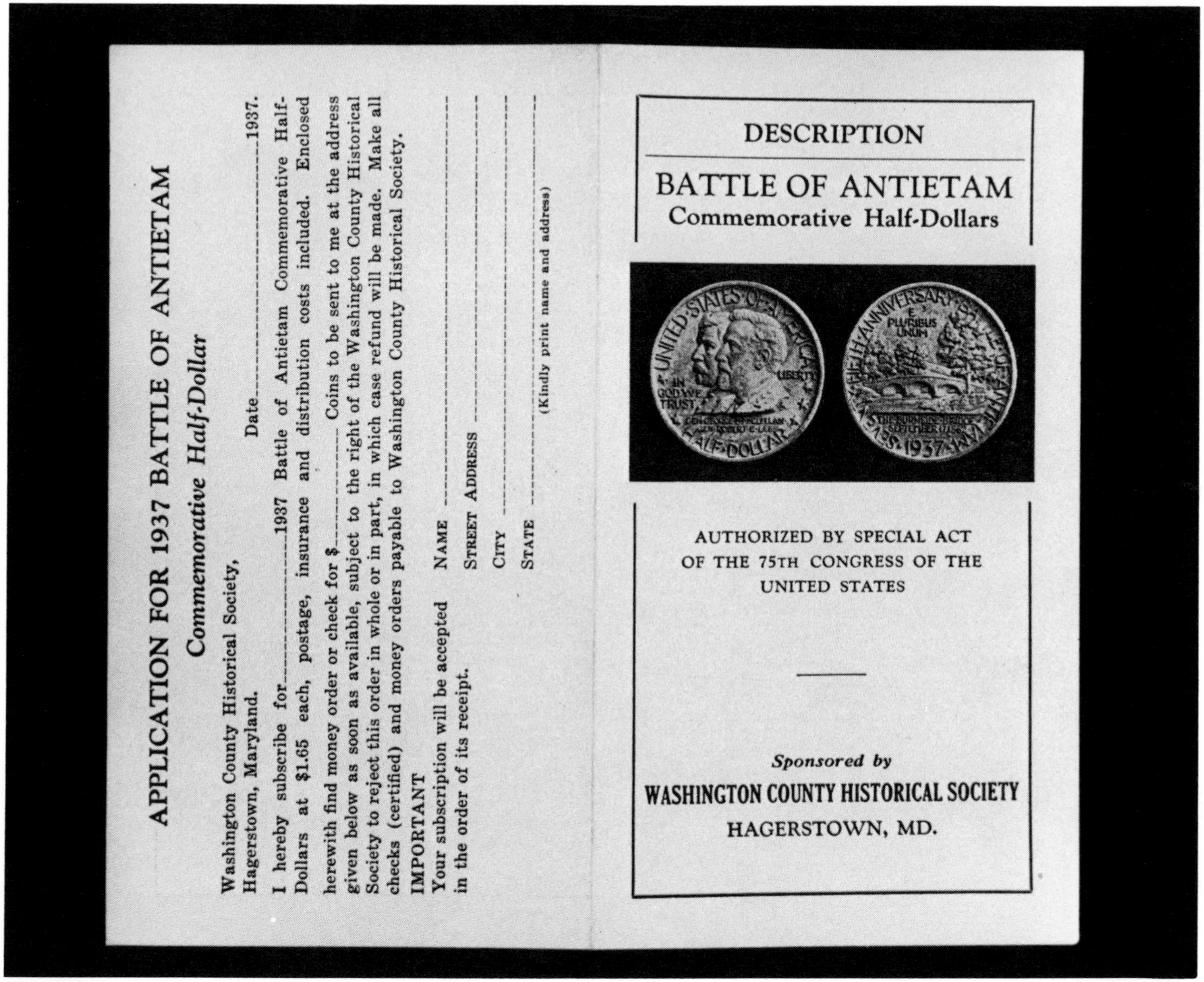

APPLICATION FOR 1937 BATTLE OF ANTIETAM

Commemorative Half-Dollar

Washington County Historical Society,
Hagerstown, Maryland. Date____________________1937.

I hereby subscribe for____________1937 Battle of Antietam Commemorative Half-Dollars at $1.65 each, postage, insurance and distribution costs included. Enclosed herewith find money order or check for $__________ Coins to be sent to me at the address given below as soon as available, subject to the right of the Washington County Historical Society to reject this order in whole or in part, in which case refund will be made. Make all checks (certified) and money orders payable to Washington County Historical Society.

IMPORTANT

Your subscription will be accepted in the order of its receipt.

NAME ______________________________

STREET ADDRESS ______________________________

CITY ______________________________

STATE ______________________________

(Kindly print name and address)

DESCRIPTION

BATTLE OF ANTIETAM
Commemorative Half-Dollars

AUTHORIZED BY SPECIAL ACT OF THE 75TH CONGRESS OF THE UNITED STATES

Sponsored by

WASHINGTON COUNTY HISTORICAL SOCIETY
HAGERSTOWN, MD.

Original application for the Antietam Commemorative Half Dollar, showing the front and back covers.

1937 BATTLE OF ANTIETAM
COMMEMORATIVE HALF-DOLLARS

Sponsored by the Washington County Historical Society

THIS coin was authorized by a Special Act of the 75th Congress of the United States fittingly to commemorate the 75th Anniversary of the Battle of Antietam, fought near Sharpsburg, Maryland, south of Hagerstown, on September 17, 1862 and universally recognized as the bloodiest one day battle of the War between the States.

There between daylight and darkness on that date approximately 25,000 Union and Confederate soldiers fell. On the Confederate side was world-famed General Robert E. Lee and his Army of Northern Virginia; opposing him was General George B. McClellan and his Army of the Potomac. In the last analysis the titanic struggle was one between a great master and his brilliant pupil for General McClellan had studied the science of war at West Point under General Lee.

From the following States came the soldiers that gave Antietam its fadeless glory: Alabama, Arkansas, Connecticut, Delaware, Florida, Georgia, Illinois, Indiana, Kentucky, Louisiana, Maryland, Massachusetts, Michigan, Maine, Mississippi, Minnesota, New Hampshire, New Jersey, New York, North Carolina, Ohio, Pennsylvania, Rhode Island, South Carolina, Tennessee, Texas, Vermont, Virginia, West Virginia and Wisconsin.

After 75 years, the "Lee - McClellan" Antietam Half-Dollar re-unites these two great Commanders. Designed by William Marks Simpson, noted sculptor of Baltimore, Maryland, the obverse side bears the profiles of General Lee and General McClellan—the reverse, the Burnside Bridge for the possession of which hours of bloody struggle ensued.

Because of the appropriateness of this issue the world-wide fame of General Lee and the honored place General McClellan will always hold in our National History it is the objective of the sponsoring agency that these coins shall pass directly into the hands of interested citizens and private collectors thereby avoiding the possibility of speculation.

It is anticipated that the coins will be minted and ready for distribution on or before August 1, 1937, and because of the already evidenced demand it is suggested that you forward your order without delay.

PARK W. T. LOY, Chairman,
Board of Directors
Washington County
Historical Society,

and

Secretary,
United States Antietam
Celebration Commission.

Inside of the application for Antietam Commemorative.

Original circular distributed prior to the exposition commemorating the Hagerstown and Antietam battlefield.

Back of the circular.

Accessories: Unknown, but would include whoever originally portrayed the generals.

Modus Operandi: Simpson completed his models in April 1937, and as Paul Manship (sculptor member of the Federal Commission of Fine Arts) had photographs of them on April 16, the Commission approved them the same day. Though the celebration's sponsors hoped to have the coins on hand on or before August 1, 1937, the Mint did not ship them until more than a week after that, and the first specimen (according to Taxay's *History* . . ., p. 241) went to President Roosevelt on August 12. In all, the legal maximum of 50,000 were coined, plus 28 reserved for assay.

Celebration or no, brochures or no, publicity or no, the coins languished even at $1.65 each, and eventually the Historical Society returned 32,000 as unsold; net mintage, 18,000.

Collateral Evidence: Many survivors, even those in pristine choice mint state, are not well struck up in center of reverse; the area most affected is the central top part of the bridge.

No proofs have been confirmed to exist; specimens (probably matte) have long been rumored to exist, and were probably made for John R. Sinnock.

We reproduce the brochures for the half dollar and for the National Antietam Commemoration; these are exceedingly rare.

This low mintage Antietam issue has to be considered an excellent investment, especially in the gem states. It was formerly considered an easy issue to obtain such, but many of the coins sold then and now as gems are well short of that grade.

THE ARKANSAS CENTENNIAL HALF DOLLARS

Obverse

Reverse

The Corpus Delicti: Alias *The Arkansas.*

Clues: Dates 1836–1936 allude to the centennial of admission of Arkansas to the Union (June 15, 1836). The two watered-down Art Deco heads are more enigmatic. What looks vaguely like either a prizefighter or an Aztec chieftain, though with a feathered headdress, is evidently intended for a Quapaw Indian since this friendly tribe formed the greater part of the population of what became the Territory of Arkansaw. As the female head wears a Phrygian cap, we can assume that it is intended for a 1936 version of Ms. Liberty. There is no clue to the type of plant forming her garland; appropriate leaves could include apple, oak, hickory, sweet gum, or cypress—or, most of all, perhaps, cotton.

Reverse symbolism is extremely complicated, in some ways more so even than on the Texas coins, though not quite so crowded in execution. Behind the eagle is a diamond-shaped symbol derived from the state flag, referring to Arkansas' diamond field (then the only one in the United States) in Pike County. (On Burr's original sketch for the coin, the actual state flag was shown behind the eagle, allegedly referring to federal protection of the

state—but this was an obvious attempt to defuse possible objections to the Confederate symbolism (see below).) On this diamond symbol are 13 stars, which do not refer to the 13 original colonies, though possibly the designer and the Centennial Commission intended that gullible "damyankees" should make such an erroneous assumption. Any local yokel could identify these as the upper half of the complete array of 25 stars in the state flag. (Arkansas was 25th in order of admission.) Within the diamond are four more stars, the three lower ones representing the three flags which had flown over the Territory (Spain, France, and the United States), and more obscurely, also representing Arkansas' position as the third state to be carved out of Louisiana Purchase lands. Above the three is the largest star of all, representing the state's participation in the Confederacy. Its position suggests that the "South Will Rise Again"; a notion common to folklore statewide and throughout the South. In addition, the Rising Sun behind the eagle and state flag device has been taken locally to mean the Rising South. That would automatically suggest that its seven longest rays (above the state flag emblem) mean the seven original seceding states (South

Carolina, Mississippi, Florida, Alabama, Georgia, Louisiana, and Texas), while the six shorter rays flanking the eagle mean the six rebel states which joined later (Virginia, Arkansas, North Carolina, Tennessee, Missouri, Kentucky). In that context, showing only the top 13 stars on the diamond emblem would suggest to locals not the 13 original colonies but the 13 seceding states.

Fantasy? Not in the least. During the Great Depression of 1929–37, this writer (W.B.) was a boy in the South (Arkansas 1934–5, Texas 1935–6, West Virginia 1937–41), and everywhere one heard pro-Confederate sentiment taking such forms as "Those damyankees in New York and Washington messed around with our tax money and the stock market, and now because of them we ain't got grocery money or jobs to earn any. We did better than that under Jeff Davis. All we need now is somebody to start the march on Washington—we'll be marching right there behind him!" And there was always the inevitable "Save your Confederate money, boys, the South will rise again!" Is it unreasonable to assume that this sentiment was known to the Arkansas Centennial Commission and their local-talent artists Edward Everett Burr and Emily Bates? Certainly local people would have interpreted the coin designs this way, and the Commission must have known it. We do know that the reverse design elements had most of the described symbolic meanings, because Burr spelled them out in correspondence with H.P. Caemmerer, of the Federal Commission of Fine Arts (Taxay, p. 146). The only conjectural element, in fact, is the identification of the Rising Sun with the Rising South—and this is more obvious than a lot of what Burr had painstakingly described.

Date below HALF DOLLAR is that of issue of the particular coins; the D or S mintmark is at lower right.

Opportunity: Local statewide celebrations, the most important being in Little Rock, honoring the Centennial. The coins were authorized by the Act of May 14, 1934.

Motive: Fund raising for local celebrations. We suspect also that the 1936 date would be taken as the 75th anniversary of Arkansas joining the Confederacy; naturally, this could not be put into print, though it was certainly known locally.

Suspects: Edward Everett Burr, designer, long a resident of Little Rock. His original sketches are shown in Taxay (p. 144). Emily Bates, also from Arkansas, made the models from Burr's sketches,

but after her first versions were rejected, she remade them following sketches by Lee Lawrie of the Federal Commission of Fine Arts, who finally approved them in the name of the Commission.

Accessories: Lorado Taft, sculptor, in whose studio Emily Bates was then working (in Chicago); Taft was a friend of both Burr and Bates, and most likely (as Taxay suggests) advisor and intermediary between them and the Commission of Fine Arts. Taft may even have given Miss Bates some technical aid in translating Burr's sketches into acceptable relief models. Senator Hattie Wyatt Caraway (D.-Ark.) was elected to fill her late husband's Senate term, served side by side with Senator Joseph T. Robinson, sponsored the authorizing bill, and initiated the correspondence with the Federal Commission of Fine Arts, once her bill became the Act of May 14, 1934.

Modus Operandi: As soon as Ms. Bates's models were approved, they were forwarded to the Medallic Art Company for reduction. Despite the centennial date of 1936, the Centennial Commission wanted to begin offering the coins at once, so the first batch was made in Philadelphia during May 1935 and enthusiastically enough received in Arkansas to be sold out before the end of September. As requests were still being received for the coins, the Commission decided to reorder, and as the authorizing act permitted coinage to be made at the branch mints, this was specified. By now the Commission was operating under the advice of the Texas coin dealer B. Max Mehl, who bought up the entire late batch (3,000 Philadelphia coins, October; 5,500 each from Denver and San Francisco, November 1935). Presumably Mehl got them at a discount, as he continued the original $1 apiece issue price for the Philadelphia coins, though in January 1936 he began offering the 1935 D and S coins at $2.75 and raised the Philadelphia price to $2. (If you already had the 1935 Philadelphia, Mehl would sell you the D and S pair at $5.)

During the actual centennial year of 1936, the Commission retailed the coins at first at $1.50 each, later at $6.75 per set of three mints. Many of the coins went in bulk lots to dealers. At year's end, the Commission offered the retail concession to the highest bidder, and the successful firm was Stack's of New York. Thereafter, the 1936 issue was readily obtainable for a price anywhere except in Arkansas, whose residents had to buy them from "damyankee" coin dealers; the 1936 set quickly acquired the sobriquet of "Orphan Issue."

The 1937 three-piece sets were sold in specially made cases as illustrated below. Stack's reserved 500 sets for distribution in Arkansas, and disposed of the other 5,000 to collectors nationwide, at $8.75 per set. The case is black with gold lettering; the advertising insert is blue.

These same cases were used for the 1938 sets, which went at the same price. When the supply of cases was exhausted, a different type was made up, without marking; this type, about 4″ × 5″, had a paper covering imitating wood grain, light tan in color, with a fake velour bottom inner lining of either black or green, containing the slots for three coins, Philadelphia at bottom, D and S above. This type of case was used for the 1939 sets, which Stack's offered at $10 apiece and which vanished almost immediately owing to the low mintage.

The following tabulation is a convenient summary:

Authorized:	500,000, per Act of May 14, 1934.
Minted, total:	95,300
Returned for re-melting:	9,600
Net mintage, total:	85,700

Beyond doubt, this issue, with the Boone, Oregon and Texas, did more to contribute to the later discredit of commemorative halves than all the rest put together. When Congress passed the Act of August 5, 1939, revoking all previous authority to manufacture commemorative coins under previous acts, the immediate occasion was indignation over the Arkansas 1939 sets, which enriched coin dealers and speculators, and which no longer had any relevance to Arkansas since the centennial celebrations were long over with.

Collateral Evidence: Many of the 1938 and 1939 sets, and a considerable number of the 1937 sets, appear dull. This is possibly partly due to the cases of issue, partly to the physical characteristics of the dies. (We cannot ascribe it to the blanks, as different batches from different sources were used by the three mints.) Some of the 1935 coins are also dull; the 1936 sets appear by and large to be the easiest ones to find in what looks like choice uncirculated. However, many of all these dates, especially from the branch mints, have coins weakly struck in central reverse, as illustrated. (Compare with that shown at the beginning of this section.)

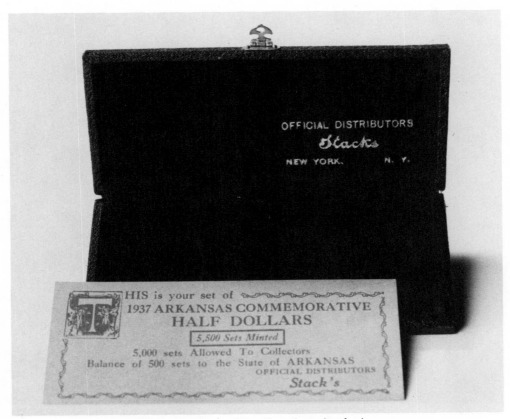

Original case which held set of Philadelphia, Denver, and San Francisco minted coins.

DATE	MINT	COINED	RESERVED FOR ASSAY	MELTED	NET MINTAGE	ISSUE PRICE
1935	(P)	13,000	12	--	13,000	$1.00
1935	D	5,500	5	--	5,500	1.00
1935	S	5,500	6	--	5,500	1.00
1936	(P)	10,000	10	350	9,650	1.50
1936	D	10,000	10	350	9,650	1.50
1936	S	10,000	12	350	9,650	1.50
1937	(P)	5,500	5	--	5,500 ⎫	8.75
1937	D	5,500	5	--	5,500 ⎬	per
1937	S	5,500	6	--	5,500 ⎭	set
1938	(P)	6,000	6	2,850	3,150 ⎫	$8.75
1938	D	6,000	5	2,850	3,150 ⎬	per set
1938	S	6,000	6	2,850	3,150 ⎭	
1939	(P)	2,100	4	--	2,100 ⎫	$10.00
1939	D	2,100	4	--	2,100 ⎬	per set
1939	S	2,100	5	--	2,100 ⎭	

Enlarged photo showing detail of a flatly struck reverse.

Mailing envelope used by the Arkansas Centennial Commission to distribute the 1935 and 1936 Arkansas commemorative half dollars.

Back of mailing envelope.

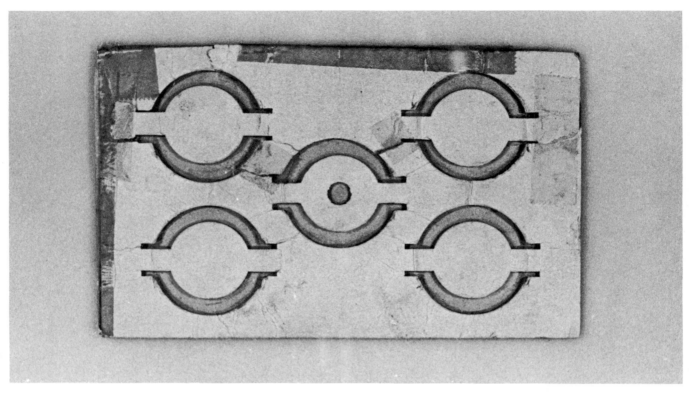

Coin holder used by the Arkansas Centennial Commission to distribute the 1935 and 1936 Arkansas commemorative half dollars.

First day cover with Arkansas 1936 Centennial stamp.

As branch mint coins were rarely allowed to leave the sets, most are in mint state, and the above-mentioned weakness must not be confused with wear. If there is doubt, check for mint luster on the weak areas. Coins with full breast feathers should command a premium.

A single matte proof of 1935 Philadelphia is reported. This coin was seen by Wayte Raymond. It should have full breast feathers.

Slabaugh mentions a "hub impression" of the 1935 s reverse, in bronze. We have not seen this piece, and suspect that it may possibly be confused with the die trial of the 1935 reverse, with an s mintmark punched directly into the piece, evidently to show where it should be located. This item is on a broad thick irregular copper or bronze planchet; it first came to our attention in 1959, when Q. David Bowers (as Empire Coin Co.) first published it (*Empire Topics* 6, May–June 1959.). It is pictured in Appendix A of Judd, 6th edition, p. 253.

There exist two matte proof 1938 sets struck at the Philadelphia Mint. Both were made for John R. Sinnock before the dies were shipped to the Denver and San Francisco Mints. Upon inspection all three coins will not compare in strike with the Robinson-Arkansas because that issue possesses more die relief. Simply compared with a business-strike '38 set, the difference cannot be missed.

To date we have seen about 50 sets dated 1937–38 in the black cases described above, the lids of which are all dated 1937. About the same number of 1939 sets are found in the uninscribed boxes. A few 1935–36 coins are found in original envelopes of issue; the holders, unfortunately, are those same uninscribed Dennison mailers. We illustrate one (it held a 1936 set) with the original envelope; any such set with the envelope is an extreme rarity.

Closely associated with the coinage is the 3¢ purple stamp released beginning June 15, 1936, for the Centennial. Designer is not credited, probably meaning that it was a collaboration. It is listed as Scott 782, Type A255. In all 72,992,650 were issued. We show both the stamp and one of the 376,693 first day covers, the latter a specially close tie-in as its recipient was the source of many of the original holders and envelopes for the coins herein illustrated.

THE ARKANSAS–ROBINSON HALF DOLLAR

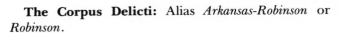

Obverse

Reverse

The Corpus Delicti: Alias *Arkansas-Robinson* or *Robinson*.

Clues: Senator Joseph T. Robinson (D.-Ark.) had come to prominence originally in the House of Representatives (1903–13), being elected governor of Arkansas in 1913 but resigning at once to take a Senate seat, which he held until his death (July 4, 1937). In 1928, he was nominated for Vice President as Al Smith's running mate; from 1933 to 1937 Robinson was Senate Majority Leader, responsible for promoting passage of many New Deal bills, and generally thought of in Arkansas as a public benefactor, or in a common phrase of the time, "the best thing since sliced bread." This sentiment ensured the Senator's place on this coin's obverse. The eagle side is the same found on the regular Arkansas Centennial coins, pages 13–19. Initial K at lower right (below the B of ROBINSON) stands for Henry Kreis, designer, sculptor.

Opportunity: When the Texas Centennial Commission introduced a bill into Congress in 1936 to authorize five new reverses for the Texas half dollars, the Arkansas Centennial Commission at once demanded three for their own coin. After the Texas bill failed, that for Arkansas was amended to permit one alteration on reverse, not less than 25,000 nor more than 50,000 coins to be made of the new design, over and above those made or still to be made of the original design; and it passed, becoming the Act of June 26, 1936, Public Law 831 (74th Congress).

Motive: Originally, rivalry with the Texas commission and, beyond doubt, That Five Finger Word.

Suspects: Henry Kreis, designer, sculptor.

Accessories: The Arkansas Centennial Commission, which specified the portrait of Robinson.

Modus Operandi: The authorizing act specified that the change was to be made in the reverse, but as the original act creating the Arkansas halves in 1934 did not specify designs, the Commission interpreted the eagle side to mean the obverse and gave Henry Kreis the contract to make Senator Robinson's coin portrait. Robinson was then very much alive and at the height of his career; however, nobody bothered to object that portrayal of a living person on coins had been illegal since 1866, especially with the precedents of Alabama's Governor Kilby and Virginia's

Senator Carter Glass (pp. 143 and 173). As the authorizing act specified that the coins were to bear the date 1936 no matter in what year they were struck (to discourage issue of multiple date varieties), the Robinson coins have this date on both sides.

After the Federal Commission of Fine Arts approved the new design on December 23, 1936, Kreis' model went to the Philadelphia Mint, and the coins were struck in January 1937. In all 25,250 plus 15 reserved for assay were struck. These coins went to the Commission's official distributor, Stack's, who marketed them at $1.85 each in specially imprinted Eggers holders (capacity not over 5 coins each). For details about these holders, see below.

Sales continued, though they dwindled with a generalized distrust of commemorative coins. A. Kosoff purchased the remaining 8,000 Robinsons, so that none had to be returned for re-melting; but this hoard has long since been dispersed.

Collateral Evidence: We illustrate the special imprinted holders.

According to an eyewitness, per the late Sol Kaplan, the first few specimens struck were satin finish proofs. The very first one made was caught by the press operator in gloved hands (to avoid its falling against anything), who passed it on to another witness (not identified except that he was not a numismatist!), who dropped it, leaving a minute nick in field above TR of TRUST from when it struck the rim of a container. This piece was set aside; then the next three strikings were earmarked for Senator Robinson, Mrs. Robinson, and President Roosevelt. The actual Number One striking (detail illustration) was enveloped along with at least four other satin finish proofs to be given later to a representative of the Arkansas Centennial Commission. At least four of the proofs went from the Commission to the illustrious numismatist Wayte Raymond. (However, Stack's has no record of ever having handled any, despite being official distributor.) Wayte Raymond's four examples went from his estate to the New Netherlands Coin Company, which auctioned one of them as NN 61:572 (June 30, 1970).

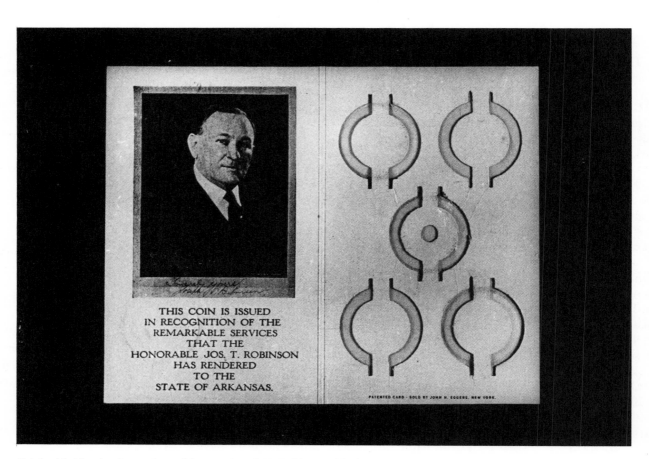

Original holder showing a photo of Senator Joseph T. Robinson with slots that could hold up to a five coin order.

Obverse   *Reverse*

Obverse (left) and reverse (right) of the very first piece struck of the rare Arkansas-Robinson satin finish proofs.

Satin finish proofs are, needless to say, exceedingly rare. Their surface is entirely unlike the normal frosted mint surface of business strikes, being somewhat nearer to that found on 1909 Lincoln cents and Roman finish 1909–1910 gold coins, but not identical to either. However, any reader believing himself fortunate enough to have one of these proof Robinsons is advised to compare his coin with the business strike pictured at the head of this chapter and with the Number One satin finish proof pictured above. Critical areas include Senator Robinson's hair above and immediately before ear, central feathers, motto scroll where it passes over feathers, and ridges on claws. The enlarged areas from the Number One proof are most instructive on comparison with regular coins!

One of these exceedingly rare genuine proof specimens was sold recently (1979) for $8,900, which should be considered a steal.

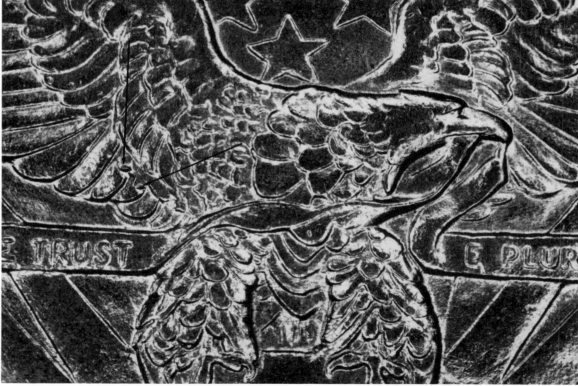

This blown-up photo (top, obverse) shows that poorly defined areas like the middle and upper part of Senator Robinson's hair appear to have been double-struck. The blow-up of the reverse (bottom) shows the sharpness of strike and the slight nick on the eagle's right wing above the word TRUST.

THE SAN FRANCISCO–OAKLAND BAY BRIDGE HALF DOLLAR

Obverse

Reverse

The Corpus Delicti: Alias *Bay Bridge.*

Clues: Once again, it is a matter of guesswork which side should be called the obverse. We follow tradition, like Slabaugh and Taxay, and list the side with the bear as the obverse. Biologists classify the animal as a California grizzly (*Ursus arctos horribilis*), and local history buffs will tell you that Jacques Schnier (whose initials js are in right field) used Monarch II, "last of the grizzlies," as his model for the California state emblem. Well-nourished and sleek though he seems on the coin, Monarch II spent 26 years in a cage in San Francisco's Golden Gate Park, for which reason this coin came in for much adverse criticism on the grounds that a caged animal is no fit symbol for liberty (which word appears under his feet). On the other side, the Bay Bridge stretches from a point over the Embarcadero (with the famous Ferry tower in foreground: the old beside the new, as the opening of the bridge rendered ferry traffic obsolete), towards Yerba Buena Island.

(The present Treasure Island, which would have been visible, is not represented because it is an artificial island and had not yet been completed.) Beyond Yerba Buena Island, the other half of the Bay Bridge stretches out, very sketchily represented, towards Emeryville, Oakland and Berkeley—represented by cross-hatching—and in the extreme distance are the Oakland–Berkeley hills. In the left field are two steamships, too sketchy to identify as to type; they are apparently there only for reasons of balance. The whole composition is stylized but without the finesse of the best Art Deco; note the uniform parallel waves and the nearly uniform evergreen trees. On the original plaster model this was exaggerated to near stereotype. Purists would have reason to complain of inaccuracy in details both of the bridge, the location of Yerba Buena Island (which should have been to the south of the bridge rather than to its north as depicted on the coin), and the contours of the hills; but the whole is intended more as emblematic than documentary.

Photographs of the plaster models of the obverse and reverse of the Bay Bridge coin. Note the absence of the "S" mint mark by the bear's paw above the letter A in HALF.

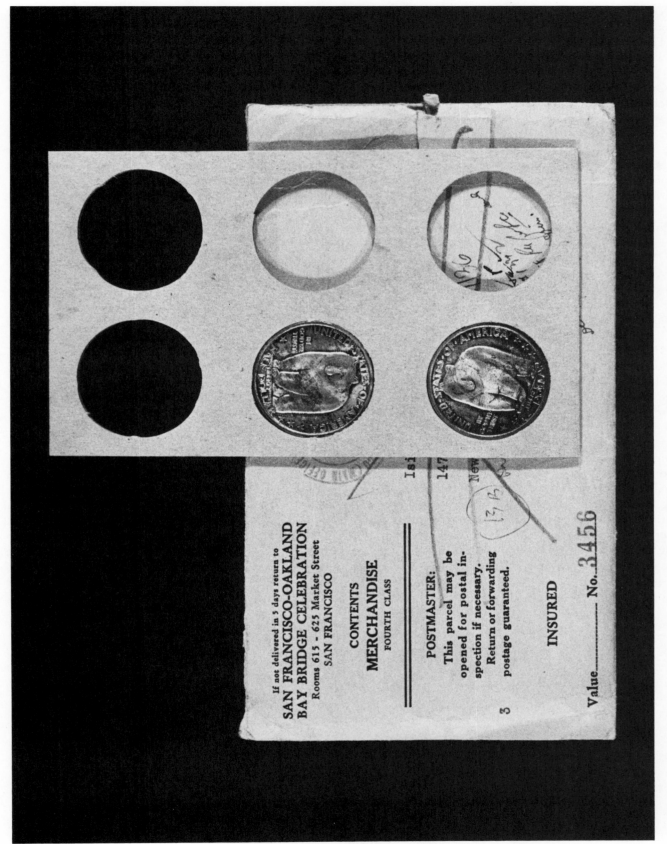

An original mailing envelope and the cardboard insert used by the San Francisco Citizens' Celebration Committee to distribute this issue.

The four obverse stars are apparently only ornamental.

The s mintmark is in field to left of Monarch's paws, above A of HALF.

Opportunity: Opening the bridge to traffic, with celebrations on November 12–14, 1936, anticipated long before and commemorated by the Act of June 26, 1936, which authorized 200,000 coins.

Motive: Local pride, and to help finance the celebration, or rather to recoup on costs, as the coins mostly sold after the celebration ended.

Suspects: Jacques Schnier, local artist, sculptor, designer.

Accessories: The San Francisco–Oakland Bay Bridge Celebration and/or San Francisco Citizens' Celebration Committee, Frank R. Havenner, chairman.

Modus Operandi: Schnier's original sketches, (shown in Taxay, p. 234) showed much smaller lettering, both mottoes flanking the bear, but these had neither his initials nor the four ornamental stars. The Federal Commission of Fine Arts received them on July 22, recommending larger lettering on the 31st; similarly, its sculptor member, Lee Lawrie, recommended a more realistic treatment of the bear's snout when Schnier's plaster models arrived on September 24. In addition, Havenner telegraphed Acting Mint Director O'Reilly for permission to omit the Latin motto and place IN GOD WE TRUST where it had been; this was approved, and the revised models (illustrated) were promptly approved in turn. There are enough differences between them and the coins as issued to raise the question of how much alteration was done at the Philadelphia Mint.

Though the authorizing act had specified a maximum of 200,000 to be coined, only 100,000 (plus 55 reserved for assay) actually left the mint. The Celebration people offered the coin for $1.50 apiece, some via the Clearing House Association, others at kiosks near the Bay Bridge entrances where motorists could pick them up without leaving their cars.

Sales came to a standstill, and in 1937 some 28,631 pieces of the first and only batch were returned to the Mint for re-melting, leaving a total of 71,369 as net mintage. A considerable proportion of these received careless handling, so that really choice survivors are very scarce.

Collateral Evidence: No proofs are reported, though specimens may have been made for John R. Sinnock.

Reportedly, some were distributed in small envelopes; authentic imprinted envelopes of this kind have not been met with. Others were sold directly from rolls, without adequate wrappers of any kind, again accounting for the unsatisfactory condition of many of them. The only authentic holders we have seen are as illustrated, and they are of the highest rarity with the original mailing envelopes.

Today, this issue is looked upon as plentiful. That remark holds only if one disregards quality. Most survivors are nicked and scratched; many have been poorly cleaned, as is common with coins bought by the general public. Gem quality specimens are few.

A hoard of 1,800 pieces exists in the hands of a small investor group. All 1,800 were bought as gem specimens. Those examined by A.S. ranged from About Uncirculated to Uncirculated, none really choice. Many had been cleaned and most were either barely mint state or borderline cases.

THE DANIEL BOONE
BICENTENNIAL ISSUES

Obverse

Reverse

The Corpus Delicti: Alias *Boone*.

Clues: The unidentified bust with fringed collar on the obverse of this coin is meant to be Chief Big Turtle, né Daniel Boone (1734–1820). It is not a portrait but an imaginary idealized figure, not in the slightest degree resembling any of the four contemporaneous descriptions of Boone, nor yet Harding's portrait of Boone (made in 1818), nor even Albin Polasek's bust of him (ca. 1925) in the New York University Hall of Fame. For the actual source, see *Suspects* and *Accessories*, below.

On reverse, the pseudo-Boone is represented as with the Shawnee Chief Black Fish (dressed in some other tribe's regalia) in a historically impossible palaver, allegedly discussing the treaty that was to put an end to the nine-day siege of Fort Boonesborough, in Transylvania (!), part of what is now Kentucky. "Boone" is holding a scroll representing the treaty, together with a musket. Chief Black Fish, who had just adopted Boone as his son (an act which led to Boone being accused of disloyalty), without the expected peace pipe, holds his tomahawk in such a position as to suggest that Boone has just informed him that his fly was open. Behind them are vague

suggestions of an embankment and buildings, intended for Boone's blockhouse fort.

Mint mark D or S, on 1935–38 issues, is placed behind the Chief's heel. We have not found a satisfactory explanation for the phrase PIONEER YEAR, unless that was meant to connect the coin with some publicity releases by the Daniel Boone Bicentennial Commission. Where normally the bicentennial dates 1734–1934 would be expected, only DANIEL BOONE BICENTENNIAL appears. The reason for this is that when the late 1935–38 issues came out (August 26, 1935) a supplemental Act of Congress added the original bicentennial date 1934 above PIONEER YEAR, while the date of issue remained at bottom.

Opportunity: The Daniel Boone Bicentennial Commission, of Lexington, Kentucky, under chairmanship of C. Frank Dunn (with the advice and consent of the Boone family), prevailed on the illustrious Senator Alben Barkley (D.-Ky., later Vice President) to push a bill through Congress, which would authorize mintage of 600,000 commemorative half dollars celebrating Boone's 200th year. This became the Act of May 26, 1934.

Motive: To finance the restoration of four Boone historical sites.

Suspects: Augustus Lukeman, sculptor. The Commission chose him on a favorite son basis, presumably in part because he had been the successor to Gutzon Borglum on the Stone Mountain project.

Accessories: The Daniel Boone Bicentennial Commission, which not only specified the devices, but also insisted that Lukeman copy the Albin Polasek bust of Boone in the Hall of Fame. Lukeman's original models ignored the Polasek bust. In correspondence with C. Frank Dunn, Lukeman claimed (correctly) that the Polasek bust, being backlit, was impossible to copy in profile except in silhouette. What Lukeman did not tell Dunn was that he followed his own fanciful portrait of Boone, which in turn was based on the frontispiece in Collins' *History of Kentucky* (1847 and 1878 editions). The Commission appears to have been acting, in part, on behalf of the Boone Family Association (Col. William Boone Douglass, president). The latter had originally wished for historical accuracy, no matter how much time and research was necessary, but insisted that the Polasek bust was the only accurate one and must be followed; Douglass, the Bicentennial Commission, and Lukeman were heading for an impasse, when on August 23, 1934, the Lexington *Herald* (the very paper which Douglass claimed had studied Boone more than any other publication, and which had approved the Polasek bust) approved of Lukeman's designs. That ended the controversy; the models, which had already been approved by the Federal Commission of Fine Arts, went to Medallic Art Company for reduction, and the Philadelphia Mint began work on the original dies and hubs.

Modus Operandi: Though the authorizing act may have meant a single variety, the Philadelphia Mint interpreted it (as did the Commission) to mean that all three mints could strike the coins in several years, as with the Oregon and Texas issues. Accordingly, the first batch, struck at Philadelphia in October 1934, consisted of only 10,000 pieces. The first one was placed in a specially marked envelope, signed by the Superintendent of the Philadelphia Mint, and delivered on behalf of the Commission by Senator Barkley to President Roosevelt. Most of the others sold at $1.60 each.

Three more batches followed: 10,000 from Philadelphia in March 1935, and 5,000 each from Denver and San Francisco in May. These bore the 1935 date at bottom (as illustrated above), like the 1934; the Philadelphia coin sold for $1.10, the branch mint pieces at $1.60 each.

Fearing that public confusion might result as to the actual year of the bicentennial, the Boone Bicentennial Commission sought authority from Congress to add the date 1934 above PIONEER YEAR on all coins to be made subsequently. This became law on August 26, 1935.

An immediate consequence was creation of a rarity, or rather a pair of them. The Commission ordered additional coins in the fall of 1935, and in Philadelphia 10,000 more were made with the extra 1934 date during October; but in November the two branch mints delivered 2,000 apiece with the extra date. These were snapped up at once, becoming promptly known as the "Rare Boones," and speculators pushed the price up very rapidly. The controversy that erupted during the next few years about these pieces became extremely acrimonious. Not only was the Commission attacked, the noise reached the Treasury Department, and beyond doubt it confirmed and intensified conservative opposition to commemoratives that continues to the present day. All issues thereafter through the end of the Boones in 1938 bear this extra date, as illustrated below.

Boone reverse showing the addition of the date 1934 above the words PIONEER YEAR. This is usually referred to as the "small 1934."

As if that were not bad enough, the Commission announced that "the Boone Issue will end with the '37 set," but nevertheless went ahead and obtained 5,000 sets dated 1938. These also became rarities, not because of low mintage, but because more than half of the sets were melted as unsold. The following tabulation is a convenient summary:

Authorized:	600,000
Coined, total	108,000
Re-melted, total:	21,400
Net mintage, total:	86,600

Collateral Evidence: The majority of Philadelphia Mint issues 1934–37 inclusive will show nicks, scratches or poor cleaning. On the other hand, the rarer branch mint issues normally come in full mint state and often in choice condition: not only free of any signs of abuse, but benefiting from proper housing. (Exceptions are mostly from recent cleaning.)

There is a set of the three 1937 coins with matte finish, which has been represented as matte proofs. These are extremely rare and show more detail than on the business strikes. These MS-70 coins must be seen to be fully appreciated. Each of them possesses a double strike with sharp, squared letters—especially notable on the PIONEER YEAR inscription. In other words, there isn't the usual roundness on the lettering, dates or mint marks.

On the other hand, there exist a few 1937 s coins struck from a brilliantly polished obverse die, with mirrorlike fields. These are very rare and suspected of being some kind of presentation pieces.

The only holders located to date are those same standard Dennison coin holders, with the rubber-stamped imprint of C. Frank Dunn; these are of the highest rarity. As they could be readily imitated, one of the authentic ones is pictured.

A philatelic tie-in was not to come for some years; this was the Kentucky Statehood Sesquicentennial

Photos show the excessively rare 1937 Denver-minted matte proof coin. This is part of a set that was made for the then chief engraver of the U.S. Mint, John R. Sinnock.

DATE	MINT	STRUCK	RESERVED FOR ASSAY	REMELTED	NET MINTAGE	ISSUE PRICE
1934	(P)	10,000	7	—	10,000	$1.60
1935	(P)	10,000	10	—	10,000	1.10
1935	D	5,000	5	—	5,000	1.60
1935	S	5,000	5	—	5,000	1.60
Act of August 26, 1935: Small 1934 added on reverse						
1935	(P)	10,000	8	—	10,000	1.10
1935	D	2,000	3	—	2,000⎫	$3.70 per
1935	S	2,000	4	—	2,000⎭	pair
1936	(P)	12,000	12	—	12,000	1.10
1936	D	5,000	5	—	5,000	1.60
1936	S	5,000	6	—	5,000	1.60
1937	(P)	15,000	10	5,200	9,800	*
1937	D	7,500	6	5,000	2,500	**
1937	S	5,000	6	2,500	2,500	***
1938	(P)	5,000	5	2,900	2,100⎫	
1938	D	5,000	5	2,900	2,100⎬	$6.50
1938	S	5,000	6	2,900	2,100⎭	per set

*The 1937 (P) was priced at $1.60 initially; after May 1937 it was available only in a pair with the Denver coin.
**Available after May, offered only in a pair with the 1937 (P) at $7.25 for the two coins. Never sold singly.
***Offered initially, separately, at $5.15. A few weeks later, available only in 3-piece sets at $12.40.

Obverse of the mirrorlike 1937–S Boone.

issue, a 3¢ violet stamp designed by William A. Roach (after Gilbert White's mural), depicting Daniel Boone and three frontiersmen. This was released on June 1, 1942. It is listed as Scott 904, Type A363, and a total of 6,558,400 were issued.

There is one other stamp that honors Boone by name. Part of the "American Folklore" series, it is a 6¢, in two shades of yellow, maroon, and black, Scott 1357, Type A779, designed by Louis Macouillard, and released beginning September 26, 1968—an odd choice of date, as the stamp mentions Boone's birth year of 1734. In all 130,385,000 were issued.

In the American Numismatic Society museum are two copper uniface die trials, the obverse without special identification but probably made on the same occasion as the reverse. This latter is from the die of the 1935 s with small 1934. Both are pictured in Judd, Appendix A, p. 252.

Envelope and coin holder used to distribute the 1934 Boone issue.

THE BRIDGEPORT, CONNECTICUT, CENTENNIAL HALF DOLLAR

Obverse

Reverse

The Corpus Delicti: Alias *Bridgeport* or *P.T. Barnum*.

Clues: In this very Art Deco composition little really calls for explanation except the date 1836 (for a city founded in 1639!) and the choice of P.T. Barnum, of all imaginable people, for portrayal. The date 1836 alludes to incorporation of Bridgeport as a city; the head of Barnum has less to do with his "There's a sucker born every minute" cynicism (however applicable this might have been to commemorative coin fanciers in the 1930s) than to his philanthropic benefactions to the city. It appears, among other things, that Barnum (b. Bethel, Ct., July 5, 1810; d. April 7, 1891), "the man who lured the herd," laid out tree-lined streets in what eventually became greater Bridgeport, and reserved a grove of eight acres which is now known as Washington Park; he is credited with stimulating the growth of industry in the Bridgeport area, making possible its present reputation as the chief industrial city of Connecticut.

On the reverse is the most modernistic eagle ever put on a U.S. coin—or, so far as we know, on a coin of any nation. At lower right, below RT of LIBERTY, is Henry Kreis' incused initial K.

Opportunity: Local celebrations in Bridgeport; Act of Congress, May 15, 1936, which amazingly authorized indefinite continuance of mintage so long as each coin bore date 1936!

Motive: To help defray the cost of the local celebrations.

Suspects: Henry Kreis, designer.

Accessories: Bridgeport Centennial, Inc., in charge of the celebrations.

Modus Operandi: The Federal Commission of Fine Arts approved Kreis' sketches about July 17, 1936, after which Kreis' models went to Medallic Art

Co. of New York for reduction to half dollar size. During September 1936, the Philadelphia Mint struck 25,000 (the minimum figure) plus 15 reserved for assay. Bridgeport Centennial, Inc., which was in charge of the celebrations, distributed the coins to local residents through Bridgeport banks, and to out-of-town buyers through the First National Bank and Trust Company of Bridgeport. In a perhaps unwise effort to discourage speculation and insure fair distribution, the committee in charge attempted to limit purchases to not over five coins per customer, at $2 per coin. As a result, almost 1,000 pieces remained unsold, and no further orders followed.

During the late 1950s this batch of unsold remainders came on the market, and was purchased by Allen Johnson, son of Toivo Johnson (the East Holden, Maine, coin dealer, famous in that decade). Johnson, in the early 1970s, sold part of the hoard to a Kansas City dealer, the rest of it to First Coinvestors, Inc. Despite the attempt to exclude speculators from the roster of purchasers, there are several hoards of one to perhaps a dozen rolls each.

Collateral Evidence: No proofs are traced, though several were probably made for John R. Sinnock. The Bridgeport Centennial Commission distributed single specimens in dark blue and gold cardboard boxes. These have the city arms and two diagonal gold bands on the top cover. Inner cover at top has an inscription about P.T. Barnum (blue ink on gold paper); inner bottom half contains the slot for the coin. Larger holders are similar but have slots for three coins. At least 100 of each type of holder survive.

One of us (A.S.) noticed that if one inverts the reverse, the eagle comes to resemble a shark with open mouth and tongue and two dorsal fins; more fanciful minds make the shark appear to be laughing, presumably at its prey, namely those of whom one more is "born every minute."

THE CALIFORNIA DIAMOND JUBILEE HALF DOLLAR

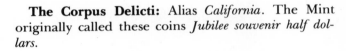

Obverse

Reverse

The Corpus Delicti: Alias *California*. The Mint originally called these coins *Jubilee souvenir half dollars*.

Clues: Squatting on obverse is a gold miner with a pan, inspecting gravel from a stream for possible gold flakes or nuggets—a method in use since remote antiquity and usual among the forty-niners. The DIAMOND JUBILEE 1925 inscription refers to the 75th anniversary of California's admission into the Union as a state, September 9, 1850, as part of the Compromise of 1850. On reverse, the grizzly bear (*Ursus arctos horribilis*) represents the California Republic's bear flag under General John C. Frémont, 1846–50—said to symbolize strength and independence.

Opportunity: The San Francisco Citizens' Committee (Angelo J. Rossi, chairman) wanted souvenir coins for a celebration fondly hoped to be at least as important as the Monroe Doctrine or the Pan Pacific. Senator Samuel Morgan Shortridge (R.-Cal.) and Rep. John Raker (D.-Cal.) pushed the authorizing bill, but Rep. Albert H. Vestal of the House Coinage Committee (pressured by the Mint Bureau) was

against any further commemorative acts. When the Vermont senators pushed a bill to authorize such coinage for the Battle of Bennington, Vermont, a cause dear to President Coolidge's heart, Rep. Raker offered an amendment, February 16, 1925, to authorize the California Jubilee coin. This was passed, the amended bill eventually becoming the Act of February 24, 1925.

Motive: Fund raising for the big local celebrations in San Francisco and Los Angeles.

Suspects: Jo Mora, local sculptor commissioned by the Citizen's Committee, which appears to have chosen the actual designs. Chairman Rossi sent Mora's initial sketches on May 4, 1925 to Mint Director Grant, who forwarded them to the Federal Commission of Fine Arts on May 8. Despite disapproval by James Earle Fraser (who recommended firing Mora as "inexperienced and amateurish"), Mora's finished design was eventually approved, June 20, probably for lack of time to hire either Robert Aitken or Chester Beach (Fraser's choices), not to mention the much greater cost of their fees. The grizzly bear came under especially strong criticism because its trunk was disproportionately short in relation to its leg length.

Accessories: Unknown.

Modus Operandi: The Mint made the necessary reductions of the models to half dollar size and prepared working dies during July; these went to San Francisco (the mintmark s is at bottom of reverse) where 150,000 coins were struck between August 1 and 26, 1925. The San Francisco Clearing House Association and its sister in Los Angeles offered the coins to the public at $1 apiece. We know that the first batch left the Mint not later than August 26 because a specimen was exhibited on that date at a meeting of the Pacific Coast Numismatic Society. (*The Numismatist*, November 1925, p. 591.) Despite all the high hopes, however, the Citizen's Committee was unable to sell even the entirety of the first batch, and no more were ordered. In tabular form:

Authorized:	Not over 300,000
Coined:	150,000 plus 200 reserved for assay
Returned for melting:	63,606
Net mintage:	86,394.

A small number went (to VIPs and possibly Citizen's Committee members?) in holders to which were attached red, yellow and green ribbons, similar to the ribbon illustrated. We have not seen any of these holders; the report derives from Slabaugh, p. 68.

At least one matte proof, without the s mintmark, is reported; this we have not been able to examine to date. If the report is correct, the coin must have been specially made at Philadelphia before the dies went to San Francisco. Presumably it too went from the J. R. Sinnock estate to its present East Coast holder.

Early struck satin finish specimens exist that are far better struck than normal impressions, with sharp inner rims and extra detail on garment and pelt; the fields are not truly mirrorlike but show unusual gloss with raised die striations. They are rare, and one of us (A.S.) believes that they are probably the only survivors qualifying at the gem

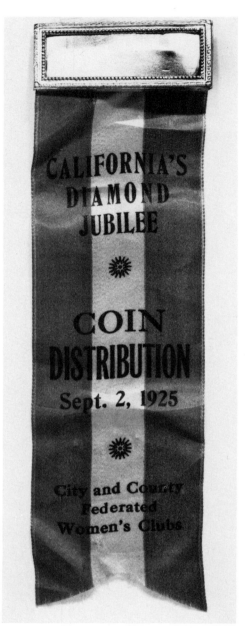

Ribbon worn by the California Diamond Jubilee Coin Distribution Committee. Attached to the ribbon (not shown here) was a holder which held a commemorative half dollar.

level. Gem uncirculated specimens are becoming less available; many of the survivors came from non-numismatic sources, and were carelessly handled or badly cleaned.

THE CALIFORNIA–PACIFIC INTERNATIONAL EXPOSITION HALF DOLLARS

Obverse

Reverse

The Corpus Delicti: Alias *San Diego.*

Clues: Here again, it's a matter of guesswork which side was originally intended for the obverse. For lack of better evidence, we will follow the *Red Book,* Taxay and Slabaugh, and assume that the side with the California state seal adaptation is the obverse—though normally the statutory legend and denomination come on reverse. Despite the word LIBERTY, the seated female is meant to be Minerva, goddess of wisdom, the same depicted on the Pan-Pacific fifties. She holds spear and shield, but no olive branch for peace (all the more odd, because Minerva was the Roman name for Athena, who taught the Greeks to grow olives!). On her shield is the aegis, the goatskin bag to which is affixed the head of the Gorgon Medusa; above it the goldminers' slogan EVREKA (which should be pronounced *Hew-RAY-ka* and means about the same as the current bumpersticker slogan "I FOUND IT!"). Overlapping the shield is a cornucopia, symbolic of the state's prodigious amount of natural resources, both

agricultural and mineral. In front of her spear is the California grizzly bear. Behind them are a square-rigged schooner in full sail and a miner wielding a pickaxe; behind everything else, mountains. The design looks less crowded than it sounds, but that is only because the miner and ship are microscopic and usually so faint as to be all but invisible. Robert Aitken's monogrammed initials appear at the lower left.

On what we take to be the reverse is one of the very rare instances of a building making a good coin design—or, rather, two buildings. These began life as the State of California buildings in Balboa Park, San Diego, erected for the Exposition named in the legend. That with the dome is the Chapel of St. Francis; the other is the California Tower. Surrounding them is a motif said to suggest Spanish mission architecture, though to people more familiar with medieval and Renaissance gold coins, it would be readily recognizable as a tressure. Similar tressures (four arches separated by angles) were found on the *mouton d'or* of Henry V (ca. 1420), and on

Portuguese *cruzados* of Alfonso V (late 15th century), though a possibly more likely antecedent is certain large Spanish silver coins of Philip II (late 16th century).

The mintmark—s on coins dated 1935, D on those of 1936—is found at bottom, below T of TRUST.

Opportunity: The California-Pacific International Exposition, generally counted as a world's fair though not so listed in the World Almanac, was the second such exposition to be held in San Diego (the first was the Panama-California Exposition in 1915), and one of the biggest of all: 1,400 acres in Balboa Park, costing about $20,000,000 and attracting about 3,750,000 visitors. Slabaugh says that in a sense the authorization of this coin for the Exposition made amends for San Diego's having no commemorative coin in 1915. Actually, it is unlikely that anyone had complained since California had had more commemorative coins authorized than any other state. This San Diego coin is a unique departure from tradition in another sense: When the Exposition authorities became apprehensive that part of the 250,000 coins authorized by the Act of May 3, 1935, would not sell, they induced their friends in Congress to pass a special Recoinage Act as of May 6, 1936 to authorize the unsold residue to be re-melted and recoined into a new variety dated 1936.

Motive: That Five Finger Word; specifically, to have something to sell to souvenir hunters at the Exposition, and in two varieties to coin collectors.

Suspects: Robert Aitken, sculptor.

Accessories: Emil Klicka, Treasurer of the Exposition Commission handling the coins.

Modus Operandi: After the Federal Commission of Fine Arts approved Aitken's models on July 5, 1935, they were shipped to the Medallic Art Company for reduction, after which (in what must have been inordinate haste) the reductions went to Philadelphia for manufacture of original dies, hubs, and working dies, which in turn were sent back to San Francisco. The San Francisco mint struck 250,000 coins in August 1935, which went in a penultimate stage of this game of musical chairs to the Bank of America in San Diego, which handled the distribution. Despite all the Exposition publicity, only 68,000 coins were sold at $1 each, some 2,000 more remaining in the Exposition's vaults.

After the Act of May 6, 1936, the unsold remainder (some 180,000 coins) went to the Denver Mint for re-melting and recoinage into 1936 D San Diego halves. These did even worse: only 30,000 coins were sold at $1.50 each, leaving 150,000 to be re-melted after the Exposition closed its gates. In fact, not all the 30,000 listed as sold actually moved at the Exposition; some of them were retained by Emil Klicka, who raised the price to $3 apiece in 1937 and sold them to coin collectors.

In tabular form:

Authorized:	Not over 250,000
Coined, 1935 s:	250,000 plus 132 assay coins
Returned for recoinage:	180,000
Net mintage, 1935 s:	70,000
Coined, 1936 D:	180,000 plus 92 assay coins
Remelted, 1936 D:	150,000
Net mintage, 1936 D:	30,000

We are unsure if sheer greed was the motive, or merely a desire to end a bad situation, balancing the books by taking part payment in coins, but two large hoards were made at the time. One of the managers of the Exposition had a hoard of 31,050 pieces of the 1935 s issue; this was found and dispersed after 1966. The vast majority of really uncirculated survivors came from this source. One of us (A.S.) has positive information of the existence of a full mint sack of 1936 D coins; this was last offered for sale in 1937, and it is at present in an estate.

Collateral Evidence: This is the only issue to have been struck at two different branch mints but not also at Philadelphia. Specimens dated 1935 are known which show only a featureless blob where the s mintmark should be. Clear s mintmarks are, if anything, more unusual.

We have not seen the copper trial piece of the 1935 reverse, so we have no idea if it bears the s mintmark. If not, it was probably made before the dies were shipped west from Philadelphia.

On the 1936 D coins, weak striking is the rule, as in the facing illustration. Compared to the 1935 s, the upper half of the California Tower is almost featureless. Full sharp strikings of the 1936 D are very rare—and it is not often that a business strike commemorative coin can be called rare!

Weakness on Minerva's knees is common on both dates, though more so on 1936 D. If you are in doubt whether your coin is fully mint state, look for mint frost on the weak areas.

Two matte proofs of 1935 s are reported: one seen by Wayte Raymond and the other in the John

Obverse

Reverse

Note the weak striking on the 1936 version of the San Diego Commemorative, especially on the almost featureless upper half of the California Tower. Compare this with the 1935 version.

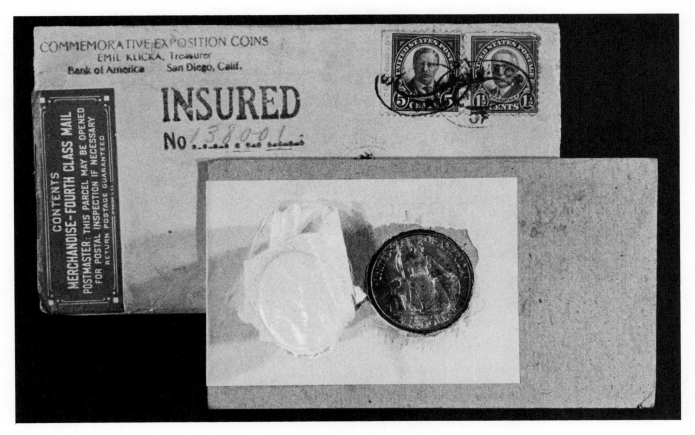

This is one of the original coin holder and envelope combinations used to distribute the San Diego issue.

R. Sinnock estate. Neither of these is available to be photographed. One would expect both to show more detail than the business strike in the facing photograph, especially on Minerva's drapery and helmet, and probably also on the buildings.

Two original holders have been found, but as they are unprinted, they could be readily imitated; the safest documentation is original envelopes such as that pictured.

The philatelic tie-in is the purple 3¢, Scott 773 (Type A250), showing the Exposition's buildings in Balboa Park, prominent among which are the same two shown on the coins. We are unable to account for the date 1535–1935 on the stamp; Juan Rod-

The California-Pacific International Exposition philatelic tie-in—Scott 773, type A250.

ríguez Cabrillo did not reach the harbor until 1542, nor was the bay named until 1602. The earliest settlement dates only from 1769, when Mission San Diego was built. Historical accuracy aside, the stamp must have been popular, as some 100,839,600 were distributed. The designer is not credited.

In the R.E. Cox collection was a die trial of the 1935 reverse on a thin undersized copper planchet. This was lot 2307 of the 1962 New York Metropolitan sale; it is pictured in Appendix A of Judd, p. 253.

THE CINCINNATI HALF DOLLARS

Obverse

Reverse

The Corpus Delicti: Alias *Cincinnati.*

Clues: In this very Art Deco composition, the portrait represents—very much after a fashion, as it is idealized almost to unrecognizability—Stephen Foster (b. Lawrenceville, now part of Pittsburgh, Pennsylvania, July 4, 1826; d. New York City, 1864). Behind Foster's neck are linked initials co for Constance Ortmayer, the designer. We have not been able to trace the ultimate source of the phrase AMERICA'S TROUBADOUR.

On reverse, the female holding a lyre is supposed to personify Music; the date 1886 was chosen on the basis of no historical event whatever, in order to obtain a suitable year for convincing Congress to authorize the coin, "to commemorate the 50th anniversary of Cincinnati, Ohio, as a center of music, and to commemorate Cincinnati's contribution to the art of music in the United States for the past 50 years," to quote the authorizing act. These false claims were at once used as grounds for rejection by the Federal Commission of Fine Arts, whose chairman Charles Moore wrote on May 13, 1936, complaining about them to Mint Director Nellie Tayloe

"Ma" Ross. For starters, Stephen Foster had no connection with the musical life of Cincinnati; his only relevance to the city was that he worked there as a bookkeeper in his brother's firm for three years in the 1840s. In addition, as Moore pointed out, Cincinnati had become the locale for musical festivals beginning in 1873 with the May Festival Association, organized by George Ward Nichols, and conducted by the illustrious Theodore Thomas, using a chorus of over 1,000 voices assembled from 35 midwestern musical societies. Following this initial success, Thomas became director (1878–81) of the newly founded Cincinnati College of Music, and in later years he acquired the title "Musical Missionary" by taking the Cincinnati Symphony Orchestra (itself an outgrowth of the biennial festivals) on nation-wide tours, gradually creating an appetite in audiences from Massachusetts to California for symphonic music, at a time when most people's musical experience consisted of village band concerts, singing around the parlor piano, or watching song-and-dance routines done in Uncle Tom shows or blackface minstrel shows. (There were, of course, no phonograph records, and to the average young person of the day a completely professional violinist was as exotic as a performer on the Tibetan trumpet today.)

So that if any commemorative coin were to have been legitimately planned to honor Cincinnati's immense contribution to American cultural life, it should have borne dates 1873–1923 or 1873–1973, and it should have portrayed Theodore Thomas. (As authorized, it would have more appropriately portrayed Tom Melish and a bank vault.)

Unfortunately for rationality, historical accuracy and any sense of the fitness of things, the "Cincinnati Musical Center Commemorative Coin Association" (unknown to any of the Cincinnati musical groups then or later) put pressure on the Treasury to overrule the Commission of Fine Arts, and the design was adopted as is.

Mintmark s or D will be found below the date 1936.

Opportunity: Pressure from the above-mentioned Association on Congress induced passage of the Act of March 31, 1936, authorizing this issue. There were neither local celebrations nor any attempt to coordinate publicity for the coin with any musical events in Cincinnati; as it was an even-numbered year, there was not even a May Festival to tie in with publicity for the coins, let alone to justify the Act's wording.

Motive: That Five Finger Word.

Suspects: The Cincinnati Musical Center Commemorative Coin Association, Thomas G. Melish, chairman. This group consisted not of friends of music but of coin collectors, and they had only one idea in mind: enriching themselves by publicizing and distributing a limited issue which could be priced into orbit by speculators.

Accessories: Miss Constance Ortmayer, the designer. She is demoted from "Suspect" to "Accessory" because here the Association is clearly the culprit; she may not even have known of the cynical and venal aspects of the operation.

Modus Operandi: In July 1936, 5,000 sets were struck at the three mints, with 5 extra reserved for assay at Philadelphia and Denver, 6 extra at San Francisco. The first 200 coins produced at each mint were caught by an operator wearing soft gloves, to avoid nicks or scratches; this operator then placed each piece into a specially marked envelope, in order of manufacture, and the coins went thereafter to the Association, which placed the numbered sets into specially marked black cardboard holders. These show notarized statements that the coins within were the 6th (or 48th, or whatever) coins produced at each mint of this issue; besides the notary's signature and seal, they bear the signature of Thomas G. Melish. Accompanying letters originally went with these "special striking" sets; they were either given or sold for undisclosed prices to VIP friends of Melish and his gang. The remaining 4,800 sets were placed into the same kind of holders (the usual Wayte Raymond type, with celluloid strips in openings to prevent the coins from falling out) but minus the numbering or documentation.

As the issue was oversubscribed before the August 1936 issue date, those who got theirs at the announced $7.75 issue price were the lucky exceptions. Asking price thereafter was $45 and it rapidly climbed to $75—roughly the equivalent of $600 in 1980 dollars! Cartoons had in the meantime been published ridiculing the commemorative market, showing speculators buying coins from Commissions at $5 and offering them at once for $10 to collectors rushing to line up for them.

After the issue sold out, the Association attempted to obtain Congressional approval for a second mintage to be dated 1937, but the bill failed to pass. Possibly because of this issue, Congress was becoming less and less enthusiastic about commemorative coin proposals; the Cincinnati authorizing act was the last in which the phrase "at the mints" was to be used in this period.

Collateral Evidence: No proofs have been confirmed to exist. Sets in original numbered holders are extremely rare; these appear to be the ultimate source of the few absolute gem survivors from all three mints. Possibly 50 sets remain in original unnumbered holders; these tend to have bag marks. Denver coins are found in choice uncirculated more often than Philadelphia and vastly more often than San Francisco strikings, aside from those first 200.

Many specimens are lightly struck so that the designer's initials co are faint or invisible (see illustration).

Specimens such as that pictured here, with initials plain, are seldom available. This obverse is also notable for die scratches behind head, near TED.

Counterfeits are mostly high-quality casts made from a genuine specimen. Aside from the peculiar surface (which is unlike ordinary mint bloom), these show raised granular defects especially on cheek and in field near TROUBADOUR (see the respective illustrations of these areas). On reverse, there are

The marks seen in back of Stephen Foster's head, especially those below the letter D in UNITED, are die scratches. These raised lines were transferred from the die surface to the coin blank or planchet during striking. What appears to be two circles in the field in back of Mr. Foster's head are the designer's initials.

This blow-up of the obverse surface of a counterfeit Cincinnati reveals telltale granular defects.

This blow-up of the reverse surface of a counterfeit Cincinnati shows raised die file marks.

Blow-up of a counterfeit's reverse surface shows granular raised bubbles around the date.

raised die file marks at CINCINN, and more of the same kind of granular raised "bubbles" around date and mottoes.

As an investment, this set is a great one. However, this applies only to sets in truly gem state: full original mint luster, no ugly bag marks and sharply struck. Occasional individual coins qualify at this level, but sets seldom do. For some unknown reason, more Denver Mint gems have survived than Philadelphia or San Francisco specimens.

A set in which all three coins are gems should be snapped up at once as a fantastic find. (This remark holds true even if as many as 200 sets survive in original numbered holders—an extremely unlikely upper limit.) Assembling a gem set from individual coins could be a profitable endeavor.

THE CLEVELAND CENTENNIAL/ GREAT LAKES EXPOSITION HALF DOLLAR

Obverse

Reverse

The Corpus Delicti: Alias *Cleveland*.

Clues: Moses Cleaveland (1754–1806) was a lawyer, Revolutionary War general, and later state congressman from Canterbury, Connecticut. He became one of the directors and surveyors for the Connecticut Land Company, which bought 3,267,000 acres of the "Western Reserve" area in what is now northeastern Ohio; he laid out the city later to be named after him (it dropped its extra "a" about 1830, becoming known as Cleveland). This city was incorporated in 1836 (hence choice of this date for centennial celebrations).

Initials BP below shoulder are those of Brenda Putnam, the coin's designer.

On reverse we find the five Great Lakes with their nine principal cities marked by stars, that for Cleveland (at the bottom compass point) largest, less for city size than for emphasis as the city most directly alluded to in commemoration. Ms. Putnam's original sketches showed a drastically curved horizon, with the other compass point on it somewhere in Canada,

miles above Lake Superior; it also represented the cities—only six, not nine—by buildings, but the change to stars came at once on suggestions by Lee Lawrie of the Federal Commission of Fine Arts. We have not found documentation, but we suspect that the compass was intended to show Cleveland as the center of industry within a radius of approximately 900 miles, which area would include not only the other Great Lakes cities (Duluth, Milwaukee, Chicago, Detroit, Toledo, Toronto, Buffalo and Rochester) but also, if the circle were completed, St. Louis, Washington, New York and Boston!

Opportunity: The Cleveland Centennial and Great Lakes Exposition was held in Cleveland from June 27 to October 4, 1936, on a 125-acre lakefront site, "a Glamorous Spectacle of Supreme Significance, . . . Presenting Outstanding Attractions Worthy of a World's Fair . . . presenting achievements of the Arts and Sciences in understandable ways (!) . . . portraying the drama of Industry and Commerce in fascinating and colorful manners . . .

unfolding the romance of Iron and Coal (!!) in impressive methods . . . " to quote press puffery for the $25,000,000 event. This provided Thomas G. Melish with another automatic opportunity for pressuring Congress for a commemorative coin, which was duly approved, "to commemorate Cleveland's contribution to the industrial progress of the United States for a century," in the orotund phrases of the Act of May 5, 1936.

Motive: That Five Finger Word. Melish was a coin collector, and we have already sampled his machinations with the Cincinnati issue. However, as the Cleveland issue was in connection with a legitimate celebration, and as 25,000 (minimum) to 50,000 (maximum) were authorized, Melish's sales strategy had to be very different: the coins would have to be aimed at the Exposition visitors and the general public at $1.50 apiece, not at his own coterie of greedy speculators.

Suspects: The Cleveland Centennial Commemorative Coin Association, Thomas G. Melish, treasurer.

Accessories: Brenda Putnam, designer; and the unnamed artist who provided the only known portrait of General Cleaveland from life, which was Ms. Putnam's immediate source.

Modus Operandi: As soon as the Commission of Fine Arts approved the design, June 2, 1936, Medallic Art Company of New York reduced Ms. Putnam's models to half dollar size and shipped them to the Philadelphia Mint, where 25,000 were struck in July 1936 (with an extra 15 reserved for assay). When this batch actually sold out, the remaining 25,000 (again with an extra 15 reserved for assay) followed in February 1937. (Technically the latter should have been dated 1937, but that would have required an amendment to the authorizing act, which called for the entire mintage to be dated 1936.) There is no way the 1936 and 1937 strikings can be positively told apart.

Collateral Evidence: No proofs are reported. As with the Cincinnati sets, by Melish's orders, the first

A rare circular describing the Great Lakes Exposition Cleveland Centennial.

Circular and coin envelope housing coins sold at the exposition.

Front of coin holder displaying both the obverse of the 32nd and the reverse of the 33rd coins struck.

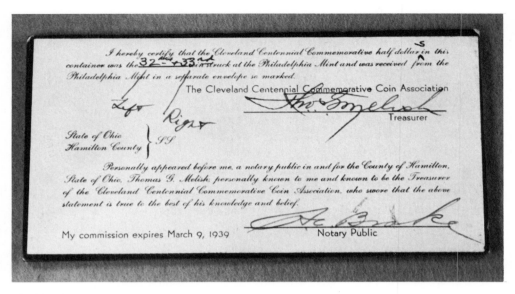

Back of holder showing documents, notary seal, and signatures.

The Western Reserve Numismatic Club counterstamped a number of Cleveland Commemoratives in 1941 and again in 1971 for the club's 20th and 50th anniversaries.

Here is a blow-up showing the details of the 1971 counterstamp that celebrated the Western Reserve Numismatic Club's 50th anniversary.

200 coins to be struck were specially caught in gloves by the press operator, and placed in numbered envelopes in the order of manufacture. When these 200 reached the Association, they were inserted into special black cardboard Wayte Raymond type holders (mostly one per holder, rarely two: nos. 32–33 occupy a single holder), on the back of which is a notarized statement as to the order of striking, signed by the notary and by Melish; these 200 were sent out with individual accompanying letters. The dies were not polished, nor were the coins treated in any special way; nevertheless, they are better strikings than any later ones. We have examined nos. 6, 14, 32–33, and a few later ones; about 20 are estimated to survive in the original notarized holders. They are unusually sharp but not prooflike. Early numbered holders, possessing one coin, have sold for $800.

Specimens were sold at the Exposition (some in numbered envelopes—we illustrate no. 738—and others in black holders of the same kind as were used for the special strikings, but unnumbered and without notarization) by various Ohio banks, and by the Association (from Melish's own address). The entire mintage was sold, so that none went back for melting. At present we know three in Exposition envelopes and about 35 in unnumbered holders.

During its 20th anniversary celebration in 1941, the Western Reserve Numismatic Club of Cleveland counterstamped exactly 100 Cleveland half dollars with small round dies as illustrated; these portray General Cleaveland. No details are available of this operation, as it was then illegal; the counterstamp dies were promptly destroyed after the 100th striking, and early holders of the counterstamped coins were not about to talk publicly about them. As a result, we are unable to name either the diecutter or the instigators of the project.

Another and still rarer counterstamp was affixed to Cleveland half dollars in 1971, this for the 50th anniversary of the Western Reserve Numismatic Club. Only 13 (Slabaugh says 20) Cleveland halves were countermarked, together with a small number of silver dollars, foreign coins, tokens, and silver bars. The illustration and enlarged detail are self-explanatory, though owing to the double striking it may be difficult to read either FIFTY YEARS 1971 in field or the name MOSES CLEVELAND (sic!) below waist. We have not found the diecutter's name for this project either, nor those of the promoters.

How rare is the Cleveland Great Lakes Exposition Half Dollar? This issue is hardly likely to become a rarity; many hoards exist. We personally know one comprising 22 rolls (440 pieces!); another hoarder admits to holding 1,000 specimens. The Cleveland is always available for a price, even in gem state. We suspect, though, that in later decades many survivors will fall victim to cleaning which will permanently lower the number of choice or gem specimens.

THE COLUMBIA, SOUTH CAROLINA, SESQUICENTENNIAL HALF DOLLAR

Obverse

Reverse

The Corpus Delicti: Alias *Columbia*.

Clues: A figure of Justice with scales and sword, but for once no blindfold, stands in a plaza; in the background, the Old State House and date 1786, the New State House and date 1936. On reverse is a stylized palmetto tree (the state emblem), with two bunches of arrows in a saltire pattern tied to its base by a broad ribbon. (These arrows were much clearer on the original model, pictured in Taxay, p. 180.) A lopped oak branch lies at its feet; around are 13 stars, ostensibly for the 13 original colonies. This peculiar emblem does not yield up its iconographic meaning without some background material. On June 28, 1776, General Clinton and the British fleet attempted to seize Fort Moultrie on Sullivan's Island in Charleston (South Carolina) Harbor. Ft. Moultrie was constructed of palmetto logs, in which the British naval missiles buried themselves, so that after some 12 hours of bombardment, the score stood at

under 12 colonists killed, but hundreds of Britishers; minor damage to the palmetto logs, but drastic damage to the British oaken ships from the shells continually fired from Ft. Moultrie. So, the arrows tied to the palmetto tree indicate the latter's military connotations. (A similar device of crossed arrows was found on the five-pound notes issued by South Carolina Provincial Congress, dated June 1, 1775; and the palmetto dominates the seal on ten-shilling notes dated April 10, 1778—significantly with the besieged Ft. Moultrie in the background.) As for the 13 stars, their obvious connotation is the 13 original colonies, of which South Carolina was one; but we cannot rule out here, any more than with the Arkansas, the local connotation identifying the 13 stars with the 13 seceding states.

Mintmark D or s for Denver or San Francisco will be found below Ms. Justice's foot; Philadelphia coins, of course, have no mint mark.

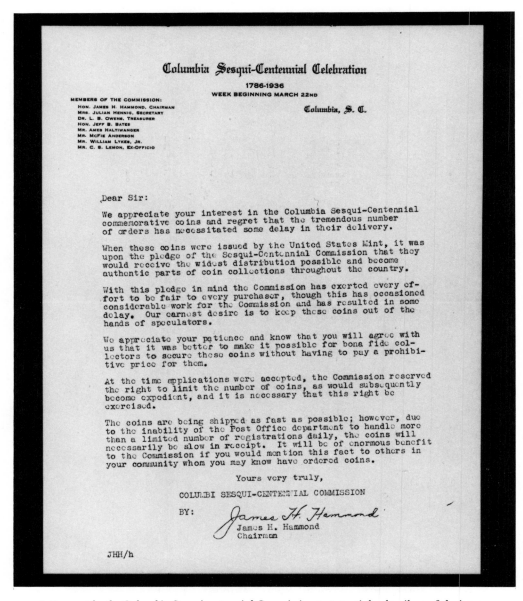

Letter sent by the Columbia Sesquicentennial Commission to potential subscribers of the issue.

Opportunity: Local celebrations in Columbia, South Carolina, March 22–29, 1936. The mayor appears to have appointed the membership of the Columbia Sesquicentennial Commission, which was to distribute the coins, and which presumably exerted pressure on Congress for passage of the authorizing act (March 18, 1936).

Motive: Local pride, and That Five Finger Word. The Commission Chairman, Hon. James H. Hammond, insisted that "When these coins were issued by the U.S. Mint, it was upon the pledge of the

Sesquicentennial Commission that they would receive the widest distribution possible . . . Our earnest desire is to keep these coins out of the hands of speculators."

Suspects: A. Wolfe Davidson, then a 32-year-old student sculptor at Clemson College, who was appointed as designer by the Commission.

Accessories: The Columbia Sesquicentennial Commission (Hon. James H. Hammond, chairman;

COST OF COIN

$2.15 each.
$6.45 set of three.

TREASURER,
Columbia Sesqui-Centennial Commission,
% Columbia Chamber of Commerce,
Columbia, S. C.

I hereby subscribe for .... Columbia, South Carolina,
Sesqui-Centennial Commemorative Half Dollars and enclose herewith MONEY ORDER or
CERTIFIED CHECK for $........ Coin to be forwarded to me at the address given
below, as soon as available, subject to right of committee to reject this order in whole or in part, in
which case refund will be made.

Date........................1936.

APPLICATION FOR COLUMBIA, SOUTH CAROLINA,
SESQUI-CENTENNIAL HALF DOLLAR

NAME.........................
STREET ADDRESS.........................
CITY.........................
STATE.........................

SUBSCRIPTION APPLICATION

COLUMBIA
South Carolina

SESQUI-CENTENNIAL
COMMEMORATIVE
HALF DOLLAR

1786-1936

Authorized by Special Act of Congress

This folder issued by
Columbia Sesqui-Centennial Commission
Columbia, S. C.

Subscription application (front and back) for the Columbia, South Carolina Commemorative half dollars. This is a rare find.

Columbia, South Carolina
SESQUI-CENTENNIAL HALF DOLLAR

A Commemorative Half Dollar

Has been authorized by a Special Act of Congress to be issued in connection with the 150th Anniversary of the founding of the city of Columbia, the capital of the State of South Carolina.

Number Limited

The issue is limited to 25,000 coins to be minted as follows:

9,000 Philadelphia Mint.
8,000 Denver Mint.
8,000 San Francisco Mint.

Sculptor

The sculptor whose selection has been approved by the Treasury Department and the Fine Arts Commission is A. Wolfe Davidson, of Clemson Colege, S. C. Mr. Davidson is an outstanding sculptor of the State and is, at present, engaged in sculptoring the bust of Thomas Clemson, the founder of the State Agricultural & Mechanical College.

By Subscription Only

The coins will be sold by subscription only and applications will be limited to ten sets (30 coins) to a single subscriber. Preferential consideration will be given to subscribers ordering sets of three coins.

Residents of the City of Columbia will be given the privilege of making their purchases during the first twenty-four hours after the coins are placed on sale. Mail orders will then be filled.

It is the desire of the Commission that the coin be sold to private collectors rather than dealers.

Price of Coin

The price asked for the coin is two dollars plus fifteen cents each for postage and handling ($2.15).

Orders will be accepted only when accompanied by CASH, CERTIFIED CHECK, or POSTAL OR EXPRESS MONEY ORDER.

Centerspread of the subscription application.

55

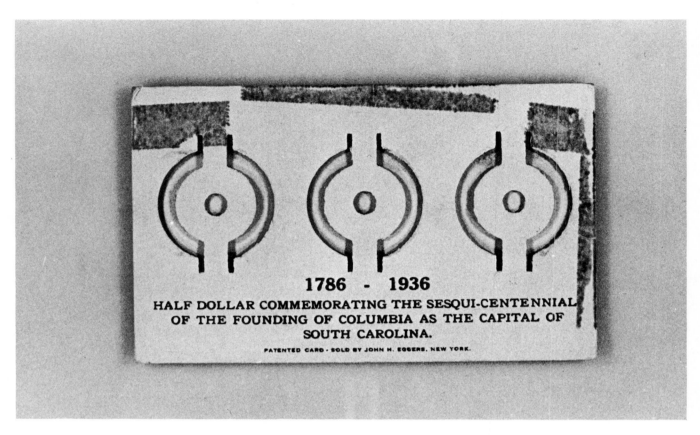

Actual cardboard mailing holder that housed a set of Philadelphia, Denver, and San Francisco minted coins.

Mrs. Julian Hennig, secretary; Dr. L.B. Owens, treasurer; Hon. Jeff B. Bates; Ames Haltiwanger; McFie Anderson; William Lykes, Jr.; C.S. Lemon, exofficio); Lee Lawrie, of the Federal Commission of Fine Arts, who supervised reworking of Davidson's models (the Commission had rejected them as of May 29) until they proved acceptable, as of July 22.

Modus Operandi: The authorizing act called for 25,000 coins to be made "at the mints," so the Commission specified 9,000 at Philadelphia, 8,000 each at Denver and San Francisco: in other words, 8,000 three-piece sets with an extra thousand for filling orders for singles. Mintage was completed in September, but not all the coins were received by the Commission until well into October. Taxay says distribution began on October 15; Slabaugh insists that the Commission decided not to begin filling orders until all the coins were on hand from all three mints, which supposedly came about in December. However that may be, coins were offered singly at $2.15 each (the 15¢ for postage and handling), or in three-piece sets at $6.45 (limit of 10 sets per customer; preference to orders of sets, and to collectors rather than to dealers). Residents of Columbia, South Carolina, were given the first 24 hours after the coins went on sale to place their own orders; latecomers were out of luck, dealers had short supplies and they would not price the coins in their advertisements. Delays in delivery of the coins from the Commission were explained in the mimeographed letter reproduced herein.

The entire mintage sold out quickly. As there has been some confusion over the amounts, we give the correct figures:

> Philadelphia, 9,000 + 7 reserved for assay;
> Denver, 8,000 + 9 for assay;
> San Francisco, 8,000 + 7 for assay.
> Total: 8,000 three-piece sets plus 1,000 extra Philadelphia coins for singles or type collections. None melted.

Collateral Evidence: The coins were shipped out in imprinted holders of the kind here illustrated; about 175 holders survive.

The accompanying brochure or Subscription Application received wide distribution during the fall of 1936. No proofs are reported, though some may have been made for John R. Sinnock.

THE WORLD'S COLUMBIAN EXPOSITION HALF DOLLAR

Obverse

Reverse

The Corpus Delicti: Alias *Columbian '92* or *Columbian '93*.

Clues: The fanciful head is intended to represent Columbus. It is signed в for Charles E. Barber, Engraver of the Mint. As no authentic portraits of Columbus exist—the earliest one is attributed to Lorenzo Lotto, 1512, some six years after the explorer's death—Barber was forced to use imaginary portraits for his prototypes. Three of these have been identified (see *Accessories,* below). The portrait immediately came in for criticism as resembling either Daniel Webster or Henry Ward Beecher; the resemblances are there but beyond doubt accidental considering the actual prototypes.

The three-masted caravel on reverse is intended to represent the *Santa María,* Columbus' flagship. George T. Morgan, the Assistant Engraver (best known because of the silver dollars he designed), appears to have copied it from a photograph of the reproduction of that ship, built in Spain for the Columbian Exposition. Morgan's initial м is concealed in the ship's rigging. Below are two hemispheres, the "Dos Mundos" or "Two Worlds" motif

originally from the Mexican Pillar Dollars or pieces of eight, which for generations had formed the bulk of circulating silver in the United States, and which were actually legal tender until May 1857. The motif refers, of course, to the Spanish possessions in Europe and points east, and to their counterparts in the New World. It promptly came in for criticism as the "ship on wheels."

Opportunity: The Act of Congress of August 5, 1892, which authorized a maximum of 5,000,000 to be coined "at the mints of the United States" to help defray the cost of completing the buildings and exhibits. The coins were to be "manufactured from uncurrent subsidiary coins now in the Treasury" (mostly half dimes withdrawn in 1873 but not melted in the meantime). This was the first of the great World's Fairs to be honored with a commemorative coin; it was scheduled to open in Chicago in October 1892, to honor the 400th anniversary of Columbus' discovery of a group of Caribbean islands, which he mistakenly thought to be part of India. (Half dollars or no, the Exposition did not manage to open until May 1, 1893, remaining in operation only until the following October 30.)

Designers' initials on the Columbian half dollar. The incused B on Columbus' truncated coat collar is the initial of Charles Barber. The raised M below the sail on the reverse is that of George Morgan.

Motive: The floundering Exposition, in financial difficulty long before its doors could open, had petitioned Congress for a $5,000,000 appropriation. What it was promised by the above-mentioned Act of Congress was "nothin' much before," half that sum in commemorative half dollars, to be sold at $1 apiece. What it got was "rather less than 'arf o'that behind," because Congress had withheld some 1,141,760 pieces of the 1893 mintage as security to cover expenses of awards medals and judges, and many of the coins they did get remained unsold, to be either spent or melted. "No reason for it, just company policy," saith the Lord unto Job.

Suspects: Charles E. Barber and George T. Morgan.

Accessories: The Board of Gentlemen Managers of the World's Columbian Exposition (H.N. Higinbotham, president; A.F. Seeberger, treasurer; F.W. Peck, finance committee chairman), and others alluded to below. The Exposition was organized as of April 9, 1890, Congress specifying Chicago as the site (Act of April 25, 1890) after much pressure from city officials in New York, St. Louis and Washington, D.C. wanting the Exposition to be held in their respective cities. On a tract of 686 wilderness acres bordering Lake Michigan and known as Jackson Park, the Exposition people had to erect some 150 buildings, accomodating over 9,000 paintings, innumerable sculptures and 65,000 exhibitors: a formidable task. The Board (through F.W. Peck) made many recommendations to the Mint for designs of the half dollars. At first, through Board member W.E. Curtis, they commissioned the Washington, D.C. sculptor U.S.J. Dunbar to model a bust of Columbus based on the Lotto painting. Mint Engraver Barber rejected it. When it became apparent that the designing itself would have to be done in the Mint, the Board suggested that Barber could adapt the portrait of Columbus from that on a recent medal by Enrique López Lorensis, which medal was duly ordered for the Mint Cabinet Collection via the U.S. Minister to Spain at Madrid. However, what arrived instead was an anonymous medal, pictured by Taxay (p. 5), and even this—being in very high relief—could never have satisfied Barber. Slabaugh says that Barber based his portrait on a photograph or medallic reproduction of the statue by Jerónimo Suñel in Madrid, which statue is in turn based on a portrait by Charles Legrand in the Naval Museum in Madrid. We have been unable to verify this. However, the actual prototype was evidently the plaster model signed O.L.W., one specimen being found in the Chicago Historical Society; its resemblance to the finished coin is so strong as to silence any doubts.

Much the same problems recurred with the reverse. At various times during the fall of 1892, the Board favored different motifs. An editorial in the October 1892 *American Journal of Numismatics* cites newspaper stories describing two devices, respectively the main Exposition building with its enormous dome, and the *Niña, Pinta* and *Santa María* sailing westward. Neither of these proved acceptable to Barber. Eventually, the Board decided on the single three-masted caravel with the two hemispheres, as in the plaster model here illustrated (also in the Chicago Historical Society). This is not credited, but is probably by the same O.L.W. as there are many stylistic resemblances to his signed obverse. When the plaster model for the reverse arrived, Barber labeled it as "uncoinable," but he evidently turned it over to Morgan for copying. O.L.W. must have used the Spanish reproduction of the *Santa María* for copying but Morgan improved on this by using a photograph of the ship—while preserving the same "ship on wheels" layout, the divided date of 1492, and the stars flanking date 1892.

Modus Operandi: The beginning of the coinage has fortunately been documented in detail. The following quotation is from the Chicago *Tribune*, November 20, 1892, page 4, column 1, an on-the-scene report about the striking of the first piece.

FIRST COINS MINTED

Prize World's Fair Souvenirs Turned Out at Philadelphia

The Second Attempt Results in the Production of the Perfect Coin

There Was a Large Gathering of Distinguished People Present

PHILADELPHIA, PA. NOV. 19 (SPECIAL). It was a $10,000 beauty that dropped today from the coin press at the United States Mint when the work of coining the Columbian Half Dollars began. Supt. Bosbyshell was on hand to represent the Government, and James W. Ellsworth of the World's Fair Commission represented that body. There was great interest manifested in the affair because of the big premiums that have been offered for certain of the coins. In addition to the first one, there were also coined and delivered to Mr. Ellsworth the 400th, 1492nd and 1892nd coins of the new Half-Dollars.

Over two thousand of the souvenirs were struck today and the work will continue until all of the 5,000,000 donated by Congress are completed. With the exception of the four valuable coins already specified, the remainder will be held at the Mint until orders for their disposal are received from the Treasury Department. The work of coining the souvenirs will not be finished much before the opening of the Exposition in May, next.

When the hour arrived, Supt. Bosbyshell was summoned to the pressroom by Chief Coiner William S. Steele, while Engraver Charles Barber, who designed the famous coin, Chief Clerk M.N. Cobb, and others, assembled as witnesses. Two dies, one bearing the impression to be stamped upon the obverse face, and the other the reverse, and the only pair in existence (!), were already in place. Foreman Albert Downing placed one of the blank planchets in the receiver and grasped the lever which raises the lower die, while Edwin Cliff, his assistant, stood at the balance wheel. Unfortunately, the first attempt was a failure—a little flaw caused the coin's rejection.

The next attempt was made more carefully for the reputation of the coiners was at stake and they had resolved that the first approved souvenir of the Exposition should be a marvel of perfection and beauty. The planchet, before being accepted, was examined under the microscope and found without a blemish. For the second time, the two workmen turned the press by hand, while the spectators waited in suspense. Again the coin was lifted from the face of the steel die and critically examined by Coiner Steele, Engraver Barber, and Superintendent Bosbyshell. Every line was sharply defined, and the strong (!) features of the discoverer of America, which adorn the coin, seemed to look approvingly on the work. Columbus himself could not have done better, and Uncle Sam's reputation as an artist (!) was vindicated.

Cardboard boxes had been prepared for the reception of the coins, much like those in which pills are sold. No finger touched the first of the souvenirs, but the pliers gently clutched it by the rim and conveyed the $10,000 lump to the box which was immediately sealed and handed to the World's Fair Commissioner (Ellsworth).

After the delivery of the first coin the foreman and his assistant continued coining by hand until they had struck 100 proof pieces, occupying about an hour in the task. Power was then applied, and the actual work of making 5,000,000 half dollars went rapidly ahead.

The new half dollars bear the portrait of Columbus according to Lotto (sic) upon one side, while upon the other is (its) discoverer's caravel, the Santa Maria, in full sail. Beneath the vessel is the date 1492 and the two supporting hemispheres representing the Old and the New World. The motto 'In God We Trust' (actually not on the coins!) and the date 1892 are the remaining details.

Commissioner Ellsworth will take back with him most of the coins for which fancy prices have been offered. The entire vintage (sic) will be shipped to Chicago and disposed of from that city. The coin was designed by Morgan (!), an Englishman, the same who planned the dollar of the daddies. The sum of $10,000 is to be paid the Columbian Commission for the first half dollar, and it was for that reason that Mr. Ellsworth witnessed the coinage. He will make affidavit to what he saw.

These are preliminary plaster models for the Columbian half dollar. Two are preliminary models for the obverse and one is for the reverse. All photos courtesy of the Chicago Historical Society.

Obverse   *Reverse*

This is the actual first attempt at stamping a proof coin. It was rejected because of a slight planchet flaw and snatched up by Colonel James W. Ellsworth.

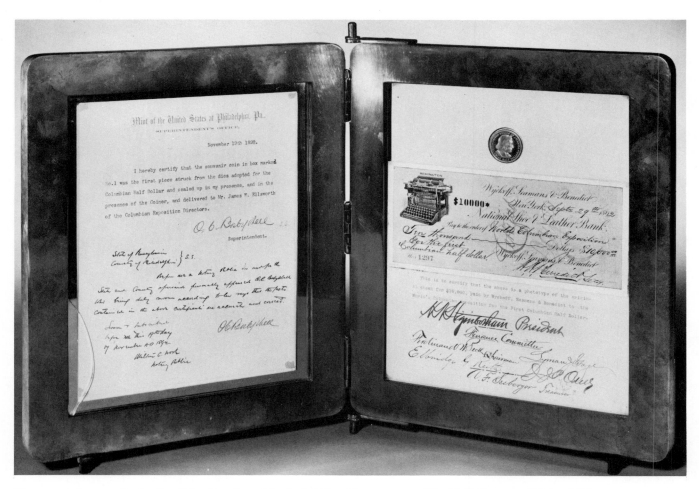

The presentation case for the first Columbian Exposition half dollar. Photo courtesy of the Field Museum of Natural History.

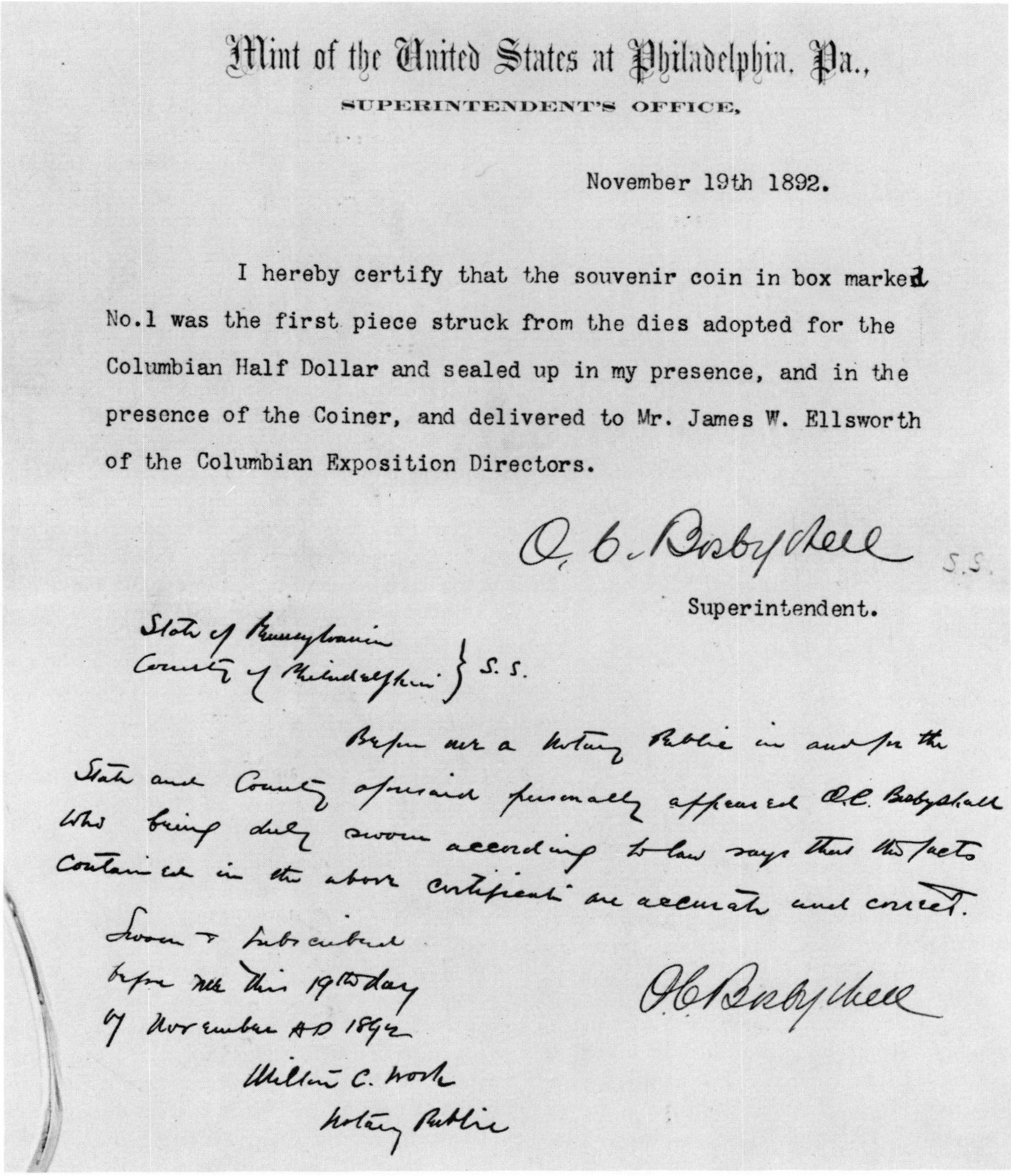

Mint of the United States at Philadelphia, Pa.,

SUPERINTENDENT'S OFFICE,

November 19th 1892.

I hereby certify that the souvenir coin in box marked
No.1 was the first piece struck from the dies adopted for the
Columbian Half Dollar and sealed up in my presence, and in the
presence of the Coiner, and delivered to Mr. James W. Ellsworth
of the Columbian Exposition Directors.

O. C. Bosbyshell S.S.

Superintendent.

State of Pennsylvania
County of Philadelphia } S.S.

Before me a Notary Public in and for the
State and County aforesaid personally appeared O.C. Bosbyshell
who being duly sworn according to law says that the facts
contained in the above certificate are accurate and correct.

Sworn & subscribed
before me this 19th day
of November A.D. 1892

William C. Work
Notary Public

O. C. Bosbyshell

Document stating that the first Columbian struck is in the enclosed holder.

Yes, that extraordinary price—$10,000 then was equivalent in purchasing power to a six figure sum today—was a publicity stunt. Col. James W. Ellsworth, later one of the most famous coin collectors in the United States (owner of, among other things, two 1804 dollars, the four 1783 CONSTELLATIO NOVA silver pieces traced back to the year of issue through Robert Morris, Thomas Jefferson and Charles Thomson (secretary of Continental Congress), a Brasher doubloon, and almost every other American rarity then known), had managed to get himself a membership on the Board of Gentlemen Managers of the World's Columbian Exposition as a fund-raising gimmick. He witnessed this event in

63

order to testify that the coin to be delivered to the firm of Wyckoff, Seamans and Benedict (the Remington typewriter manufacturers) was in fact the first one made. Actually, it was the second one struck! Newspaper stories like the above-quoted made it certain that sooner or later people would know that the Remington typewriter firm—who furnished all the typewriters at the Exposition—had bought the documented first Columbian half dollar for $10,000 and were presumably expecting eventually to make a profit. This called the public's attention to the enormous possibilities in coin collecting, and to the fact that not all coin collectors are gimlet-eyed monomaniacs.

(This is by no means the last word about Ellsworth's connection with the Columbian half dollars. See below, in the discussion about proof strikings.)

We have no specific details about times or circumstances of manufacture of the 5,000,000 business strikes aside from the following tabulation and the later story of the No. One 1893 proof.

Authorized	5,000,000
Struck November– December 1892	950,000
Struck, 1893	4,050,000 + 2,105 for assay
Withheld by Congress, February 1893	− 1,141,760
Available for sale dated 1893	2,908,240
Melted, unsold, of latter	1,359,940
Net mintage, 1893	1,548,300

The larger figure usually seen for 1893 net mintage is derived by counting the assay pieces (which had never left the mint) as part of those released. The total melted is usually given as 2,501,700 (e.g. in Slabaugh), but this figure is known to include the 1,141,760 withheld by Congress. Congress' action was regarded by the Exposition authorities as a breach of contract and a violation of the authorizing act, since the half dollars had been issued only for costs of completing the Exhibition buildings and exhibits—not for award medals and judges. As a result, the Exposition authorities no longer felt bound by Section 4 of the authorizing act, which was a "blue law" sop to the fundamentalist element forbidding the Exposition to open on Sundays. We do not understand Slabaugh's reference (p. 9) to "some 400,000 that the Exposition did not sell" being later melted, since only the larger figure given above is reconcilable with the total recorded meltage. What we would like to know is how many of the unsold

coins were spent instead during and after the Panic of 1893. It appears that the Exposition authorities used the coins as collateral for bank loans at par—amazingly, the Chicago banks charged the Exposition no interest. But after the Exposition closed and the coins remained unsold, the banks released them into circulation. It is also very probable that some of the coins which actually sold to Exposition visitors at $1 apiece were worn down as pocket pieces or later spent, either by their children, or by those same visitors feeling a financial pinch later that year.

For 1893, the year of the Exposition, was also the year of one of the greatest disasters in the history of the United States, and for millions of people a single 50¢ piece could mean the difference between eating that day and going hungry. The reason, of course, was Senator John Sherman and his House crony Rep. Richard P. "Silver Dick" Bland. Bland had become famous for pushing an act through Congress over a presidential veto in February 1878, mandating mint purchases of enormous quantities of silver bullion to make the Morgan dollars—for the benefit of the owners of western silver mines. When the original Bland Act was expiring, Senator Sherman in 1890 forced a bill through Congress (the Sherman Silver Purchase Act), which required the Mint Bureau to buy from 2,000,000 to 4,000,000 ounces of silver per month, at subsidy prices well above the world market level, and to pay for it in gold or in the new Coin Notes (alias "Treasury Notes of 1890"), which could be redeemed in gold. The mine owners shipped their silver to the mint, received Coin Notes for it, turned them in for gold, used the gold to buy silver outside for the depressed market price, sold this in turn to the mint for hefty profits, receiving more Coin Notes and turning them in for gold, in an endless chain, so that by 1893 the Treasury was nearly stripped of its gold reserves, while various international obligations had to be paid in gold, and several bond issues (also payable in gold) were coming due. The prospect that the Treasury might default on bonds threw Wall Street into a panic. A selling rush developed, prices collapsed, over 300 banks failed (by the end of 1893 the figure was 419), thousands of factories and other businesses went bankrupt, farmers could not sell their produce, taxes could not be collected, over 4,000,000 people were jobless and many were starving in the streets. (Many of the survivors joined Coxey's Army in 1894, in the first protest march on Washington, ancestor of the civil rights marches and peace marches of the 1960s.) Meanwhile the silver mine owners were becoming millionaires, and doubtless they would have shrugged and echoed Marie Antoinette's "let 'em eat cake" line had anyone been so discourteous as to point out that millions of people were without bread. President Cleveland called Congress into special session to repeal the Sherman Act, which was done only over violent protests from "Silver Dick" Bland, who evidently believed that what was good for the silver mine owners was good for the nation. (Bland was so popular, despite his role in the Sherman Act, that he became the front runner for the 1896 presidential nomination, until William Jennings Bryan made his "Cross of Gold" speech and was nominated instead!)

Under the circumstances, it is not surprising that the 28,000,000–odd visitors to the Exposition spent an average of only $1.18 apiece. And when the pinch came on them, they spent their Columbian half dollars, which is why so many of them today are found in circulated condition. Gem survivors are quite uncommon!

On January 3, 1893, the Mint began striking Columbian half dollars dated 1893. The first of these was earmarked for presentation to Harlow N. Higinbotham, president of the Exposition, who could hardly have cared less. Higinbotham was not interested in coin collecting; his sole concern with the coins was that as many as possible should be sold at double face to help bail the Exposition out of debt. Higinbotham eventually turned over his coin to the Chicago Historical Society, where it remains. (The full story of this coin, however, is so completely entangled with the history of the 104 proofs dated 1892 that we must consider them together.) With the coin is the original certificate, here illustrated.

Originally the Mint had not planned to issue any proof Columbian half dollars. Including them in the proof sets of the year would have required either that they be priced lower than the cost of a business strike Columbian half dollar on the fairgrounds, or that the prices of the proof sets be raised to a level where they felt sales would have suffered. However, the circumstances of mintage of the first hundred specimens "by hand" on November 19 indicate that they must have been true brilliant proofs, like the Number One specimen which went to the Remington typewriter people, and the newspaper story quoted above seems to us conclusive evidence that the Philadelphia Mint actually struck not less than 104 proofs dated 1892 on that same day: the initial reject (illustrated), nos. 1 through 100, and nos. 400, 1492 and 1892. (Why no. 400? Apparently because what was being commemorated was a 400th anniversary.) A comparable account exists for the Number One specimen of 1893, which we quote from William A. Pettit's booklet *The Resurrection of the First Columbian Half Dollars.*

A few minutes later Mr. Zywicki (of the Chicago Historical Society) returned from the vault. He had three large envelopes and a small round box. The little box was like a pill box, and on top of it was written "No. 1, 1893" and it was sealed on the side with red wax with a small medal pressed into the wax sealed on the side, with a portrait of Superintendent O.C. Bosbyshell, and showed that he had sealed the box. Inside the first box was a second box. On top of this box it read: "Phila. Jan. 3/93 First Columbian Half-Dol. struck in 1893. O.C. Bosbyshell, Supt. Mint U.S. at Phila."

I opened this box and inside I saw cotton. I took the cotton away, and there was the first 1893 Columbian Half Dollar—*a gray proof.* The condition was the same as the 1892, except that this one, having been exposed to the air, had turned to a gray color. After picking it up by the edges and examining both obverse and reverse, I was satisfied that this was the coin I had been looking for.

We illustrate the 1893 Number One coin with its box and wax seals on page 67.

At this point it will be useful to remind readers that the word "proof" means not a grade of preservation, but a method of manufacture. In this period, proofs were special strikings for collectors, sold to them at premiums or included in diplomatic presentations and cornerstones. Coins, to qualify as proofs, must fulfill all the following criteria: they must be struck on brilliantly polished planchets, from polished dies, and given two to four blows apiece from the dies at striking, in order to bring up relief details of the design to a clarity then unknown on ordinary business strikings. (See Walter Breen's *Encyclopedia of U.S. and Colonial Proof Coins, 1722–1977,* FCI Press, July 1977, esp. pp. 14–15, 19–21, 194–5.) This requires special mention because in addition to the 104 authentic proof strikings of the 1892 Columbian half dollar and the Number One 1893, there are many business strikings of both dates from new dies retaining initial polish, or from dies heavily repolished to efface clash marks. These are often offered for sale as the far rarer proofs, and collectors unfamiliar with the genuine article have more often than not been deceived. Illustrations following will exhibit the difference more plainly than any words can do.

On page 68, the bottom obverse and the bottom reverse belong to a proof striking (the actual Number One coin) and the above belong to a proof-like early business striking. Note particularly the details of hair, garments, sail seams, rigging generally, planking, central waves, and the raised rim where it meets the dentilated borders.

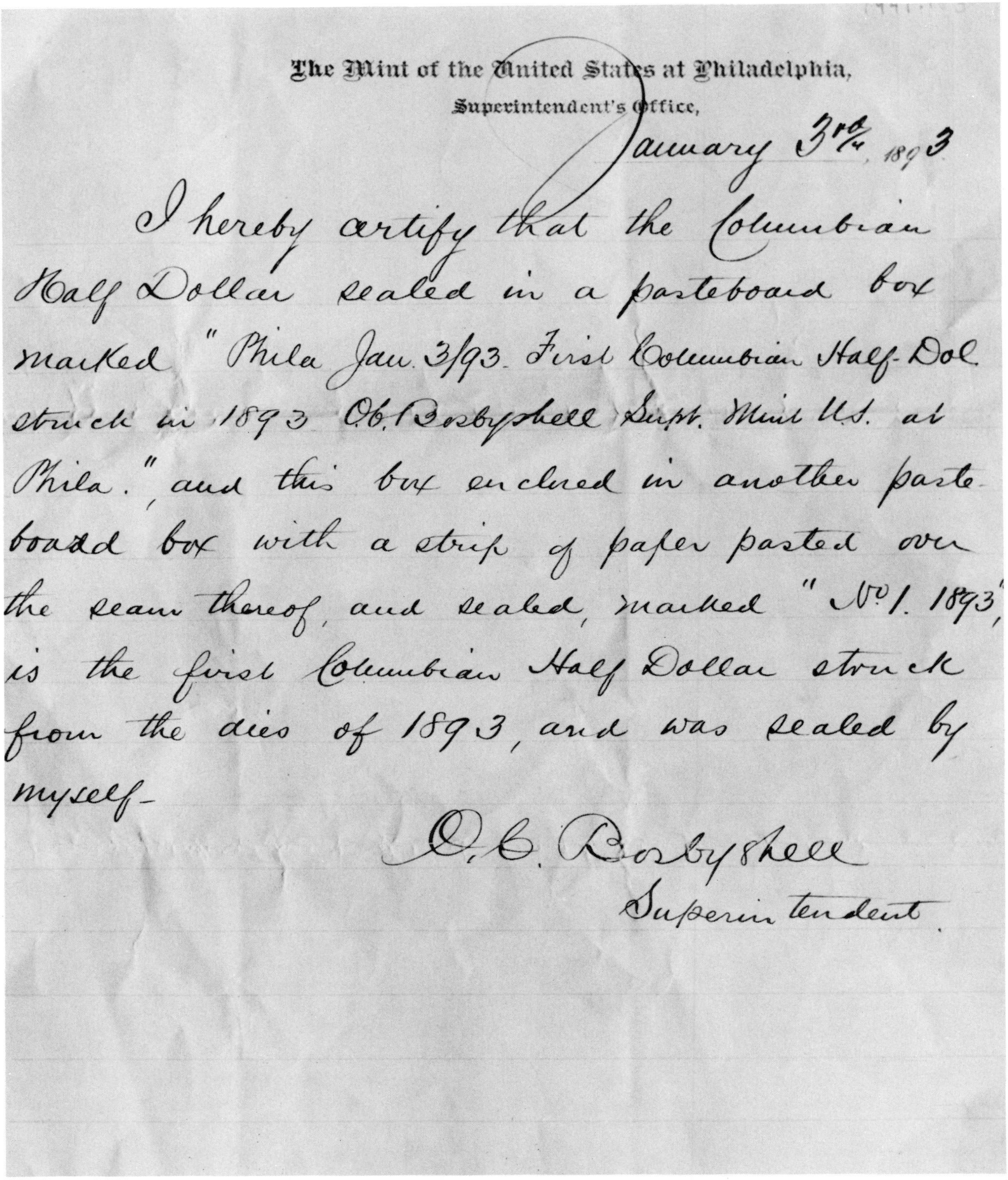

The Mint of the United States at Philadelphia,

Superintendent's Office,

January 3rd, 1893

I hereby certify that the Columbian Half Dollar sealed in a pasteboard box marked "Phila Jan. 3/93. First Columbian Half-Dol. struck in 1893 O.C. Bosbyshell Supt. Mint U.S. at Phila." and this box enclosed in another paste-board box with a strip of paper pasted over the seam thereof, and sealed, marked "No. 1. 1893," is the first Columbian Half Dollar struck from the dies of 1893, and was sealed by myself —

O. C. Bosbyshell
Superintendent.

Original mint certificate that accompanied the #1 proof Columbian now in the Chicago Historical Society. Photo courtesy of the Chicago Historical Society.

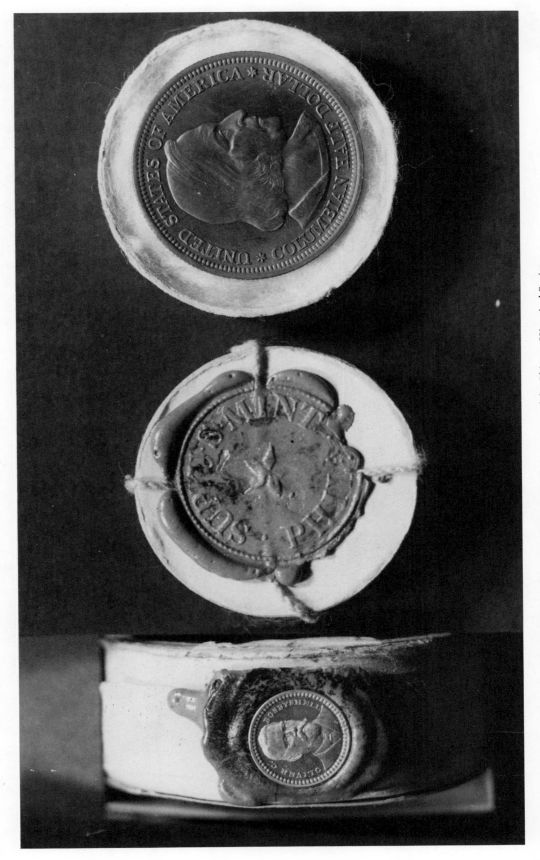

The 1893 #1 coin with its box, wax seals, and gold medal of Mr. Bosbyshell. Photo courtesy of the Chicago Historical Society.

Obverse

Reverse

Obverse and reverse of a prooflike business striking.

Obverse

Reverse

Obverse and reverse of an actual proof striking.

Top plate shows detail of a proof 1892 commemorative half dollar. Bottom photo shows same detail on an early-struck, frosted, prooflike regular issue coin. This is the sort of coin often sold to the unwary as a proof coin.

To remove the last possible ambiguity, we show other areas in enlargement. On the figure below, details of rigging and waves are obviously so much sharper in detail on the proof than on the proof-like business striking that a child could tell them apart—*once he has had his attention drawn to them.*

We return to the circumstances of mintage of the proofs, and to Col. Ellsworth's singular role in their unauthorized, unwanted, unwelcome, clandestine and contract-breaking manufacture and distribution.

Before the first piece was struck, possibly weeks before, Col. Ellsworth asked Mr. Higinbotham to sign an order addressed to the mint personnel in charge of the initial striking, instructing Superintendent Bosbyshell to give Ellsworth the first 100 specimens to be struck after the Number One coin

earmarked for the Remington typewriter people. Higinbotham immediately told him this was impossible because on August 20, 1892, a Mr. J.K. Robinson had contracted to subscribe to the first 500 pieces to be struck, paying the regular $1 apiece. Since he was the first subscriber, Mr. Higinbotham felt morally obligated to fulfill his request. Ellsworth attempted to induce Higinbotham to change his mind—in vain. The most that Higinbotham would do was to write a letter to Bosbyshell asking him to single out numbers 1, 400, 1492, 1892, and the last one to be struck, sealing each coin separately with his own signed certificate accompanying them. (The certificate for No. 1492 is appended.)

Armed with this letter, but with no other authorization, Col. Ellsworth directed the mint superintendent to produce the Remington coin as a proof striking; to strike the next 100 specimens as proofs, having each one enveloped and numbered; to strike the 400th, 1492nd and 1892nd coins in proof, likewise separately enveloped and furnished with his signed certificates; and to strike the first 1893 coin in proof. How he managed this is unknown. One of us (A.S.) firmly believes that he brought imaginary verbal orders from Higinbotham to strike the extra proofs, after the authorizing letter had been written, because they were needed for presentation purposes for Mrs. Higinbotham, the wives of the other Directors, and the ladies of the families of the railroad officials. Whatever his actual story to the Superintendent of the Mint, clearly it worked, and it was completely contrary to Higinbotham's intention.

There is a still more singular circumstance. Recall that the newspaper article cited earlier had mentioned that the actual first specimen (not the one that went to the Remington people) was rejected because of a planchet flaw. It is strange that Albert Downing, the most knowledgeable and experienced foreman of the coining room at the Philadelphia Mint, would have selected such a blank without inspecting it, especially for a coin known at the time to be earmarked for sale at $10,000—numismatics' most expensive specimen till 1941. Wouldn't the actual first specimen, permanently identifiable by the planchet defect, be a grand prize for even a collector of the prestige and wealth of Col. James W. Ellsworth? Is it not possible that either Ellsworth himself selected the blank with this in mind, or at best that it was a happy accident? And after that, if Col. Ellsworth requested that the actual first be placed in the envelope marked #2 and included with the 101 proofs to be struck that day, why should Superintendent Bosbyshell deny his request?

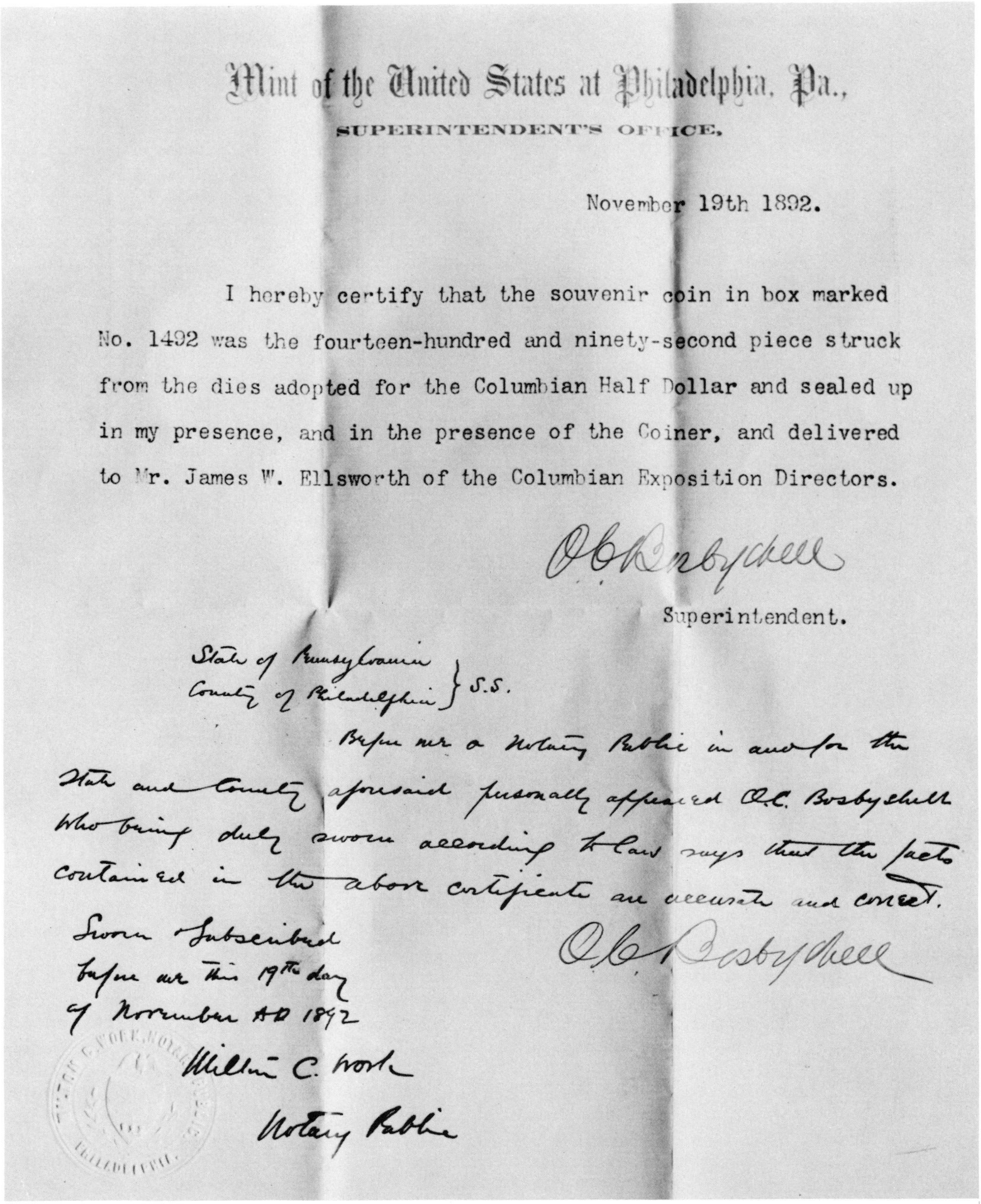

Mint of the United States at Philadelphia, Pa.,

SUPERINTENDENT'S OFFICE,

November 19th 1892.

I hereby certify that the souvenir coin in box marked No. 1492 was the fourteen-hundred and ninety-second piece struck from the dies adopted for the Columbian Half Dollar and sealed up in my presence, and in the presence of the Coiner, and delivered to Mr. James W. Ellsworth of the Columbian Exposition Directors.

O.C. Bosbyshell

Superintendent.

State of Pennsylvania
County of Philadelphia } S.S.

Before me a Notary Public in and for the State and County aforesaid personally appeared O.C. Bosbyshell who being duly sworn according to law says that the facts contained in the above certificate are accurate and correct.

O.C. Bosbyshell

Sworn & subscribed
before me this 19th day
of November AD 1892

William C. York

Notary Public

The certificate for the 1492nd Columbian coin struck in proof at the Philadelphia mint. Photo courtesy of the Chicago Historical Society.

The top photo, an enlarged detail of the actual number one coin, shows the quality of strike. Compare this with the detail of number 8 proof in the bottom photo, noting the loss of sharpness even in the first strikings. Also note in the top photo Morgan's initial just above the corner of the sail in the upper right corner.

None of this came to Higinbotham's attention at the time. Instead, being no more aware of the difference between a proof coin and a first strike than the beginning collector, Higinbotham did not know that the really special strikings had been set aside, and assumed that they were all in the first keg to arrive from the mint. And so, on Christmas Day of 1892, he personally opened that keg (containing 1,000 in all) and took out 500 coins for Mr. J.K. Robinson, the first subscriber.

Unfortunately, Ellsworth was not present when the mint's third shipment arrived at the Commission's Chicago office on January 10, 1893. The keg bore the word SPECIAL on a label, and with it was a letter from Mint Superintendent Bosbyshell, dated January 4, 1893, explaining why this shipment was marked $947.50 instead of $1000, mentioning that the 100 special proof pieces had been withheld from the first keg and placed in a separate wooden box, that five had been taken out by Bosbyshell with

Official admission tickets to the World's Columbian Exposition.

Higinbotham's prior consent (total $52.50), and that in another separate box would be found the first piece dated 1893, a proof, with its certificate.

Higinbotham was infuriated, and placed *all* the special strikings in a safe deposit box in the Illinois Trust and Savings Bank, to be kept unopened until he had words with Col. Ellsworth.

No details of the confrontation are known, though one may conjecture mushroom-shaped clouds rising above the Commission offices when Ellsworth returned.

The next act of the drama showed Col. Ellsworth writing to Mint Superintendent Bosbyshell, who obligingly wrote in turn to Mr. Higinbotham suggesting that he be guided by Ellsworth's plans for disposition of the coins. There was no response.

On March 20, 1893, A.F. Seeberger, Treasurer of the Exposition, wrote to Higinbotham indicating that Ellsworth was expecting the special strikings to be delivered, because they were scheduled for presentation to the people who had given the Commission much assistance. Higinbotham's reply ignored that issue and concentrated solely on the moral aspect—how Ellsworth had requested the special coins without any authorization from Higinbotham or any other Exposition officer, and therefore that Ellsworth had no right whatever to them.

On February 3, 1894, at Mr. Higinbotham's house, the special package was finally opened by J.K. Robinson. By agreement, Robinson was to retain all the even numbered specimens, nos. 2 through 100, while the odd-numbered ones, nos. 5 through 99, were retained by Higinbotham, no. 3 going to Mrs. Higinbotham. This was the package Ellsworth had desperately wanted because it contained his dream coins, no. 2 (the actual first striking of all, preceding the Remington coin, with the planchet defect) and the 1893 no. 1, the first *official* proof. However, nobody present knew the story.

Robinson gave the #2 coin and others to a close friend who lived in Pennsylvania. In 1911, the #2 coin, along with nos. 8 and either 32 or 38 went to the friend's son, who in turn showed them to one of us (A.S.) along with the rest of his father's small collection. In a later conversation, this man said, "One of the coins came in a purple-bluish paper envelope and was numbered 2 in blue ink." To the question "Which one?" he replied, "The coin with those lines or scratches above the ship." It developed that the envelopes had been thrown away because they were "torn and in a bad state"—probably tattered enough that the coins would fall out of them!—but that "the green-colored coin came in envelope 8, while the other coin was in envelope 32 or 38."

After reading the newspaper article quoted above, and carefully studying the unpublished personal correspondence of Mr. Higinbotham, the question arose—why did the Number 2 coin have planchet defects on both sides? The original Remington striking, the second made and the first perfect piece, was made available for examination at the Field Museum of Natural History. The #2 specimen proved to be identical in striking quality. However, nos. 8 and the later proofs were not as sharply impressed in the centers, especially on the vertical ribs, planking, sail seams and central waves (see photo, p. 71) because the dies were already wearing down. Also, greater care was taken in making the defective prototype and Number One. The conclusion was clear enough: Number Two was the actual Number One defective prototype, and the coin Ellsworth had wanted for himself. (None of the other proofs to date have shown any planchet defects.) In this writer's opinion (A.S.), since this is the first commemorative coin minted for the United States of America, it is far more valuable both historically and numismatically than the one in the Field Museum in Chicago.

The rare $5.00 Columbian Commemorative stamp.

Collateral Evidence: To date no original presentation cases or holders have shown up, though there are a few Columbians in cases originally intended for medals. Slabaugh's "gold imprinted black leather holder nearly round in shape, similar to a small coin purse" is apparently in this latter category. On the other hand, there are several types of original mountings.

We have no details on these, but presume they were special badges sold to groups in attendance on those days only. They are quite rare, seldom exhibited.

The portrait from the half dollar is found, minus its inscription, on one of the regular admission tickets (a selection of the different designs is illustrated). These were made by the American Bank Note Company, evidently copying the half dollar—the time element excludes its being the other way around. These tickets, but particularly the one with the Columbus head, make excellent tie-ins at convention exhibits of commemorative half dollars (quite aside from their being long popular among coin collectors).

A rarer and more desirable tie-in, however, is the $5 commemorative stamp with the half dollar portrait reversed and again without its inscription. This is Scott 245 (design A86), also designed by the American Bank Note Company, its first day of issue being January 2, 1893. Understandably, the quantity made was very limited—only 27,350—and the stamp is now a famous rarity.

THE CONNECTICUT TERCENTENARY HALF DOLLAR

Obverse

Reverse

The Corpus Delicti: Alias *Connecticut* or *Charter Oak.*

Clues: This very Art Deco design represents the Charter Oak, vaguely after one of C.D.W. Brownell's four paintings of this historic tree (completed in 1855–56, in the Connecticut Historical Society; it is pictured in Slabaugh and Taxay), with a prominent cavity in the trunk emphasized for historical reasons rather than realism. (Realism would have made the leaves less than one-tenth the size they are on the coin, compared to the trunk! This tree was about 1,000 years old and some 21 feet around near the base before lightning blasted it on August 21, 1856.) Use of this tree as a symbol for Connecticut was inevitable: in 1662, King Charles II granted the younger John Winthrop a royal charter for the colony; but when James II succeeded to the throne, he sought to recall all his predecessors' charters and to consolidate all the New England colonies into the Dominion of New England under Governor Sir Edmund Andros (1686). Andros visited the colonial authorities at Hartford on October 31, 1687, and

when at a meeting that evening he announced that he intended to seize the charter and return it to the King, all the candles were extinguished long enough for Joseph Wadsworth to hide the charter in the oak tree's historic cavity. Andros left, infuriated, but powerless as long as he did not have that document. After his patron James II was ousted in the "Glorious Revolution" a year later, the colonists in Boston seized Andros and sent him back to England in chains. The original charter was retrieved (a fragment of which remains with the Connecticut Historical Society), and the tree, ever since called the Charter Oak, became an object of veneration. After lightning felled it, its wood was used for making various historical items, including the chair still reserved in the Hartford State House for the President of the State Senate. The Charter Oak Memorial stands today on the site of the tree, at Charter Oak Avenue and Charter Oak Place. The Charter Oak, then, is a symbol of Connecticut's colonial independence—cut from the same bolt of cloth as the more ferociously radical activist variety represented by the Sons of Liberty in Massachusetts.

Obverse   *Reverse*

The excessively rare Connecticut matte proof that was once in the collection of chief mint engraver John R. Sinnock.

One of the original coin boxes in which the Connecticut commemorative half dollars were housed.

On the reverse, thirteen stars for the 13 original colonies form a semicircular arc around the eagle, though they are so faint as not to be visible on some strikings. This leaves only the dates 1635–1935 un-explained. Historians have long taken 1635 as the official date of foundation of the Colony of Connect-icut, mostly because in that year John Winthrop the younger (later Royal Governor and recipient of the charter from Charles II) had been named governor on the strength of letters patent from the Earl of Warwick. There had been Dutch settlers in the area for a generation before, and English Puritan settle-ments since 1633, but no formally organized central government before Winthrop.

Opportunity: The Connecticut Tercentenary Commission (Samuel Fisher, chairman) sought ap-proval of an issue of commemorative half dollars in connection with statewide celebrations to be held in 1935. The bill to authorize the mintage became the Act of June 21, 1934.

Motive: To aid in financing the celebration.

Suspects: Henry Kreis, sculptor. Though the au-thorizing act specified that the government was "not to be subject to the expense of making the models for master dies or other preparations for this coin-age," this was nevertheless openly violated, as the designing was a Public Works Administration proj-ect. For once we not only condone, we applaud, as the result was immensely satisfactory. This is one of the best designs in the series.

Accessories: Paul Manship, the illustrious sculptor who supervised Kreis. Theodore Sizer, Assistant Di-rector, Fine Arts Department, Yale University, wrote to the Federal Fine Arts Commission strongly urging approval, and defused any possible objections to the exaggerated leaf size on the perfectly good grounds that in this type of stylization the leaves had to be enlarged to show at all as design elements. (Sizer was one of the members of the Tercentenary Commit-tee.)

Modus Operandi: The Fine Arts Commission ap-proved Kreis' models as of February 4, 1935; the Treasury concurred on February 6, after which the models went to Medallic Art Company for reduction. As the authorizing act specified 25,000 coins, the Philadelphia Mint struck that quantity in a single batch, with 18 extra reserved for assay, during part of April and May 1935. They went on sale through the Tercentenary Committee at $1 apiece; the entire

issue sold out and there was no hint of scandal at any time.

Collateral Evidence: Many of these coins went to the general public, and as a result many of them are in none too satisfactory condition, being nicked, scratched, or poorly cleaned. A critical area appears to be the upper part of wing, legs, and claw pads; look for mint frost if any of these are weaker than on the specimen pictured.

Matte proofs exist; the only one we have physically handled is from the John R. Sinnock estate, via lot 2055, 1962 ANA Convention auction. Four or five others are reported. As they could be fraudulently simulated by pickling or sandblasting ordinary un-circulated specimens, we show an enlargement of the authentic proof. No specimen with less detail sharp-ness than this—or with the same granularity *within* nicks or dents as elsewhere in fields—is acceptable.

The normal coins were distributed in small boxes covered with silver foil, and bearing the state arms in dark blue ink, one coin per box. About thirty of these original boxes of issue survive; there are slight variations in the state arms. Unfortunately, we have not had long enough access to any of these to photo-graph the varieties.

A fine philatelic tie-in is the Connecticut Ter-centenary or "Charter Oak" 3¢ stamp, Scott 772, Type A249. This comes in violet (one variety being called rose violet) and its designer is not credited. Released April 26, 1935, it went to the public in a total issue of 70,726,000. The tree is obviously based on the Brownell painting, but this time minus cavity, enlarged leaves, or stylization.

The Connecticut Tercentenary or "Charter Oak" 3 ¢ commemora-tive stamp.

THE DELAWARE SWEDISH TERCENTENARY HALF DOLLAR

Obverse

Reverse

The Corpus Delicti: Alias *Delaware, Founding of Swedish Delaware Tercentary, 1936 Delaware, 1937 Delaware, 1938 Delaware.*

Clues: According to C.L. Ward, chairman of the Delaware Swedish Tercentenary Commission, the ship side is obverse, and represents the *Kalmar Nyckel* (Key of Kalmar—a port city in southeastern Sweden). This ship, with its sister the *Fogel Grip*, brought settlers for the New Sweden colony to Delaware Bay, in an area already claimed by both the English and the Dutch. They arrived in March 1638, hence this date below the ship. They settled at "The Rocks," building Fort Christina (now a park in Wilmington); they named the fort after the then 11-year-old Queen Christina, later to be notorious throughout Europe both for her extreme intellectuality and for her intransigently unconventional lesbian lifestyle. Slabaugh (p. 136) has sketched the complex story of boundary disputes near Delaware Bay (comparable to those between the Israelis and the P.L.O.) which were not to end until 1750, by which time the New Sweden colony had been taken over first by the Dutch and then by the English, only to become in

1776 part of the Sovereign State of Delaware, first to ratify the Constitution in 1787.

The three diamonds dividing 1638–1938 from other lettering allude to the state's three counties of Kent, New Castle, and Sussex, as well as (very approximately) to their conformation, and to the state's minuscule size and great fertility—apparently the acres of diamonds symbolism being taken seriously enough to give the state the sobriquet of "Diamond State" even though no diamonds are actually mined therein.

Initials CLS behind the stern of the ship are for Carl L. Schmitz, designer, sculptor. Not enough details are visible on the flags to tell, but presumably they're meant to be flags of Sweden. A model of the ship is part of the monument in the Fort Christina area.

On reverse, the sun's rays piercing the clouds (presumably symbolic of divine protection despite adversity) shine on the Old Swedes Church (Holy Trinity) at Wilmington. This was erected in 1698–99, dedicated in the latter year, and remains open today as (allegedly) the oldest Protestant church building still in use for worship in the United States.

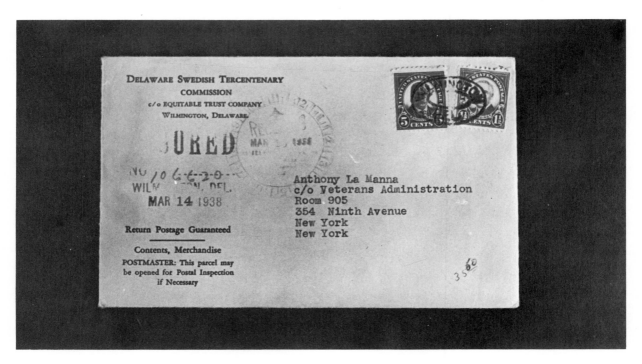

Envelope holding coin holder—with slots for five coins—used by the Delaware Swedish Tercentenary Commission to distribute the Delaware Commemorative half dollar to its subscribers.

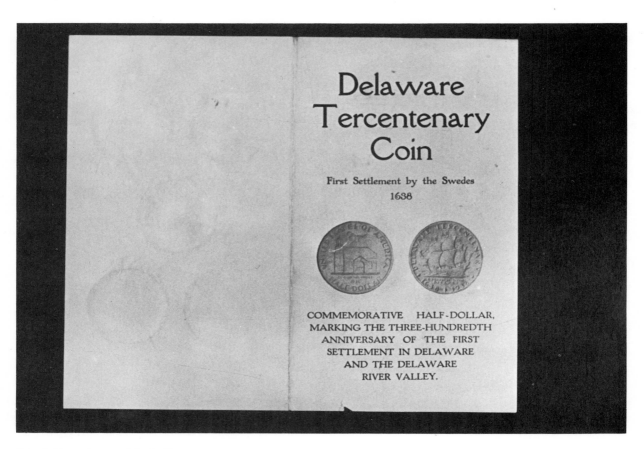

Coin holder—front and back sides.

80

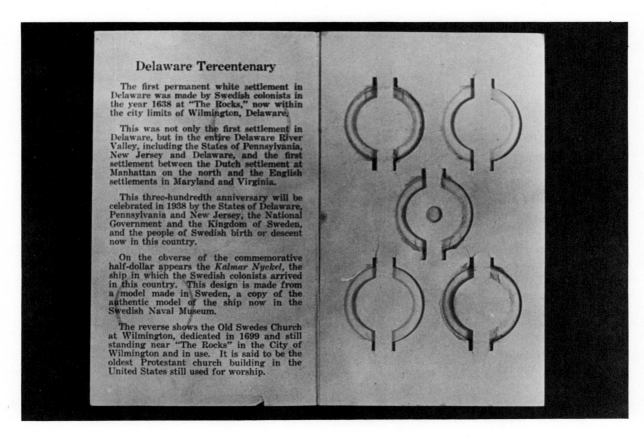

Coin holder—center spread.

Its location—near "The Rocks," very close to where the *Kalmar Nyckel* dropped anchor at landfall—made it a natural choice for inclusion in the commemoration, though the way it is represented on the coin is very different from the way it looked in 1699: the arch on the side dates only from 1750, the tower and belfry only from 1802.

Date 1936 below the church is that of the coin's authorization.

Opportunity: Local celebrations statewide, scheduled for summer of 1938; Act of Congress, May 15, 1936.

Motive: Local pride, and to help finance the celebrations by advance sales.

Suspects: Carl L. Schmitz, local German-American designer and sculptor, winner of a competition for the coin design sponsored by the Delaware Swedish Tercentenary Commission. (There were some 40 entries; prize $500, judges being John R. Sinnock, Engraver of the Mint, and the renowned sculptor Dr. Robert Tait MacKenzie.)

Accessories: Whoever took photographs of the Old Swedes Church and of the accurate scale model of the *Kalmar Nyckel* in the Swedish Naval Museum.

Modus Operandi: After the Act of Congress authorizing the coinage came the competition; Schmitz was adjudged the winner in November, but his name was not publicly announced until the Federal Commission of Fine Arts approved his models, which they did on December 14, subject to minor revisions improving the historical accuracy of the church architecture. Schmitz executed these corrections (which did not include removal of the post-1699 arch or bell tower!), after which the models went to the Medallic Art Company of New York for reduction to half-dollar size, thence to the Philadelphia Mint, which struck 25,000 (plus 15 reserved for assay) in March 1937. This accounts for early advertisements of these coins as *1937 Delaware*, despite their 1936 and anticipatory 1938 dates. As the authorizing act gave 25,000 as the minimum coinage, but specified neither maximum nor expiration date so long as the designs remained unchanged, Delaware halves could have been struck in indefinitely large quantities at until the Act of August 5, 1939 stopped any further issue. In actuality, only the one batch was struck, and not all of these were sold, so there was no reason to make others.

The Delaware Swedish Tercentenary Commission marketed the coins at $1.75 each from Room 318, Equitable Trust Company, Wilmington, presumably using this bank's vaults for storage.

Of the solitary batch of 25,000 half dollars, some 4,022 eventually went back to the Mint for re-melting, leaving a net mintage of 20,978.

Collateral Evidence: About 80 original holders are known; these are the regular five-coin Eggers holders, specially imprinted for the Commission.

The vast majority of survivors are weakly struck in centers despite the coin's low relief. It is very unusual to find one in which the gable above the arch is completely clear, or in which the vegetation near the lower part of the tower is without blurring, or in which the clouds or the mainsail are free of flatness.

Proofs are not reported, though probably some were made for John R. Sinnock. On the other hand, there are brilliantly proof-like pieces from polished dies, and these may have been specially made for presentation.

Because the local celebrations were planned to be held by New Jersey and Pennsylvania in addition to Delaware, as well as nationwide among people of Swedish descent, numerous commemorative medals were struck in the United States and in Sweden. No comprehensive catalogue of these is known to us. Two tie-in items are familiar, however, and these could be used for effective exhibits.

One of these is the Swedish-Finnish Tercentenary stamp, depicting Stanley M. Arthur's painting "Landing of the First Swedish and Finnish Settlers in America." This is the red-violet 3¢, Scott 836 (Type A308), first issued June 27, 1938, to the extent of 58,564,368 specimens; the first day covers (postmarked Wilmington, Delaware, of course) numbered 225,617.

The other—and for years far better known—is the Swedish commemorative 2 Kronor of 1938, Yeoman 61, the same size as the half dollar, portraying King Gustav V on obverse, and the crown above the *Kalmar Nyckel* on reverse. The legend NOVAE SUECIAE SUECIA MEMOR means "Sweden is mindful of New Sweden" (i.e., of her first colony in the New World); the dates 1638–1938 have the obvious explanation. In all, 500,000 were coined, and the late Wayte Raymond was among those who promoted this coin as a tie-in along with the Norse-American medals of 1925 and several other pieces tangential to commemorative coins.

Locating a specimen with a clean-surfaced center sail and the sail located in the exact center of the coin obverse, plus a reverse with a fully struck triangular top section above the church door (that resembles a wide arrowhead that appears to be pointing to the clouds above the church) would be a real find. Most specimens were flatly struck in this area on the reverse, while the sail usually shows slide marks or fine scratches on its surface. There exist proof-like specimens struck from a highly polished set of dies, possibly for presentation purposes: these should command a premium.

Here is another issue which is believed to be easily located. However, top quality pieces are becoming difficult to find, and the present available supply is somewhat thin and not as plentiful as believed.

THE ELGIN CENTENNIAL HALF DOLLAR

Obverse

Reverse

The Corpus Delicti: Alias *The Elgin, Pioneer.*

Clues: The obverse head is a copy of "Head of a Pioneer" by Trygve Rovelstad, a statue pictured in Taxay, p. 217. Another version of it is the head of the rifleman in the group of pioneers found on reverse, itself a small copy of the still unfinished Pioneer Memorial at Elgin, Illinois, also by Rovelstad. His initials TR are under the beard on obverse. The only other feature requiring explanation is the date 1673. On the original medal (pictured in Slabaugh, p. 127), which depicted the same statue in far clearer detail than the coin, the dates were given as 1835–1935, for the centennial of the city of Elgin. We have been unable to learn who insisted on substituting 1673; this date is irrelevant to the events honored on the coin, being that of the year in which Joliet and Marquette first entered what is now Illinois on their missionary work.

The statue deserves additional comment. On the coin, it is never clearly enough brought up to show necessary details; which is why, among other things, it is usually referred to as a group of four pioneers when actually there are five, the fifth being the baby in its mother's arms. Around the statue's base, above a long bas relief depicting workers and Indians, is the inscription "To the men who have blazed the trails, who have conquered the soil, and who have built an empire in the land of the Illini." Necessity of including statutory inscriptions made it impossible to show even part of this dedication. Slabaugh says that Rovelstad's medal, apparently issued in 1935 in connection with the actual Elgin Centennial, ultimately inspired introduction of the bill in Congress seeking to authorize this half dollar.

Opportunity: As above, resulting in the Act of June 16, 1936 (along with the Albany and Gettysburg issues).

Motive: To finance construction of the full-sized Pioneer Memorial. This has yet to be completed, though the foundation for it was laid in 1934! It is in Davidson Park, Elgin, on the site of the log cabin of James and Hezekiah Gifford, who settled there about 1834 and who founded and named Elgin. Once completed, if ever, it will consist of the group of bronze figures in heroic size (about 12 feet tall) atop a granite base eight feet tall. Here we do not have the excuse of political problems which delayed for still longer the completion of the Stone Mountain Memorial; the explanation is as yet unknown.

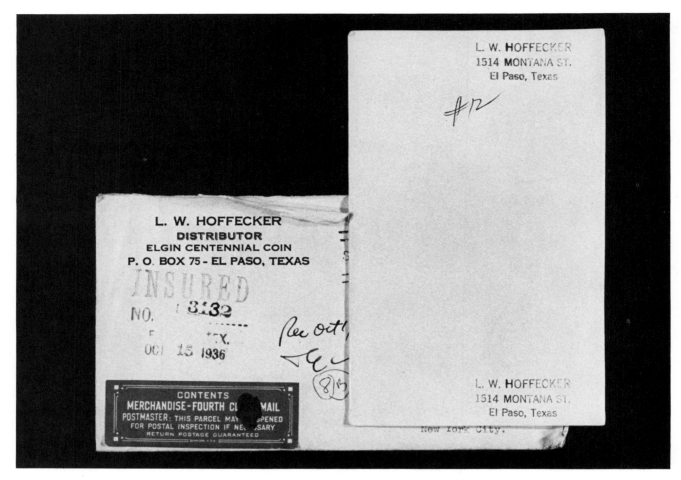

Original mailing envelope with an unprinted coin mailer used by L. W. Hoffecker to distribute the Elgin Commemorative half dollar.

Suspects: Trygve A. Rovelstad, local sculptor, designer of the coin and earlier of the medal as well as of the Memorial itself.

Accessories: The Elgin Centennial Monumental Committee; L.W. Hoffecker, coin dealer of El Paso, Texas, distributor of the coins.

Modus Operandi: Rovelstad's original sketches for the coin showed the rifleman's head in ¾-face, seen from below; the Federal Commission of Fine Arts approved them as of July 17, 1936, provided that the obverse head be shown in profile. Rovelstad completed his models by August 15, and they were approved on the 21st, going at once to Medallic Art Company of New York, which made the reductions to half-dollar size. The Philadelphia Mint completed the mintage during October: 25,000 pieces (maximum allowed), plus 15 reserved for assay.

L.W. Hoffecker actually sold 20,000 of these coins during the rest of the year, at $1.50 each, returning 5,000 to the mint for re-melting in 1937. His rationale for so doing was that demand had come to a standstill, and the unsold 5,000 would otherwise end up in the hands of speculators.

The vast majority of survivors, even those which have not been poorly cleaned, are not well struck; it is very unusual to find one in which the pioneers on reverse all have facial details. Should you notice a small polished area between the A of AMERICA and the young pioneer's head, don't panic. This is a die polishing mark—that is also seen on the reverses of the Huguenot, Oregon Trail, and Monroe half dollars.

Collateral Evidence: No proofs are reported, though some may have been made for John R. Sinnock.

Only a single holder has been met with to date; this is an unprinted holder of the usual coin-mailer type, with Hoffecker's rubber-stamped address.

84

THE BATTLE OF GETTYSBURG HALF DOLLAR

Obverse

Reverse

The Corpus Delicti: Alias *Gettysburg*.

Clues: Though he used different models for his Union and Confederate soldiers, somehow designer Frank Vittor managed to make them lookalikes, seemingly brothers, with remarkably similar facial expressions. Whatever he may have intended to convey by this concept, what he managed to communicate was a reminder that the Civil War did in fact pit father against son and brother against brother. This duality theme continues on reverse, where the fasces (for the power of life and death, i.e., sovereignty of the State) divides the Union and Confederate arms. Oak and olive branches, supposedly for war and peace, tend more to connote authority and victory: We are not allowed to forget that the Reconstruction with its brutal exploitation followed on the heels of the war between the states. Inscriptions here are self-explanatory except for BLUE AND GRAY REUNION, which alludes to the event mentioned below under *Opportunity*. The dates 1863–1938 define the 75th anniversary of the Battle of Gettysburg, generally considered to be the turning point of the Civil War,

but the date 1936, for a coin struck in 1937, demands explanation. The Act of June 16, 1936, which authorized this coinage, seems to provide that explanation, but use of the 1936 date produced exactly the same kind of confusion as with the Delaware Swedish Tercentenary coins.

Opportunity: The Blue and Gray Reunion, scheduled for July 1–3, 1938 (i.e., the exact anniversary dates of the battle), brought together on the battlefield site numerous surviving members of the G.A.R. (Grand Army of the Republic) and the U.C.V. (United Confederate Veterans), ostensibly "to affirm the unity of the United States in the turbulent modern world," but in actuality to renew old acquaintanceships, to talk over the times when each shared in what seemed a desperate heroic enterprise. This gathering appeared important enough at the time that President Roosevelt showed up and dedicated the Eternal Light Peace Memorial, with its perpetual flame. Promoters of this Reunion had pressured Congress into authorizing the coinage, June 16, 1936.

Motive: Local pride, apparently to create souvenirs for the attending veterans, and possibly also to help finance the Reunion.

Suspects: Frank Vittor, designer and sculptor, of Pittsburgh.

Accessories: The Pennsylvania State Commission, of Gettysburg.

Modus Operandi: The Commission did not even hire a designer until 1937. Frank Vittor completed his initial sketch models in mid-March of that year; Mint Director Nellie Tayloe "Ma" Ross submitted photographs of them to the Federal Commission of Fine Arts, March 15, and they were approved subject to very minor corrections (removal of the insignia from the Confederate soldier's collar, removal of the stars from the Union arms). During June 1937, the Philadelphia Mint coined the legal maximum, 50,000 pieces, plus 28 reserved for assay.

These coins were sold at $1.65 each by the Pennsylvania State Commission, both before and during the Reunion. Those remaining unsold were turned over to the American Legion; and those 23,100 that the Legionnaires could not dispose of at $2.65 each went back to the mint for re-melting, leaving a net mintage of 26,900.

No proofs are reported, though specimens may have been made for John R. Sinnock, Engraver of the Mint.

Collateral Evidence: Many survivors show bag marks, nicks or scratches—signs of mishandling that appear most noticeably on soldiers or shields. True gem quality specimens are very rare and an excellent investment when available.

Some of the coins were distributed in unprinted white three-coin holders. Not many of these have remained with the coins since issue time, but obviously this type of holder could be procured elsewhere; it is unsafe to assume that any given one is original without other documentation.

THE GRANT
MEMORIAL ISSUES

Obverse—no star.　　　*Obverse—Grant with star.*　　　*Reverse*

The Corpus Delicti: Alias *Grant Star Half, Grant Plain Half, Grant Star Dollar* and *Grant Plain Dollar,* respectively.

Clues: The following apply to all varieties of both the dollar and the half-dollar. The dates 1822–1922 refer to the centennial of birth of General (later President) Ulysses Simpson Grant, whose dissolute portrait (after a Mathew Brady photograph) adorns the obverse. The tiny letter G between those dates is actually a monogrammed LGF for Laura Gardin Fraser, the illustrious sculptor who modeled these coins. On the gold dollar this detail is very difficult to see even with a good magnifying glass—one of her few miscalculations.

Reverse depicts a small frame house at Point Pleasant, Ohio, near Cincinnati, where Grant was born on April 27, 1822. Laura Gardin Fraser worked from photographs of the house taken before it was restored, showing two stands of trees omitted on the centennial medal.

The log cabin label was affixed to this design by Andrew W. Mellon, then Secretary of the Treasury, who so described it in his annual report for fiscal 1922. As Slabaugh has pointed out, Mellon confused this frame house with a log cabin Grant built over 30 years later on his wife's farm near St. Louis.

We confess puzzlement over why General "Unconditional Surrender" Grant had to appear on two different commemorative coins, and why he ties for third place with Jefferson (behind Washington and Lincoln) in the number of different issues of paper currency portraying him. We can understand why Washington, "Father of His Country," has always been a favorite for currency portraiture, and why Lincoln the Liberator and Martyr followed him, and why Jefferson, the author of the Declaration of Independence, followed them. But why Grant? Grant was as controversial in his day as Richard Nixon was in his. Forced to resign his army commission after the Mexican War owing to alcoholism, which was then regarded the way heroin addiction is now, Grant succeeded at only one thing (his Civil War generalship) until the Republican Party nominated him for the presidency (solely on the basis of his war record), in which he ran in a campaign which was unrivaled for dirtiness until 1972. Once elected, Grant produced a record as one of the worst presidents of all. He apparently could not believe that any of his sycophantic friends could either be incompetent or dishonest, yet many were both. Even after others began warning him, he could not believe that the people who gave him exorbitantly expensive gifts could have ulterior motives. Yet the record speaks for itself: Jay Gould bought off various presidential assistants in his notorious attempt to corner the gold market. Orville Babcock, Grant's private secretary, was implicated in the Whiskey Ring and the abortive attempt to annex Santo Domingo. William Belknap, his Secretary of War, was convicted of taking bribes. Grant himself offered the post of Chief Justice of the Supreme Court to the notorious "Boss" Conkling (Senator Roscoe Conkling, of New York), and he publicly consorted with the even more notorious robber baron Jim Fisk, "Boss" Tweed's crony, implicated (until Fisk was murdered) in wholesale buying of judges and bribery of legislatures. We are not implying that Grant was wicked, merely that he was a victim of the Peter Principle: As president, he had gone to a level where he was completely beyond his competence, and he is and was a poor choice to be honored on U.S. coins or currency.

Numerologists, incidentally, are likely to have a field day with the Grant coins. Grant was born in 1822; there are 2 varieties apiece of the 2 denominations of commemorative coins portraying him, authorized by Act of 2/2/22.

Opportunity: Little is known of the behind-the-scenes activity as the correspondence has not survived; what is known is that the House, on October 17, 1921, passed a bill on behalf of the Ulysses S. Grant Centenary Memorial Commission authorizing the issue of 200,000 "souvenir" gold dollars, to be sold by the Commission during 1922. However, the Senate Committee on Banking and Currency was probably aware of the sales fiascos of previous gold dollar souvenirs, and even more aware of the tiny amount of gold then in the mint. (Note that in 1917–19 the only gold coins struck were the McKinley commemoratives; in 1920 small quantities of $10s and $20s and in 1921 a small batch of $20s—fewer than in most years before the war.) The Committee accordingly protested and refused "to sequester so much gold" for this coinage, and recommended that the bill be amended to authorize instead 10,000 gold dollars and 250,000 half dollars. In this amended form it passed the Senate on January 23, 1922, the House concurring on January 26; President Harding signed it into law February 2.

Motive: The Centenary Commission wanted these coins to help finance the construction of memorial buildings in Georgetown and Bethel, and a five-mile highway from New Richmond to Point Pleasant, all these being Ohio locales associated with Grant's pre-war years.

Suspects: The Ulysses S. Grant Centenary Memorial Commission specified the designs to Laura Gardin Fraser. As her husband James Earle Fraser was sculptor member of the Federal Commission of Fine

Arts, he had the responsibility of choosing the artist to design and model the coins. Her success with the Alabama made her a logical choice for this assignment.

Accessories: Mathew Brady, whose photograph of Grant was Mrs. Fraser's immediate source.

Modus Operandi: As early as February 24, 1922, James Earle Fraser submitted Laura's model for the gold dollar obverse to the Centenary Commission, which promptly approved it. Less than two weeks later, her models for the half dollar were complete and approved; that for its reverse was also to be used (in greater mechanical reduction at the mint) for the gold dollar reverse. On March 3, James Earle Fraser wrote to Charles Moore, Chairman of the Federal Fine Arts Commission, officially approving the designs; when Moore concurred, they went to the mint, and before March 31, the gold dollar coinage was completed.

The Grant Centenary Commission had requested that 5,000 of the 10,000 gold dollars show a special mark. Since there was no historically significant numeral or emblem available which tied in directly with Grant, an incused star was chosen. (They might have had in mind the General's uniform stars, though this was never mentioned as a possible meaning.) As soon as the coins showed up for public sale, in April, people began remembering the special marks on the Alabama and Missouri half dollars, and adverse criticism cited the venality of this procedure. However, both batches of gold dollars sold out, the "star" coins at $3.50 each, the "plain" at $3 each.

In the meantime, the Mint completed the first batch of 100,000 half dollars. Much to the Centenary Commission's surprise, this contained a bonus: 5,000

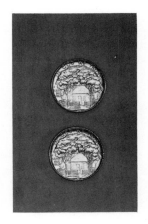

Grant gold dollars.

of the coins had an incused star similar to that on the dollars. From April 1922 to the end of the year, the Commission offered the half dollars at $1 apiece, star or no star; as sales lagged, they lowered the price of the remaining 29,000-odd halves in December 1922 to 75¢ each for the "plain" variety (in lots of 10 or more) and raised the "star" coins to $1.50 each. Sales of both were stopped as of January 1, 1923, and the Commission returned the unsold coins to the mint for re-melting.

The following tabulation is a convenient summary:

Authorized, Gold Dollars: Not over 10,000
Coined: 5,000 with star, 5,000 without, plus 16 for assay
Melted: None
Net Mintage: 5,000 with star, 5,000 plain

Authorized, Half Dollars: Not over 250,000
Coined: With star, 5,000 plus 6 for assay
                Without star, 95,000 + 55 for assay
Melted: 750 with star; 27,650 plain
Net mintage: With star, 4,250; plain, 67,350

Collateral Evidence: At least four matte or sandblast proof half dollars with star are known to exist. One of these was in the J.R. Sinnock estate. A second was offered by the late Charles E. Green of Chicago during the 1950s; this is believed to be the coin later in the R. E. Cox collection. A third was lot 417 of the S. A. Tanenbaum collection. One of these two went to Herbert Tobias, who still had it in recent years. The fourth is in a private collection. Four matte or sandblast proof half dollars without star are reported, but we have not examined any.

Matte proof gold dollars with stars are rumored to exist but we have not examined any.

Sharpness on all the matte proofs is considerably greater than on even the uncirculated half dollars illustrated herein, notably on Grant's hair, beard, uniform, and the reverse leaves, roof and siding. In addition, these coins will show neither the die striations nor any mint frost. Counterfeits have been offered as matte proofs, but they are so much inferior in detail sharpness as to rule out acceptance. The same remark holds for chemically treated coins.

Trial pieces of the gold dollars exist in white metal and brass; owing to Treasury Department policy (which cites a mythical law mentioned in the Dr. Judd book on patterns), we have not kept any record of location of these. The same remark holds for the obverse trial pieces of the half dollar in copper, white metal and brass, and for the white metal trials of the reverse die.

Many specimens of the Grant Plain half dollar survive in barely or marginally uncirculated state, others in lower grades; evidently some were kept as pocket pieces or spent. Gem specimens are not easy to locate, however. The gold dollars are more often found in choice mint state, and there is not much difference between them in scarcity reckoned in terms of numbers offered. We are unable to understand the pricing practice which pretends that the "plain" is much rarer than the "star" in the gold dollars.

About 1935, a Bronx dentist purchased several hundred Grant "plain" half dollars and punched stars into them to simulate the rarer issue, which was then the highest priced of all commemorative silver coins ($65 as against $3.50 for the "plain"). Even in recent years, these coins (and possibly others made by different parties for the same reason) have been showing up to plague collectors. Illustrations of the genuine and the faked stars will show more clearly than words the differences.

Many collectors have heard that the test of a genuine Grant "star" half dollar is "die breaks at chin and tie." This is a misconception; what actually happened was that very early in the life of the obverse die found on almost all genuine Grant "star" coins, it clashed against a reverse without a blank planchet between them, and (as the illustration of the genuine clearly shows) impressions from the spaces between clumps of leaves appear between chin and G and in field just right of tie; and at tops of F DO there are clash marks from the very top of the trees. On some specimens these are less obvious than on that here pictured. These never show on the fakes altered from Grant "plain" coins. Nor have they been reported on any ordinary Grant "plain" halves. (It is possible that cast counterfeits may exist, made from genuine Grant "star" coins; but these can be detected in the same ways as other casts—weight, specific gravity and microscopic surface texture.)

Two varieties of reverse of the genuine Grant "star" are known. It is uncertain if this means two reverse dies. In what we take to be the first reverse (or reverse state), there is little or no spacing between leaves in the areas indicated by arrows on the illustration. In what we take to be the second, "Variety II," the reverse die has obviously been much repolished, probably to remove clash marks. This process has left plain openings among the leaves, in the four areas indicated by arrows. Lettering in E PLURIBUS UNUM has been much thinned out, and the

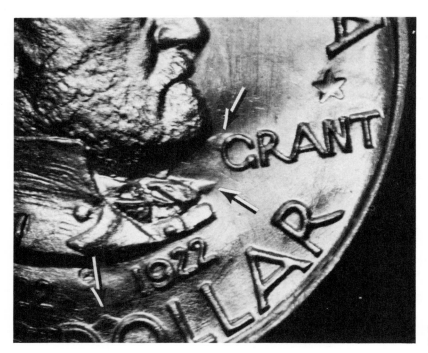

Genuine Grant star struck from clashed dies. Arrows indicate clash marks.

This star was privately added to a genuine Grant no star issue. Note doubled G *in* GRANT.

This is a variety I reverse, struck from a normal reverse die.

This is a variety II reverse which, according to A. Swiatek, was struck from a clashed and repolished reverse die. Note small L *in* PLURIBUS *and open spaces in the leaves indicated by the arrows.*

Obverse of counterfeit Grant gold dollar. Note blurry relief details.

Reverse of counterfeit Grant gold dollar. Again, note blurriness.

top of L is lower than the tops of P-U; the upper stroke of E appears longer than the two lower strokes; and the thinning out of these letters produces other subtler differences apparent on inspection.

We assume either that the repolished die is a later state of the original die, produced after they had clashed (the same accident that marred the obverse), though we have been unable to trace the clash marks on reverse; or that the normal reverse is a new die substituted for the clashed reverse. Mint records are no help here. According to *The Numismatist,* December 1946, p. 1423, there were supposedly 8 obverse dies in all, 3 with the star. This seems an excessively large number for the mintage, especially as very few Grant "star" coins are reported without the clashed obverse die and one of us (W.B.) has never authenticated one; it seems unlikely that 99+ percent of a total mintage of 5,000 should have been from one obverse die, the remaining few dozen from two others. More suspiciously still, over 95 percent of Grant "plain" coins come from a single obverse die, with the doubling on G of GRANT and the peculiar die striations in left, lower, and right obverse fields (as shown in the illustrations of the coin with faked star). That strongly suggests that the Mint used only one obverse die for the "star" coins, seen before and after the clashing accident; and one or at most two obverse dies for the Grant "plain." Normally the Mint used the minimum number of dies compatible with issue of acceptable coins. At this period the number of impressions the Mint normally could expect from a pair of half-dollar dies was in the neighborhood of 200,000; it had been in the excess of 150,000 since long before the Civil War. If the Mint made as many as eight obverse dies for the entire authorized Grant mintage, it must have been anticipating a per-die life of about 31,250, which is very low. For obvious reasons of economy, most of the dies made would not have been used; why would they even have been made? It is possible that whoever was quoting mint records may have been misreading "obverses" when "working dies" was meant.

The only safe procedure, then, is to look first for the clash marks on any Grant "star" half dollar offered you; then if they are present, check for indication that the piece is a struck coin rather than a cast. If they are absent, it is imperative to check the appearance of the star. One of us (A.S.) maintains that the star will be identical in appearance on all genuine Grant "star" coins from either obverse die—without or with the clash marks; the star was punched into the working hub from which all three

(?) obverse dies were made, then ground away for making the other five (?) "plain" obverse dies. This would have been easier to do on the working dies. No more definite conclusions are possible until more specimens have been examined of "star" coins without the clash marks, and of Grant "plain" coins without the doubling on the G. On the genuine "star" coins, the incuse star (below level of field) is asymmetrical: its lower left point is thin and narrow, its lower right point is notably wider and rounded, and the surface within the star itself is uneven with odd internal detail. None of these remarks applies to the stars added by the dentist.

Counterfeits are known of the Grant gold dollars without stars, but to date all seen are casts looking much like the one pictured on the preceding page. Relief details are so blurry compared to the genuine, and the surface is so different in texture, that these forgeries should not be much of a threat.

No original holders, boxes, or accompanying literature have been located.

The Grant postage stamp, 8¢ olive-green, Scott 589 (Type A163), might be collected as an interesting comparison item, but it was not made for the centenary; Scott gives the date of issue as May 29, 1926, and it is in fact part of the new series of presidential stamps designed by Charles Aubrey Huston to replace the old 1908–09 designs. Huston's stamps began appearing in October–November 1922, the 11¢ first (October 4, 1922) followed shortly by the 5¢, 15¢, 25¢, and 6¢ in November. Had the Post Office wished to do anything for the Grant Centenary Commission, nothing would have been simpler than to issue the 8¢ Grant during 1922, but a delay of three and a half years is a little long even for the Post Office!

The Grant 8¢ postage stamp—Scott 589, Type 163.

THE HAWAIIAN SESQUICENTENNIAL HALF DOLLAR

Obverse

Reverse

The Corpus Delicti: Alias *Hawaii* or *Captain Cook.*

Clues: The bust in naval uniform represents Captain James Cook, discoverer (so far as the European/American world was concerned) of the Sandwich Islands, later known by their true name of Hawaii. The object after CAPT. is a compass, its needle to the north so that the Captain is shown as facing westward, towards the islands which he discovered (January 18, 1778) and on which he was murdered thirteen months later (February 14, 1779). The sculptor used the compass as a symbol of Cook's feats as a navigator and explorer. The eight triangles in lower field (formerly referred to as volcanoes) represent the eight largest islands in the Hawaiian group. Behind the shoulder is Chester Beach's circular monogram. Both the flowing lettering and the wavy border are meant to allude to the sea.

On the reverse, the landscape represents part of Waikiki Beach fronting on Mamala Bay, with Diamond Head in the background. Instead of the present beachfront hotels, there are only occasional grass huts and coconut palm trees. Standing on a promontory, facing in the general direction of Pearl Harbor, is a native warrior chieftain (not meant for King Kamehameha I, as it is sometimes erroneously believed) wearing a feather cloak and holding a barbed spear. To show that his intentions are peaceful, his hand is extended in welcome. Behind him is another coconut palm. The sesquicentennial dates and Latin motto (again in flowing letters meant to suggest the sea) complete the design.

Opportunity: In conjunction with sesquicentennial celebrations then being planned throughout the Islands, local groups came up with the idea of establishing a Captain Cook Memorial Collection, to be housed in the Archives of Hawaii. This collection was to be financed in part by proceeds from the sale of these half dollars. Accordingly, Commander Victor Stewart Kaleoaloha Houston, the Delegate to Congress from the then Territory of Hawaii, sponsored a bill which would authorize coinage of 10,000 souvenir half dollars for these purposes; this became the Act of March 7, 1928.

Motive: As above. There was never any scandal about these coins.

Suspects: Chester Beach, sculptor; Miss Juliette Mae Frazer of Honolulu, designer; Bruce Cartwright, Jr., who contributed preliminary sketches of reverse; V.S.K. Houston, who demanded dozens of minute changes, the major one being removal of the chief's anklet of shark teeth, as "pertaining to a dancer instead of a warrior."

Accessories: Josiah Wedgewood, whose cameo of Captain Cook (pictured in Slabaugh, p. 84) was then owned by Bruce Cartwright, Jr., Chairman of the Captain Cook Sesquicentennial Commission. Chester Beach claimed that the actual prototype was an "original painting by Dance in the gallery of the Greenwich Hospital, London." If so, this must have been the source of Wedgewood's cameo design, as the major change was to make Cook face the other way, slightly de-emphasize his nose, and very slightly emphasize his brow ridges. Though the warrior is not meant to represent any known individual, Cartwright's design must have been influenced by the statue of King Kamehameha I near the Royal Palace in Honolulu, as depicted on the 3¢ stamp, Scott 799 (Type A271), released October 18, 1937. (Some 78,454,450 were distributed.) This stamp makes an excellent tie-in for displays.

Modus Operandi: Either Commander Houston was owed a lot of favors by his fellow Congressmen

The Hawaiian Sesquicentennial overprint stamps.

in and out of the House Coinage Committee, or there was some kind of behind-the-scenes influence

exerted by the White House, because Houston submitted preliminary sketches for the half dollar to Charles Moore of the Federal Fine Arts Commission no later than November 2, 1927—well before he got around to introducing his bill in Congress (December 5, 1927). Though James Earle Fraser (then a consultant, no longer a member of the Commission) recommended that Anthony de Francisci do the models, the Commission finally decided on Chester Beach, who accepted the assignment on March 12, 1928. Taxay, pp. 127–131, quotes Houston's and the Mint's criticisms with Beach's replies—leaving the overall impression, at this late date, that Houston was an old fussbudget who should never have had any veto power over a professional artist's designs. The wonder is that Beach's designs, as they reached the Mint, had any strength left. As of May 9, Treasury Secretary Andrew W. Mellon approved the models.

During June 1928, the Philadelphia Mint struck 10,000 half dollars. Under terms of the authorizing act, these could have been made at any or all the branch mints, and it is a little surprising that they were not made in San Francisco, like previous commemoratives referring to the Far West.

They went to the Captain Cook Sesquicentennial Commission in Honolulu, which arranged with the Bank of Hawaii, Ltd., to distribute the coins at $2 apiece—the highest initial cost of any commemorative issue until that time. The small issue was allocated as follows:

> 50 sandblast or matte proofs, for special presentation (see below).
> 200 normal strikings, withheld for presentation.
> 4,975 for sale on the Islands. Not over five per customer.
> The remaining 4,975 for sale in the "States" (the mainland).

Distribution began October 8, 1928. The issue was quickly exhausted, and demand has outstripped the supply from the beginning. One of us (A.S.) has heard from two sources considered very reliable that of the 4,975 earmarked for distribution in Hawaii, some 1,500 never reached the public, but were bought directly from the Bank of Hawaii, Ltd., and retained in vaults in two different banks in Hawaii to the present day. These two hoards, if released today, would probably have only a brief effect on the overall market, owing to the extreme demand for gem uncirculated specimens.

Collateral Evidence: The majority of survivors, though not frankly circulated, will show evidence of careless preservation; they come nicked, scratched and most often poorly cleaned. The spots most likely to show rubbing (demoting the coins to below full mint state) include Captain Cook's cheek, the roll of hair over his ear, hair above temple, shoulder above truncation, and the warrior's fingers, thighs and knees.

There is no way of identifying the 200 presentation pieces except by documentation.

Aside from the case in which the American Numismatic Society's proof specimen has always been housed, no original holders are known.

Courtesy of Gordon Medcalf, this writer (W.B.) has seen a typescript of the original roster of 50 recipients of the proofs, from the Archives of Hawaii. This list was also reproduced in the December 1928 *The Numismatist,* p. 734. An old copy of it in Lester Merkin's possession had early penciled annotations; these were quoted in the *Encyclopedia of Proof Coins,* p. 222. An updated version follows: Asterisks denote those now located (1978) in private hands; daggers denote those now located (1978) in museums.

1. Edgar Henriques, Executive Secretary, Captain Cook Sesquicentennial Commission.

*2. Bruce Cartwright, Jr., Chairman, Captain Cook Sesquicentennial Commission; Robert van Dyke.

3. Dr. Albert E. Gregory, Commissioner.

4. Albert Pierce Taylor, Commissioner.

5. Bishop H.B. Restarick, Commissioner.

*6. Col. C.P. Iaukea, Commissioner; Anthony Swiatek; H. Lincoln Vehmeyer. This piece was displayed at the 1976 ANA Convention.

*7. Prof. Ralph S. Kuykendall, private collection, seen in 1976 in New York.

*8. Juliette Mae Frazer, Robert van Dyke, Alfred J. Ostheimer, Superior Galleries, private collections.

9. Hon. Wallace R. Farrington.

10. Miss Marie von Holt.

†11. Hawaiian Historical Society.

†12. Bernice Pauahi Bishop Museum, 1355 Kalihi St., Honolulu.

13. Hon. Gerald H. Phipps.

†14. Archives of Hawaii.

15. B.C. Stewart.

†16. United States National Museum, "not delivered." Now in the Smithsonian Institution.

17. British Admiralty.

18. Rt. Hon. S. M. Bruce.

19. The Hon. T.R. Bavin.

†20. The British Museum.

*21. President Coolidge, private collection.

†22. King George V of England. Presumably with the Royal Collections, Windsor Castle.

23. Lord Sandwich.

24. Andrew W. Mellon, Secretary of Treasury.

25. Rear Admiral George S. Marvell, USN.

*26. Major General Fox Conner, USA, his grandson, a Florida dealer, private collection.

27. The American Numismatic Association. (Where is it now? Not seen at the Colorado Springs museum when I visited it. [W.B.])

28. Capt. Leveson-Gower, R.N., D.S.O.

29. Capt. Gerald Cartwell Harrison.

30. Commodore —— Swabey.

31. Capt. John Greenslade.

32. Hon. Dwight F. Davis, Secretary of War under President Coolidge.

33. Sir Joseph Carruthers.

34. Sir Henry Newbolt.

35. Prof. Frank A. Golder.

36. Judge F. W. Howay.

37. Verne Blue ("not delivered").

†38. Kauai Historical Society, Lihue, Kauai.

39. James A. Wilder.

40. Unassigned. Later given to Hon. Lawrence M. Judd.

41. Theodore B. Pitman.

42. Dr. Peter H. Buck.

43. Hon. Maurice Cohen.

44. The Right Hon. J.G. Coates.

†45. National Museum, Wellington, New Zealand.

46. Hon. John C. Lane.

†47. The American Numismatic Society. (Pictured in the *Encyclopedia of U.S. and Colonial Proof Coins,* p. 222.)

*48. Edward L. Caum, private collection, Mitchell Proctor (John Dean Coin Co.), Gary Filler (Chattanooga Coin Co.), James N. Anthony.

49. J. Frank Woods.

*50. Commander Victor Stewart Kaleoaloha Houston, private collection.

In addition to these, there are two orphans not traced to their original owners:

*x. Waldo Newcomer, Col. E.H.R. Green, various dealer intermediaries, R.E. Cox, 1962 N.Y. Metropolitan Convention Sale, lot 2125, Alfred J. Ostheimer, Superior Galleries, Neggen Estate Sale, February 16–18, lot 1252, private collection. This was originally thought to have been no. 2, because Waldo Newcomer had bought much of the Cartwright collection prior to 1933. There is also the possibility that the owner of no. 8 has confused it with this piece.

*y. —— Bauer (coin dealer in Hawaii), Krause,

The obverse and reverse of the rare #6 Hawaiian sandblast proof. A specimen similar to this sold for $15,000.00 at a 1979 auction in California.

Tom McAfee, private collection. Since this piece came to Mr. Bauer from a non-numismatic source in Hawaii, presumably its provenance could be narrowed down considerably from the 33 available numbers.

There are also several forgeries purporting to be proofs, but made from ordinary business strikings. To people unfamiliar with the genuine article, these could be dangerously deceptive. To avoid any possible confusion, we illustrate one of the documented proofs (no. 6) above, in enlargement. Comparison of this piece with a normal business strike will be of considerable interest. (However, it should be mentioned that at least two of the forgeries had their pickling or sandblasting applied to coins showing nicks and scratches, so that the adventitious finish showed *within* the nicks!) On the genuine, note the additional detail on Cook's garments and hair, and in the chief's helmet, face, feather cloak, muscular definition and toes; there is more contour detail visible in Diamond Head, on the fern and on both leaves and trunk of the coconut palm tree behind the chief, perhaps most clearly of all on the palm leaves.

From one extreme to the other, we turn from the proof to the counterfeits. Earlier counterfeits were made by casting, and they show porosity as well as fuzziness of relief detail. More recent counterfeits—much more dangerous—can be identified, by the raised marks near WE TRUST, above US of PLURIBUS, and right-hand volcanoes, in the photomacrographs on the following page (supplied by ANACS August 12, 1977).

Though there were no commemorative stamps issued for the Hawaiian Sesquicentennial, a direct philatelic tie-in may be found in the Hawaiian overprints. These are found on the regular 2¢ carmine (Type A157) and 5¢ dark blue (Type A160). They were placed on sale as of August 13, 1928 at post offices in Hawaii and at the Postal Agency in Washington, D.C. Of no. 647 (the overprinted 2¢) only 5,519,897 were issued; of no. 648 (the 5¢), only 1,459,897. Very rarely, vertical pairs of 2¢ occur with 28mm spacing between the overprints, rather than the normal 18mm—so that the overprint will be much higher on one stamp than on the other.

It is possibly more than coincidence that in 1942–43 the Bureau of Engraving and Printing, which had made the overprinted stamps, made overprinted currency for use in Hawaii and some parts of the South Pacific during World War II. These all had brown seals and HAWAII overprints on both sides; the denominations were $1 Silver Certificates and $5, $10 and $20 Federal Reserve Notes (San Francisco district). They are described in full in Chuck O'Donnell's *Standard Handbook of Modern U.S. Paper Money* (6th ed., pp. 18, 88, 134–5, 161, and 164).

A detail of a counterfeit Hawaiian. Note the raised marks above both U*'s of* PLURIBUS *as well as the deep valley between* PLURIBUS *and* UNUM. *None of these markings are present on the genuine issue.*

A detail of a counterfeit Hawaiian. More recent counterfeits can be identified by raised marks near WE TRUST. *Also beware of specimens whose reverse is prooflike. They were definitely not struck at the Philadelphia mint.*

THE CITY OF HUDSON, NEW YORK, SESQUICENTENNIAL HALF DOLLAR

Obverse

Reverse

The Corpus Delicti: Alias *The Hudson.*

Clues: It is arbitrary which side is designated as obverse. The mayor of Hudson had originally suggested a bust of Hudson for obverse device, the city seal for reverse. Beach himself referred to the ship side as obverse (Taxay, p. 165–6); we will follow his view. Buried in the waves below the ship is the word HUDSON, referring less to the city than to the explorer Henry Hudson (an Englishman, though the Dutchmen in New York liked to Hollandize his name as "Hendrick"). His ship, the *Half Moon* (again alias *Halve Maene* among the Dutch patroons), rides at full sail, with a crescent (?) moon in field representing its name, and two unidentifiable flags from mainmast and foremast. If it is intended as a crescent moon just past new, then the ship sails east back to Europe at sunset; if a waning moon before dawn, the ship is heading westward. The small circular emblem in field is Chester Beach's monogrammed CB as designer.

On the other side is the city seal of Hudson, New York, with the quaint device of King Neptune riding backwards on a spouting whale, whose eye is represented as being about where its blowhole should be. Neptune is briefly clad in a wisp of cloth "blowing in the wind." Behind them is a triton blowing his or her horn. ET DECUS ET PRETIUM RECTI ("Both an ornament and a reward of the righteous man") is the village's motto. Anniversary dates 1785–1935 allude to the incorporation of this settlement, originally called Claverack Landing (there is still a nearby village of Claverack and an extensive district known by that name).

Opportunity: On a "monkey see, monkey do" basis, dozens of bills seeking to authorize commemorative coinages for this village or that county or the other local exposition went to the House Coinage Committee, and four of them were actually reported out during the year 1935. For reasons unknown, probably the usual "you vote for my bill

Detail of Hudson counterfeit. Note raised marks around the letters MERI *on this specimen made outside the mint.*

and I'll vote for yours" arrangement, that for Hudson, New York, was voted into law, becoming the Act of May 2, 1935 simultaneously with one for coinage for Providence, Rhode Island.

Motive: Local pride, mingled with That Five Finger Word.

Suspects: Chester Beach, sculptor, designer; Mayor Frank A. Wise of Hudson, New York, who specified the city seal as a major device; the City Council, who conferred with Wise for the choice; Rep. Philip Arnold Goodwin (R.-NY), long-time president of the Greene County Historical Society, representing Coxsackie and the entire Greene County area, who sponsored the bill for his friends in Hudson, about seven miles downriver.

Accessories: The unknown designer of the Hudson city seal, which (from the copy reproduced in Taxay, p. 163) may date back to 1785 or a few years later.

Modus Operandi: When Rep. Goodwin had to locate a sculptor who could design the newly authorized coins, he wrote to Charles Moore of the Federal Commission of Fine Arts. Moore recommended Laura Gardin Fraser and four others. Mayor Wise countered with the name of John Flannagan, who had designed the Washington quarter dollar; though the Commission consented, in the end Chester Beach got the assignment, possibly because he was the only one whose work the Mint would readily approve who was willing to do the models for only $1000—lower than most of the earlier fees mentioned by Taxay for designing commemorative coins. Beach completed the models in slightly over a week, and they were promptly approved, going during the first week of June to Medallic Art Company for reduction to half dollar size. The Commission of Fine Arts had approved them on May 28th. In unusual haste even for these issues, the Mint completed the working dies in June and struck 10,000 coins (reserving 8 extra for assay), delivering the entire batch on June 28 to the First National Bank & Trust Co. of Hudson, on the

Detail of Hudson counterfeit. Note defects on city motto.

mayor's orders, on behalf of the "Hudson Sesquicentennial Committee," probably the mayor and city fathers.

Ostensibly the coins were to be on public sale at $1 apiece, beginning on June 28. By July 2, it was announced that the entire issue was sold. We have learned in intervening years that most of them were hoarded, speculators later releasing small quantities at much higher prices. One of us (A.S.) knows families in the Hudson area who retain nine original rolls (180 pieces); these families are unwilling to sell in the foreseeable future. Other smaller hoards have been dispersed in recent years, but the coin remains far more difficult to locate, especially in gem state, than its mintage would suggest, and in all likelihood many hundreds, possibly over 1,000, remain squirreled away in upstate bank vaults. The announcement that these coins had "sold out" in five days, followed by offerings at greatly increased prices, gave rise to much adverse criticism; yet the coin has remained in great demand ever since.

Most survivors are in rather less than choice state; and even those in gem condition are weak on King Neptune's face, leg, motto, hull, and central sails. If you are in doubt as to whether your coin is in full mint state, look for mint frost on those weak areas.

Collateral Evidence: Two matte proofs are reported, one of them from the John R. Sinnock estate. They are better struck than most of the normal business strikes. However, they can be readily imitated by pickling or sandblasting normal coins, so authentication is mandatory; we have already seen treated or processed coins purporting to be matte proofs.

Two original holders are reported; we do not have full descriptions of these.

Dangerous counterfeits of this issue are known. If a coin offered to you shows any of the raised marks on the enlarged illustrations (note especially around MERI, and on city motto), it is to be rejected. If in doubt, have it sent to ANACS for authentication.

One could, by stretching a point, consider the 2¢ carmine Hudson-Fulton Celebration stamp (first released September 25, 1909, in the amount of 72,634,631 normal, and 216,480 imperforates) as a tie-in, especially as this stamp depicts the Half Moon. These are respectively listed as Scott 372 and 373, the design being Type A143.

In the R.E. Cox collection was a set of three copper uniface impressions from the hub used for making the ship die. They are very slightly different. The set went as lot 2306, 1962 New York Metropolitan sale. One is pictured in Judd, Appendix A, p. 253.

THE HUGUENOT–WALLOON TERCENTENARY HALF DOLLAR

Obverse

Reverse

The Corpus Delicti: Alias *Huguenot.*

Clues: HUGUENOT HALF DOLLAR alludes, supposedly, to the 300th anniversary of the arrival of 110 Walloons (thirty families of Lowlands Huguenots, the French name for Calvinists) aboard the ship *Nieuw Nederlandt* in the Hudson River region of upstate New York. However, the accolated portraits are not relevant to this event (which had led to the controversial purchase of Manhattan Island from local Indians for trinkets said to be worth 24 Lyon Dollars). That labeled COLIGNY is an imaginary portrait of Admiral Gaspard de Coligny (1519–1572), who was killed in the St. Bartholomew's Day massacre, August 24, 1572, no more and no less a martyr than the other thousands of Calvinist extremists who perished at the same time, but in no way connected with any settlement in North America, let alone one occurring 52 years after his death. The other one, marked WILLIAM THE SILENT, is an equally paradoxical choice. Willem I, prince of Orange (1533–1584), became ruler of the Dutch with the avowed intention of ridding his people of Spanish viceroys, Spanish troops and Spanish taxes. He was less concerned about the religious issue (the conflict between Catholic Spain and the Protestant

Lowlands) than about rule by foreigners who could not even speak Dutch. For reasons of policy, Prince Willem had in 1573 joined the Calvinist church, and the year before he was assassinated, he married Admiral de Coligny's daughter Louise; these are his sole connections with Calvinism per se. This leaves unfounded all claims that he was a "martyr for the cause of Protestantism," let alone any claims of a relationship between him and the Dutch settlements in New York. Historians agree that Willem's assassination served the purpose of furthering Spanish rule in the Netherlands, not religious indignation.

The M on Coligny's shoulder refers to Mint Engraver Morgan, who made the original dies.

The reverse displays a fanciful three-masted ship, supposed to represent the *Nieuw Nederlandt* bound for America, in 1624—hence the dates and inscriptions. NEW NETHERLAND refers to the settlements in upper New York state and neighboring New Jersey, 1621–1664.

Opportunity: A seemingly innocuous organization calling itself the Huguenot-Walloon New Netherland Commission, under Rev. Dr. John Baer Stoudt, chairman, promoted the idea of commemorative coins and stamps for this tercentenary. The authorizing bill attracted little attention in Congress and was routinely passed into law as of February 26, 1923, after Rep. Albert H. Vestal, House Coinage Committee chairman, had approved it.

Motive: The Commission was actually a front for the Federal Council of Churches of Christ in America, which wanted the coins as a fund-raising project. Rev. Stoudt just happened to be a coin collector as well as an amateur artist. It is therefore not at all impossible that Stoudt suggested the idea to the Council people. We do not know if they were unaware of its unconstitutionality, or if they simply believed they could get away with their project by rushing the coins onto the market before protests could become effective.

But as soon as news of the coins appeared in print, protests began. Other churches who would not receive a cent from the enterprise attacked the issue as sectarian and therefore unconstitutional. Anticlerical and ad-hoc patriotic groups united in dedication to the principle of separation of church and state attacked the issue as religious propaganda in violation of the First Amendment and therefore unconstitutional. Many of their arguments sound as though written by Madalyn Murray O'Hair forty years later. However, any petitions for withdrawal of the coins or repeal of the authorizing act must have been ignored by the government, as no action followed.

Suspects: Rev. John Baer Stoudt, who provided the original concept and its rationalization of Coligny and Willem I as "martyrs" as well as sketches for the devices. (The ship design is entirely Stoudt's fantasy, on both the coin and the stamp, though Morgan's original rejected model showed it facing the other way.) George T. Morgan, Engraver of the Mint since Barber's death in 1917, and Assistant Engraver for forty years before that, completed the work slowly and fumblingly, so poorly that the Federal Fine Arts Commission rejected it! This was doubly ironical in that Morgan had originally told Congressman Vestal that the work should be done entirely within the Mint, citing Barber's tired old lie about how outside artists invariably made their coin models in too high relief to stack or to strike up properly. Relief problems aside, Morgan had to complete revised models under supervision of an outsider named James Earle Fraser, which fact must have been doubly and trebly humiliating in that Fraser's initial was then adorning

the current 5¢ nickel, while neither Barber's nor Morgan's was on any regular issue coinage then in production. This was Morgan's last work as he died the following year.

Accessories: Whichever people in the Federal Council of Churches conferred with Rev. Dr. Stoudt to agree on the choice of Coligny and Willem I for the obverse design.

Modus Operandi: The Philadelphia Mint struck a total of 142,000 Huguenot half dollars in February and April 1924, plus 80 reserved for assay, out of the 300,000 originally authorized. By arrangement with the Huguenot-Walloon New Netherland Commission, the Fifth National Bank of New York obtained the coins at face value, and began offering them (over the above-mentioned protests) at $1 apiece. Partly owing to pressure from the Federal Council of Churches, the churchgoing public actually bought 87,000 of the coins. The remaining 55,000 were eventually released into circulation at face value, probably unsaleable owing to the protests and attacks. Survivors are apt to be VF to AU or sliders, dull and cleaned; look for mint frost on cheek. Die polishing marks (shiny areas) near the OT of HUGUENOT are common features of one reverse die and not damage to your coin.

Collateral Evidence: A single matte proof is reported, but we have not yet seen the piece.

No holders, cases, or accompanying literature have survived.

A single uniface brass trial impression of a reverse die is known; for reasons earlier mentioned, we have no record of its location.

The tercentenary was commemorated by three different stamps, all issued on May 1, 1924, all designed by Charles Aubrey Huston. Among these, the 2¢ commemorates the landing at Fort Orange (which would have been a better subject for the coin), and the 5¢ shows the Jan Ribault monument at Mayport, Florida (though we have not heard of any attacks on the Post Office for this sectarian item). Only the dark green 1¢, Scott 614, Type A178, is a true tie-in, Rev. Dr. Stoudt's ship design appearing here in a close copy of the version on the coin. Some 51,378,033 of these stamps got into public hands, probably without needing too much help from the Federal Council of Churches especially as the latter was unlikely to derive any revenue from their sale.

The Huguenot-Walloon Tercentenary 1¢ commemorative stamp—Scott 614, Type A178.

THE ILLINOIS CENTENNIAL HALF DOLLAR

Obverse

Reverse

The Corpus Delicti: Alias *The Lincoln.*

Clues: From the beardless (pre-1860) bust of Lincoln, one might guess the focus to be on some anniversary from the martyred President's life; however, the legend clearly indicated instead state-wide and local (county) centennial celebrations. Relevance of the defiant eagle is impossible to establish; it may have been copied, loosely, from Morgan's pattern dollar design of 1882, found with the "Second Schoolgirl" or "Shield Earring" head. However, the motto STATE SOVEREIGNTY NATIONAL UNION is that of Illinois; the eagle turns away from the rising sun, i.e., toward the west, as did the people who migrated there from the East Coast in search of vast tracts of farmland. Note also that the olive branch for peace is prominent, but that there are no arrows for war: their presence on a coin designed during the concluding months of World War I might have been considered just a bit raw.

Opportunity: Congress authorized the mintage of 100,000 special half dollars by Act of June 1, 1918, the proceeds to be used for helping finance county centennial celebrations throughout the state.

Motive: As above. This was to be the first of the state centennial commemoratives to be authorized.

Suspects: George T. Morgan, Engraver of the Mint after Barber's death, designed the obverse; the Assistant Engraver, John R. Sinnock, designed the reverse. The prime mover was the Illinois Centennial Commission; we have not located the names.

Accessories: Morgan's bust of Lincoln is his translation of a photograph of Andrew O'Conner's heroic statue of Lincoln, unveiled in Springfield in August 1918, as part of the centennial ceremonies. It is also beyond any conceivable challenge Morgan's masterpiece. An unintentional accessory—at least to forcing revision of lettering and placement of mottoes—was Treasury Secretary W.G. McAdoo, who (through his mouthpiece Mary O'Reilly, Acting Director of the Mint), in June 1918, disapproved the original models and insisted on the arrangement as adopted on the coins, except that he wished the Illinois motto replaced by E PLURIBUS UNUM. We have not been able to ascertain who overruled McAdoo in the matter of the Illinois motto; presumably pressure was brought by the head of the Illinois Centennial Commission and possibly also by other Treasury officials.

Modus Operandi: Despite McAdoo's adverse views, the Philadelphia Mint struck its full authorized quota of 100,000 pieces in August 1918, with 58 extras being reserved for assay. At the beginning of the mintage, "set-up trials" were made in copper and nickel, and on these the designs are only partially brought up. Reportedly, at least one specimen also exists in "white metal," from a collector with "mint connections," which may mean that it came from the John R. Sinnock estate, like many other similar items. There are at least two satin finish proofs, and the issue may also exist in matte proof finish; any such specimens will have much more sharpness of detail on hair and feathers than the piece pictured above, especially in the breast area.

All 100,000 went to the Commission and many were sold at $1 apiece. Others appear to have been spent, as many circulated specimens now survive. Several thousand remained in a vault in a Springfield, Illinois bank, and were released during the bank panic of the 1930s, some of them going to dealers at not much above face value; the rest were probably spent.

Distinguishing truly mint state specimens is a problem, as many are weakly struck on Lincoln's cheekbone and the hair above it, as well as on many feathers and on the grass around the rock. A magnifying glass should enable you to ascertain if these areas have been rubbed.

The only official holders we have heard of are the bronze shield-shaped badges with ribbon, identified as the official badge of the Illinois Centennial.

THE IOWA STATEHOOD CENTENNIAL HALF DOLLAR

Obverse

Reverse

The Corpus Delicti: Alias *Iowa.*

Clues: Obverse design is an adaptation of the state arms, with 29 stars above the eagle, indicating Iowa's rank as 29th state to enter the Union. On many specimens the motto is not too clearly brought up; its full text is OUR LIBERTIES WE PRIZE AND OUR RIGHTS WE WILL MAINTAIN. Reverse device is the old state capitol in Iowa City, called the Old Stone Capitol. At lower right border, between a final A of statutory inscription and final R of DOLLAR, is AP, for Adam Pietz, Assistant Engraver of the Mint.

Opportunity: The presence of a new administration (that of Harry S. Truman) gave promoters of this and other commemorative issues some hope of passage of authorizing acts; accordingly, the Iowa State Centennial Committee under Governor Blue exerted pressure in Congress, 1945–46, so that on July 15, 1946, a bill passed the House. President Truman—doubtless favorably influenced by the coin's being for a state centennial rather than some local commercial enterprise—signed it into law on August 7, 1946.

Motive: Local pride, mostly; for once that Five Finger Word appears to have been conspicuously absent.

Suspects: Adam Pietz, sculptor, Assistant Engraver of the Mint.

Accessories: Whichever members of the State Centennial Committee suggested the devices; it is also possible that the designers of the Iowa Territorial Centennial stamp of 1938 (on the following page) might belong here, as its Old Stone Capitol motif—without the plaza outbuildings or sidewise stairs—was echoed on the coin.

Modus Operandi: On September 13, 1946, Nellie Tayloe (Ma) Ross, the Mint Director, submitted designs (without mention of the artist's name) to the Federal Commission of Fine Arts. On September 16, Governor Blue told the Commission that his Centennial Committee had already approved the designs. The next day Gilmore Clarke, chairman of the Commission of Fine Arts, recommended that legs be added to the eagle and that the plaster models be resubmitted. On October 1, Acting Director of the Mint Leland Howard submitted plaster models, with the talons added as requested, but this time he informed the Commission that the artist was Adam Pietz. Six days later, Gilmore Clarke indicated that the Commission "imposes no objection to the minting of the coin"—but mostly in view of the late date of submission of models.

During November 1946, the Mint struck 100,000 pieces plus 57 reserved for assay; these were shipped at once to the Iowa Centennial Committee at the State House in Des Moines. The Committee made extraordinary efforts to exclude speculators. Initial price was $2.50 to Iowa residents, $3 to outsiders. Iowans were apportioned coins according to county and population, and the coins were sold through local banks via a lottery system. Would-be purchasers selected numbered tickets; if their numbers were drawn in the lottery, the holders could present their tickets to the local distributing bank, these tickets awarding the right to make purchases, though not guaranteeing that coins would be available. If a given bank's allotment was exhausted earlier, would-be buyers would have to wait until some other bank, unable to sell its own allotment, shipped duplicates.

Some 5,000 specimens were reserved for out-of-state sales at $3, any unsold local coins being earmarked for the same purpose. These were all sold within a few weeks, as were the 94,000 intended for local sales. For the state sesquicentennial in 1996, and for its bicentennial in 2046, 500 coins each were set aside. Half of each batch is intended for presentation to VIPs during the celebration dates, by orders of the Governor and the Centennial Commission.

Despite these tactics, or possibly partly because of them, the Iowa half dollars sold out completely, without a speculative market ever developing. Cheques had to be addressed to State Treasurer, State House, Des Moines (*The Numismatist* 2/47:167). The coins were first illustrated in *The Numismatist* 4/47:296.

Collateral Evidence: No holders have been met with and possibly none were made for initial distribution of the coins.

The Iowa Territorial Centennial Stamp.

No proofs or special presentation strikings are even rumored.

There are two philatelic tie-ins, but the connection of the first is at best secondary; this is the 3¢ violet "Iowa Territory Centennial" issue, Scott 838 (Type A310), featuring the same building as the coins. This stamp was released on August 24, 1938, a total of 47,064, 300 being issued.

The other one is the Iowa Statehood Issue, featuring state flag and map; this is the 3¢ deep blue, Scott 942 (Type A389), issued to the quantity of 132,430,000. First day covers for the 1938 stamp, dated August 24, postmarked Des Moines, were issued to the amount of 209,860; for the 1946 stamp, dated August 3, 1946, they were issued postmarked Iowa City, to a total of 517,505—the largest in its own day except for the 1939 World's Fair 3¢.

This issue is always available for a price! Its investment potential is considered good, provided that your specimens are in truly choice or gem state and that the details of the eagle's head and neck are well struck. Nicked or weak examples of this coin are not recommended.

THE ISABELLA QUARTER DOLLAR

Obverse

Reverse

The Corpus Delicti: Alias *Isabella Quarter.*

Clues: The crowned female bust is Barber's fanciful portrait of Queen Ysabela (Isabella) "la Catolica," possibly remotely after some uncredited old engraving. There is little resemblance between her crown and that of the Spanish kings or queens, nor are the details of her snood and garments particularly authentic, at least if one may judge from the surviving coins portraying her with King Fernando. Reverse is supposed to represent an idealized spinner, holding a distaff with yarn in her left hand, dangling a spindle from her right. Both these attributes were intended as symbolic of woman's major industry at the time of Queen Ysabela (even as when the coins were made)—making fabrics for garments, bedlinens, etc. The old phrase "the distaff side" (of a family, etc.) refers to this view.

The inscription BOARD OF LADY MANAGERS requires somewhat more extended explanation. This was a group of women designated by the promoters of the Exposition to publicize what were thought to be specifically female interests. It was organized in opposition to the Board of Gentlemen Managers, largely because of pressure from Susan B. Anthony (then president of the National American Woman Suffrage Association). Ms. Anthony lobbied in both

houses of Congress, finally presenting a petition to Senator Orville Platt (R.-Conn.), which appears to have done the trick, and the Board of Lady Managers became a reality, as part of the authorizing act.

Unfortunately, after the choice of Mrs. Potter Palmer for its head, the Board could no longer be taken seriously. Mrs. Palmer was the wife of the hotel tycoon after whom the Palmer House Hotel was named; she was a commanding figure in Society (capital S) in Chicago. She was notorious for incredible extravagance in dress and her husband kept her tottering by draping her in some $500,000 in diamonds (probably over $10 million at today's prices) at all public gatherings. The medallic portrait in Slabaugh communicates some slight idea of the image this peacock displayed. True that her Board of Lady Managers did coordinate exhibits by women; true that they supervised the Women's Building (which was designed by a woman); true that Mrs. Palmer suggested to Congress that some $10,000 of the money given to the Board of Lady Managers should be paid out in commemorative quarter dollars; nevertheless she and her Board were continually overruled by both the Mint and the Board of Gentlemen Managers, especially when any decisions were in the least degree controversial. No proper gentlemen of that day would have considered for a moment that

Obverse and reverse of Isabella proof quarter.

women could manage anything on their own, and unfortunately one of Mrs. Palmer's decisions, if tolerated, would have lost the Exposition a considerable amount of money. This was the case of the "Egyptian Village" girls, whom Mrs. Palmer considered obscene and sought to expel. They were actually local girls with dark eyes, tan makeup, pseudo-Oriental costumes, and a belly-dance act probably more decorous than those performed today in local nightclubs. Slabaugh quotes the old story that the Exposition opened on May 1, and by May 2 everyone had heard about the "Egyptian Village" girls. Mrs. Palmer and her Board were overruled, partly because this exhibit was one of the few real moneymakers.

Motive: Fund raising for the Board of Lady Manager's projects at the Exposition; and, in a more dim and inarticulate way, recognition that even a group of women could have a commemorative coin issued through their influence.

Suspects: Charles E. Barber. Mrs. Palmer wrote to Mint Director Leech early in March 1893 (just after the authorizing act had been passed, March 3), recommending that the commemorative quarter dollars portray Queen Ysabela, presumably because she was Columbus' patroness. Leech wrote to her on March

17 to the effect that this could be most effectively done by forwarding an "effigy," not hiring any sculptor or modeller. However, as there was no female engraver in the Mint, Mrs. Palmer (possibly at Susan B. Anthony's recommendation) ignored Leech and commissioned the New York artist Caroline Peddle to design the coin. Miss Peddle submitted two hasty sketches, the obverse with a nearly full face enthroned figure of the Queen, the reverse with a nine-line inscription (both are reproduced in Taxay, p. 6), but as Mrs. Palmer had attempted to bypass Barber, there was no way in which Miss Peddle's designs could have been approved. Her enthroned figure was replaced by Barber's fantasy head; and the Board's alternate choice of the Women's Building at the Exposition for reverse device was, on good grounds, rejected by Barber (his sketch is also in Taxay). In the end, Barber designed both sides.

Accessories: Mint Director Leech; Philadelphia Mint Superintendent O.C. Bosbyshell, who always agreed with Barber.

Modus Operandi: Production began June 13, 1893. As with the 1892 half dollars, the 400th, 1492nd and 1892nd pieces struck were selected and documented by the Mint, and forwarded to the

114

Chicago Historical Society; we have not found out what happened to the first one, though we recall rumors that it also sold for an extremely high price like the 1892 half dollar. The following tabulation is self-explanatory:

Authorized: 40,000
Coined: 40,000 + 23 assay
Melted: 15,809
Net mintage: 24,191

It appears that 103 of these were proofs: the first 100 and nos. 400, 1492 and 1892. That gives us 24,088 business strikes in addition to the 103 proofs. These coins were originally offered at $1 apiece, but after the Exposition closed some were being sold by coin dealers at 35¢ each. Evidently some went into circulation or were worn down as pocket pieces, as we have seen some in Fine to AU; the majority of uncirculated pieces have been cleaned, many of them so often or so poorly as to reduce their grade to AU. Gem specimens are now difficult to locate.

As most proof Isabella quarters have been doubted at one time or another, collectors are advised that the piece illustrated on the preceding page is one of the proofs of such high quality as to be beyond reasonable question. Note the extra sharpness of detail in centers: on the Queen's hair, her ruffled collar, her brocaded or embroidered garment, the lappet of her snood, the folds in the spinner's sleeve, the locks of her hair, the twists in her yarn, the continuous line from distaff to spindle even where it crosses her thigh. Proofs also have brilliant mirror surface in the triangular field area just left of the fist holding the distaff, at the very center of reverse. Unfortunately, some proof-like early business strikes also have this area mirrored; but no coin authenticated as a proof of this issue lacks it.

THE JEFFERSON AND McKINLEY LOUISIANA PURCHASE GOLD DOLLARS

Thomas Jefferson obverse.

William McKinley obverse.

Reverse

The original case of issue for the Louisiana Purchase gold dollars.

A Louisiana Purchase gold dollar in its case of issue accompanied by a gold mounting.

Obverse and reverse of a counterfeit of the McKinley Louisiana Purchase gold dollar. Note the lack of detail and sharpness on the portrait of McKinley.

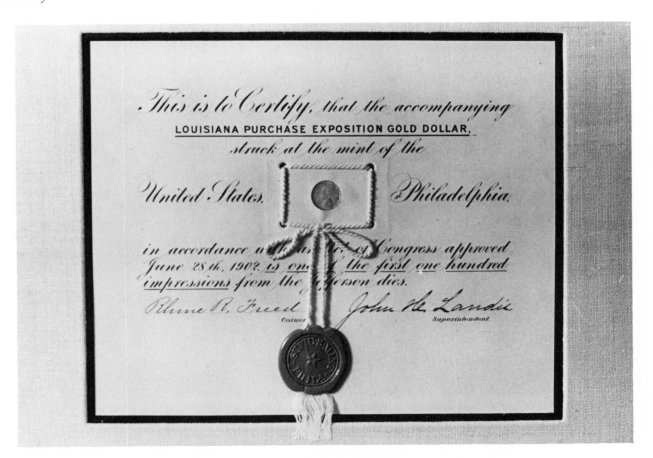

Original cardboard holder with accompanying signed certificate housing a genuine proof Louisiana Purchase Commemorative gold dollar. Note the original dark red wax seal.

"Louisiana Gold" souvenir tokens.

The Corpus Delicti: Alias *Jefferson 1903, McKinley 1903.*

Clues: Jefferson's portrait is recognized by the cravat and periwig; his facial features, inaccurately rendered by Charles E. Barber, have acquired a resemblance to Napoleon Bonaparte, the other party in the Louisiana Purchase transaction. McKinley's portrait is recognized by the bowtie. On reverse, the olive branch—if that is the plant intended—may refer to this 828,000 square mile territory's acquisition by peaceful means; the dates 1803–1903 refer to the Purchase and the Exposition's scheduled opening.

Opportunity: On June 28, 1902, Congress passed an appropriations bill, including a $5,000,000 rider financing the forthcoming Louisiana Purchase Exposition. Some $250,000 of the five million were to consist of gold dollars commemorating the exposition and to be sold on the site. These were originally intended to be made and marketed in 1903, but as usual with World's Fairs in these decades, opening was delayed until the following year, and nobody was about to raise a fuss that the centennial year was over with.

Motive: To help raise funds for the Louisiana Purchase Exposition, held at Forest Park in St. Louis (a 1,272-acre site, largest exposition site ever in its time), April 30–December 1, 1904.

Suspects: The Exposition's Souvenir Coin Department; Charles E. Barber.

Accessories: Barber copied the Jefferson portrait from John Reich's Indian Peace Medal of Jefferson (1801), a specimen of which was then reportedly in the Mint Cabinet collection. The McKinley portrait was from life; McKinley had sat for his portrait on Barber's presidential medal. As portraiture, it is idealized compared to the stamp (on the following page); as a composition, the medal had managed to

receive the sarcastic accolade of "deadly!" from no less than Augustus St.-Gaudens.

Modus Operandi: Originally the gold dollars were only to portray Jefferson as the president in charge when the territory was sold to the United States. In the meantime, President McKinley, who had signed the Exposition into law as of March 3, 1901, was assassinated at another Exposition in September 1901. Through some unrecorded agreement, a new obverse die portraying McKinley was made. It is not definitely known which dollars were first struck, only that they were distributed simultaneously in equal quantities. In December 1902, some 75,000 dollars were struck with an extra 80 held for assay; 50,000 of these went to the St. Louis Subtreasury as of December 22, 1902, to be held until Exposition officials "complied with the requirements of the law" (whatever that might have meant—posting bonds?) (*The Numismatist* 2/03:60). In January 1903, 175,000 more were struck, with an extra 178 reserved for assay, giving a total of 250,000—the entire authorization. Half were Jeffersons, half McKinleys; all bore the 1903 date. It is impossible to distinguish the December 1902 striking from those of January 1903.

They were offered at $3 apiece, but relatively few moved. Certainly the homely case of issue did not help, as the illustration shows.

Whatever the cause, relatively few moved. It is likely that the price stimulated sales resistance; they were not well-publicized, and they were competing with the Exposition's own mint-made medal, which was nearly silver dollar size and much more attractive.

In an effort to drum up public interest, Farran Zerbe circulated wooden postcards portraying them (the Slabaugh book, p. 22, shows one of these, full of wooden puns); tie-in sales were made with the M.E. Hart & Co. "Louisiana Gold" souvenir ½ and ¼ dollar tokens. (With one or more gold dollars, the souvenirs were sold at 75¢ the pair; separately, they cost double.)

Many of the gold dollars were made into stickpins, bangles, charms, brooches, or the like, destroying their numismatic value because the findings were soldered onto the gold coins. Still others were sold with separate mountings into which the coins could be harmlessly inserted, such as that shown on p. 118.

A tie-in of another kind was the pair of stamps portraying Jefferson and McKinley. These are respectively the 2¢ Jefferson, Scott 324 (Type A131), of which 192,732,400 in all were released, and the 5¢ McKinley, Scott 326 (Type A133), of which 6,926,700 were distributed. Both these were offi-

The 2 ¢ Jefferson—Scott 324.

The 5 ¢ McKinley—Scott 326.

cially released for the first time on the Exposition's first day, April 30, 1904.

Packaging or no, mountings or no, tie-in sales or no, the coins languished, only some 35,000 being sold in all, presumably in equal numbers. The bare statistics (250,000 coined, 215,250 melted) need some amplification. If the numbers of survivors are about equal (and their relative frequency of appearance certainly suggests so), it would follow that the numbers melted were also approximately equal. In tabular form:

Authorized:	125,000 each type
Coined:	125,000 each type
Melted:	215,250 total, or about 107,625 each
Net mintage:	about 17,375 each type

Of these, the first 100 of each type were brilliant proofs. They were originally distributed in large cardboard pages with certificates signed by J.M.

Landis, Superintendent, and Rhine R. Freed, Coiner, Philadelphia Mint. Each was certified to be one of the first hundred pieces coined of the issue; each had a penciled serial number at one corner. A matched pair, one of each type, in the original holder of issue, was recently offered at $22,000. Probably some of the holders became damaged, as several of the proof dollars (more Jeffersons than McKinleys, for some reason) have been lately met with in ordinary envelopes, or—as with the #5 McKinley—in a plastic holder with the documentation; this last was lot 2061, 1977 ANA Convention sale, at $2,800.

Some alleged matte proofs have shown up lately in what are supposed to be their original cardboard pages. In fact, they've turned out to be brilliant proofs obscured by waxed paper protective coverings.

In recent years, numismatic counterfeits have shown up. The surface and blurry device details as on the accompanying illustrations (p. 119), compared with that on p. 117, will enable quick identification of suspected coins.

THE LAFAYETTE SILVER DOLLAR

Obverse   *Reverse*

The Corpus Delicti: Alias *Lafayette*.

Clues: The heads of Washington and Lafayette appear jugate—here actually cheek to cheek, in a singularly appropriate testimony not only to their joint role in the Revolution but to their relationship in life. The childless Washington and the then extremely handsome young Lafayette were closer than brothers throughout the war. It might have been even more appropriate to portray them as they appeared then, rather than decades later, but possibly no engraved portrait of Lafayette of that time was available to go with those of Washington by Pierre Eugène du Simitière.

We may take Lafayette's pose on the statue, as depicted on the coin, to represent him in triumphal procession rather than charging against the enemy —note his sheathed sword, like a Highland pipe major's baton, serving as a standard rather than brandished unsheathed as a weapon.

The words PARIS 1900 refer to the Paris Exposition. For the other inscriptions, see below.

Opportunity: Congress authorized these coins as of March 3, 1899, as part of our government's participation in the 1900 Paris Exposition, and in commemoration of the centennial of Washington's death.

Motive: To defray part of the cost of completion of Paul Wayland Bartlett's (1865–1925) equestrian statue of Lafayette, then under construction in Paris for display at the Exposition.

Suspects: The Lafayette Monument Committee (Robert J. Thompson, secretary); Charles E. Barber.

Accessories: Barber copied an engraving or photograph of the familiar Jean Antoine Houdon bust of Washington (1785) for his lifeless head of the President. His prototype for the head of Lafayette—as for the entire composition—was beyond doubt Peter L. Krider's Yorktown Centennial Medal (1881), pictured in Slabaugh.

EQUESTRIAN STATUE OF LAFAYETTE.

The school children of the United States raised the money to pay for this statue, which is to be presented to France on July Fourth, next, with elaborate ceremonies.

The equestrian statue of General Lafayette used for the coin's reverse.

LAFAYETTE DOLLAR.

OFFICE OF THE LAFAYETTE MEMORIAL COMMISSION

CHICAGO, December 8, 1899.

TO THE PUBLIC:

Within the next few days there will be struck at the United States Mint in Philadelphia the most unique and significant coin issued in modern times. It is the Lafayette Dollar authorized by Congress in aid of the Lafayette Monument.

This coin, which is a legal tender dollar, bears upon its face in bas-relief a double medallion of the heads of Washington and Lafayette and upon its reverse a miniature reproduction of the equestrian statue of Lafayette used for the Monument. The inscription on the dollar explains its purpose (struck in commemoration of Monument erected by school youth of United States to General Lafayette, Paris, France, 1900).

The Lafayette Dollar thus serves not only to aid the Memorial work but forms a new and beautiful tie between the two great republics of Europe and America, and therefore the coin must be regarded as an international emblem. It constitutes a most desirable souvenir and memento of the Children's Monument to the "Knight of Liberty," the Universal Exposition of 1900 at Paris, and the opening of the twentieth century. The limited number issued will make these coins extremely rare and in very great demand.

The first coin to be struck of the 50,000 will be presented to the President of the French Republic.

Popular subscriptions for these coins will now be entered, and honored in the order received. The price fixed on them by the Commission is two dollars. All orders for coins must be accompanied by payment in full and be in the hands of the Commission on or before DECEMBER 20, 1899, on which date the popular subscription closes. Drafts, currency or Money Orders will be accepted in payment. Drafts and Money Orders must be made payable to Edwin A. Potter, Treasurer of the Commission.

The Commission reserves the right to limit the number of coins (above fifty) allotted to each subscriber. ORDERS FOR ONE COIN SHOULD BE COMBINED AND SENT IN ONE SUBSCRIPTION, ENABLING THE COMMISSION TO DELIVER TO ONE ADDRESS. IF POSSIBLE, SEND THROUGH LOCAL BANK OR EXPRESS OFFICE.

Inquiries and subscriptions for coins to be addressed to Robert J. Thompson, Secretary, in care of American Trust & Savings Bank, Chicago.

THE LAFAYETTE MEMORIAL COMMISSION.

WM. R. DAY,	MELVILLE E. STONE,
WM. B. ALLISON,	CHAS. A. COLLIER,
EDWARD EVERETT HALE,	EDWIN A. POTTER,
W. T. HARRIS,	CHAS. G. DAWES,
ARCHBISHOP IRELAND,	ALEX. H. REVELL,
JOHN W. MACKAY,	FERDINAND W. PECK,

ROBERT J. THOMPSON.

The letter sent by the Lafayette Memorial Commission to possible subscribers of America's only commemorative dollar coin.

The Lafayette reverse, B variety with long stem on palm branch.

Krider, a Philadelphia engraver known for a variety of tokens and medalets in the 1870s and '80s, had in turn copied the well-known Caunois portrait medal of General Lafayette (1824).

The reverse device is Barber's version of an early sketch of the Bartlett statue, including Bartlett's name on the base (disproportionately large on the coin)—a rare concession on Barber's part, and possibly intended to represent Barber's disavowal of the equestrian figure. As the statue was completed several months after the coins were struck, it differs noticeably from Barber's version, particularly in having the sword held aloft and the horse's tail shorter and bound up. Newspaper stories (e.g., New York *Herald,* July 1, 1900) invariably published photographs of one or another of the sketches, but these are all later than Barber's source.

Modus Operandi: For some months in 1899, nationwide campaigns induced school children to contribute pennies (one or several cents each) towards the $50,000 needed to fulfill the U.S.A.'s pledge towards completion of the monument. In honor of their efforts, the finished coins bore the inscription ERECTED BY THE YOUTH OF THE UNITED STATES IN HONOR OF GEN. LAFAYETTE PARIS 1900. As the coins were struck in 1899, the date 1900 was officially interpreted not as the year of mintage (which would have violated the Mint Act of 1873), but as the year of the Paris Exposition and of the erection of the monument. Even this interpretation of the date violates the same Mint Act, which demands that all U.S. coins bear a date representing the year of mintage, which means that the Lafayette dollars are technically undated and therefore illegal!

Originally, the Lafayette Monument Committee requested that Congress authorize production of 100,000 half dollars, which would be sold at a premium, the profits going to defray the cost of the monument. Later, Secretary Thompson changed his mind and advocated a silver dollar as a better souvenir. With this amendment, the authorizing bill went through Congress without difficulty, becoming the Act of March 3, 1899. On December 14, 1899, the exact day of the centenary of Washington's death, the 50,000 production coins (with 26 extra for assay) were struck, taking something over ten hours of press time. The first specimen struck, after the precedent established by the Columbians and the Isabella Quarter, received an offer of $5,000, but by

Obverse counterfeit Lafayette dollar.

prearrangement it went instead into an elaborate presentation case at the order of President McKinley, to be taken by Secretary Thompson (appointed Special Commissioner of the United States to the President of the French Republic by the State Department for the purpose) aboard the *S.S. Champagne,* destination Paris. Thompson presented it to President Loubet of France on February 22, 1900.

Photographs of the casket were released on that day but we have not been able to locate one.

During the remainder of December 1899 and well into 1900, the Commission attempted to sell the coins at $2 apiece. In February 1900 the Commission moved its headquarters from the Equitable Building in Chicago to No. 20 Avenue Rapp, Paris, leaving the actual distribution of the coins to be handled

The Lafayette reverse, C variety with short stem on palm branch.

through the American Trust & Savings Bank of Chicago. The first batch was offered by subscription solicited by the Commission in care of that bank, a week before the actual striking of the coins (originally planned for December 12), as the accompanying announcement (p. 125) shows.

Comparatively small numbers sold to coin collectors, and after the Exposition closed its doors, the bank held large quantities unsold. As early as January 1903, specimens were being peddled at $1.10 apiece. *(The Numismatist* 1/03:24, referring to a Providence, Rhode Island, collector obtaining four at that exact price.) Many of the others were evidently spent, as survivors are far more often found in Fine to AU condition than in mint state; in fact, pristine specimens (full mint state without evidence of cleaning) are very difficult to locate at any price. Some 36,000 were disposed of in one way or another, the remaining 14,000 being returned to the mint, where they remained in vaults until 1945. About that time the Omaha coin dealer Aubrey Bebee heard of their existence in mint vaults and attempted to buy them, only to learn that in the meantime they had been melted.

What little the Commission had managed to raise through sale of the dollars at a premium was diminished by a lawsuit filed against them by one Henry Hornbostel, demanding architect's fees for plans he had submitted for a pedestal to the monument, which plans had been disapproved by the Paris jury. Without admitting any misdeeds, the Commission paid Hornbostel an amount said to be equal to his out-of-pocket expenses as part of an out-of-court settlement.

Collateral Evidence: As far back as 1925, a few alert students noted that more than one distinguishable die variety existed. Research by George H. Clapp (the Alcoa president notable for his large cent collection in ANS, his conchology collection in the Carnegie Institute, and his multimillion-dollar gifts to universities) and Howland Wood (the counterfeit expert) led to the identification of four die varieties from three obverse and four reverse dies. We are able to illustrate two of the four reverses here.

The following die descriptions follow Clapp and Howland Wood.

Reverse counterfeit Lafayette dollar.

Obverse 1. AT in STATES high; point of Lafayette's bust above top of L; small point on bust of Washington. With Rev. A, B, and C.

Obverse 2. A in STATES high; final A of AMERICA double punched at left foot. With Rev. C.

Obverse 3. Final s in STATES low, AT repunched; both F's defective; AMERICA poorly spaced, RI close; pellet between OF · A is closer to A than to F; point of Lafayette's bust is beyond right top of L. With Rev. D.

Reverse A. Palm branch with 14 long leaves and long stem; point of lowest leaf above 1 of 1900; B below Y in BY. With Obv. 1.

Reverse B. Palm branch with 14 shorter leaves and long stem; point of lowest leaf over space between 1 and 9. With Obv. 1. Later, cracked through legend.

Reverse C. Palm branch with 14 medium leaves and short stem bent down; point of lowest leaf above center of 9. With Obv. 2.

Reverse D. Palm branch with 15 thin leaves and short stem, bent up; point of lowest leaf above center of 9. With Obv. 3.

These make the following combinations:

Clapp-Wood 1. Obv. 1, rev. A. Scarce.
Clapp-Wood 2. Obv. 1, rev. B. Probably least scarce.
Clapp-Wood 3. Obv. 2, rev. C. Rare.
Clapp-Wood 4. Obv. 3, rev. D. Very rare.

Swiatek 5. Obv. 1, rev. C. Very rare.

Specimens not matching any of the above are most likely to be counterfeits. The counterfeit pictured here, with its rude, irregularly placed letters, AR about touching, F of LAFAYETTE defective at base, probably was cast from a Clapp-Wood 2. It was identified by Ed Fleischmann of ANACS at the 1977 ANA Convention (Atlanta, Georgia). The owner of the two silver Pan–Pacific fifties has shown me (A.S.) an authentic brilliant proof Lafayette dollar. No other is even *rumored*!

THE
LEWIS AND CLARK
EXPOSITION
GOLD DOLLARS

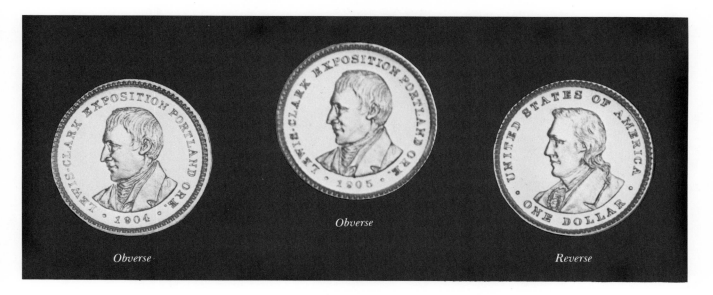

Obverse ·   Obverse   Reverse

The Corpus Delicti: Alias *Lewis and Clarks.*

Clues: In this, our nation's only two-headed coin, the obverse is legally the date side, and this side portrays—after a fashion—Captain Meriwether Lewis, who had been Thomas Jefferson's secretary despite his appallingly poor spelling. The side with ONE DOLLAR supposedly portrays Captain William Clark. In the usual strikings, it is difficult to tell one from the other (the coins illustrated above are better struck than average) and collectors have generally not bothered to object. The obverse inscription LEWIS-CLARK EXPOSITION PORTLAND ORE. is almost self-explanatory (see below). Dates are 1904 and 1905.

Opportunity: The Act of Congress of April 13, 1904, created the Exposition—for once not an "international exposition"—honoring the Corps of Discovery which explored the Northwest, 1803–06, under their two Captains. Part of the appropriation enabling the Exposition to begin was furnished by a

clause authorizing 250,000 gold dollars to be struck for resale on the site.

Suspects: Charles E. Barber and the Exposition heads, whose names have not been located.

Accessories: Charles E. Barber appears to have copied the Charles Willson Peale portraits of Lewis and Clark in Independence Hall, Philadelphia.

Modus Operandi: During September 1904, the Philadelphia Mint struck 25,000 Lewis and Clark dollars (with an extra 28 being reserved for assay). They remained in the vaults for nearly a year, as the Exposition did not open until June 1, 1905. When it did open, Farran Zerbe—who had been heard to brag unwisely "I am the only man who ever sold 50,000 dollars at $3 apiece," referring to the Louisiana Purchase coins—set up an exhibit of his coin collection (the nucleus of that which later formed the Chase Manhattan Bank Money Museum)

In April 1905, long before the exposition officially opened, the Lewis and Clark issue was offered for sale by this dealer. This ad claimed that even at this early date, the supply was nearly exhausted.

A month later, in the May 1905 issue of The Numismatist, *the same advertiser offered Lewis and Clark gold dollars at "6 for $10." One must wonder how he restocked or even managed to get the coins no one else was able to obtain.*

in the Manufacturers Building on the exposition site, and began peddling the Lewis and Clark dollars at $2 apiece. No original holders have been located to date. (*The Numismatist* 8/05:239-241.)

In the meantime, the mint made 35,000 dollars dated 1905, with 41 extras reserved for assay, during the months of March and June 1905. By the time the Exposition closed, on October 14, 1905, only 9,997 of the 1904s had been sold, and only 10,000 of 1905s; the other 1905s never left the mint.

By some kind of skulduggery, the details of which have never been made public, a coin dealer in Portland, Oregon, operating under the name of D.M. Averill & Co., at 331 Morrison Street, obtained a quantity of 1904 gold dollars before the Exposition opened, and began advertising them in *The Numismatist* as early as October 1904. (*The Numismatist* 10/04:316, 11/04:352, 12/04:385—where a typographical error reduced the price from $2 to $1—and 1/05:33, again at $2.) Averill also obtained specimens of the 1905 issue before anyone else, and offered them at $2 each while raising the 1904s to $2.50 on the grounds that "These are nearly exhausted." (*The Numismatist* 4/05:130, 5/05:165 and later issues, where the 1905s were offered at 6 for $10.)

Motive: The proceeds of sale were earmarked for completion of the bronze memorial to Sacagawea, alias Mrs. Toussaint Charbonneau: she was part-time guide and full-time interpreter between the Corps of Discovery and the Indian tribes, negotiating with them for horses necessary to cross the mountainous areas between the end of the Missouri River and the Pacific Ocean, and convincing various tribes that the expedition was not in fact a war party.

Some survivors are proof-like. A few authentic proofs are known of the 1904, one in the Smithsonian Institution (from the Chief Coiner, Rhine R. Freed, December 19, 1904), one in ANS, possibly 5 or 6 in private collections. These coins are more sharply impressed than normal business strikings, having received at least two blows from the dies; they are notable for having much more hair detail than the ordinary run of production coins, and all border beads are clearly distinct from each other and from the surrounding rim. Proofs of the 1905 issues are much rarer, one being in the Smithsonian, and possibly four others in private hands, with a doubtful fifth in ANS.

Aside from the quantity turned over to Averill (presumably by the Exposition heads), those unsold at the Exposition were returned to the mint and melted. In tabular form:

Authorized:	250,000 in total (for both dates)
Coined:	1904, 25,000; 1905, 35,000
Melted:	1904, 15,003; 1905, the 25,000 which had not left the mint
Net mintage:	1904, 9,997; 1905, 10,000

Counterfeits were made in the early 1960s: most were confiscated by the U.S. Secret Service, but it is possible that a few may survive in private hands. These are somewhat porous, and the lettering and devices are, if possible, cruder than the originals; in particular, the lettering is irregularly placed. If in doubt, check the illustration here, or submit your coins to ANACS or INSAB.

Collateral Evidence: As early as 1901, when the new "Bison" notes (the $10 Legal Tender, Series of 1901) were being designed at the Bureau of Engraving and Printing, there was talk of the forthcoming Exposition; and to help generate interest in it, according to Gene Hessler, Walter Shirlaw's portraits of Lewis and Clark—not at all resembling those on the coins—were translated into engraved vignettes by the illustrious G.F.C. Smillie and placed at the ends of the original plates. And so, from about the end of 1901 through August 1925, every Red Seal $10 bore these portraits, some 133,718,000 in all.

THE LEXINGTON–CONCORD SESQUICENTENNIAL HALF DOLLAR

Obverse

Reverse

The Corpus Delicti: Alias *Lexington, Minute-Man.*

Clues: The obverse device, labeled CONCORD MINUTE-MAN, is a close copy of Daniel Chester French's "Grand Concord Man" statue (commonly called the Minute-Man) at Concord, Massachusetts. This statue depicts one of the volunteer soldiers taking part in the battle of Lexington and Concord which began the Revolutionary War on April 19, 1775; a farmer, leaving his coat on his plow, ready to leave for the battlefront at a minute's notice, musket in hand, presumably awaiting the call to arms sounded by bells in the Old Belfry at Lexington (the reverse device of this coin). This statue was French's first commission (he was then 23 years of age), and it was erected in April 1875 for the centennial celebration. President Grant attended the ceremony. On a panel below the statue, not visible on the coin but known to every schoolboy in New England, and likely to be called to mind whenever the landmark statue was seen or remembered or pictured as on the coins, is Emerson's famous stanza about the event:

By the rude bridge that arched the flood,
Their flag to April's breeze unfurled,
Here once the embattled farmers stood
And fired the shot heard round the world.

The word PATRIOT alludes partly to the statue (as representative of a generation of revolutionaries), partly to the celebration; it was a non-negotiable demand of the Concord Town Committee, one of the two which divided the designing and the payment to the artist. As the coins were meant to appear on April 19, 1925, there was an additional local allusion; April 19 has been "Patriot Day" and a legal holiday in Massachusetts ever since Governor Greenhalge proclaimed it in 1894. The remaining inscriptions are self-explanatory, though perhaps we should mention that the Concord Committee even wanted to add the date APRIL 19 on reverse!

Opportunity: Two separate town committees late in 1924 were planning sesquicentennial celebrations in Concord and Lexington. The Lexington committee sponsored legislation in Congress to authorize a commemorative half dollar (which became the Act of January 14, 1925), and on its own initiative contacted Chester Beach, offering him the commission to design the coin. (The Mint, pleased with Beach's work on the Monroe half dollar, had been recommending him to committees seeking passage of commemorative coin bills.) When the Concord committee learned of the impending passage of the bill, its members sought out Beach as well, and eventually the two committees agreed to share the expense of his fee, but in exchange they insisted on their designs being used, Concord's for the obverse, Lexington's for the reverse.

Motive: Apparently, publicity—and a modicum of fund-raising—for the two major local celebrations.

Suspects: Chester Beach, sculptor; the Concord town committee (Judge Prescott Keyes, chairman; Harold Orendorff, publicity); the Lexington town committee (Edward C. Stone, attorney; Hallie C. Blake, finance chairman); Philip Holden, artist and designer in Concord.

Accessories: Daniel Chester French, sculptor of the "Minuteman" statue. French was still alive, in his seventies, in the Concord area, and Chester Beach consulted with him as to the propriety of adding the words CONCORD MINUTE-MAN. French not only approved, he gave Beach a photograph of the statue for use in making his original plaster models. (We would also list the architect of the Old Belfry in Lexington if anyone knew his name.)

Modus Operandi: After an amazing amount of petty niggling demands by the two committees, changing from week to week, Beach finally managed to produce designs satisfactory to both committees. His nearest prototype, for layout, was Philip Holden's drawing, though minus the 13 stars in the obverse sky; this is reproduced in Taxay, p. 83. Buildings are always a difficult problem in coin design, and Beach's solution was to use a photograph from a low angle—probably the camera was on the ground—furnished by Edward Stone. After working day and night for some weeks, Beach submitted plaster models to the Federal Commission of Fine Arts, February 14, 1925; James Earle Fraser, as sculptor member, approved them at once, but protested that the committees had made most unsuitable choices of subject matter.

One of the original wooden holders with its inked stampings—minuteman on top and Lexington's Old Belfry on bottom.

The models went to the Philadelphia Mint, which rushed the coins into production during April and May 1925. Apparently the first strikings were available for the celebration on Patriot Day. A joint enterprise called the United States Lexington-Concord Sesquicentennial Commission made up of members of the two town committees handled the sales. Harold Orendorff, the Concord publicity chairman, arranged for the Concord National Bank and the Lexington Trust Company to do the actual distribution.

In tabular form:

Authorized: Not over 300,000
Struck: 162,000 + 99   reserved
                   for assay
Returned for melting: 86
Net mintage: 161,914

Many of the coins were sold in small wooden boxes, with sliding tops, like that illustrated on the preceding page. These had on top a rubber-stamped picture of the Minute Man statue in blue ink; owing to weathering, the ink has faded, varying from dull blue-black to pale graying blue. On the base of each box is a similar stamped picture of the Old Belfry, in the same color ink. Over 125 of these coins are around in the original boxes; they are among the least rare original holders for commemorative coins, but they are still very scarce and desirable.

Collateral Evidence: At least one matte proof is reported, but it is not yet available for examination. As its source was reportedly the J. R. Sinnock estate, the coin is quite probably as described.

Survivors tend to be weak on hat, chin, musket and often also on garment details. The coins are not often found in low grades, but there are many sliders and borderline cases, and many that have been

The Lexington-Concord Commemorative 5 ¢ postage stamp—Scott 619, Type 183.

poorly handled—nicked or scratched up, or badly cleaned by subsequent non-numismatic owners.

An interesting tie-in to this issue is the commemorative 5¢ stamp, dark blue, Scott 619, Type A183, issued April 4, 1925; designer is not credited, but it looks like Charles Aubrey Huston's work. Some 5,348,800 were distributed. Huston (or whoever it was) used a different photograph of Daniel Chester French's statue, and added Emerson's four lines on flanking panels.

THE LONG ISLAND TERCENTENARY HALF DOLLAR

Obverse

Reverse

The Corpus Delicti: Alias *Long Island.*

Clues: The two accolated busts represent a Dutch settler and an Algonquin Indian, respectively symbolizing the Dutch settlement on Jamaica Bay (1636), named Breuckelin (later anglicized to Brooklyn), and the 13 tribes of Indians living on Long Island when Henry Hudson discovered it. Below the Indian's chin is the monogram of the designer, Howard Kenneth Weinman (son of A.A. Weinman who had designed the then current Mercury dime and Walking Liberty half dollar), who thus became part of the second father-and-son team ever to design U.S. coins. (The first, of course, was William and Charles E. Barber, successive Engravers of the U.S. Mint.) On reverse is a Dutch three-masted ship, presumably meant for one of those that brought settlers over to Breuckelin, but nowhere identifiable by name.

Opportunity: Local celebrations in May 1936, sponsored by the Long Island Tercentenary Celebration Committee (a.k.a. the Long Island Tercentenary Committee: Louis C. Wills, chairman; John W. Smith, secretary; DeWitt A. Forward, treasurer; National City Bank of New York, Peoples' Trust Branch, 181 Montague Street, Brooklyn, depository). These people exerted enough political clout to

have the commemorative coin authorized as of April 13, 1936, to "commemorate the 300th anniversary of the founding of the first settlement on Long Island, New York." The coins were to "bear the date 1936, irrespective of the year in which they were minted or issued"; they were to be struck at "a mint" (rather than "at the mints"—hence no mintmark varieties), and issued not later than April 13, 1937, to a maximum of 100,000 pieces.

Motive: Presumably, fund raising for the celebrations, though the coins did not arrive until August, or a couple of months after the celebrations ended.

Suspects: Howard Kenneth Weinman, designer.

Accessories: The Long Island Tercentenary Committee, above.

Modus Operandi: As early as April 2, or nearly two weeks before the bill became law, the Committee appointed young Weinman to design and model the coin. Weinman completed his models during May 1936, and the Federal Commission of Fine Arts approved them (after demanding revision such that the two mottoes were transposed into their present position—originally the Latin motto was below the

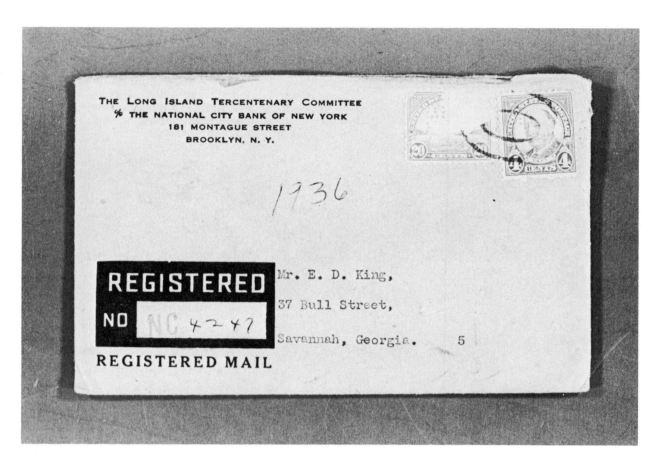

Mailing envelope used by the Long Island Tercentenary Committee to forward the coins to their subscribers.

ship) about the 24th of June. The models then went to Medallic Art Company for reproduction, thence to the Philadelphia Mint, where 100,000 coins were struck (plus 53 reserved for assay) in August.

The Committee distributed the coins through various banks in New York City and Long Island, at $1 apiece. Despite almost no advertising, they managed to sell 81,773 pieces before the April 13, 1937 deadline, the remaining 18,227 being returned to the Mint for re-melting.

Collateral Evidence: No proofs are reported, though some may have been made for John R. Sinnock, Engraver of the Mint (who incidentally had to letter the incuse motto below ship). Supposedly

about 100 of these coins are known in unimprinted holders of issue, apparently the standard Dennison-type holders; but they would hardly command a premium unless one could be sure that the holders were authentic ones from the Committee, e.g., by presence of original envelopes and invoices. We show examples of the latter.

As noted in previous *Coin World* articles in 1976 and 1977, the purchase of specimens possessing deep nicks and scratches, especially on the lower central sail of the Dutch three-masted ship is not recommended. Locating a *Long Island* that is free of bag marks may be surprisingly difficult. These coins were handled carelessly at the mint and, apparently, by the distributor as well.

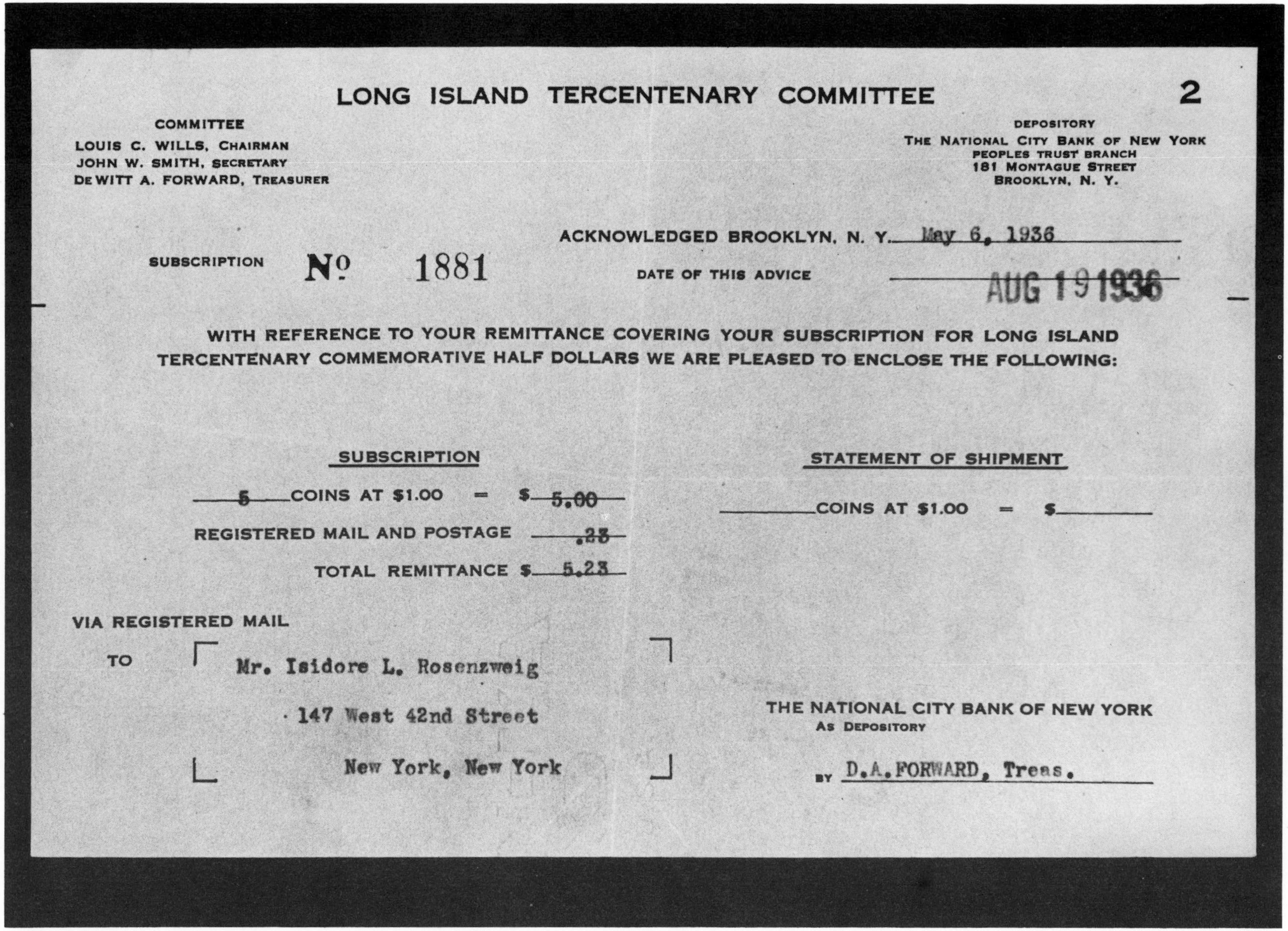

LONG ISLAND TERCENTENARY COMMITTEE

2

COMMITTEE

LOUIS C. WILLS, CHAIRMAN
JOHN W. SMITH, SECRETARY
DEWITT A. FORWARD, TREASURER

DEPOSITORY

THE NATIONAL CITY BANK OF NEW YORK
PEOPLES TRUST BRANCH
181 MONTAGUE STREET
BROOKLYN, N. Y.

SUBSCRIPTION **N⁰. 1881**

ACKNOWLEDGED BROOKLYN, N. Y. May 6, 1936

DATE OF THIS ADVICE **AUG 19 1936**

WITH REFERENCE TO YOUR REMITTANCE COVERING YOUR SUBSCRIPTION FOR LONG ISLAND TERCENTENARY COMMEMORATIVE HALF DOLLARS WE ARE PLEASED TO ENCLOSE THE FOLLOWING:

SUBSCRIPTION

5 COINS AT $1.00 = $5.00

REGISTERED MAIL AND POSTAGE .23

TOTAL REMITTANCE $ 5.23

STATEMENT OF SHIPMENT

COINS AT $1.00 = $

VIA REGISTERED MAIL

TO ⌐ Mr. Isidore L. Rosenzweig

147 West 42nd Street

New York, New York ⌐

THE NATIONAL CITY BANK OF NEW YORK
AS DEPOSITORY

BY D.A. FORWARD, Treas.

This subscription and invoice accompanied each of the Long Island Commemorative half dollars.

141

THE LYNCHBURG, VIRGINIA, SESQUICENTENNIAL HALF DOLLAR

Obverse

Reverse

The Corpus Delicti: Alias *Lynchburg* or *Carter Glass.*

Clues: Senator Carter Glass (D.-Va.; 1858–1946) was one of the founders of the Federal Reserve system, and one of the unsung heroes of our nation's economic history. Because no central clearing house or rediscounting facility existed to service several thousand National Banks, among other things, any occasional tightness in the money supply was likely to occasion bank failures, factory closures, mortgage foreclosures, tax delinquencies and mass unemployment—and in those pre-welfare days, many people starved as a result. By 1907, this had happened enough times to be a source of nationwide anxiety —especially as it seemed on the verge of happening again, as by December of that year the entire National Bank system was on the verge of collapse. Emergency relief was provided by the Aldrich-Vreeland Act (1908), but it was temporary; the same conditions reappeared in 1912. Senator Aldrich proposed a national reserve association with voluntary bank membership—only to find the farm bloc opposing it on populist grounds suspiciously reminiscent of those adduced eighty years earlier during

President Jackson's stupid battle with the Bank of the United States (Jackson's victory over the Bank having precipitated eight years of hard times, like the 1929–37 depression only without the kind of relief FDR mandated). At the same time, a House committee revealed incredible Wall Street scandals: a half dozen firms, operating as a cartel, came within a hair's breadth of cornering the money market. As soon as Aldrich's bill failed of passage, Senator Glass introduced its twin, which managed to pass as the Federal Reserve Act. This set up the Federal Reserve System (popularly the Fed) as a banker's bank, performing the same services for thousands of member banks through its 12 branches as the member banks in turn provided for depositors. It also empowered the Fed to issue its own paper currency, and to manipulate the money supply, buying and selling bonds in the open market, to prevent financial panics like those of 1837, 1857, 1873, 1893, or 1907; not that it was too successful here, as events of 1921 and 1929 proved. This latter disaster induced Senator Glass to create and push passage of the Glass-Steagall Act of 1933, creating the Federal Deposit Insurance Corporation (to help protect depositors from bank failures) and making other necessary repairs and improvements in the Fed. It is thus only fitting that Glass became the only person in American history to have both his signature on U.S. paper currency (during his tenure as President Wilson's Secretary of Treasury) and his portrait on a U.S. coin—this Lynchburg half dollar. (And the latter was over his own protests, approved by the Treasury Department despite its open violation of the Act of April 7, 1866 forbidding portrayal of any living individual on U.S. coins or currency!)

Glass' portrait was chosen as device by the Lynchburg Sesquicentennial Association, even as he had been named its honorary president. A portrait of John Lynch (founder of the town, chartered in 1786—hence the date on reverse) would have been more appropriate, according to the Federal Commission of Fine Arts, but none is known.

On reverse, Ms. Liberty extends a hand in welcome; behind her is part of Monument Terrace, with the Confederate Monument (above 19 of 1936) and the old Lynchburg Courthouse at the top. This view for many years was the first sight to greet visitors as they entered Lynchburg at Union Station; it is still perhaps the most distinctive feature of the city.

Opportunity: The Lynchburg Sesquicentennial, otherwise "Lynchburg in Old Virginia Celebrates its 150th Birthday," October 12–16, 1936; Act of May 28, 1936.

Motive: Local pride. As the coins were offered at $1 apiece, with a limit of ten per customer, clearly there was little room for That Five Finger Word here.

Suspects: Charles Keck, designer.

Accessories: The Lynchburg Sesquicentennial Association, Fred McWane, secretary. This group debated the merits of Keck and John Brcin as possible designers; Charles Moore of the Federal Commission of Fine Arts praised both, but emphasized Keck's special qualifications—he had already designed several previous commemorative coins; accordingly, the Association gave the commission to Keck, along with the $1000 figure named by the Commission (July 1, 1936).

Modus Operandi: Keck's models were completed before July 28, on which day they went from Acting Director of the Mint, Mary O'Reilly, to the Commission, which approved them on the 29th. The Philadelphia Mint struck the full authorized amount, 20,000 coins, plus 13 reserved for assay; these were

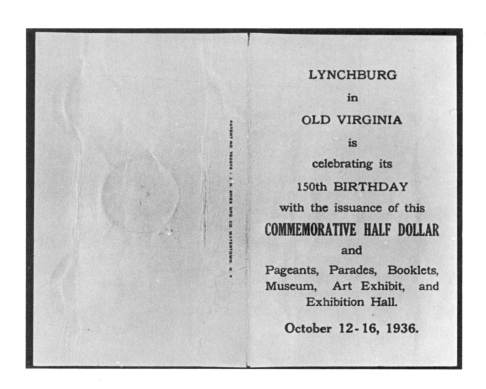

Front and back of original holder.

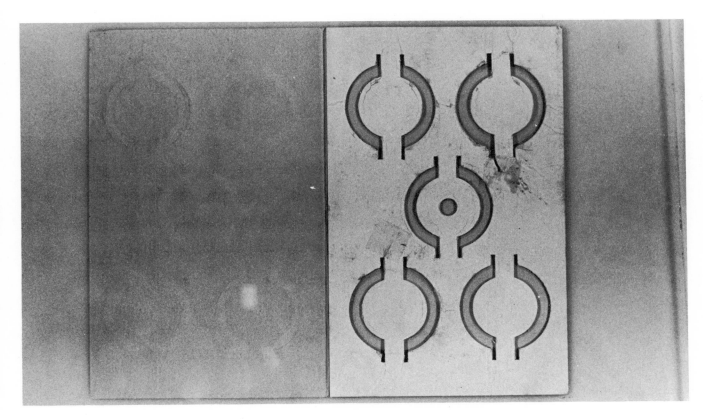

Centerspread of original holder.

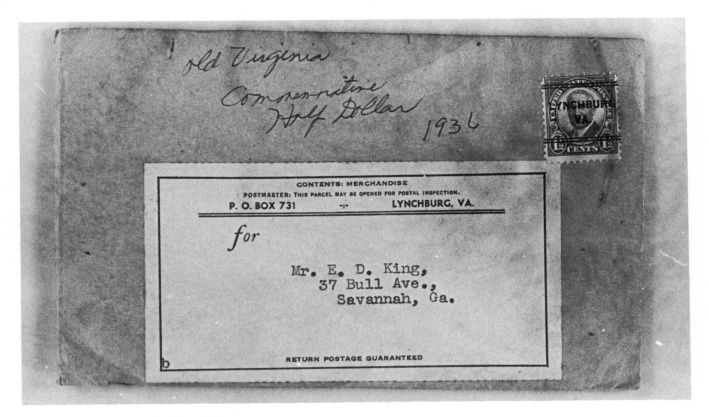

Mailing envelope used to distribute this issue.

released as of September 21, in time for the local celebrations. Locals got them for $1; outsiders received them by mail at $1.25.

The entire batch sold out, mostly as singles, a smaller number in five-coin presentation packages (limit of two packages per customer).

Collateral Evidence: We illustrate one of the buff-colored original holders of the issue. About 100 of these are known to survive.

No proofs are reported, though some may have been made for John R. Sinnock.

Survivors in gem state are increasingly difficult to locate, and increasingly often simulated by lower quality coins with plain nicks and scratches, especially left of Senator Glass' ear and on Ms. Liberty's thighs. The latter are not recommended.

THE MAINE CENTENNIAL HALF DOLLAR

Obverse

Reverse

The Corpus Delicti: Alias *Maine.*

Clues: Obverse depicts the state arms. However they may have been officially blazoned, they are here represented as "Argent, a moose couchant, behind him a pine tree, all proper; supporters, Agriculture with scythe, Commerce with anchor; crest, the Blazing Star with motto DIRIGO." DIRIGO means "I direct" or "I lead" and it has been the state motto since the state joined the Union (March 15, 1820). Note that the moose and the pine tree are defined by sunken outlines, but modeled in relief within them—the technique first met with on Egyptian stelae and tomb carvings of the same period as the pyramids, and revived (to great controversy) in 1908 with Bela Lyon Pratt's new half eagle and quarter eagle designs. Note also the symbolism in representing "Commerce" by a seaman with anchor: Maine's fisheries and lobster trappers were always extremely important in its economy, even while it was a part of Massachusetts (ca. 1658–1820). The moose apparently represents the fur trade, the pine tree the trade in timber and forestry products; the scythe suggests some above-ground crops, though Maine is possibly more famous for its potatoes. The wreath on reverse is made up not of the expected spruce and birch but of some kind of long-leaf pine, to go with its "Pine Tree State" nickname and the pine tree in the state arms.

Opportunity: The Act of Congress of May 10, 1920, authorized 100,000 of these coins to be made for sale at the Maine Centennial Celebration in Portland.

Motive: Apparently, to help defray the cost of the Maine Centennial Celebration. Rep. John A. Peters (R.-Maine) thought that the coins would simply go into circulation, and informed Congress of his wishful thinking on April 21, 1920, while the bill was still under consideration: this curious view was not shared by other legislators, nor by the Celebration people, who sold the coins at $1 apiece.

147

Obverse of a Maine Commemorative half dollar struck from dies that were heavily clashed and relapped.

Reverse of coin struck from clashed and relapped dies.

Obverse of a fraudulent Maine matte proof. A well struck business striking was used, but the coin is not double-struck, which is one major prerequisite of all genuine matte, sandblast, and brilliant proof U.S. commemoratives.

Reverse of the fraudulent Maine matte proof.

Suspects: Rep. John A. Peters, who submitted the proposal and the sketch, on behalf of the officials in charge of the Maine Centennial Commission; Anthony de Francisci, who made the original models from the sketch—reluctantly and without inspiration; George T. Morgan and/or John R. Sinnock, who altered these models in the process of translating them into master dies and hubs. On the model, the moose and pine tree are in relief, not in the "Egyptian" technique. This was probably to minimize the relief of the coin and improve its striking quality—evidently a necessary step, as most examples are still weak on those details.

Accessories: Unknown.

Modus Operandi: During "late summer" 1920 (September?), the Philadelphia Mint struck 50,000 specimens, plus 28 reserved for assay: these were delivered to the State Treasurer, as by the time the order was completed, the Centennial Celebration was over. More than half were actually sold by the State Treasurer's office within a few months, after which sales slowed down enough so that there was no talk of ordering the remaining 50,000 authorized. During ensuing months through part of 1921, the coins were continuously offered for sale until all were sold. Nevertheless, a fair number of these found their way into circulation, as Rep. Peters had predicted, and others were kept as pocket pieces, so that many survivors are found as low as Very Fine and occasional ones in Fine condition. Pristine specimens are now fairly difficult to find, aside from those being offered singly from a hoard which originally numbered 400 pieces. Specimens in which the two faces on Messrs. Agriculture and Commerce can be made out are rare; the piece pictured on the preceding page is a better than average striking, and the two faces on it are blurred. Do not expect to find central details on the pine tree, as the original model (pictured by Taxay, from the National Archives) does not have them.

In May 1978 specimens were discovered from dies that had been heavily clashed and relapped. The markings are plainest between the shoulder of Agriculture and the motto DIRIGO, and on reverse below and to left of the word MAINE. Regrinding of both dies made some letters seemingly thinner and slightly irregular in placement, but it also had the unintentional, though welcome, side effect of improving the striking quality by slightly lowering the relief.

Collateral Evidence: Matte proof strikings have been reported. One examined at the 1979 ANA Convention was genuine; the others are definitely fraudulent. One of the more dangerous fraudulent pieces is pictured on p. 149; it was apparently made from an unusually well struck business striking by sandblasting. Note that the details of garments on the two supporting figures are vague and indefinite compared to those on the clashed-die example pictured on the preceding page.

THE MARYLAND TERCENTENARY HALF DOLLAR

Obverse

Reverse

The Corpus Delicti: Alias *Maryland.*

Clues: The ¾-facing bust labeled CECIL CALVERT is that of the second Lord Baltimore (after whom the city is named); the reverse features his arms (paly of 6, argent and sable, a bend counterchanged—as on Baltimore's own coins), quartered with his wife's (a cross botony), as those were adapted for the arms of the State of Maryland. We have not been able to ascertain why the mantling or the triple crest were used, though the coronet and flags (above the helmet) appear on the Lord Baltimore Denarium or "Penny" of 1658. The reason Baltimore (1609–75) is portrayed is that he received the immense land grant (some 10,000,000 acres of what is now called Maryland) from King Charles I, ruling it as a benevolent despot, but according his subjects religious freedom at a time when it was not to be found anywhere else in the English-speaking world except Rhode Island.

The two supporters apparently represent Labor (with the spade) and Fisheries (with the fish). Next to Labor's foot are initials HS for Hans Schuler, the designer. As for the motto, FATTI MASCHII PAROLE FEMINE ("Deeds are manly, words are womanly"), that belongs to the State of Maryland, which to date has not shown any disposition to repudiate this sexist rubbish. The date 1634 is that of arrival of the 200-odd colonists at St. Mary's, the first group to settle in Maryland after Lord Baltimore obtained his grant.

Opportunity: The Maryland Tercentenary Commission in Baltimore induced its friends in Congress, notably Senator Phillips Lee Goldsborough (a former Republican Governor and a friend of President Roosevelt, who later appointed him to the board of directors of the FDIC), and Senator Millard Tydings (D.-Maryland), to speak for the bill which sought to authorize coinage of commemorative half dollars for the Tercentenary celebrations to be held statewide that summer and fall. This bill became the Act of May 9, 1934; it was the first commemorative coinage act to mention the Director of the Mint as responsible for the mintage, or to mention that the coins were to be sold above face value.

Obverse   *Reverse*

The excessively rare Maryland Tercentenary matte proof from the collection of the chief mint engraver, John R. Sinnock.

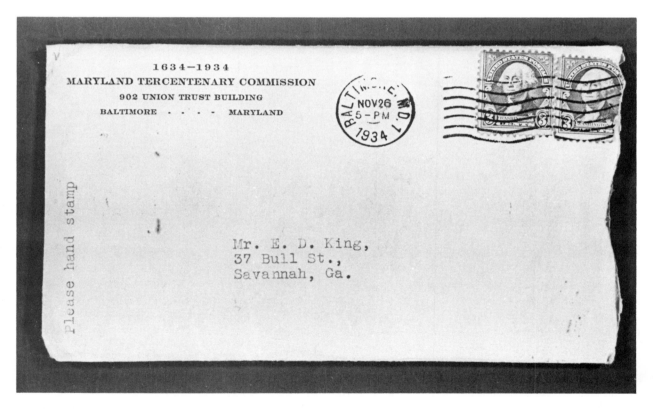

Envelope sent to interested individuals by the Maryland Tercentenary Commission.

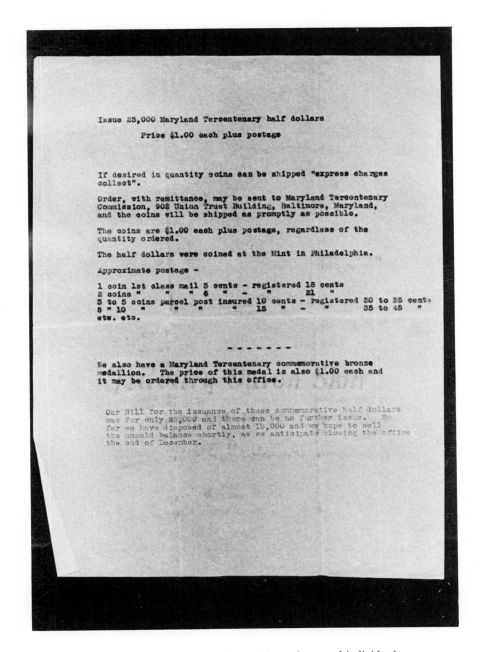

Issue 25,000 Maryland Tercentenary half dollars

Price $1.00 each plus postage

If desired in quantity coins can be shipped "express charges collect".

Order, with remittance, may be sent to Maryland Tercentenary Commission, 902 Union Trust Building, Baltimore, Maryland, and the coins will be shipped as promptly as possible.

The coins are $1.00 each plus postage, regardless of the quantity ordered.

The half dollars were coined at the Mint in Philadelphia.

Approximate postage -

1 coin 1st class mail 3 cents - registered 18 cents
2 coins "   "   6 " - "   21 "
3 to 5 coins parcel post insured 10 cents - registered 30 to 35 cents
5 " 10 "   "   "   "   15 " - "   35 to 45 "
etc. etc.

- - - - - - -

We also have a Maryland Tercentenary commemorative bronze medallion. The price of this medal is also $1.00 each and it may be ordered through this office.

Our Bill for the issuance of these commemorative half dollars was for only 25,000 and there can be no further issue. So far we have disposed of almost 15,000 and we hope to sell the unsold balance shortly, as we anticipate closing the office the end of December.

Letter sent by Maryland Tercentenary Commission to interested individuals.

Motive: Fund raising for the celebrations.

Suspects: Hans Schuler, sculptor; the Maryland Tercentenary Commission.

Accessories: Gerard Soes, whose early painting of Lord Baltimore was Schuler's source. However, even that does not excuse the Puritan collar worn by Lord Baltimore, the Cavalier of Cavaliers. Schuler would have done better to go to Lord Baltimore's own coins, which show a very different portrait.

Modus Operandi: As usual, excessive haste prevailed in making the models. Schuler's preliminary models were completed as of May 9, 1934, and arrived at the Philadelphia Mint on May 10. A few minor revisions became necessary—notably, removal of thirteen stars from obverse field—and the revised models were approved during the last week of May, being sent at once to the Medallic Art Company of New York for reduction to half dollar size. The Philadelphia Mint made 25,000 coins (plus 15 for assay) during July 1934. The Maryland Tercentenary Commission managed to sell almost 15,000 of

The normal striking for the Maryland Commemorative obverse. Note the cheekbone, eyebrows, and nose.

the coins at $1 apiece by mid-November 1934, mostly to locals; during the following month they moved about 5,000 more at the same price. During 1935 the remaining 250 rolls (5,000 coins) were offered at 75¢ apiece; about 2,000 pieces went at this figure, the remainder being dumped at 65¢ each. One of us (A.S.) has been in touch with representatives of several Maryland families who purchased 20 rolls at 65¢ per coin; these specimens remain off the market, being held for sentimental reasons.

Collateral Evidence: Matte proofs of this issue exist; the number is unknown but has been estimated at four. To date three different ones have been examined: (1) Ex Wayte Raymond. (2) Ex J.R. Sinnock estate, 1962 ANA Convention Sale, lot 2053. (3) Ex J.R. Sinnock estate, 1962 ANA Convention Sale, lot 2054. One of the latter two is illustrated on page 152. On comparison with the exceptionally sharp business strike shown at the head of this section, we at once realize the extreme danger

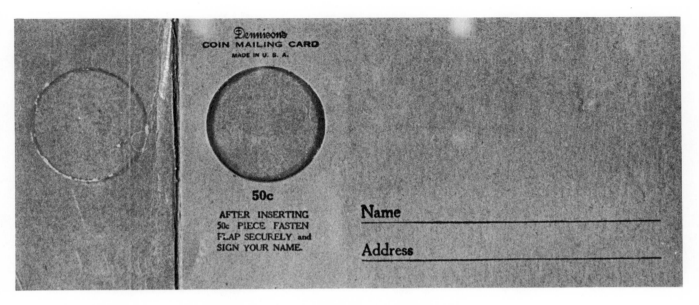

This issue was distributed in a standard Dennison coin holder, as was the 1934 Texas issue.

The Maryland Tercentenary 3¢ postage issue—Scott 736, type A326.

posed by normal business strikes which have been pickled or sandblasted.

Actually, the vast majority of survivors are weaker impressions, which would become weaker still if fraudulently treated to simulate proofs; compare the illustration of the proof and the ordinary striking below it. Note especially hair, eyebrows, and cheekbones.

About ten original holders are known, as illustrated above, but they are not in any sense distinctive and could easily be imitated, being in fact standard Dennison coin holders.

The philatelic tie-in shows the ships *Ark* and *Dove* in which the colonists sailed to Maryland in 1634. It is a 3¢, carmine rose, Scott 736, Type A236, designed by Alvin R. Meissner, first released as of March 23, 1934, and distributed to the number of 46,258,300.

THE McKINLEY MEMORIAL GOLD DOLLARS

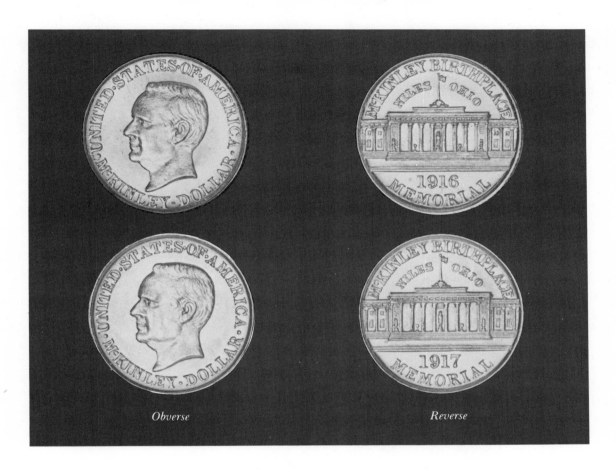

Obverse   *Reverse*

The Corpus Delicti: Alias *1916* or *1917 McKinley*.

Clues: The building on reverse is intended as a facing view of the McKinley Birthplace Memorial in Niles, Ohio; the most charitable view must characterize it as inaccurate and incompetently done. The portrait is evidently intended for William McKinley, but Barber appears to have been trying (as Taxay says) to make it as different as possible from that on the 1903 coins.

Opportunity: The Act of Congress of February 23, 1916, authorizing construction of the McKinley Birthplace Memorial, specified that not over 100,000 gold dollars of special commemorative designs could be made at the Philadelphia Mint only, and that

afterwards the dies must be destroyed. (This would have been required under the provisions of the Mint Act of 1873, but for unknown reasons the framers of this 1916 bill thought reiteration necessary.) Why 1916? This is uncertain; possibly it took the local citizens in Niles fifteen years to get around to realizing that their assassinated President's birthplace could become a tourist attraction; possibly the target was 1917, 75th anniversary of McKinley's birth.

Motive: To help defray costs of construction of the McKinley Birthplace Memorial.

Suspects: Charles E. Barber (designer of the obverse); George T. Morgan, Assistant Engraver of the U.S. Mint (designer of the reverse, but best known

Obverse of a genuine 1917 McKinley proof gold dollar.   *Reverse of a genuine 1917 McKinley proof gold dollar.*

for the silver dollars of 1878–1921); and the heads of the National McKinley Birthplace Memorial Association, especially Col. Joseph Butler (see *Modus Operandi* below).

Accessories: Unknown.

Modus Operandi: The original plan was for 100,000 commemorative silver dollars to be sold nationally by the Association, and a bill to that effect was before Congress in January 1916. At a hearing January 13, before the House Committee on Coinage, Weights and Measures, Col. Joseph Butler of the Association testified in objection to the proposal for silver dollars. Someone had evidently reminded him that McKinley's original election was as the gold standard candidate, and so Butler said "If you will recall the fact, McKinley was elected in 1896 mainly on the question of the gold standard. I think that was what elected him . . . I want to ask that these dollars be gold instead of silver." And the bill was accordingly amended, averting a gaffe as ridiculous as that which had portrayed William Windom on the 1891 $2 Silver Certificates. (Windom was a ferocious advocate of the gold standard and an implacable opponent of the silver mine owners who were trying to elect William Jennings Bryan: he was portrayed on the $2 certificate because he had died in office as President Benjamin Harrison's Secretary of Treasury, and the bill was chosen because extensive counterfeiting of the 1886 Series required recall and

reissue with changed design.) Like Windom, McKinley was portrayed on money only because he had been killed in office.

The Philadelphia Mint struck 20,000 gold dollars (with 26 extra reserved for assay) during August and October 1916. These two strikings cannot be distinguished. During February 1917, 10,000 (plus 14 extra reserved for assay) followed, from the new 1917 dies. The Association began offering the 1916s at $3 apiece, either unaware or choosing to forget that the 1903 and 1904–5 gold dollars were impossible to market in any quantity at that figure. By 1917, even the Association realized the futility of this pricing policy, and dumped a total of 10,000 of the coins at a lower figure to the Texas dealer, B. Max Mehl, who offered them to collectors at $2.50 apiece.

It is uncertain whether Mehl's consignment consisted only of 1917s or of a mixture of the two dates. In either event, the Association returned 10,023 of the 1916 dollars to the mint for re-melting, producing the following tabular results:

Authorized:	100,000 maximum
Coined:	1916, 20,000; 1917, 10,000
Melted:	1916, 10,023
Net Mintage:	1916, 9,977; 1917, 10,000

Despite this record of actual mintage and distribution, the 1917 coin is a little harder to find than the 1916. Proof-like specimens exist of both dates; in addition, there are at least a half dozen proofs of the

Blow-up showing the crudity of the die work.

1916 (including one in the Smithsonian Institution) and five of the 1917 (including one in a Philadelphia estate, and one in 1977 ANA:2062). The piece pictured here is one of the proofs; the definition of detail is far superior to that on business strikings previously shown, in which the rims are rounded, the hair definition is apt to be vague and many letters weak at tops or bottoms, whichever is nearer to the borders. Dates were evidently added to the working dies, as they differ in spacing; note that the 7 is much farther from the 1 on the business strike (serif of 7 is vertically above center of R on the proof, vertically above curve of R on the business strike; other dies are possible).

Note the crudity of die work: the side frame of a window extends up to the roof, the Doric column

159

Obverse of a genuine McKinley business striking.

Reverse of a genuine McKinley business striking.

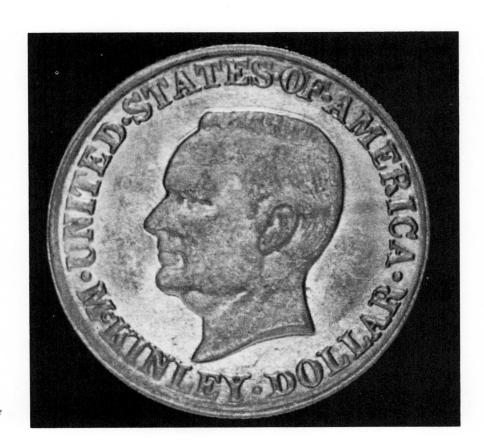

Obverse of a counterfeit McKinley made outside the mint.

Reverse of a counterfeit McKinley.

capitals are mere blobs, and there are other evidences of carelessness, as shown on the enlarged detail.

Counterfeits exist of the 1917 and possibly also of the 1916. Because so many of the genuine dollars are weak strikings, a detailed comparison is necessary; we therefore illustrate (p. 160–161) first the genuine (from a die with 17 well apart), then the counterfeit (17 very closely spaced, and with far less hair visible than on the genuine).

THE MISSOURI CENTENNIAL HALF DOLLARS

Obverse

Reverse

Obverse, 2★4 variety.

Reverse

The Corpus Delicti: Alias *Missouri 2★4, Missouri 2 by 4.*

Clues: The dates 1821–1921 refer to the centennial of Missouri's admission into the Union as the 24th State, August 10, 1821, following Maine as 23rd, as part of the Missouri Compromise Act of 1820. Though usually identified merely as "a frontiersman," the bust of a young man in deerskin jacket and coonskin cap was originally intended to represent Daniel Boone, who had died in 1820 at the age of 86. On the first variety, the 2★4 in left field again alludes to Missouri's rank as 24th State and 24th star on the flag. On reverse, the 24 stars have the identical meaning—apparently on the principle that some ideas need to be repeated to get into others' heads; the remainder are more obscure. A white frontiersman with rifle and powderhorn (apparently on the old theory that "the only good Injun is a dead Injun") appears to be sending away the

Indian, whose shield and peace pipe are mere impedimenta. Taxay quotes James Montgomery (chairman of the Missouri Centennial Exposition) as having suggested both Boone's portrait and the Indian (originally to be sitting at Boone's feet facing the river), to signify that "the white man had supplanted the Indian in Missouri Territory," as though this was something to brag about. On the coin, the pose is theatrical and suggests a quite different situation—the caption that immediately springs to this writer's mind (W.B.) is "Straighten your loincloth and get on stage, buddy—that's your *cue!*" In exergue, the name SEDALIA designates the site of the Exposition and State Fair for which these coins were made. Near the rifle butt, the peculiar monogram (like a stylized movie camera on a tripod) is meant to be RA, the initials of Robert Aitken, the sculptor.

Opportunity: The Act of Congress of March 4, 1921—Warren G. Harding's inauguration day, a singular choice. Harding must have signed it as a lame-duck item left over from the previous (66th) Congress.

Motive: To raise funds for the Missouri Centennial Exposition and State Fair, August 8–20, 1921.

Suspects: James Montgomery, chairman of the Exposition; Robert Aitken.

Accessories: Uncertain. It has been conjectured that the portrait of young Daniel Boone may have been remotely inspired by the Albin Polasek bust of Boone in the New York University Hall of Fame. (As it faces the viewer, this bust is backlit, and the only way to obtain a profile view is in silhouette.)

Modus Operandi: The Federal Commission of Fine Arts hired Robert Aitken (a safe choice because of his earlier commemorative coin designs) during the last week of March 1921. Aitken's earliest sketches (pictured in Taxay) embodied James Montgomery's suggestions. Montgomery had originally wanted the Missouri Great Seal for the reverse, but Aitken found that in half dollar size it would produce an impossibly crowded and dull composition. On May 26, Charles Moore, chairman of the Fine Arts Commission, telegraphed Aitken, approving of the "Daniel Boone head" and the "reverse with two standing figures." The latter was evidently Aitken's own concept, as nothing like it was found among Montgomery's suggestions; in fact, the Missouri Centennial Exposition Committee's advertising continued all summer long to feature Aitken's sketch of the Great Seal, evidently unaware that Aitken had abandoned it! Because the coins had to be ready in early August, Aitken had his models reduced to coin size by the Medallic Art Company in New York, and the hubs so produced were sent directly to the Philadelphia Mint. James Montgomery had the idea of marking some part of the issue with a distinctive emblem or inscription as a way of selling more coins; the Mint accordingly placed the 2★4 on the first working obverse die, from which 5,000 coins were struck in July. Afterwards, the 2★4 was ground off this die, and 45,000 more coins followed in the same month, plus 28 extra for assay.

Distribution began during the first week of August 1921. The Exposition and State Fair sold the plain coins, the Sedalia Trust Company marketed the 2★4s. Several were displayed a few weeks later at the ANA Convention in Boston. No original holders have been seen or described.

A single 2★4 matte proof striking has been reported, but even ten years later it remains unavailable for examination.

Though the coins were well liked, national distribution through numismatic channels appears to have been very limited, and not many were sold at the brief Exposition—possibly because of little advance publicity, possibly because then and later relatively few people in that Depression year felt they could afford the pieces, even at $1 apiece for either variety. In tabular form:

Authorized:	250,000 total
Coined, 2★4:	5,000 (all were sold)
Coined, plain:	45,000 plus 28 for assay
Re-melted, plain:	29,600
Net mintage, plain:	15,400

No original holders are reported.

Possibly because of the financial pinch during the 1921 crisis, possibly also during the 1929–36 Depression years, many of the Missouris were spent; others were kept as good-luck pocket pieces. As a result, few pristine gems remain. Grading is difficult, because the striking quality of most of them is less than satisfactory. It has been estimated that not more than 400 of either variety survive in choice mint state.

THE MONROE DOCTRINE CENTENNIAL HALF DOLLAR

Obverse

Reverse

The Corpus Delicti: Alias *The Monroe.*

Clues: The accolated busts labeled MONROE and ADAMS represent President James Monroe and his Secretary of State (later also President) John Quincy Adams. Their names are separated—or maybe that should read joined—by two links of chain. This refers to their unanimity in promulgating the so-called Monroe Doctrine; a doctrine developed by Quincy Adams, but proclaimed by Monroe in his Presidential message of December 2, 1823. The s below the date is the San Francisco mintmark—the entire mintage was struck there.

What appears on reverse to represent the continents of North and South America proves on closer examination to depict two female figures. Ms. North

America holds some kind of branch (too vague to be identified as to species) in her left hand while her right hand offers a twig to her contortionist sister, Ms. South America, who holds a cornucopia. The position must have been a considerable strain to the model, if there was any. This lady sits with her left elbow resting halfway up her right thigh, her left forearm resting along the thigh and rotating to the left, while her upper right arm is extended well behind her back to accommodate the cornucopia. (If you think this position is easy, just try it.) The scale indicates, too, that though both females have adult proportions, Ms. North America must have been at least a foot taller than her sister. (The wonder is less that the figures are disproportionate than that they could be made at all, however.)

Centennial dates flank a scroll on which rests a quill pen, its nib pointing north, probably alluding to the Doctrine manuscripts and to the legend MONROE DOCTRINE CENTENNIAL. Faint lines in the field represent ocean currents. Clockwise, from upper right, these are the Gulf Stream, the North and South Equatorial Currents, the Brazil Current, the Falkland Current near Cape Horn (or Ms. South America's right foot and left calf, above ES), the West Wind Drift (at S ANG), the Humboldt Current (at her knees), the Pacific South and North Equatorial Currents (with the Equatorial Countercurrent between them, extending to MO), and the California and Alaska Currents. (The Japan Current would have been concealed at ROE.) We suspect, but cannot prove, that the reason for showing ocean currents was to represent the unending flow of imports and exports between the two continents, unimpeded by foreign powers. The whole composition has a very Art Deco feeling, though its lettering is of older style and suggests only a little of the flowing look of Art Nouveau. At lower right is a circular monogram intended for CB—Chester Beach, the designer and modeler. The words LOS ANGELES refer to where the celebration was to take place.

The Monroe Doctrine's reputation as a sacred cow dates back to its formulation; its guiding principle goes back to 1797, when Washington's Farewell Address specified noninterference and opposition to European encroachments in the Western Hemisphere. When Washington made this speech, he was alluding to British and Spanish territorial claims in North America. When the revolutions of 1812–24 in various parts of Latin America ended uniformly in the overthrow or capitulation of Spanish viceroys and establishment of republics, the U.S.A. recognized them one and all—for consistency, also recognizing various military juntas and even the Empire of Brazil under Dom Pedro; anything but more European colonies. This was the immediate background of the Doctrine; its precipitating cause was the various resolutions by the Holy Alliance of Austria, Prussia, and Russia (later echoed by France under Louis XVIII and Charles X) to "put an end to the system of representative government" and restore the Spanish rule throughout Latin America, in the name of the Divine Right of Kings. Canning, the British Colonial Secretary, proposed a joint declaration by Britain and the U.S.A. condemning the Holy Alliance's proposal; Jefferson and Madison favored such a declaration, but John Quincy Adams insisted instead on a unilateral one by the U.S.A., and got his wish. In its own day, the Doctrine was recognized as an unenforceable gesture without legal standing,

calling on foreign powers (i.e., Spain and Russia) to avoid any further interference in what would now be called the internal affairs of the banana republics, and to cease attempting to make colonies out of unclaimed parts of western North America.

By 1831, the Doctrine was a dead letter, as Britain seized parts of the Guianas, while the Russians and British (Hudson's Bay Company, mostly) had already occupied parts of California and coastal areas farther north. After the Mexican War, the Doctrine appeared largely as a saber-rattling U.S. attempt to keep a monopoly on colonialism in the Western Hemisphere. Though neither a treaty nor part of international law, the Doctrine was officially recognized in the two Hague Conventions of 1899 and 1907. A curious theme for a celebration in 1923.

Opportunity: The motion picture industry sponsored something called the American Historical Revue and Motion Picture Historical Exposition, to be held in Los Angeles in 1923. Because of the success of some previous coin tie-ins with expositions, some of the film colony promoters sought to have a commemorative coin, but they were in considerable difficulties finding a suitable occasion to commemorate on it. The obvious one (the Boston Tea Party of 1773) could not be tortured into even the vaguest relevance to California, let alone to Los Angeles. When Rep. Walter Franklin Lineberger (R.-California) introduced the bill on December 18, 1922, his nearest excuse was a fabricated story to the effect that Monroe's manifesto had allegedly prevented France, England and Russia from trying to acquire California from Mexico. This was somehow to be a reason for having the Los Angeles Clearing House awarded a monopoly on distributing the coins. Predictably, the latter clause met opposition, most vigorously from Rep. Louis Cramton (R.-Michigan); and in the Senate, Sen. Frank Greene (R.-Vermont) voiced what was later to become a common objection to commemorative coins: " . . . The question is not one of selling a coin at a particular value or at a particular place. The question is whether the United States Government is going to go on from year to year, submitting its coinage to this—well—harlotry." However, despite these objections, the bill became law on January 24, 1923.

Motive: There certainly was some kind of Exposition held in Los Angeles in June 1923, in one of the football stadiums; however, it was not one of the better known ones, and little is recorded about it. Choice of the Clearing House (the association of local banks) as sole distributor was apparently to dissociate the issue from motion picture studios, and the whole idea appears to have been publicity and good will, perhaps stimulating tourism and convincing everyone that the motion picture colony had public interests at heart, etc. Fill in the details yourself and call it P.R. or hype, as you please.

Suspects: Chester Beach, sculptor.

Accessories: F.B. Davison, Director-General of the Exposition. This man, probably in consultation with some of the film people, decided on the devices. Originally, the reverse was to have shown maps of the North and South American continents, but Chester Beach and James Earle Fraser decided to personify the continents, and the Federal Fine Arts Commission agreed to this idea, approving Beach's models as early as March 8, 1923, Mint Director Scobey and Treasury Secretary Mellon concurring on the same day. However, on July 23, 1923, Ralph Beck complained to the Mint that the reverse of the new coins copied his 1901 Pan-American Exposition seal. His complaint was perfectly valid; Taxay illustrates the seal, and Slabaugh pictures a medal copying it. This device had been used in many different contexts during the Exposition and afterwards, especially by steamship lines and other businesses engaging in imports or exports between the U.S.A. and Latin America, so much so that presumably Beach thought it to be a part of the vernacular of common motifs along with Uncle Sam, Father Time, Santa Claus, Baby New Year, etc. In any event, there is no record of a lawsuit or of any other action on Mr. Beck's complaint.

Modus Operandi: The San Francisco Mint completed the bulk strikings during May and June 1923; the coins were on sale well before the end of June,

through the Los Angeles Clearing House, and presumably some were available at local banks, at $1 apiece. Later in the year, sales slumped, and the member banks began releasing the coins into circulation. We have not been able to ascertain why only 274,000 were actually delivered to the Clearing House people instead of the entire allotment, nor yet how many were sold at double face. From the evidence of the coins, probably over 90 percent either were released at face value, or some of those that had been bought at $1 each were kept as pocket pieces, or spent by inheritors, or they were spent during the Great Depression of 1929–37. Most survivors show some signs of circulation, and more than half those offered as "uncirculated" are sliders, cleaned or in some other way unsatisfactory. Despite the Fine Arts Commission's thoroughly favorable report on the design (as quoted by Taxay, pp. 67–8), the coins did not strike up well; that pictured at the head of the chapter is fully uncirculated, but like most others it can be so graded only because the weak areas are covered with mint frost.

Collateral Evidence: No holder, original case, or envelope or accompanying literature has been reported.

A copper trial piece has been seen, as well as a uniface trial impression of reverse on an oversize flan.

Two matte proofs are reported, but to date neither one has been available for examination.

The orange 10¢ Monroe stamp, designed by Charles Aubrey Huston, Scott 562 (Type A164), might be considered as a tie-in, as it was first issued January 15, 1923, in plenty of time for the Exposition. However, like the Grant earlier mentioned, it is actually part of the regular 1922–23 Presidential Series.

THE NEW ROCHELLE, NEW YORK, HALF DOLLAR

Obverse

Reverse

The Corpus Delicti: Alias *New Rochelle*.

Clues: We can hardly improve on the explanation furnished by this coin's designer, Gertrude K. Lathrop, in *The Numismatist*, April 1937, p. 305. "New Rochelle . . . was settled in 1688 by French Huguenots from La Rochelle, France. One year later a tract of 6,000 acres, the land upon which New Rochelle now stands, was sold by John Pell to Jacob Leisler, who was for a short time Governor of New York. Leisler was commissioned by these French Huguenots to obtain the land. One of the conditions of sale was that Jacob Leisler, his heirs and assigns, should give to 'John Pell his heirs and assigns Lords of the said Manor of Pelham . . . as an Acknowledgment to the said Manor one fatt calfe on every fouer and twentyth day of June Yearly and Every Year forever (if demanded).' . . . On the obverse of the coin is shown a protesting calf being delivered in payment of this debt. The model for the calf was found on the Kenwood farm of Parker Corning, Representative in Congress last year . . . Reverse shows a modern interpretation of the old conventionalized form of fleur-de-lis which has been the symbol of France since 1180. It appears on the

shield of La Rochelle from which the settlers came, and also on the shield of the city of New Rochelle." We can only add that the date 1938 is that of the celebration of the 250th anniversary, not the year of mintage of the coin, and that Ms. Lathrop's initials GKL are in the field near the calf's forefoot. Many people believe that the figure in the late 17th Century costume is meant for John Pell, but this is unconfirmed; the design can be read to mean either that the calf is being brought to Pell by one of Leisler's people, or that Pell has just accepted the delivery. Had Ms. Lathrop specifically meant the figure to represent Pell, she would doubtless have said so.

Opportunity: Local celebration in New Rochelle June 10–20, 1938, Act of May 5, 1936.

Motive: Local pride; but insofar as the Westchester County Coin Club of New Rochelle was among the coin's original sponsors, we may suspect That Five Finger Word was at work. However, Slabaugh maintains (following Amy Skipton) that funds raised by sales of the coins were used to finance the celebration.

Obverse and reverse of one of 50 New Rochelle presentation pieces struck with a single blow on a proof planchet using polished dies.

Obverse and reverse of the excessively rare New Rochelle Commemorative matte proof half dollar once owned by the chief mint engraver of the United States and later by the famous numismatist Abe Kosoff.

Suspects: Westchester County Coin Club; New Rochelle Commemorative Coin Committee (Mayor Harry Scott, honorary chairman; Pitt M. Skipton, chairman; Ernest Watson, treasurer; Jere Milleman, secretary). As originally planned, the coin club would have distributed the issue, but Congress was reluctant to approve this method of promotion, and rewrote the bill specifying the Committee (appointed by the mayor), which sold the coins through the First National Bank of New Rochelle.

Accessories: Gertrude K. Lathrop, designer, sculptor, of Albany, New York, member of the National Academy of Design and the National Sculpture Society.

Modus Operandi: The original plan was to have a wholly different design by Lorillard Wise on the coin, depicting an Indian at the shore awaiting the arrival of settlers by canoe, and on reverse the city arms. A later version of this (pictured in Taxay, p. 197) actually won the unthinking approval of the Federal Commission of Fine Arts! To their credit, they later withdrew approval at least of the side with the Indian, even as they refused to approve its successor, in which Lorillard Wise attempted to depict Bonnefoi Point in Echo Bay (Long Island Sound) where the Huguenot refugees landed in 1688. In mid-November 1936, Pitt Skipton saw a specimen of the Albany commemorative half dollar, and at once commissioned its designer, Gertrude K. Lathrop, to design the New Rochelle coin. She and Skipton simultaneously came up with the "Fatt Calfe" motif; her designs were approved by the Federal Commission of Fine Arts in February 1937. During April 1937, the Philadelphia Mint struck 25,000 specimens (the maximum allowed by the authorizing act) plus 15 reserved for assay, thus producing yet another date-confused item like the Delaware and Gettysburg: authorized in 1936, struck in 1937, for an event of 1938. The coins sold at $2 each; some 9,749 unsold pieces were returned to the Philadelphia Mint for re-melting, leaving a net mintage of 15,251.

Fifty presentation specimens were struck with a single blow on a proof planchet, using polished dies, for coin collecting members of the Commemorative Coin Committee; they were issued in small, dark red presentation boxes (photograph unavailable) and each accompanied by a bronze medal. One of the earliest of these to be auctioned was lot 1707, 1958 ANA convention sale, reappearing as Hydeman: 694; this had a document certifying that it was the 8th coin struck, presented to William S. Dewey, then president of the Westchester County Coin Club.

In addition, a smaller number (estimated by A.S. as 10 to 14) of matte proofs were struck. One of these came from the John R. Sinnock estate, via lot 2056, 1962 ANA Convention; it is presently in the collection of one client of A.S.

It is extremely probable that the above coins will be simulated by fakes. Presentation coins could be imitated by polishing ordinary production strikings; look for polishing marks especially on devices, and for detail definition considerably less sharp than that illustrated. Matte proofs could be imitated by sandblasting ordinary coins, but again detail definition will be inferior. The genuine must be double struck as illustrated. If it is not, don't look any further. What you are looking at is a fake.

Presentation prooflike specimens may also be confused with early business strikes from dies retaining initial polish. The latter might not have the extra sharpness on central rib of flower, or on the calf's skin.

Many subsequent owners subjected the proof-like presentation pieces to numismatic abuse—either cleaning (all too often with baking soda or other abrasives) or by dipping them in a cleaning solution and drying them with a cloth or paper towel that contained foreign (and hence destructive) substances. One individual, believing these pieces were proof-like specimens, collected 22 presentation pieces over a 26 year period. Unfortunately, he never knew what he actually possessed, and recently sold 20 pieces to a West Coast dealer for $8,000. When he spoke to one of us (A.S.) at a recent convention, he was informed that his remaining two coins were definitely presentation pieces and should be valued at $3500+ *per* coin! Fortunately or unfortunately, depending on how you view the situation, the dealer who sold the coins was also not aware of what they were. Some of the individuals who possess a proof-like New Rochelle might be in for a nice surprise. However, let us hope it is not one of the lesser-valued early business strikes as previously mentioned. (Forward to Anthony Swiatek, P.O. Box 343, Kew Gardens, New York, should you be in doubt.) Proof-like specimens of U.S. Commemorative half dollars are rare. In most cases, they are excessively rare. The aforementioned business strike in the gem state (MS-65) should be worth at least $2000+.

This issue was well distributed but long remained easy to locate in ordinary uncirculated or slider grades because speculators didn't exploit it. However, truly choice or gem survivors are very difficult to locate, are rarely auctioned and constitute a good investment.

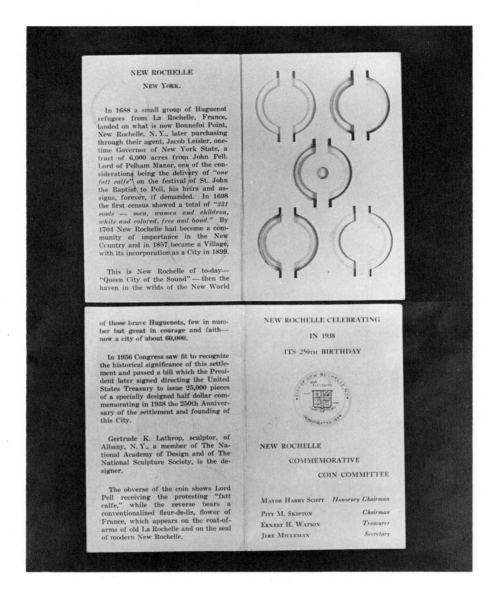

Original mailing holder used to mail three or more New Rochelle Commemoratives. Holders also exist that housed only one or two coins.

Locating a fully-struck specimen of this issue will be a very difficult task. The center petal of the fleur de lis on the reverse possesses what appears to be a vertical line which is the main vein or midrib, whose function is to transport materials throughout the petal via side veins. This area is nearly always struck a little flat and appears to be worn. Again, finding fully struck specimens where the midrib is fully struck in the center of the petal—provided the coin is in strict choice and especially gem condition—will be most rewarding.

THE NORFOLK, VIRGINIA, BICENTENNIAL HALF DOLLAR

Obverse

Reverse

The Corpus Delicti: Alias *Norfolk.*

Clues: Obverse device is the Norfolk city seal. Below the stylized waves are a plough with a row of young plants (possibly peanut plants, as Norfolk is in a major peanut-growing area), and below these in turn three wheat sheaves—these details are often vague on normal strikings. Mottoes ET TERRA ET MARE DIVITIAE TUAE and CRESCAS mean, respectively, "Both land and sea are your riches" and "May you grow" or "May you prosper." Though no documentation exists, the cable border separating the outermost legend from the city seal may allude to ship's ropes (appropriate for this naval town), and the two scallop shells flanking the date almost certainly continue the maritime theme. On reverse, the ornate object is Norfolk's Royal Mace, presented to the Borough of Norfolk in 1753 by Lieutenant Governor Robert Dinwiddie, formally accepted by the Common Council in 1754 and cherished ever since as the city's greatest historical treasure. (It is in fact the only Royal Mace ever presented to an American city during Colonial times; it was removed and hidden during the Revolution and the Civil War, and remains most of the time in a bank vault, seldom exhibited.)

Flanking the 1636 date, which is that of the original Norfolk Land Grant, are two dogwood sprigs. In lower field, the monogram is WM(S) + MES, for William Marks Simpson and his wife Marjorie Emory Simpson, the coin's joint designers.

Opportunity: As with a couple of other Southern commemoratives (the *Alabama* and *Stone Mountain*), this issue was posthumous, the local anniversary celebrations being long over with by the time it was authorized. Originally, the Norfolk Advertising Board and Norfolk Association of Commerce (the celebration's sponsors) had sought a commemorative coin, but the Senate (fed up with such coins) changed the bill to call for a medal, in which form it became the Act of June 26, 1936, but became a dead letter at once—the promoters wanted coins, not medals. Senator Carter Glass promised the Simpsons that he would make another attempt, and this was successful, becoming the Act of June 28, 1937.

Motive: Local pride, mostly.

Suspects: The Norfolk Advertising Board and the Norfolk Association of Commerce.

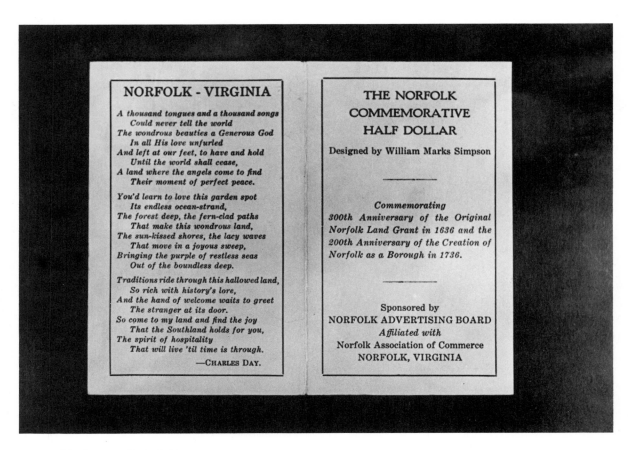

Front and back cover of coin holder.

Accessories: William Marks Simpson and his wife Marjorie Emory Simpson.

Modus Operandi: Mr. Simpson furnished photographs of the coin models to the Commission of Fine Arts, September 26, 1936. Lee Lawrie, sculptor member, was more enthusiastic than with most such proposed designs. On the 29th, the Commission approved the designs subject to minor revisions in the lettering. But as Congress did not finally authorize the coin for nine months more, nothing was done. When the Act passed, Simpson reworked his models, submitting photographs to the Commission on August 10, and received approval as of August 14.

As the Act of Congress authorized a maximum of 25,000, this amount was struck at Philadelphia (plus 13 reserved for assay); as the Act specified the date 1936, the coins retained it even though they were not struck until September 1937.

Issue price was $1.50 each. The Norfolk Advertising Board acted as distributor, and attempted to discourage speculators by limiting purchasers to not over 20 coins apiece. They returned 5,000 coins to the Philadelphia Mint for re-melting in 1938, and another 3,077 later on, leaving a net mintage of 16,923.

Collateral Evidence: No proofs are known, though some may have been made for John R. Sinnock, Engraver of the Mint.

Original holders had a capacity for five coins, probably the regular Eggers type; we illustrate the two imprinted sides, which are on light green paper. Note that in a predictably sexist manner, the sponsoring organization named only William Marks Simpson as designer, omitting any mention of his wife as co-designer, despite her initials on the coin. About 40 of these holders are traced today.

We also illustrate the order blank.

As many of these coins were sold to the general public, survivors are often in less than pristine condition; look for wear or signs of scratching on sails.

Any further issue of any of the above commemorative coins was prevented by Congressional passage of the Act of August 5, 1939, which forbade

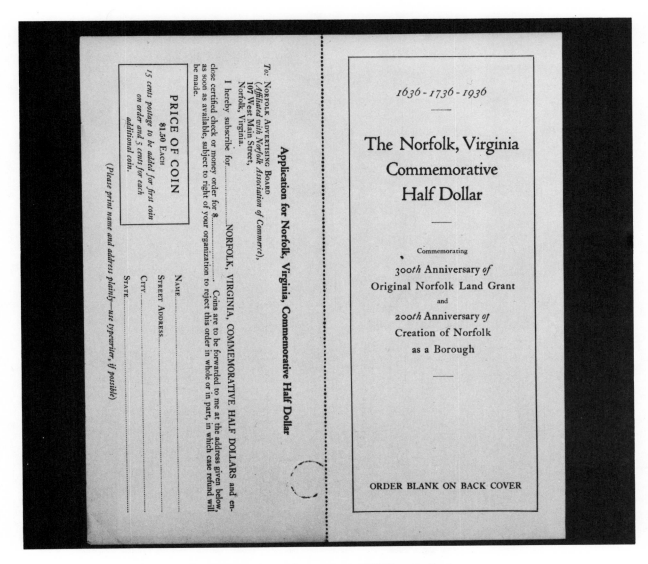

1636 - 1736 - 1936

The Norfolk, Virginia Commemorative Half Dollar

Commemorating

300th Anniversary of
Original Norfolk Land Grant

and

200th Anniversary of
Creation of Norfolk
as a Borough

ORDER BLANK ON BACK COVER

Application for Norfolk, Virginia, Commemorative Half Dollar

To: NORFOLK ADVERTISING BOARD
(*Affiliated with Norfolk Association of Commerce*),
107 West Main Street,
Norfolk, Virginia.

I hereby subscribe for .... NORFOLK, VIRGINIA, COMMEMORATIVE HALF DOLLARS and enclose certified check or money order for $ .... Coins are to be forwarded to me at the address given below, as soon as available, subject to right of your organization to reject this order in whole or in part, in which case refund will be made.

PRICE OF COIN
$1.50 EACH

15 cents postage to be added for first coin on order and 5 cents for each additional coin.

NAME ....

STREET ADDRESS ....

CITY ....

STATE ....

(*Please print name and address plainly—use typewriter, if possible*)

Original application for the Norfolk Commemorative. Photo courtesy of William R. Devine.

further issue of any previously authorized commemorative half dollars. This was mainly aimed at the major perpetrators of abuses—the promoters of the Texas, Oregon, Boone and Arkansas issues.

This is another low mintage issue that many believe is easily located. That may have been true when there was no serious demand for the commemorative series. Had ten rolls made their appearance at a coin show you would hear from dealers that the show was flooded with Norfolks. At this instant, were fifty rolls ever to hit the market, they would be absorbed like water into a dry sponge. The demand is here to stay and it is that great! Many are beginning to realize the potential of the series. Thus the coin is now becoming difficult to locate in true gem state. One of us (A.S.) has been offered a roll of this issue from time to time. The coins were not gems as described, but had had their luster dipped away. Upon comparison with a pristine specimen, the difference was obvious. Experimentation (by A.S.) has shown that when any half dollar is dipped twice or improperly cleaned once—possibly by keeping the coin in the solution for too long—the original mint-given brilliance will be gone forever.

175

THE OLD SPANISH TRAIL HALF DOLLAR

Obverse

Reverse

The Corpus Delicti: Alias *Spanish Trail.*

Clues: "Cabeza de Vaca" is Spanish for "head of a cow," and as no portrait is known of the explorer Alvar Núñez Cabeza de Vaca, the punning device of a cow's head dominates the obverse. The proper surname is Núñez, under which name libraries still catalogue his classic text *Los Naufragios,* "The Shipwrecked Men." Cabeza de Vaca was a kind of title or agnomen, like the Roman Nero or Germanicus, borne instead of a matronymic surname. There are two stories about why the explorer used it. L.W. Hoffecker, designer of the coin, said that the explorer's grandfather had used cows' skulls as trail-markers, after which practice the family adopted it. Slabaugh quotes an alternative version to the effect that the first Cabeza de Vaca was a 13th century shepherd ancestor, who received the title from the King of Navarre for showing his forces a hidden mountain pass through which they made a successful rear attack on Moorish enemy armies. However, Slabaugh does not say why this name was chosen: was the trail to the mountain pass marked by cows' skulls?

On reverse, the map represents some part of what little has been identified of Núñez's westbound journey (its exact extent is not known and may have included points as far west as California). Misleadingly, it shows the trail as totally overland and mostly in straight lines, joining cities that did not exist until generations after Núñez's expedition: San Agustin (St. Augustine), Jacksonville and Tallahassee, Florida; Mobile, Alabama; New Orleans, Louisiana; Galveston, San Antonio and El Paso, Texas. In actuality, Núñez was treasurer of the Panfilo de Narvaez expedition (1527–42), which made landfall with over 200 men in the West Indies in 1527, wintered there, and proceeded to Florida in the spring of 1528, in a vain quest for gold. What with tropical diseases, hostile Indians and alligators, they abandoned the quest, improvising five crude boats. Narvaez's crew abandoned Núñez to his fate, only to be blown out into the Gulf of Mexico; Núñez and about 80 men were washed ashore near Galveston, Texas, November 1528, settled there among friendly Indians and sent scouts to find the nearest Spanish settlements in Mexico from which a rescue party could be organized. That was the good news; the bad news is that their wait lasted for 7½ more years. Their scouts never reached Mexico, and Núñez's people later endured the most extreme hardships: starvation, disease, slavery, torture and even cannibalism. Only four of the original 200 survived. The whole grim story of catastrophe and heroism is found in

Counterfeit Spanish Trail coin whose surface looks like stucco under high magnification.

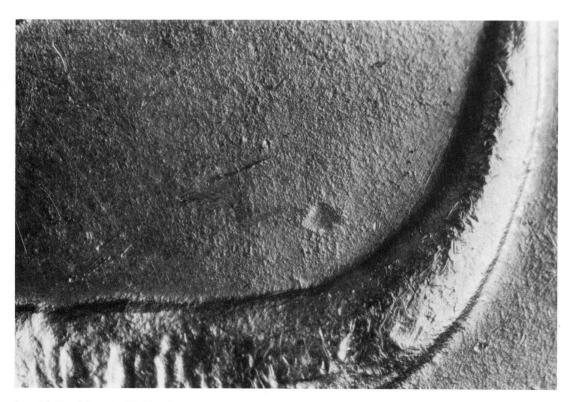

Spanish Trail Counterfeit (detail).
Blow-up of obverse displays minute cavities in the coin.

Spanish Trail Counterfeit (detail).
Note raised lines and shallow depressions on this counterfeit coin. Such will be visible on every coin in the same location.

Spanish Trail Counterfeit (detail).
What can you observe about the reverse of this counterfeit Spanish Trail specimen?

Los Naufragios, published in 1542 and still read today.

The plant in central reverse is a yucca tree in bloom, a common sight in the area, though considering the climate of west Texas and possible further points west on the Trail, a saguaro cactus might have been more appropriate. It appears to have been chosen for design purposes. Dates 1535–1935 refer to fairly arbitrary quatrocentennial dates; it was actually in April 1536 that a Spanish viceroy's patrol in the Province of Sinaloa (Mexico) saw Núñez and his sidekick, Estebanico the Moroccan, coming out of the northern no man's land, at which point they stood in astonishment until Núñez asked them the Castilian equivalent of "Take me to your leader." At the margin, between date and Key West, are initials LWH for L.W. Hoffecker.

Opportunity: Local celebrations, principally sponsored by groups in El Paso, which was thought to be the end of the Trail. Chief among these were the Texas Memorial Committee and the El Paso Museum Committee, which used friendships with Texas congressmen to induce passage of the authorizing bill, which became the Act of June 5, 1935.

Motive: Fund raising to further the work of the Museum. For once, no venality appears to have been involved, only praise. No scandal attached itself to Hoffecker (chairman of the Museum Committee), despite his being a well-known coin collector. (He was later president of the American Numismatic Association.) Collectors did not receive favored-party treatment in distribution of the coins; speculators got none of them.

Suspects: L.W. Hoffecker, designer; Edmund J. Senn, El Paso sculptor, who translated the sketches into plaster models.

Accessories: The Texas Memorial Committee, which objected to use of the naked or fleshless skull of a cow, the nasal bones making what they thought to be a displeasing conformation. In a singular quibble, since cabeza means head rather than merely skull, they ordered that the design be developed so that the eyes are partly filled in, the nose partly fleshed out and—on the plaster model at least—skull sutures remain partly visible.

Modus Operandi: As the authorizing act of June 5, 1935, called for no more than 10,000 coins, the Philadelphia Mint struck this number in September 1935, reserving 8 more for assay. The Museum Committee distributed the half dollars at $2 apiece. As many of them went to the general public, survivors are apt to be nicked, scratched, poorly cleaned or rubbed; gem specimens are very few. The entire issue was sold out in a short time and has remained in continuous demand.

Collateral Evidence: Two matte proofs (fine grain) exist. One of these was first reported by Wayte Raymond; the other came from the John R. Sinnock estate. This writer (W.B.) saw one of the two about 1956; it has an almost chalky look, with unsuspected fine detail on cow's head and yucca tree, even the blossoms surmounting it being sharp, far more than on the uncirculated piece illustrated.

At the other extreme are the counterfeits. They are apparently made by a high pressure casting process, and show porosity, both negative and positive —negative being minute raised bumps, looking almost like stucco under high magnification, while positive show up as minute cavities in the coins. There are, on the more modern counterfeits, raised lines and shallow depressions which show on every specimen in the same location; these are plainly visible on the enlarged detail photographs on pp. 178–179. If you are in doubt, have the suspected specimen checked by ANACS.

No original imprinted holders or presentation cases are known. Apparently, the Museum Committee in El Paso (pronounced locally "El Peso" as if it meant Dollarsville instead of mountain pass) sent the coins out in regular Dennison mailers.

THE OREGON TRAIL
MEMORIAL HALF DOLLARS

Obverse

Reverse

The Corpus Delicti: Alias *Oregon.*

Clues: The Indian—no single tribe is represented —stands with blanket and bow, but without peace pipe, his gesture seemingly warning the westward-bound whites, "So far and no further." (His position has been irreverently compared to that of a traffic policeman demanding "Halt!") Behind him is a map of the United States on which a line of Conestoga wagons is headed for what is now the State of Washington; but the map shows no state boundaries. On issues possessing mintmarks, the D or s for Denver or San Francisco appears right of the F in HALF. A Conestoga wagon heading for the setting sun, drawn by oxen led by a pioneer, his wife and baby within, dominates the reverse. Behind it is the joint monogram JE/LGF for the designers, James Earle Fraser (reverse) and Laura Gardin Fraser (obverse). There is no stated reason for the five stars—perhaps they represent states or territories crossed enroute from St. Joseph, Missouri on the way west.

Opportunity: The Oregon Trail Memorial Association, Inc., a New York corporation, for reasons best

known to itself, sought in early 1926 to have Congress authorize no less than 6,000,000 commemorative half dollars. In the grandiloquent language of the bill, these were "to commemorate the heroism of the fathers and mothers who traversed the Oregon Trail to the Far West with great hardship, daring, and loss of life, which not only resulted in adding new States to the Union, but earned a well-deserved and imperishable fame to the pioneers; to honor the 20,000 dead that lie buried in unknown graves along 20,000 miles of the great highway of history; to rescue the various important points along the trail from oblivion and to commemorate by suitable monuments, memorial or otherwise, the tragic events associated with that immigration, erecting them either along the trail itself or elsewhere in localities appropriate for the purpose, including the City of Washington . . ." Possibly because the stated purpose was nationalistic rather than obscurely local, the House Coinage Committee reported the bill favorably, and it became the Act of May 17, 1926.

Motive: Unquestionably, That Five Finger Word. ("Gimme a G! . . . Gimme an R! . . . Gimme an E,

E, D!!") Though this coinage was one of the greatest artistic triumphs ever to be released by the Mint, it became one of the most flagrant abuses of the commemorative coinage privilege, along with the Boone, Texas and Arkansas issues. The promoters' subsequent activities in exploiting coin collectors and the general public eventually led to the unpopularity of commemoratives in Congress and ultimately to adamant Treasury Department opposition to any further commemorative issues, no matter how worthy the cause to be memorialized, no matter who represented the sponsoring commissions.

Suspects: The Oregon Trail Memorial Association, Inc., though presumably less its nonagenarian figurehead president (the pioneer Ezra Meeker, 1830–1928, who made the trek himself in 1851) than its finance committee and its attorneys and publicity agents. Scott Stamp & Coin Co., New York, must share some small part of the guilt for acting as the major distributor to coin people.

Accessories: As this was not a crime against art, only against the public purse, the Frasers qualify at worst as accessories before the fact. (The Association had originally, on Mint recommendation, approached Chester Beach, who went as far as making several sketches (Taxay, pp. 119–120); but Beach eventually gave up the assignment, which is just as well.

Modus Operandi: Laura Gardin Fraser completed both obverse and reverse models, the reverse after drawings by James Earle Fraser from about July 30, 1925.

For unknown reasons, the compass above DOLLAR in her original model (Taxay, p. 121), was removed. The Federal Commission of Fine Arts, seeing photographs of the two models, reacted with unprecedented enthusiasm, thereafter pointing to these as standards which later commemorative artists would have to approach if they wanted Commission approval. Charles Moore of the Commission telegraphed approval of the models to Mint Director Grant as of August 5. To save time, as the Association wanted the coins at once, the models went to Medallic Art Company for making mechanical reductions to half dollar size. These went to the Mint during the same month. During September 1926, the Philadelphia Mint struck 48,000 specimens, which promptly went to the Association. These were later named the "Ezra Meeker issue," which circumstance enables us to deduce the reason for the 1926 date: it was exactly 75 years after Meeker's

initial trek. In 1907, Meeker had left his Oregon home and retraversed the entire Oregon Trail in a covered wagon with ox team, to publicize it to people along the way, in the process fixing its exact location for erection of future memorials, plaques, etc.

The initial 1926 (Philadelphia) batch was well-received, and most were sold, so that the Association requisitioned additional coins to be struck at San Francisco, expecting that the collectors who bought 1926 Philadelphia coins would turn out in similar or greater numbers for the second variety. The San Francisco Mint complied, striking the coins during October and November.

But from there on it was downhill all the way. Few of the 1926 s coins sold at $1 apiece. The Treasury then ordered the mints to make no more until the 1926 s's sold, which is why none followed in 1927.

In 1928, the Philadelphia Mint struck another 50,000 pieces, but the earlier Treasury orders kept the coins in the vaults for another five years. Only in 1933 were the remaining 1926 s's re-melted, enabling release of the 1928 batch. These were offered in July 1933, hastily dubbed the "Jedediah Smith Issue," but there were few takers at $2 apiece. In that depression year, $2 was a lot of money; it would have bought a Sunday-best shirt, or, in many locales, a week's groceries, if anyone had the cash at all. (If anyone is interested, Jedediah Smith (1799–1831) was one of the more famous western explorers; he and two companions, ca. 1828, were the first white men to cross the Sierra Nevada and the Great Salt Lake Desert. He was murdered by Indians on the Santa Fe Trail.)

Through God only knows what manner of political manipulation, the Oregon Trail Memorial Association managed to obtain approval of a new 1933 Denver issue for sale at the Century of Progress Exposition, naming coins after the latter. As Scott Stamp & Coin Co. had only managed to sell 6,000 of the 1928s, mostly to speculators and investors, the 1933 D coins numbered only 5,250 including probably five or six assay pieces, establishing a pattern to be followed thereafter: small batches of 3,000 to 12,000 apiece, preferably different mintmark varieties, year after year, aimed less at the general public than at speculators. (And if Congress had not passed an Act on August 5, 1939, forbidding any future issues of commemoriatives authorized before March 1939, there would probably be Oregon Trail coins dated 1980.) The Association's reputation was already bad, but worse was to follow.

Scott Stamp & Coin Co. managed to sell most of the 1933 D coins, and after the remaining 242 were melted, the Association ordered a new batch for

1934, also from the Denver Mint. These coins received the unwieldy name of "Fort Hall, Fort Laramie and Jason Lee Issue," so that few people paid any attention to these names thereafter. Sales remained sluggish at $2 apiece, despite all Scott's could do. Nearly half of each variety for the next two years had to be earmarked for patriotic societies, which attempted to sell them to their own mailing lists; the idea was that these people somehow might not have heard of the earlier issues and thus not have developed as much sales resistance as coin collectors. Slabaugh adds that as late as 1943, the American Pioneer Trails Association was still trying to sell 1936 Philadelphia and 1937 D Oregon Trail coins. The Association abandoned this project in 1937, and in the same year dropped its attempt to have Scott Stamp & Coin Co. market the remainder. The 1936 s Oregons bore the name "Whitman Mission Coin," after Marcus Whitman (1802–47), a missionary like Jason Lee, both of whom founded missions in the Oregon Territory attempting to tell the local Native Americans that the Great Spirit no longer favored their ancestral modes of worship, and that they should instead adopt white men's religion, white men's taboos, white men's attitudes towards work, whiskey, and women. It is just as well that these names became forgotten.

Issues from 1937 through 1939 were offered directly to the public by the Association in an attempt to bypass the middlemen; but to no avail, and the affair became scandalous. The very day that the Association announced a new limited edition of coins—at $1.60 for 1936 and 1936 s (the "Marcus Whitman" issue), $1.60 again for 1937 D—the speculators got there on the first day and doubled or trebled the prices to ordinary collectors. In 1938 and 1939, the coins were offered by the Association in three-piece sets (Philadelphia, Denver, and San Francisco) at $6.25 and $7.50 per set respectively, with the same result. Numerous protests to the Association and the Mints followed, and these protests are believed to have been among those that led to Congress passing the above-mentioned Act of August 5, 1939, ending the enterprise after a little over 264,000 Oregons had been struck out of the authorized six million.

In tabular form:

Authorized:	Not over 6,000,000
Coined, total:	264,419, including about 174 assay coins
Melted, total (exclusive of assay coins):	61,317
Net mintage, total:	202,928

By dates and mintmarks (Philadelphia (P), no mintmark on coins; Denver, D; San Francisco, S):

DATE	MINT	STRUCK	RESERVED FOR ASSAY	RETURNED FOR RE-MELTING	NET MINTAGE
1926	(P)	48,000	30	75	47,925
1926	S	100,000	55	17,000	83,000
1928	(P)	50,000	28	44,000	6,000
1933	D	5,245?	5?	242	4,998
1934	D	7,000	6	—	7,000
1936	(P)	10,000	6	—	10,000
1936	S	5,000	6	—	5,000
1937	D	12,000	8	—	12,000
1938	(P)	6,000	6	—	6,000
1938	D	6,000	5	—	6,000
1938	S	6,000	6	—	6,000
1939	(P)	3,000	4	—	3,000
1939	D	3,000	4	—	3,000
1939	S	3,000	5	—	3,000

Original sketch for coin's reverse by James Earle Fraser.

Collateral Evidence: No original holders for the 1926–1934 coins have been met with, though it is possible that they may exist especially for the 1934 D and later coins distributed by patriotic societies. Later holders were nothing special; we illustrate the only types seen to date, evidently originally made for the 1936 issue, but used later as well. (Note that the one marked "1938 PDS" was originally marked "1936 P," and altered by a later hand, probably at the Association.)

To date about 40 three-piece holders for 1936 (P), and mixed-date coins, are known, and about 20 each of the 1938 and 1939 holders for three-piece sets, all with written dates. The single-coin holder for 1936 (P) is the only one seen to date. It is quite likely that such holders could be imitated, still more likely that blank holders could be either written or imprinted. Documentation such as the envelope illustrated would be valuable evidence not only of the coin's source, but also of authenticity of coins and holders.

The 1945 envelope is included for documentary evidence of the claim that the Association was still

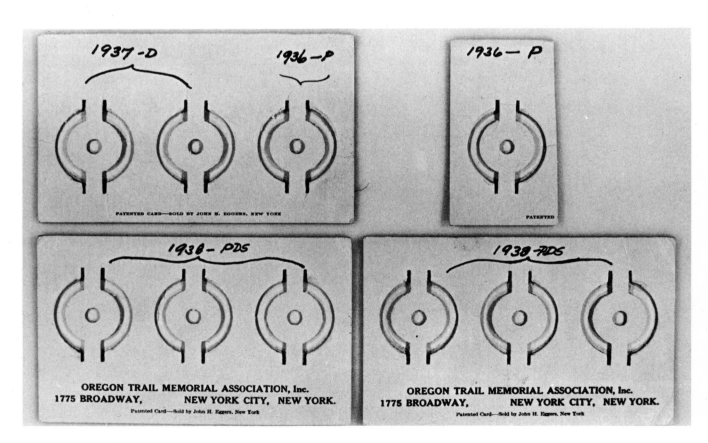

The Oregon Trail Memorial Association distributed the Oregon Trail Commemoratives in coin mailing holders as illustrated above.

184

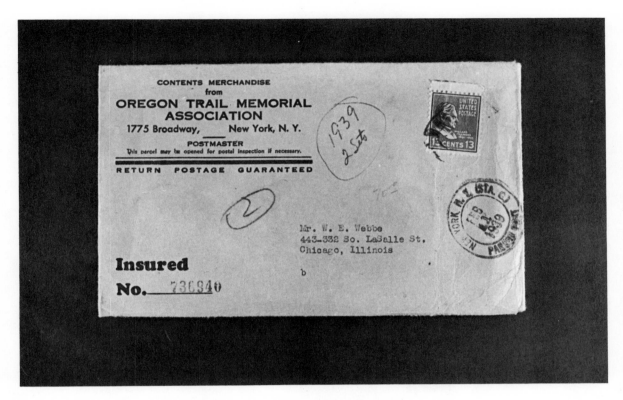

Envelope that housed two 1939 Oregon Trail Commemorative half dollar sets.

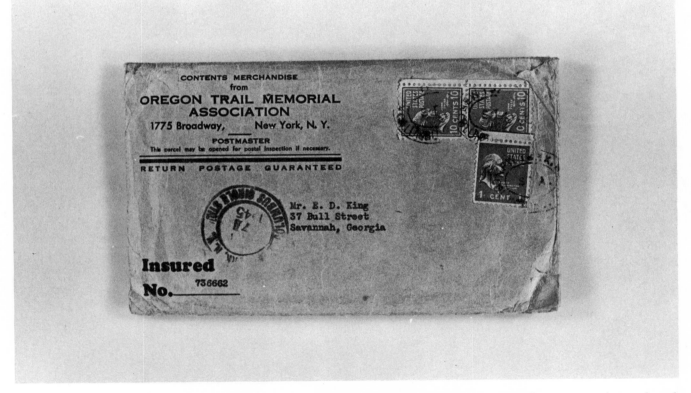

Oregon Trail Commemoratives were being offered for sale long after Congress had prohibited their manufacture, as can be seen from the date on this envelope.

Two specimens of the excessively rare matte proof 1926 Oregon Trail exist. This specimen was once owned by John R. Sinnock, chief engraver of the U.S. Mint, and Aubrey Bebee, owner of the famous 1913 Liberty Nickel.

The normal striking for the 1926 Philadelphia doesn't reveal the Indian's thumb or first finger because this was the way the dies were designed. The '26 S and other issues to follow would show them, though. However, the depth of the strike varies with each date.

selling back issues (1936–37 dates) long after Congress had prohibited further manufacture of Oregon coins.

Physical characteristics of the genuine coins vary widely. The 1926 Philadelphia has poor detail on the Indian's bow hand, foot, and sometimes also on the feathers. (See photo of matte proof.) Make sure that your coin has mint luster on these details to qualify as a full uncirculated specimen.

The Bebee (1948) matte proof, of the 1926 P issue, of which two exist, is now in the collection of one of us (A.S.).

Other reported proofs must be documented, as they could be imitated by pickling or sandblasting business strikes. However, these will not be double struck!

The single issue most easily obtained in gem mint state at present is the 1926 s, evidently from quantities bought by speculators and investors just before the remainder went back for re-melting.

Coins dated 1928 are apt to be better struck than either 1926 issue.

The 1933 D coin has the lowest net mintage. Three speculators retain, among them, to the present day, 20 rolls, in all 400 coins. They are not sharp strikings, as is characteristic of the date. Note especially the flatness on the pioneer's body.

Most of the 1934 D coins are better struck than any of the others in this series that ran from 1926–1939. The only possible exceptions are a few 1936, '36 s and '37 D specimens. For an example, compare the illustrated '34 D with the 1926 shown earlier.

When the announcement appeared that only 5,000 of the "Whitman Mission" issue (the 1936 s) Oregon half dollars would be produced, Scott Stamp & Coin Co. sold out the entirety within ten days and several months later offered to repurchase any offered at $10 apiece! No large hoards are known. These are often nearly as well struck as 1934 D.

The 1934 D issue showing the Indian's thumb and first finger.

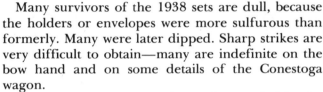

The Oregon Territory Commemorative 3¢ stamp—Scott 783, Type A256.

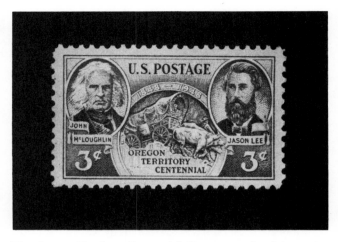

The Oregon Territory Centennial Commemorative 3¢ stamp— Scott 964, Type A411. See pp. 239–240.

Many survivors of the 1938 sets are dull, because the holders or envelopes were more sulfurous than formerly. Many were later dipped. Sharp strikes are very difficult to obtain—many are indefinite on the bow hand and on some details of the Conestoga wagon.

The same remark, to a lesser degree, holds also for the 1939 set.

A 1939 matte proof three-piece set is known, but surfaces and details on the three coins are most suspicious, and we think its owner will have extreme difficulty proving the set came that way from the three mints.

There are two philatelic tie-ins, either of which would make a beautiful addition to an exhibit of commemorative coins. The first of these is the 3¢ purple Oregon Territory issue, Scott 783 (Type A256), first released July 14, 1936, "in commemoration of the 100th anniversary of the opening of Oregon Territory," to the extent of 74,407,450 pieces. The designer is not identified, but (s)he was doubtless familiar with the coins, using the map, trail, Conestoga wagon, and Indian themes—with the Indian's headdress the same as that on the coins.

The other one is of a later period, "issued to commemorate the centenary of the establishment of Oregon Territory," and portraying Dr. John McLoughlin (whom we will see on the Ft. Vancouver half dollars) and the missionary Rev. Jason Lee. This brown-red 3¢ stamp, Scott 964 (Type A411), was first released August 14, 1948, designer uncredited, to the amount of 52,214,000 pieces. Again, the Conestoga wagon is shown, with a pioneer leading the oxen pulling it.

THE PANAMA–PACIFIC INTERNATIONAL EXPOSITION HALF DOLLAR

Obverse

Reverse

The Corpus Delicti: Alias *Pan-Pac Half.*

Clues: Ms. Liberty (so identified by her Phrygian cap) scatters flowers from a cornucopia held by her naked child. Unaccountably, Ms. Liberty has most often been mislabeled Columbia, which name would mean only the tutelary genius of the lands discovered by Columbus. Equally unaccountably, the child has nearly adult proportions, though to be of that height compared with Ms. Liberty and the flowers, (s)he must have been about four years old. Beyond them, the sun sets between the southern (Yerba Buena or San Francisco) and northern (Marin County) outcroppings of the Golden Gate, shown as they might have been before 1848—minus buildings or bridge. Between the sun and the date 1915 is a conventionalized wave motif, alluding to the Exposition's maritime themes. Left of the date is the s

mintmark of San Francisco, though in actuality many of the Exposition's coins of all denominations were struck on the Exposition grounds rather than in the "Granite Lady" (as the mint building was then known). The inscription is a conveniently abbreviated form of the exposition's official title. On reverse, oak and olive branches flank an eagle which is an imitation of Morgan's. The olive branch is traditional for peace, though either ironical or imperceptive for 1915 when World War I was already underway. We have not heard any explanation of the oak branch which makes any sense, and considering Charles E. Barber's role in the design, possibly there is none. As a sop to Congress, which in 1908 had furiously demanded restoration of the motto IN GOD WE TRUST on St. Gauden's gold coins, this is the first commemorative coin to bear either of the mottoes; possibly the framers of the authorizing act, or

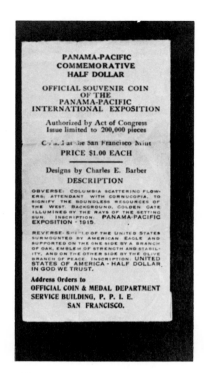

PANAMA-PACIFIC
COMMEMORATIVE
HALF DOLLAR

OFFICIAL SOUVENIR COIN
OF THE
PANAMA-PACIFIC
INTERNATIONAL EXPOSITION

Authorized by Act of Congress
Issue limited to 200,000 pieces

Coined at the San Francisco Mint
PRICE $1.00 EACH

Designs by Charles E. Barber
DESCRIPTION

OBVERSE: COLUMBIA SCATTERING FLOW-
ERS; ATTENDANT WITH CORNUCOPIA, TO
SIGNIFY THE BOUNDLESS RESOURCES OF
THE WEST. BACKGROUND, GOLDEN GATE
ILLUMINED BY THE RAYS OF THE SETTING
SUN. INSCRIPTION. PANAMA-PACIFIC
EXPOSITION · 1915.

REVERSE: SHIELD OF THE UNITED STATES
SURMOUNTED BY AMERICAN EAGLE AND
SUPPORTED ON THE ONE SIDE BY A BRANCH
OF OAK, EMBLEM OF STRENGTH AND STABIL-
ITY, AND ON THE OTHER SIDE BY THE OLIVE
BRANCH OF PEACE. INSCRIPTION. UNITED
STATES OF AMERICA · HALF DOLLAR.
IN GOD WE TRUST.

Address Orders to
OFFICIAL COIN & MEDAL DEPARTMENT
SERVICE BUILDING, P. P. I. E.
SAN FRANCISCO.

The Panama-Pacific Commemorative 50¢ piece, $1, and $2½ coins were distributed in paper envelopes with a description of the enclosed coins printed on the envelope.

Treasury Secretary McAdoo (who had to approve the designs), or the engravers, or all of them, remembered the public protests attending the appearance in 1907–08 of the mottoless coins.

Opportunity: As early as July 1914, two bills were already pending in the Senate which sought to authorize souvenir coins (commemoratives). One, introduced by Senator Elihu Root (R.-New York, and recently Nobel Laureate for Peace), would have mandated issue of quarter dollars celebrating a century of peace (!) and the opening of the Panama Canal. The other was the Panama-Pacific Exposition Company's bill, providing for silver half dollars and gold dollars, quarter eagles, and $50 coins, for the Exposition to be held in San Francisco in 1915. This bill eventually became the Act of January 16, 1915. It included an appropriation for designing the coins, presumably to be paid to whichever artist provided models satisfactory to Treasury Secretary McAdoo.

Motive: Fund raising for the Exposition; see *Modus Operandi* below.

Suspects: Charles E. Barber, Engraver of the Mint; William Malburn, Assistant Secretary of Treasury, who sought to have all the design work done in

the Mint (i.e., by Barber), and who managed to convince McAdoo to reject Paul Manship's design for the half dollar and Evelyn Longman's for the quarter eagle—McAdoo was only with great difficulty persuaded to accept the outsiders' designs for the gold dollar and $50 coins.

Accessories: Farran Zerbe (see below, under $50).

Modus Operandi: Sometime between February 1 and 8, 1915, Malburn persuaded McAdoo that the half dollars should be designed entirely within the Mint. By February 13, Acting Mint Director Dewey wrote to A.M. Joyce, Superintendent of the Philadelphia Mint, that he had already delivered Barber's designs for the half dollar to Malburn— quick work, to say the least! Malburn obtained Secretary McAdoo's approval on March 22, and during the ensuing two months the master dies, hubs, and working dies were prepared in the Philadelphia Mint. At some unknown date in this period, trial strikings from the adopted dies, without s mint mark, were made at Philadelphia: not over four in copper, six in silver, two in gold. One of the two gold strikings is in the Norweb collection, ex King Farouk; the other was in the Brand estate, sold early in the 1970s by A. Kosoff, along with a silver and a copper specimen without the s. At least one of the silver strikings was recovered during the 1950s as a normal Pan-Pacific half dollar; *have you examined yours?*

The Panama-Pacific International Exposition, celebrating the opening of the Panama Canal (by the *S.S. Ancon,* August 15, 1914), was set up late in 1914 through early 1915 on a 635-acre site near the Marina in San Francisco; some of Bernard Maybeck's buildings erected for it still survive, notably the colonnade at the Exploratorium at the foot of Lyon Street.

As its total cost was in excess of $50 million, larger than that of any other national or regional exposition until the 1939–40 New York World's Fair, it had to explore every possible means of attracting visitors by the millions (after its opening on February 20, 1915, there were some 19,000,000 in all). Commemorative coins were only a small part of the whole publicity venture; but as the exposition was taking place in a mint city, what more natural than to have presses and personnel from the San Francisco Mint to demonstrate the minting process? Local newspaper people were on hand, and the strikings went on accompanied by great festivity. (For other details see *Modus Operandi* section under the $50 coinage.)

In all, 200,000 were authorized to be made, all at the San Francisco Mint (this being the first commemorative half dollar ever to be made at a U.S. branch mint, and the only one to be struck in the presence of the public). Despite the immense publicity, only 60,000 were actually struck, all in June 1915, plus 30 assay coins; and of the 60,000, only 27,134 were actually sold, the remaining 32,866 being returned to the mint for melting. At least half of the survivors have been cleaned, impaired, or frankly circulated; gem specimens are very difficult to locate.

One scarce variety shows plainly double punched mintmark s (north).

Individual half dollars were sold at $1 apiece, most of them in small paper envelopes bearing an unfortunate resemblance to workmen's pay envelopes, with a description of the enclosed coin.

The text was similar to that on the pasteboard tickets in the copper frames. A very small number went out in small plush cases similar to those for the short sets. We have seen possibly ten envelopes and 18 of the single-coin plush cases.

Collateral Evidence: Satin finish proofs are rumored to exist with the s mintmark, but to date neither of the two coins reported has shown up.

Philatelic tie-ins for the entire Pan-Pacific series consist of the four-piece sets of Pan-Pacific Exposition stamps, as follows:

Green 1¢, Scott 397 and 401 (Type A144), respectively perforated 12 and 10, the latter scarcer, respectively issued beginning January 1, 1913 and December 13, 1914, depicting Vasco Núñez de Balboa. In all, 334,796,926 were issued, of which only tiny quantities were on first-day covers. Color variants exist—dark green to yellow-green.

Carmine 2¢, Scott 398 and 402 (Type A145), respectively perforated 12 and 10, the latter scarcer (particularly uncancelled), respectively issued beginning January 18, 1913 and February 2, 1915, depicting the Pedro Miguel Locks of the Panama Canal. In all 503,713,086 were issued, of which still tinier quantities were on first-day covers. Color variants exist—from light carmine (orange-red) to lake (bluish red).

Blue 5¢, Scott 399 and 403 (Type A146), respectively perforated 12 and 10, the latter scarcer (particularly uncancelled), respectively issued beginning January 1, 1913 and February 6, 1915, depicting the Golden Gate at sunset with boats. In all 29,088,726 were issued, of which the few first-day covers reported of Scott 399 show also the 10¢ and 1¢, and yet fewer first-day covers are reported of Scott 403.

Orange 10¢, Scott 400 (orange), 400A (orange-yellow), either perforated 12, and 404 (orange, perforated 10), all Type A147, were issued respectively beginning January 1, 1913, August 25, 1913, and July 17, 1915. All are very scarce uncancelled. A total of 16,968,365 were released, and the very rare first-day covers (January 1, 1913, San Francisco) are of Scott 400 only. Specimens of all the above are known with San Francisco (Exposition Station) cancellations showing various dates in 1915 and MODEL POST OFFICE PANAMA PACIFIC INTERNATIONAL EXPOSITION.

Almost all survivors have been cleaned (some with abrasives), nicked or scratched. Truly gem or choice specimens are therefore extremely difficult to locate and many offered as such (even at $12,000+!) are actually sliders, just like those offered at $900 as ordinary Uncs. So, the only thing you can do is either learn to grade the coins offered you, or trade only with dealers you trust—preferably you should do both. If you've learned to grade the coins that are being offered to you and have found a dealer you can trust, we'd like to say that this coin, in sharp pristine Unc. only, is recommended for investment.

THE PANAMA–PACIFIC INTERNATIONAL EXPOSITION GOLD DOLLAR

Obverse *Reverse*

The Corpus Delicti: Alias *Pan-Pac Dollar*.

Clues: The head of a man wearing a cap, often mistaken for a baseball player, is intended to represent one of the laborers who helped build the Panama Canal. On reverse, the two dolphins are meant to symbolize the meeting of the Atlantic and Pacific Oceans. s mintmark, for San Francisco, is below space between DO of DOLLAR.

Opportunity: Same as for the half dollar, above, p. 190.

Motive: As for the half dollar, above, p. 190.

Suspects: Charles Keck, designer; William Malburn, Assistant Secretary of Treasury, who wanted to have all the designs done by Barber (above, p. 190), and who accordingly made specious objections to Keck's original designs featuring Poseidon with trident. See Taxay, pp. 27, 31.

Accessories: Farran Zerbe (below, under the $50).

Modus Operandi: After Malburn had unaccountably rejected Keck's original designs, the artist sent three others—one depicting Balboa, though little resembling the 1¢ stamp created for the Exposition, the other two showing the laborer's head respectively with and without wreath on his cap. Secretary McAdoo chose the latter early in March 1915. Medallic Art Company of New York reduced the adopted models to gold dollar size, and the Philadelphia Mint prepared hubs and dies.

Silver trial pieces, at least one on thick and two on thin flans, without s mintmarks, were struck at some unnamed date in the spring 1915, before the working dies went to San Francisco. One of the two—the thicker one—has an extraordinary knife-rim, almost as though a collar had been added to the finished coin; this working die had cracked in two places. This coin was part of lot 2030 of the Palace Collections of Egypt, the 1954 auction of King Farouk's

193

$1 Panama-Pacific trial piece struck in silver at the Philadelphia mint before the working dies went to San Francisco.

Panama-Pacific Gold $1 envelopes—two varieties.

coin collection after the Nasser regime had deposed him. It had earlier been owned by Farran Zerbe, William H. Woodin, and a variety of dealers; subsequently also by Dr. J. Hewitt Judd and Frankie Laine, the singer. It was formerly on display at the Chase Bank Money Museum. It is now owned by a client of A.S.

There were also at least eight gold strikings in a single set, without s mintmark, some with reeded edges, others with plain, in various states of die breakage. There are also uniface impressions of both obverse and reverse dies, without s mintmark, in white metal, bronzed.

A report attributed to Farran Zerbe has it that these—like the silver strikings—were made for Treasury Secretary William Gibbs McAdoo, who collected coins.

Of the regular strikings for distribution at the Exposition, 25,000 were authorized to be struck, and the full amount was made with 34 extras reserved for assay, during parts of May, June and July 1915.

They were offered for sale at $2 apiece, though a Coin & Medal Department price list of the Exposition's numismatic items says $2.25. Possibly, the $2 price was instituted after Zerbe's group met with sales resistance at the higher figure. After November 1, 1916, 10,000 unsold specimens were re-melted, leaving a net mintage 15,000.

Collateral Evidence: Proofs are reported of the regular issue with s mintmark; to date the count stands at one or possibly two reeded-edge pieces and one plain edge coin without s mintmark, brilliant with mirror-like fields. One brilliant proof with the mintmark is also reported, but this we have not seen.

A very few specimens are known in the original envelope, similar to that used at the Exposition to house the half dollars; see illustration.

We have seen possibly 30 in individual cases of issue, uniform with those made for the half dollars.

Beware of counterfeit specimens as illustrated. Observe the sharpness of striking and lack of detail in areas such as the lettering, the hair detail on the laborer and the reverse dolphins.

A rare die variety exists with obvious double-punched s, one of the two punchings below and to right of the other (southeast).

194

Obverse of the Panama-Pacific $1. Note the overall sharpness of the striking, especially the sharpness of the lettering and the hair and ear of the laborer.

Reverse of the gold $1 coin displays same sharpness of striking, especially on the lower dolphin and mint mark.

This is a counterfeit Panama-Pacific $1 gold coin. Obverse side.

Reverse of counterfeit $1 gold coin.

THE PANAMA–PACIFIC INTERNATIONAL EXPOSITION QUARTER EAGLE

Obverse   *Reverse*

The Corpus Delicti: Alias *Pan-Pacific 2½*.

Clues: Columbia—wearing an ambiguous head-dress that might conceivably have been intended to represent a liberty cap—rides sidesaddle and facing backwards on a hippocampus, which is to a horse what a mermaid is to a woman. In her free hand is a caduceus, said to represent the medical breakthrough of Col. William C. Gorgas' successful campaign with the U.S. Army Medical Corps to put an end to the malaria and yellow fever epidemics which had halted all previous canal-building attempts. According to Slabaugh, the hippocampus itself alludes to commerce through the Canal; this requires elaboration, and the best we can do is to surmise that it alludes to the Canal as making possible the transportation of land-based goods (normally by draft horses) by water (as the fish body swims): the mythological equivalent of a ship, though its original symbolism was very different. Mintmark s is in exergual space, far to right of date. On reverse, Morgan's defiant

eagle probably alludes to the necessity of keeping the Canal open during World War I; the whole composition is meant to suggest a Roman legionary standard, which was a pole surmounted by some such device, distinctive to each of the various legions or army divisions.

Opportunity: As with the half dollar and gold dollar.

Motive: As with the half dollar and gold dollar.

Suspects: Charles E. Barber, designer. George T. Morgan, the long-forgotten Assistant Engraver of the Mint (remembered then only among coin collectors, for the silver dollar of 1878–1904), contributed the eagle on reverse; it reappears, though with different appurtenances, on the Lincoln half dollar. Also, William Malburn.

Accessories: Farran Zerbe.

Envelope in which the Panama-Pacific $2½ gold coin was issued.

Modus Operandi: Originally, Col. Harts, of the Federal Commission of Fine Arts, recommended Miss Evelyn Longman to design the quarter eagle. Her design, according to her letter of January 27, 1915, to Acting Mint Director Dewey (quoted by Taxay, p. 30), was to have shown an eagle's head on one side, a cluster of California fruits on the other, with denomination expressed as 2½$ rather than 2½D. However, not even sketches have been located to date. But during the first week of February, despite the Commission's approval of her designs, she learned of Malburn's decision that the designing should be done entirely within the Mint (i.e., by Barber), and on March 8, Barber received notice that he was to design the quarter eagle as well as the half dollar. We have not been able to learn details of the illness Slabaugh cited as responsible for Ms. Longman's not being chosen: but in any event it would have been secondary to William Malburn's policy of excluding outsiders.

Presumably Barber's quarter eagle design was approved on March 22 along with his half dollar, though details are lacking. Trial impressions of obverse (uniface), without s mintmark, are known in

Note lack of detail on head and neck of hippocampus, as well as the breast of Columbia and her headdress on the obverse of this counterfeit $2½ gold piece.

copper and brass: Judd, Appendix A, though, unaccountably pictures the obverse of a 1926 Sesquicentennial quarter eagle.

The Act of January 16, 1915, specified a maximum of 10,000 to be coined. Accordingly, during June 1915, 10,000 were coined, plus 17 reserved for assay. These were offered for sale on the Exposition grounds at $4 each; only 6,749 sold, and the other 3,251 went back to the mint for re-melting.

Collateral Evidence: Proofs may have been made without or with s mintmark, but to date the single brilliant proof (mirrorlike field, frosty devices) without s has not been verified.

Original envelopes of issue are extremely rare; one is illustrated here. No specimen has been met with in presentation cases aside from those which were part of three-piece or five-piece sets.

For unknown reasons, the majority of survivors show varying degrees of wear; Extremely Fine and About Uncirculated are the most common grades. Pristine mint state examples are less often found in this denomination than in the fifty-dollar pieces, despite the latter's propensity for falling out of owners' hands and accumulating rim dents. It is necessary, also, to distinguish wear from weak striking; the details most often weakly struck include heads of Ms. Columbia and of the hippocampus, his (?) shoulder and her thighs, and the eagle's neck and legs. Full mint state specimens will show mint frost on even these weak areas. Really sharp specimens are rare. Many specimens offered in the usual 11 piece commemorative gold sets made up during the last fifty years fall short of mint state, as do many offered as "BU" or "ChBU," or "Gem BU."

One of us (A.S.) has seen lustrous counterfeit specimens. Again, note the quality of strike and lack of detail (aside from other detecting marks present on the coin's surface which can easily be observed with a magnifying glass).

Observe the workmanship on the eagle, standard, and pole on this Panama-Pacific counterfeited $2½ gold piece.

THE PANAMA–PACIFIC INTERNATIONAL EXPOSITION FIFTY-DOLLAR PIECES

Obverse   *Reverse*

Obverse   *Reverse*

The Corpus Delicti: Alias *Pan-Pac Fifties* round and octagonal.

Clues: The goddess Minerva or Athena wears the crested helmet found on numerous depictions of her in ancient Greek coinage; it is (as usual) pushed back off her face, to signify peaceful intentions. We have not found the exact Greek coin used as prototype of this head, though the crested helmet is of the Athenian type, and there are numerous silver coins of Velia and Corinth showing her in this type of helmet, sometimes wreathed as here, often with other devices on it. Most such types have a long tailpiece to the crest, which is omitted here. She is depicted as wearing mail (plate rather than chain)—a strange anachronism; on her shield is MCMXV (1915), only the second use of Roman numerals for date in United States coinage history (the first was the various types of St. Gaudens double eagles of 1907). Why Athena or Minerva? She was the goddess of wisdom, skill, agriculture, horticulture, spinning and weaving, among other things, and she taught her followers to grow and use olives, whose oil was long indispensable in cooking and providing light by night. All these were important in California. On reverse is her owl, seated on a branch of long-leafed pine, possibly meant for ponderosa to judge from the enormous cones. In field between the cone farthest to right and inner border of long and short beads (often called the Morse code circle) is mintmark s. Below the branch, vertically above the R of FRANCISCO, are the initials RA for Robert Aitken, the designer. Both sides of the octagonal coin, but not the round, show an additional border of dolphins, said to be symbolic of the continuous water route created by the completion of the Panama Canal. Criticisms of these designs have been numerous and mostly irrelevant, based on total misreading of the iconography. Treasury Secretary William G. McAdoo began it (at the behest of Assistant Secretary William Malburn) with stupid claims that Pallas Athena meant nothing on a U.S. coin unless she could be identified with liberty, and that Athena's owl would never mean anything at all to us. Others sneered that the coin designs either ignored the Panama Canal or implied that the Canal was built for the convenience of dolphins. In actuality, the choice of Athena was an obvious bow to the cultural and educational aspects of the Exposition; her owl is an obvious symbol for watchfulness, something especially appropriate during the early years of World War I while the United States nervously worried about possible hostile action from Germany and being abruptly forced into war; the pine branch alludes to some of California's most majestic trees and indirectly to the lumber and paper industries dependent on them; and dolphins are the friendly companions of many boats enroute to or from the Canal. To depict even one of the locks recognizably would have produced an impossibly crowded design, and to depict one type of ship rather than another would surely have brought accusations of favoritism —or worse had the ship been foreign. And to those who objected that California redwood would have been preferable to pine, the obvious answer is that birds are seldom found in redwood trees. The Indians justly believed redwoods to be unfriendly to other life forms (you will not find any other vegetation growing among them!), so that use of this species on a coin would have symbolized paranoia

as the price of long life—a theme more appropriate to the McCarthyist 1950s than to 1915.

Choice of both round and octagonal formats for this denomination, which also came in for criticism at the time, consciously reflected use of both Humbert octagonal $50 coins and Wass-Molitor round fifties as a major part of California's circulating medium in the 1850s.

Opportunity: As with the lower denominations.

Motive: Ditto.

Suspects: Robert Aitken, designer. William Malburn and Secretary McAdoo deserve to be named here, for between them they nearly forced the discarding of the design in favor of some unbearably dull thing by Barber. As it was, McAdoo objected to various minor features, and only last-minute action by Aitken forestalled its replacement. On March 3, as Taxay points out (p. 31), Acting Mint Director T.P. Dewey asked Barber to submit sketches "as rapidly as possible," but in the meantime Aitken submitted a revised model directly to McAdoo, who could find no further grounds for rejecting it. (Possibly, too, Aitken or Daniel Chester French, then chairman of the Commission of Fine Arts, had managed to explain the coin's iconography to McAdoo in language simple enough that even he could understand it, which might account in turn for the latter's willingness to approve Barber's preposterous mythological design for the quarter eagle.)

Accessories: Farran Zerbe—see below.

Modus Operandi: During preparations for the Exposition's opening, the Philadelphia Mint shipped a 14-ton hydraulic press to the fairgrounds for the specific purpose of striking these pieces. (We have not been able to ascertain how they managed it: probably it went disassembled by ship.) Hub impressions (reversed, without mintmark) were made of both sides of the octagonal type, on large round planchets—60mm in diameter.

On June 15, the first octagonal pieces were struck, at a ceremony which attracted VIPs from all over the country. This had been arranged by Farran Zerbe, then possibly the best known numismatist in the United States. Zerbe had enough political clout to have himself put in charge of the Exposition's Coin and Medal Department, which was named in the authorizing act as responsible for receiving and distributing the commemorative coins, souvenir medals, award medals and diplomas to be given exhibitors by the International Jury of Awards. Zerbe set up his own collection (over 20,000 specimens after he included additions) in a trellised display area of the Palace of Liberal Arts on the Exposition grounds labelling it *Zerbe's Unique Money of the World.* It became one of the more popular displays, and the coins, each with its own story appended, were probably seen by several million visitors between the Exposition's opening February 20 and its close on December 4, 1915. This collection, with other coins obtained in subsequent years, formed the basis of the Chase Manhattan Bank's Money Museum. Beyond doubt, between this exhibit and the public sales of the coins, Zerbe's efforts did more than anyone else's for decades to put coin collecting on the map. (See Frank Morton Todd, "The Coin Outlasts the Throne," in *The Story of the Exposition,* vol. IV, 1921.)

At the ceremony, Mint Superintendent T.W.H. Shanahan struck the first octagonal coin. This went into a five-piece set (half dollar, dollar, quarter eagle and both fifties), which contained the #1 specimens of the other denominations; the set was housed in a special gold presentation case made by Shreve & Co., and was presented to Charles C. Moore, president of the Exposition. This set went from Moore's estate through Earl Parker to R.R. Johnson, who exhibited it at a convention in the Jack Tar Hotel in San Francisco in 1967, with all the documentation. Unfortunately, in 1968 the set was stolen, but was recovered and sold by Ron Gillio for a reported $150,000.

Moore himself struck the second piece. Nos. 3 through 29 were then struck by other dignitaries, including Rep. Julius Kahn (R.-Cal.), who had sponsored the authorizing bill (Act of Jan. 16, 1915), San Francisco's Mayor James Rolph, Jr. and Farran Zerbe. Nos. 30 through 100 were struck later that same day by various employees of the San Francisco Mint. Shanahan had made the erroneous claim on striking the first piece that he was "about to strike the first 50-dollar coin ever issued under authority of law in the United States." He was unaware, like most numismatists until recent years, that the original octagonal fifties issued 1851–53 by Augustus Humbert, either as United States Assayer of Gold or as the United States Assay Office of Gold, were issued under authority of law, specifically the Act of September 30, 1850, and that it was under this authority that Humbert obtained his hubs from the Philadelphia Mint (the original dies being the work of Charles Cushing Wright under federal contract), and that the dies bore the inscription UNITED STATES OF AMERICA identically to those on coins from regular branch mints. (Proof of this was found at the Archives in recent years; Humbert submitted reports to the Director of the Mint on the same forms as those supplied other branch mints, and in fact his operation was a provisional branch mint, which received regular dies in 1852 (for 1853 use) from Philadelphia, to strike gold and silver coins should the technical problems of refining California gold be solved in the meantime.) It was thus more appropriate than anyone even then suspected that octagonal fifties should be coined in San Francisco, only a few miles from where their ancestors had been coined 64 years earlier, almost to the day.

During the months of June, July and August, the remaining gold fifties were coined. According to Slabaugh, after the first 62 round fifties were coined, the dies broke in striking the 63rd—as did the remaining pairs of dies then on hand. Coinage had to be delayed until more dies arrived from Philadelphia.

The authorizing act specified 3,000 fifties: 1,500 each of the octagonal and round types. Sales went well enough to convince the authorities to strike the entire authorization, with 9 extras reserved for assay of the octagonal type, 10 extras of the round. However, the high prices of these coins severely limited the numbers to be sold. According to Exposition price lists, a single $50 coin could be had for $100, but this price entitled the buyer to the half dollar, dollar and quarter eagle free of additional charge.

The complete five-piece sets (including both fifties) cost $200—the buyer's choice of copper frame or leather case again free of extra cost. A complete double set, mounted to show both obverse and reverse, cost $400 for the ten pieces and their copper frame. This could be obtained in hinged or unhinged versions.

Zerbe continued pushing these pieces at customers throughout the Exposition. After it closed, he moved the coin exhibit to the Palace of Fine Arts and continued the Coin and Medal Department as a sales agency until May 1, 1916.

From then until November 1, 1916, Zerbe continued to sell the Exposition's commemorative coins by mail order; after this date, by request of Exposition officials and under authority of Treasury Secretary McAdoo, the remaining coins went back to the Mint for re-melting. In all, 855 octagonal fifties and 1,017 round ones were re-melted, leaving a net mintage of 645 octagons and 483 rounds.

Collateral Evidence: One of us (A.S.) has seen a specimen of each type of fifty-dollar piece struck in silver, without s mintmark, in a private collection.

Panama-Pacific Official Coins and Medals

◻ ◻ ◻

HALF DOLLAR SILVER
Columbia, Eagle. Designed by Charles E. Barber,
60,000 coined, $1 each.

ONE DOLLAR GOLD
Head of Labor. Designed by Charles Keck,
25,000 coined, $2.25 each.

TWO AND ONE HALF DOLLARS GOLD
Columbia on Sea Horse. Designed by Charles E. Barber,
10,000 coined, $4 each.

FIFTY DOLLARS GOLD. Round and Octagonal
Minerva, Owl. Designed by Robert Aitken, N. A.
Limited to 1500 each shape, delivered in leather cases, $100 each.

COMPLETE SETS
Complete Set of designs one each $½, $1, $2½, and choice of $50 (round or
octagonal) $100.
Complete Set including both shapes $50, as illustrated, $200.
Complete Double Set, mounted to show both obverse and reverse, $400.
Special display frame, as illustrated, or fine leather presentation case, delivered with
Complete Sets without additional charge.

SMALL SETS
One each $½, $1 and $2½ in leather presentation case, $7.50.

SPECIAL QUANTITY PRICES
Six each, $½ and $2½, $25.
Six each $½, $1 and $2½, $37.00.

COIN JEWELRY MOUNTINGS
Special mountings for the insertion and removal of coins without injury will be supplied
with coins at the following price per coin, extra.
For Half Dollar, Band mountings for charms, sterling silver or sterling gold plated, 50c.
For Gold Dollar, Gold plated band for charms, stick pins, or brooch pins, 50c; solid gold,
band mountings for charms only, $1.25.
For Two and One Half Dollars Gold, Gold plated band mountings for charms, 50c; same,
solid gold, $1.50.

Panama-Pacific
Official Medal

Authorized by Congress, designed by
Robert Aitken, and produced at the Gov-
ernment Minting Demonstration at the
Panama-Pacific International Exposition.

Bronze: Bright, Oxidized, Antique,
Statuary or Gold Plated, each 25c.
With loop for charms, 50c. Coin
silver, $1.00.

OFFICIAL ENGRAVINGS
In the government's demonstration of the process of making paper money at the Exposition
there was produced extraordinary examples of engraving and plate printing, seven different
subjects, 7 x 10 inches, the set of seven, postpaid, 35c.

Address orders to: *Coin and Medal Department*
Panama-Pacific International Exposition
San Francisco, Cal.

The Exposition price list.

204

The very rare Panama-Pacific Exposition double coin set mounted to show both obverse and reverse under glass in a velvet tray with a hammered metal frame.

The special Charles C. Moore presentation case, which housed the first-struck five-piece set.

Panama-Pacific Commemorative Coins

□ □ □

To Bankers:

The notable series of coins that were authorized by Congress to commemorate the opening of the Panama Canal were produced at the San Francisco mint during the latter part of the year and have had a very successful distribution during the few months they have been on sale.

The novelty of designs, limited issue and denominations — particularly the $50 gold pieces, the first to be issued by our government—have made the series one of curiosity and popular interest that has been appreciated by banks for the local commendation and publicity a display of a set commands.

The limited number of sets that remain are now offered to banks in a special and rich display case (with hang-up and easel back) as illustrated and priced herein. Your consideration is requested for a set of these coins for your bank, not only from the immediate advantage to come from the publicity to be commanded but as a permanent possesion of the bank that should enhance in value and interest since the issue is limited to not over fifteen hundred sets. Special descriptive matter for local press will be sent.

The prices as established will be maintained and any remainder will be destroyed at the mint. The sale will be continued for the distribution of the remainder — but not later than the close of the post-Exposition period, May 1st, 1916.

Coins will be forwarded by prepaid insured carrier and remittance need not be made until coins are received. Make remittance payable to Panama-Pacific International Exposition Coin Department. Your commissions will have our prompt and careful attention.

Coin and Medal Department
Panama-Pacific International Exposition
San Francisco, Cal.

One's last chance to purchase the Exposition sets was May 1, 1916.

About 25 "short sets" (no fifties) survive in cases. About 60 five-piece sets (including both fifties) survive in original leather cases. About 30 are known in copper frames. It is almost certain that some of them were added in recent years to empty copper frames. Sets containing coins that were cleaned or rubbed have doubtless been assembled. These short set frames are all different than the housing used on the Moore "number one" set. The Moore set contains a detachable easel-type velvet plaque with a gold panel that identifies the coins as the first struck in each denomination. On the back of this assembly is another plaque explaining that this assembly was presented to Charles C. Moore for his services to the Exposition. This can all be seen in the three pictures on p. 206.

Four double sets are known, and there are reports of others. One of the double sets, possibly that owned by Robert L. Hughes, brought $70,000 in the 1978 ANA Convention sale. Another had appeared in the Kensington sale, December 1975. A third realized $92,500 in the 1979 ANA Convention sale (lot 562). Supposedly, 12 sets were made, but we cannot trace that many today. These three are the only double sets known to have appeared at public auction.

As expected among commemorative coins that found their way into hands of the general public, many fifties of both types fall well short of mint state. We have seen them as low in grade as Very Good (expensive pocket pieces, these!); many are in Very Fine to About Unc., cleaned, scrubbed, occasionally with retooling in fields to efface recipients' initials, or more often banged up at edges from being dropped. Pristine pieces—without rubbing anywhere (look at Athena's cheek, hair, upper parts of helmet, wreath, date, owl's legs, upper parts of wings, brows and beak), without traces of cleaning, without edge or rim dents—are much scarcer than anyone has suspected; to date they have not brought prices much in advance of cleaned or nicked uncirculated examples, though they are much more difficult to obtain.

These have long been considered the caviar and truffles of the United States commemorative issues, especially in original cased sets.

PILGRIM TERCENTENARY HALF DOLLARS

Obverse

Reverse

Obverse

Reverse

The Corpus Delicti: Alias *Pilgrim 1920* or the *Pilgrim 1921,* respectively.

Clues: The unidentified man in the conical hat is intended as an idealized (actually fanciful) portrait of Governor William Bradford (1590–1675), author of the *History of Plimmoth Plantations,* who spent most of his last 36 years riding herd on a crew of extremist Jesus followers, for whom Christmas was too pagan to be celebrated, and who gave a grisly meaning a few years later to the term witch hunt. (They had fled England in 1620 because King James I, head of the Established Church of England, found their rejection of bishops' authority treasonable.) The book he holds is intended for the Bible; his costume is meant for that of the Puritans of his day (the broad collar is near

Rare 1921 Pilgrim variety I of which fewer than 75 pieces are believed to survive. Note conical hat that seems too large for Governor Bradford.

The original holder for the 1920 Pilgrim Tercentenary half dollar. This is quite a rare item.

enough, though we question the authenticity of the ruffled cravat below it). This also accounts for the word PILGRIM in the inscription. Below Bradford's elbow, the initial D represents not a mintmark but the initial of the designer, Cyrus E. Dallin.

On reverse, the ship is intended to represent the Mayflower in full sail, though its small triangular flying jib (at extreme left, from the bowsprit to a stay extending from the foremast) is an anachronism which is fortunately lacking in Charles Aubrey Huston's stamp design (p. 212). Inscriptions and dates are almost self-explanatory: 1620 for the landings at Plymouth Rock and Provincetown, 1920 not for the opening of the Pilgrim Tercentenary Celebration but for the actual anniversary, which happened to be the date of authorization of the coins. (Those struck in 1921 had this date added in the left field to conform with the Mint Act of 1873, making three dates in all on each coin.)

Opportunity: Various local celebrations throughout New England during 1920–21, honoring the Pilgrim Fathers, were the occasion of the Pilgrim Tercentenary Commission's sponsoring a bill to authorize coinage of commemorative half dollars. Representative Joseph Walsh (R.-Mass.) introduced the bill. During a House debate, on April 21, 1920, Rep. Warren Gard (D.-Ohio) questioned the number of coins to be authorized: 500,000, or five times as many as for the Maine Centennial? Rep. Walsh said that the number of coins corresponded with the occasion—500,000 for a tercentenary, as against 100,000 for a mere centennial. This brought gales of laughter for his "queer sense of arithmetic" (Taxay's phrase). Rep. Albert H. Vestal (R.-Indiana), of the House Coinage Committee, said that the figure of 500,000 was a "misprint" for 300,000. This explanation apparently satisfied Congress, as the bill passed without further controversy, becoming the Act of May 12, 1920.

Motive: To raise funds for the Commission, presumably for its various local celebrations.

Suspects: Cyrus E. Dallin, Boston sculptor, who designed the coins and made the models. (A galvano of his original plaster model is, or at least recently has been, hanging on the wall of the Mayflower Coffee Shop in the Statler Hilton Hotel in New York City.) Its crudity of lettering is less noticeable on the coin—until one uses a magnifying glass; this may be

ascribed to haste, the entire composition being completed during August 1920, owing to demands between the Tercentenary Commission and the Mint that the coins be made at the earliest possible date. The Federal Commission of Fine Arts complained to Mint Director Baker about this situation and recommended that in the future a minimum of three months be allowed for designing and modeling; but no official action followed, nor was Dallin allowed time to revise the lettering.

Accessories: The Pilgrim Tercentenary Commission, which furnished sketches to Dallin.

Modus Operandi: The Philadelphia Mint struck the first batch of 200,000 half dollars during the month of October 1920. They were shipped at once to the National Shawmut Bank of Boston, which offered the coins at $1 apiece beginning in November on behalf of the Commission. Sales continued during the winter and spring of 1921, in enough quantity that the Commission ordered the remaining 100,000 to be struck; these latter had to bear the date 1921. The Mint accordingly coined them in July 1921. Unfortunately, another financial panic followed, many were left jobless and sales slumped. The Commission eventually returned a sizable quantity of both dates to the Mint for remelting. In tabular form:

Authorized:	300,000 total (both dates)
Coined, 1920:	200,000 + 112 assay pieces
Melted:	48,000
Net mintage, 1920:	152,000
Coined, 1921:	100,000
Melted:	80,000
Net mintage, 1921:	20,000

Collateral Evidence: Two matte proofs of the 1920 issue are reliably reported. One of them came from the John R. Sinnock estate (Sinnock was Morgan's successor as Engraver of the Mint, and had a fabulous collection of offbeat and excessively rare mint productions); the other had been obtained by Ira S. Reed in Philadelphia, who—like William Idler a generation earlier—disposed of numerous similar items from his Mint connections.

A single matte proof of the 1921 issue was reported years ago, by Wayte Raymond; this has not been available for examination.

Bill Brown just discovered a 1920 struck from a heavily clashed reversed die—parts of G RU (from IN GOD WE TRUST) are visible in field just above

The Pilgrim Tercentenary 1 ¢ Commemorative issue—Scott 549, Type 152.

stern. Probably the clashed obverse die was discarded before this piece was made.

A pair of dies also clashed during manufacture of the 1921 issue, producing two varieties. The earlier of these we here call "State II." "State II" has a lump before Bradford's nose, other smaller lumps behind the head, above the hat brim, below RU of TRUST, etc. Also, the hat brim is incomplete behind the head. The reverse shows RU just above the stern, similar to the 1920 but not from the same die. Only one of these is known (found by A.S.).

This was evidently followed at once by what has become known as "Variety II," on which the reverse has been replaced by one showing no clash marks. This was published in the February 27, 1974, *Coin World*. Ed Fleischmann used photographic superimposition to demonstrate that the lumps before Bradford's nose and near RU correspond to the sail detail and that those behind his head match parts of the waves. The striations near the 1921 date are apparently the result of a pressman's attempt to efface the clash marks. This variety is very scarce.

The only original holder seen to date is one not from Massachusetts at all, but from one of the local celebrations in Rhode Island. It came with the ticket as illustrated.

An interesting and far less difficult tie-in to the half dollar is the stamp issued December 21, 1920, to commemorate the Pilgrim Tercentenary celebrations. The designer was Charles Aubrey Huston. It is listed as Scott 549, Type A152. It is fortunately not rare; a total of 196,037,327 got into public hands.

THE FOUNDING OF PROVIDENCE, RHODE ISLAND, TERCENTENARY HALF DOLLARS

Obverse

Reverse

The Corpus Delicti: Alias *Rhode Island.*

Clues: Nowhere does the coin refer to Providence (originally Providence Plantations); only a knowledge of local history will allow one to infer that the Art Deco obverse design (loosely after Providence city arms but minus the city motto WHAT CHEER) alludes to the landing of Roger Williams, June 24, 1636. At left, a Narragansett Indian extends his fantastically elongated hand, palm down, in a welcoming *mudra* (symbolic gesture said to mean approval or [this is] good) to the exiled ex-Puritan dissenter Roger Williams. Williams stands, Bible in hand, in a canoe from which a musket barrel end extends, apparently somewhere in Narragansett Bay. Behind the Indian is a stylized maize (corn) plant; under it, on coins from branch mints, is the D for Denver or the S for San Francisco. Dates 1636–1936 allude to the tercentenary of Roger Williams' purchase of land from local Indians to set up his religiously tolerant farming

settlement. Williams said of this place, "In a sense of Gods mercifull Providence unto me I called the place Providence." Mingling the sun's rays with LIBERTY was deliberate symbolism for religious freedom, a major theme of the coin and the celebration.

The reverse loosely copies the state arms. Those enormous flukes on the anchor were constant on the dozens of versions of the colonial seal, found on paper money as early as 1710. However, the motto HOPE was only a substitute for the actual motto, IN TE DOMINE SPERAMUS or "In Thee, O Lord, we hope." This was probably to avoid repetition, as the colonial motto was echoed in Brown University's motto IN DEO SPERAMUS and Salmon P. Chase's translation of the latter (late 1863) which he directed to appear thereafter on U.S. coins as IN GOD WE TRUST. That fact may account for the unusual prominence of the latter motto on obverse, just above the sun's rays and LIBERTY, emphasizing the symbolism of religious freedom.

Opportunity: Statewide celebrations, principally in Providence, of the tercentenary, coordinated by the Rhode Island and Providence Plantations Tercentenary Committee (Judge Letts, chairman). Enough political pressure was applied through Senators Jesse Metcalf (R.-Providence) and Peter Gerry (D.-Warwick) and Representative John O'Connell (D.-Westerly), to induce Congress to pass the authorizing bill jointly with that for the Hudson coins; this became the Act of May 2, 1935.

Motive: Local pride, and to help finance the celebrations.

Suspects: John Howard Benson and A. Graham Carey. (The latter is identified in some sources as Arthur and in others as Abraham; Slabaugh calls him Abraham on p. 108 and Arthur on p. 109.) Benson was an instructor in lettering at the famous Rhode Island School of Design, while his friend and co-designer was a silversmith. Later they became partners in a Newport stonecutting firm, so it is not really too surprising that in some ways the sculptural quality of the coin suggests stonecutting.

Accessories: Mr. Farnum, Director of the Rhode Island School of Design, who originally assigned the

The philatelic tie-in to this coin—the Rhode Island Tercentenary.

coin project to Benson and Carey after the Tercentenary Committee turned it over to him (March 1935). Judge Letts in the meantime received so many demands by local designers, however, that by September 1935 he changed his mind and ordered that a competition be set up, with a $350 prize. Of the fifty entries, the Benson/Carey collaboration was one of three finalists, and at final judging on November 6, it won, after certain alterations demanded by the Committee. Among these, unaccountably, was omission of the quotation from Roger Williams and any references to the city; comparison of the original rejected models with those accepted (Taxay, p. 169) will be most instructive.

Modus Operandi: After the Federal Commission of Fine Arts approved the models (with remarkable lack of enthusiasm) on December 20, 1935, the latter went to the Medallic Art Company for reduction, and the reductions in turn went to the Philadelphia Mint for translation into working hubs and dies. In January, the Philadelphia Mint struck 20,000 coins, the Denver and San Francisco batches following in February; so that the first sets could be offered on March 5. This tabulation says it tersely enough:

Authorized:	50,000
Coined, Philadelphia:	20,000 plus 13 reserved for assay
Denver:	15,000 plus 10 reserved for assay
San Francisco:	15,000 plus 11 reserved for assay

March 5 proved to be a day of immense noise and confusion. The Tercentenary Committee turned over 6,750 half dollars to the Providence coin dealer Horace M. Grant (Grant's Hobby Shop) for nationwide distribution. To their chagrin, he reported that he had already received 11,500 orders from all 48 states, Canada and various foreign customers, and more were expected. To fulfill the Committee's commitments to Grant, amounts allocated to local banks were reduced, and Grant himself had to buy coins back from local recipients. By 11 AM of the same day, March 5, individuals who wanted 6 or more coins were given from one to three depending on their location. By noon, the Rhode Island Hospital National Bank (acting as prime depository and distributor of the coins to the 30 participating banks) had exhausted its supply. Arthur L. Philbrick, Treasurer of the Committee, later claimed that "approximately 45,000" of the total were sold by noon, and that local residents received their coins before the

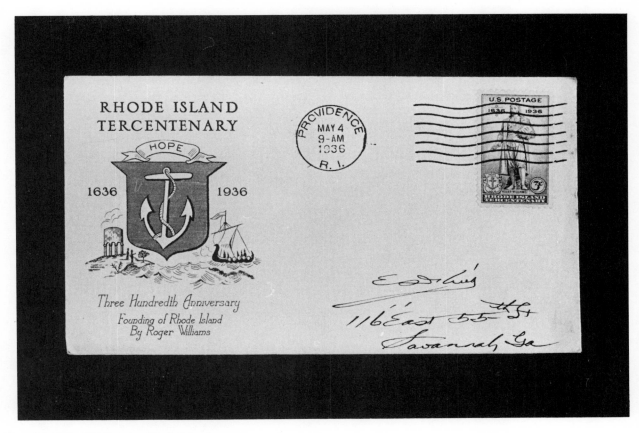

One of the 245,000 first day Rhode Island covers.

mail orders. The issue was supposedly exhausted before 3 PM.

Despite these claims, many became skeptical in ensuing weeks and months. Rumors began that this or that influential banker owned over 1,000 sets and would sell lots of five or ten sets to the highest bidder, but nobody named names. Other rumors claimed that this or that person could get you 150 sets at such and such a figure. We are unable to confirm any of these rumors, or to evaluate how much was based on sheer envy of those who were lucky enough to be ahead of others on waiting lines. Whatever the merits of the claims or the rumors, the coins have remained permanently in demand, and we know of no large hoards.

Collateral Evidence: No proofs have been confirmed to exist, though there are a small number of brilliant proof-like strikings from Philadelphia; these are rare and desirable.

No original holders for three-piece sets are known. One Dennison holder (uninscribed) has turned up for a Philadelphia single coin. Any such holders associated with Grant's Hobby Shop mailing envelopes dated March 5 or 6, 1936, would be of great interest, of course.

Counterfeits (casts) are reported, though we have not seen them; they would be detectable by the usual signs of bubbles or porosity.

The philatelic tie-in is a purple 3¢ stamp, Scott 777, Type A254, with an idealized portrait of Roger Williams and a drastically modified colonial seal with that same motto HOPE. This was released May 4, 1936, in the amount of 67,127,650. We illustrate the stamp and one of the 245,400 first day covers, the latter signed GRIMSLAND under the Newport Tower. Its design alludes not to Williams but to the Viking explorations of centuries before—explorations lately confirmed by the discovery of a medieval Norse coin in excavations in Maine.

THE ROANOKE ISLAND, NORTH CAROLINA, HALF DOLLAR

Obverse   *Reverse*

The Corpus Delicti: Alias *Roanoke, Sir Walter Ralegh, Virginia Dare–Sir Walter Raleigh,* etc.

Clues: Obverse portrays Errol Flynn posing as Sir Walter Ralegh. (The explorer's own spelling; the coin says RALEIGH because the Act of Congress authorizing the issue used that incorrect spelling, and the Commission of Fine Arts insisted that the same form be used on the coin as in the authorizing act!) Monogram WMS below truncation is that of William Marks Simpson, designer, sculptor.

The reverse depicts Eleanor Dare with the infant Virginia Dare in her arms. Behind her is a sapling of either mountain pine or some related evergreen; on either side is a small model of an old three-masted ship under full sail, said in the brochure accompanying the coins to be "similar to those in which the Colonists crossed the ocean."

Choice of all these devices reflects the event commemorated, though to deduce the connections would require a fair knowledge of local history. Ralegh (1552?–1618) held letters patent from Queen Elizabeth authorizing him to explore "remote heathen and barbarous lands." Accordingly, he outfitted two ships (evidently represented by the two on the reverse of the half dollar) to scout out possible

locales for settlements along the Atlantic coast of North America. Ralegh's people selected Roanoke Island partly because it was near to Spanish Florida, partly because the local Indians were friendly; Her Majesty named it Virginia. Slabaugh (p. 143) gives a capsule history of the ill-fated colony, as well as alluding to Virginia Dare's birth (August 18, 1587), "the first Christian born in Virginia."

Opportunity: Local Celebration at old Fort Raleigh on Roanoke Island, sponsored by a variety of civic groups and "historical associations," August 1937; Act of Congress, June 24, 1936.

Motive: Local pride, and to help finance the celebration.

Suspects: William Marks Simpson, of Baltimore.

Accessories: Unknown; possibly the Roanoke Colony Memorial Association.

Modus Operandi: As the authorizing act specified that the coins all bear date 1937 regardless of when they actually struck, this issue started out to be one of the postdated ones like the Delaware Swedish

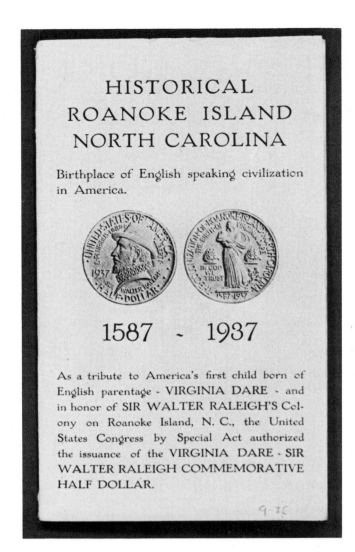

Original holder used to distribute the Roanoke Commemorative half dollar.

Tercentenary and the New Rochelle. Simpson completed the initial version of his models about September 25, 1936, differing from the coin as adopted in numerous details such as having the date 1936 on obverse, Ralegh's name in a straight line parallel to the straight truncation, and signature on reverse instead of the pine sapling. (Pictured in Taxay, p. 229.) The Federal Commission of Fine Arts approved the designs on September 30, with the stipulation that the final models be resubmitted. When this was done, the Commission balked at the spelling of Ralegh's name and remained as unwilling to yield on the point as a frontier judge, despite the artist's citing documentary evidence that "Raleigh" was the one spelling that Sir Walter never used, and that "Ralegh" was the only spelling that he consistently used from June 9, 1584, until his death in 1618. As

the Commission approved the models only subject to use of the spelling with the "i," Simpson inserted it, after which the models went to Medallic Art Co. of New York in mid-December 1936, for reduction, thence to the Philadelphia Mint. A total of 50,000 followed in two batches: 25,000 (plus 15 reserved for assay) in January 1937, and 25,000 more (with the same number of extras for assay) in June 1937. As the authorizing act gave a minimum figure of 25,000 but no maximum, more could have been made, subject to a July 1, 1937 deadline. However, sales languished even at $1.65 each, only 29,000 being sold in all, the remainder being returned to the mint for re-melting. Coins from the two batches cannot be distinguished by any known tests as yet.

Collateral Evidence: The Roanoke Colony Memorial Association marketed these coins in Eggers-type holders containing one to five pieces each, imprinted as in the illustration. About 55 of these holders are known today.

The majority of the Roanokes were sold to the general public. However, survivors are fairly common at present (1980) in choice (MS-63) to gem uncirculated (MS-65) condition because roll lots were put away in 1937. But even these are not all in gem state, since they will possess bad nicks or scratches.

Perhaps 50 proof-like presentation pieces were made; they have only ordinary sharpness. Real proofs would be sharper and rarer than these. Their satin finish somewhat resembles that on "Roman Gold" proofs of 1909–10—quite different from the occasional proof-like strikings—and as they were given at least two blows from the dies apiece, they have considerable extra sharpness of detail. The enlarged photograph of one of these satin finish proofs shows clearly how much more detail is present on them than on business strikings (such as at the head of this section). Note in particular the differing granular textures of face and coat, and the extra clarity of mustache and upper beard as well as of hair just before and behind the ear. On reverse, additional detail is visible at Eleanor Dare's hair, sleeve and cuff, point (the triangular area of the lower bodice, just below her cuff and hand) and the gathered area of draperies just below that.

A philatelic tie-in is provided by the gray-blue 5¢, Scott 796, Type A269, released August 18, 1937 (for the exact anniversary of Virginia Dare's birth). In all 25,040,400 of this Virginia Dare Issue were distributed.

There were some 226,730 first day covers, postmarked the same date, at Manteo, North Carolina.

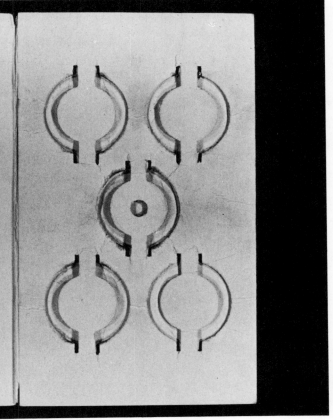

The First English Settlements in America:

ROANOKE ISLAND, N. C. --- 1585 - 1587
JAMESTOWN ISLAND, VA. --- 1607
PLYMOUTH ROCK, MASS. --- 1620

Here on the wooded bluffs of enchanting and picturesque Roanoke Island whose shores are washed by the waters of four beautiful inland sounds, English civilization in America had its birth and beginnings.

In 1937 three hundred and fifty years will have passed. In order that this truly great historical event may be fittingly commemorated, various historical associations and civic organizations have united and are planning one of the most outstanding educational, historical and religious celebrations ever staged. The celebration will be held at Old Fort Raleigh on Roanoke Island, the actual site of the first English settlement. where was born on August 18th, 1587, VIRGINIA DARE, the first child of English parentage to be born in our land.

On the obverse of the Commemorative Half-dollar is depicted a bust of Sir Walter Raleigh - the reverse shows a young mother holding her babe close to her breast, garbed in costumes similar to those that bedecked the first Roanoke Island settlers, also images of two old English sailing vessels similar to those in which the Colonists crossed the ocean.

Centerspread of the holder.

Obverse of one of the fifty presentation pieces.

Reverse of one of the fifty presentation pieces.

The Virginia Dare Issue—Scott 796, Type 269.

THE SESQUICENTENNIAL OF AMERICAN INDEPENDENCE ISSUES

Obverse

Reverse

The Corpus Delicti: Alias *Sesqui Half Dollar* and *Sesqui Quarter Eagle.*

Clues: On the half dollar, the busts are those of George Washington and Calvin Coolidge. Both were mistakes; Washington was not president of the Continental Congress in 1776, and Coolidge's portrait was illegal. By an 1866 Act of Congress, no living person could be portrayed on U.S. coins or currency; but this law had been many times violated and would be again. Washington was portrayed because he was the first president under the Constitution; Coolidge was pictured solely because he was the incumbent in 1926. The Liberty Bell and inscriptions are self-explanatory.

On the Quarter Eagle, the very Art Deco device appears to represent Ms. Liberty with liberty cap, holding the Declaration of Independence, and her torch may be intended to recall that held by the Statue of Liberty. The building on the reverse is Independence Hall, Philadelphia, with the rising sun behind it. Initials JRS are for John R. Sinnock.

Occasion: The Act of Congress of March 3, 1925, created a National Sesquicentennial Commission, and authorized mintage of commemorative half dollars and quarter eagles. (The Commission also sought approval by Congress for a $1.50 gold piece, but approval was not forthcoming, nor was authorization for a multiplicity of other commemorative coins contemplated by the Commission.)

Motive: Sales at the Sesquicentennial Exposition, held in Philadelphia from June 1 to November 30, 1926, presumably to help defray expenses.

Suspects: John R. Sinnock. Not only did this man create the quarter eagle design in such low relief that even gem specimens are hard to read under a magnifying glass (the photograph is of a matte proof and even it is unsatisfactory!), he also calmly appropriated full credit for John Frederick Lewis' design for the half dollar. The story was first revealed in Taxay, pp. 112, 115. Mint publications have continued attributing the coin to Sinnock for over fifty years.

Obverse   *Reverse*

Accessories: Asher C. Baker, Director in Chief, Sesquicentennial International Exposition Commission. He appears to have prescribed the devices to John Frederick Lewis, whose drawing of the half dollar design (in the National Archives) is reproduced by Taxay, p. 115.

Modus Operandi: The Commission of Fine Arts returned Sinnock's sketches of the quarter eagle as of March 25, 1926, recommending minor changes (deletion of the Latin motto from obverse and suggesting omission of the sun and rays from reverse); it approved Sinnock's revised sketches on April 29. There is no information about when it approved Lewis' designs for the half dollar, though the Federal Fine Arts Commission had them in hand as early as December 8, 1925. Later letters about them have unaccountably vanished. Another whitewash job? We wonder: was Lewis somehow *persona non grata* at the Mint?

During May and June 1926, the Philadelphia Mint struck the full authorized quantities of the half dollar and the quarter eagle, so that they would be ready for sale at the Exposition and especially ready for ceremonies to be held on July 4. Unfortunately, though this was one of the bigger Expositions (over 5,850,000 visitors), far fewer people spent $1 apiece on half dollar souvenirs or $4 apiece on the quarter eagles than the Commission had hoped for. The tabular results tell the story:

Authorized, half dollars:	Not over 1,000,000
Coined:	1,000,000 plus 528 reserved for assay
Returned for re-melting:	859,408
Net mintage, half dollars:	140,592
Authorized, quarter eagles:	Not over 200,000
Coined:	200,000 plus 226 reserved for assay
Returned for re-melting:	154,207
Net mintage, quarter eagles:	45,793

No original holders or literature reported.

The obverse and reverse of the excessively rare $2½ gold Sesquicentennial matte proof from the David M. Bullowa collection. It is strongly believed that John R. Sinnock, the U.S. Mint's chief engraver, had just two specimens of this coin produced.

Compare the facial features of the genuine issue (top) with those of the counterfeit illustrated below.

Collateral Evidence: The Liberty Bell device was used on the philatelic tie-in, Charles Aubrey Huston's carmine-rose 2¢ Liberty Bell stamp, Scott 627 (Type A188). First released May 10, 1926, this was issued in enormous quantities, some 307,731,900 in all reaching the public. In only one minor sense can the coin design be preferred: one can, though with extreme difficulty, make out part of the inscription

Can you tell which of the blow-ups of the reverse detail on a Sesquicentennial $2\frac{1}{2}$ is the counterfeit and which is the real thing?

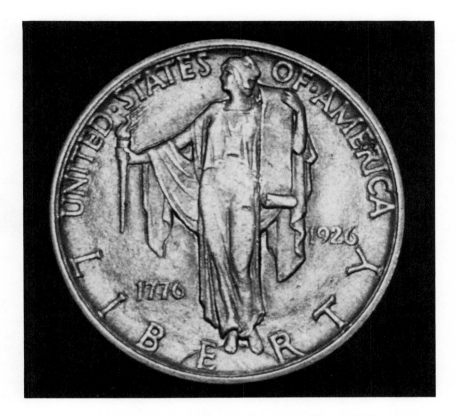

Here are the obverse and reverse of a recently discovered sharply struck counterfeit. However, on closer examination its surfaces give it away—they are quite abnormal.

on the Liberty Bell. The complete inscription reads PROCLAIM LIBERTY (THROUGHOUT ALL THE LAND UNTO THE INHABITANTS THER)EOF LEV XXV X/BY ORDER OF THE AS(SEMBLY OF THE PROVINCE OF PENNSYLVANIA FOR THE STATE H)OUSE IN PHILADA./PASS AND STOW/ PHILADA/MDCLIII. Parenthesized letters cannot be seen owing to the position of the bell, as the inscription encircles it. Lewis' reverse design was resurrected in 1948 by John R. Sinnock, still without any attempt to credit its source, for the reverse of the Franklin half dollar, though here the inscription is clearer than it was on the Sesquicentennial coin, and the inscriptions were modified for normal coinage. We can be sure that Lewis' design was the prototype, not the stamp, because of the layout and the part of the framework chosen.

Survivors among the half dollars, as with many earlier issues, seldom qualify as choice. Many are bag marked; others were nicked, scratched or poorly cleaned, or otherwise mishandled by their non-numismatic owners. Specimens often come showing frank wear, either spent or kept as pocket pieces. Even uncirculated survivors often show porosity on cheek, and most of the inscription on the Liberty Bell is too weak to be read even with a 20x glass. Specimens in gem mint state with fully legible inscription are rare and seldom offered.

Matte proofs are known of the half dollars: (1) Ex King Farouk, Edwin Hydeman (lot 695 of the Hydeman sale, 1961), R.E. Cox (lot 2124, 1962 N.Y. Metropolitan sale). (2) Ex J.R. Sinnock estate. (3) Reliably reported in 1964 by Russell Nering; was it a reappearance of the Sinnock coin? A fourth is rumored to exist. Beware ordinary uncirculated pieces sandblasted or pickled to simulate the rare matte proofs. This writer (W.B.) examined the Farouk-Hydeman-Cox coin and found that, as expected on genuine matte proofs, it has much sharper details in hair, on the elmwood yoke holding the bell and on the bell itself, than do any regular production coins.

Matte proofs are known of the quarter eagle: (1) David M. Bullowa, 1952, possibly from Ira Reed, who had a number of VIP coins from his connections at the Philadelphia Mint. This is the piece illustrated here. (2) Ex J.R. Sinnock estate.

Separate obverse and reverse die trials of the half dollar in copper have been seen; on these the designs are much stronger than on production coins. As with earlier base metal strikings, we have made no attempt to record locations lest the coins be seized.

"The Liberty Bell Stamp"—Scott 627, A188.

Separate obverse and reverse die trials of the quarter eagle are known in copper and brass. The same comments hold in entirety as for the half dollar trial pieces. They may all have come from the Sinnock estate or from Ira Reed, but the whole truth is unlikely to be known until the Treasury has ruled that any coin struck by the mints of the United States may be legally held by private citizens regardless of its irregular nature in design, alloy, inscription, weight or fabric.

On the other hand, we are not advocating that collectors become complacent about counterfeits. Two different counterfeit issues attempt to imitate the Sesquicentennial quarter eagle. The first of these is represented by the illustrations showing the upper part of Ms. Liberty and center of the building. The genuine coin is on top for both obverse and reverse. Note that on the counterfeit the facial features are cruder, letters thicker and surfaces are quite abnormal; details of Independence Hall are much sketchier even than on the genuine.

In particular, on reverse notice that no attempt is made to show internal details in any windows, lintel on door or detail in ridge atop roof.

The other counterfeit is, if anything, sharper than the genuine, but the surfaces are quite abnormal. As it was made from molds using a genuine prototype, the minor bag marks will be identical in position from one specimen to another, and the peculiar surface within and above letters is diagnostic. In case of doubt, send the coin to ANACS, 818 N. Cascade Avenue, Colorado Springs, Colorado 80903 for an authoritative opinion.

THE STONE MOUNTAIN HALF DOLLAR

Obverse

Reverse

The Corpus Delicti: Alias *Stone Mountain.*

Clues: The equestrian figures resembling Marx and Freud (the latter in hat) represent respectively General Thomas J. "Stonewall" Jackson and General Robert E. Lee. The thirteen stars around and above them allude to the 13 seceding Southern states. STONE MOUNTAIN is the name of a mountain in northwest Georgia, on which Gutzon Borglum (whose initials GB appear near the horse's tail at extreme right) had been commissioned to carve a gigantic monument, 165 feet high. The date 1925 was the legal date of issue, alluding also to the year of the 101st birthday of "Stonewall" Jackson. On reverse, the inscription MEMORIAL TO THE VALOR OF THE SOLDIER OF THE SOUTH alludes only to the Confederate troops. Scattered in the background are 35 stars: the number was originally supposed to be 34, representing the number of Union states immediately before secession. (Did someone decide to include West Virginia? This would have forced reinterpretation of the 35 stars as Union and Confederate states together as of the end of the Civil War.)

Opportunity: Originally the bill to authorize coinage specified only commemoration of "the commencement on June 18, 1923, of the work of the carving on Stone Mountain, in the State of Georgia, a monument to the valor of the Soldiers of the South, which was the inspiration of their sons and daughters and grandsons and granddaughters in the Spanish-American and World Wars." Many Northern congressmen opposed spending federal funds for coinage of anything commemorating leaders in the Southern Rebellion, and there was pressure to send the bill back to committee. Finally the text was altered, adding "and in memory of Warren G. Harding, President of the United States of America in whose administration the work was begun." In this form the revised bill became the Act of March 17, 1924; Harding's death in office was probably the only reason it managed to become law.

Motive: Fund-raising for the Stone Mountain Monumental Association. Borglum's work (not completed until 1970) was to be the South's counterpart to Mount Rushmore; it was originally planned and the commission given in 1916, but work was interrupted by World War I. His original concept is partly represented by the obverse design on the 1924 Children's Founders Roll medal, illustrated in Slabaugh, on which Jefferson Davis follows Jackson and Lee. (Davis' figure was omitted on the coins, as everyone knew that it would not be acceptable to the federal government.) There was also to be a procession of Confederate soldiers, the whole composition extending thousands of feet on the sheer northeast mountainside. Borglum and his assistants began the actual carving in June 1923, as the authorizing bill had mentioned; the head of General Lee was unveiled on January 19, 1924, Lee's 117 birthday. During the celebration 19 of the VIPs ate lunch at a table on Lee's shoulder, and people compared the project to the heroic monuments in ancient Egypt.

Despite this auspicious beginning, the project ran into difficulties at once, largely financial. The Stone Mountain Confederate Monumental Association demanded that in addition to his work on the mountainside, Borglum also design the coins. His first model was perfunctory, showing faint shadowy impressions of the Confederate soldiers in the background; the lettering would have been microscopic when the coin models were reduced to half dollar size; and the head and neck of Jeff Davis' horse obtrude, partly concealing Lee's upper leg and lower trunk, giving the impression of anatomical error. Overall, the design gave the effect of a vignette cut off from a much longer composition (which of course it was), but it was ill-adapted to the circular format of a coin. On the reverse, the necessary inscriptions alluding to Stone Mountain itself, the Confederate soldiers and IN MEMORY OF WARREN G. HARDING 1924, made an impossibly crowded composition. Predictably, when the Mint forwarded prints of these models to the Federal Fine Arts Commission, July 14, 1924, its sculptor member James Earle Fraser rejected them. Borglum revised his models and the prints went to Fraser on August 12, only to be rejected again. Borglum characterized the Commission's critique as "damn fool suggestions," and left off work on the coins to resume carving the mountain. He revised the coin models in September, only after the Association had threatened to fire him. President Coolidge disapproved of any reference to Warren G. Harding on the coins, and with the removal of this wording Borglum could produce a less encumbered design. This was approved as "barely passable" by the Federal Commission of Fine Arts as of October 10. But so much time had been wasted with the coin models that the Monumental Association felt Borglum had neglected his work on the mountainside. They quarreled with him and eventually fired him on February 26, 1925, specifically ordering him to leave his models and plans intact for the Association's further use. Borglum destroyed them in a rage, claiming that they were his property (the Children's Founders Roll Medal representing his original design does bear a copyright

notice in Borglum's name). As a result, the Association had him arrested, but he was released, and the episode made good newspaper copy for some months in 1925. Borglum washed his hands of the South and went on to carve Mount Rushmore; but in the meantime the Association had to hire Augustus Lukeman to complete Borglum's work. Lukeman had parts of the completed carving blasted away and began afresh—only to be forced to a stop by lack of funds: the fund raising effort begun with the coins had been adversely affected by the bad publicity over Borglum's departure. In 1930, the Great Depression made further work impossible, and not until 1963 was the project resumed, this time with funds from the State of Georgia. Walter Kirkland Hancock completed the carving, and the monument was dedicated on May 9, 1970. Its finished form is well represented by Robert Hallock's 6¢ commemorative stamp, released September 19, 1970 (Scott 1408, Type A822). Some 130,000,000 of these were printed.

Suspects: Gutzon Borglum.

Accessories: The Stone Mountain Confederate Monumental Association; James Earle Fraser, whose revisions had to be accepted by Borglum; President Calvin Coolidge, who insisted that the reference to Warren G. Harding had to go, despite the text of the authorizing act.

Modus Operandi: Medallic Art Co. of New York reduced Borglum's models. The Philadelphia Mint began striking coins on January 21, 1925, this date being chosen as it was "Stonewall" Jackson's birthday.

The first piece went to President Coolidge, mounted on a gold plate; others went to various VIPs. The documented 29th specimen sold for a reported $1,300 as early as 1937; what happened to the rest of that first group is unknown, but some may have been among the pieces publicly shown in May 1925, long before the official release date (July 3, 1925). Bulk strikings continued at Philadelphia through March, some 2,310,000 (out of the authorized total of 5,000,000) actually being released to the Association; the extra 4,709 mentioned in the mint report were reserved for assay.

For an issue of such unprecedented size, unprecedented publicity and promotion were essential. The Association hired the New York publicist Harvey Hill as mastermind for the campaign. One of his first projects was to induce industries to buy quantities for good will, and accordingly the Baltimore & Ohio Railroad, the Coca-Cola Bottling Company of

One of the versions of the original holders used to distribute the Stone Mountain Commemorative half dollar.

Atlanta, the Southern Fireman's Fund Insurance Co. and many southern banks, bought thousands and tens of thousands of the coins at issue price ($1 apiece), giving them away as souvenirs or premiums, or later simply spending them.

Some of the coins were distributed in special boxes similar to those more familiarly seen on the Lexington-Concord coins. Only one of these original holders has been located (see illustration, above).

Many of the coins were counterstamped with numerals and state names in abbreviation. Only in recent years has even part of the story behind these enigmatic items come to light. The summary here is derived in part from accounts by Dr. Charles R. Stearns, of Lilburn, Georgia, an expert in this area.

Part of Harvey Hill's distribution project materialized as The Great Harvest Campaign. The Governors of Virginia, South Carolina, Georgia, Florida, Alabama, Mississippi, Louisiana, Texas, Oklahoma (!), Arkansas, Kentucky and Tennessee served as campaign chairmen; North Carolina joined the program later on. Each governor assumed a sales quota based on population and bank deposits. For publicity, some of the half dollars were counterstamped to produce unique items for auction. Lettering styles indicate that nearly all the counterstamped coins were from a single source, probably the Stone Mountain Confederate Monumental Association itself; identical numeral and letter punches recur on coins with different state names.

Most of the counterstamped pieces have a serial number and the abbreviation of a state name. Within a given state the numbers will normally range from very low to well into the hundreds. Rarely are numbers duplicated, probably by accident (two each are known of TENN. 102, OKLA. 358 and VA. 202). When the counterstamped pieces appeared at public auction in 1925–6, they brought prices from $10 to well into three figures, and reportedly higher, raising funds on their own and stimulating interest in the normal coins. A letter dated December 10, 1925, from J. Wilson Gibbs, Jr., Executive Secretary in Charge of South Carolina Auction Coins, addressed to Mrs. R.E. Shannon of Blastock, South Carolina (her coin was numbered S.C. 109), explained that in South Carolina the auction prices ranged from $10 to $110, averaging $23 apiece, and recommended that before any one coin was offered, a brief speech should be made, specially mentioning that a similar coin had brought $1,300 in Bradenton, Florida!

One specimen has been seen with number 42 and no state name, but the numerals are of the same type as on the regularly seen ones; this piece turned up in Florida a few years ago, and is thought to have been a regular FLA. coin from which the state stamp was accidentally omitted. (On the other hand, appearance of others like it might require us to postulate a different stateless series.)

Close examination of specimens counterstamped TEXAS 182 and TEXAS 242 showed that the letters EXA were positioned so as to conceal overpunching over FLA. This suggests either an error corrected by the Association people doing the counterstamping, or possibly that the Florida campaign had failed to move the coins, which were then restamped for offering in Texas.

Another series of counterstamps includes state name and number with letters S.L. The explanation is unknown; a State Legislature series has been conjectured where these coins were perhaps presented to legislators to urge their support of The Great Harvest Campaign. A Florida piece of this series has G.L. instead of S.L.: an error? Unfortunately, no coin of

Another method used to distribute the Stone Mountain Commemorative. The enclosed coin was sold in 1928.

this series has as yet been traced back to its original recipient; this would be the method of choice for interpreting the initials.

A third series is found only on Tennessee coins: these have the extra letters u.d.c. for United Daughters of the Confederacy, and the serial numbers are "very high"—member or chapter numbers, perhaps?

A fourth series, of evidently different origin, has no state names; the countermarks are heavy, consisting of letter N and a number, the N with serifs. Only three specimens are located to date; N–6, from the estate of a Nashville bank employee in 1925, proves that the others in this series (with the identical letter punch) are of the same period. Slabaugh mentions N–2 and N–3; we have not examined these.

As the history of the early countermarked specimens has become better known in the last few years, specimens have begun changing hands at very high prices. Collectors are therefore warned that anyone with access to letter punches could manufacture others, in imitation of the known series, or purporting to be a still different series. Under no circumstances accept any counterstamped Stone Mountain unless it is documented.

At some unknown date, the United Daughters of the Confederacy offered quantities of Stone Mountain coins (not counterstamped) in holders of the type illustrated on the preceding page. We do not know the significance of their reference to Bernard Baruch; frankly, we were never aware that he had anything to do with coin collecting, let alone with either the Stone Mountain promotion or the United Daughters of the Confederacy. Nor have we been able to learn the year(s) of issue of these holders. The only Citizens and Southern National Bank in Georgia prior to 1935 had its headquarters in Savannah; its charter number (13068) proves that it came into existence in 1927, according to Treasury records cited by Louis van Belkum and other paper currency specialists. It is entirely possible that this bank had branches in other cities. From the appearance of the single holder known to us, there was originally a cellophane envelope stapled to the card, but this must have dried out and split, so that a modern plastic slip had to be substituted.

Promotions or no promotions, the Stone Mountain Confederate Monumental Association was unable to move even two million coins. Eventually the group had to face reality, and accordingly one million unsold half dollars went back to the mint for remelting. Many of those that had been sold went into circulation, producing the following tabular result:

Authorized:	5,000,000
Coined:	2,310,000 plus 4,709 reserved for assay
Melted:	1,000,000
Net mintage:	1,310,000

Collateral Evidence: A single matte proof has been reported, but to date it has not become available for examination.

Rare specimens show evidence of having been manufactured from doubled dies. Alan Herbert has provided a photograph of one of these, in which the doubling is plainest at date. Not to oversimplify too much, the way this occurred is similar to the cause of the very famous 1955 doubled die cent. Since World War I, to sink the devices, letters and numerals into a working die a working hub had to be placed into a press opposite the die blank, and from two to four impressions made, depending on the size of the die. But between any two impressions into a die blank from the hub, the die blank has to be annealed, as the process produces marked stress hardening. After annealing, it is replaced into the press. Occasionally a die blank goes to a different press, or it is replaced in the original press but aligned with a minute difference; in either event the result is extra outlines which show on all impressions from the working die. Dies which suffer this fate are often condemned so that specimens struck from them are scarce or rare. The Stone Mountain with doubled obverse die is no exception.

Stone Mountain Commemorative struck from doubled dies.

THE TEXAS CENTENNIAL HALF DOLLARS

Obverse

Reverse

The Corpus Delicti: Alias *Texas.*

Clues: Only because of some of the Federal Fine Arts Commission's correspondence do we even know which side of this incredibly crowded design was meant to be the obverse (it turned out to be that with the eagle, contrary to the usual practice in U.S. coins). This eagle is superimposed on the Lone Star, in reference to Texas as the Lone Star State. The oak branch with enormous acorns in his claws was a laurel branch in the original models. No reason for the change has been forthcoming. (If they wished a tree representing Texas, the economically worthless but extremely common mesquite would have been more appropriate.) The six stars flanking HALF DOLLAR probably allude to the six flags which have at various times flown over Texas (the flags themselves form part of the confusion on reverse). We are unable even to guess why the hyphens are in UNITED–STATES–OF–AMERICA.

As for the reverse, the problem is to know where to begin in making sense out of this jumble. Miss Winged Victory of 1934 holds an olive branch in her right hand while her left rests on a miniature replica of the Alamo, the historic burnt-out church in Alamo Plaza, San Antonio, which figured so largely in the Revolution of 1835–36. (It was fortified, occupied by revolutionaries in December 1835 and besieged by the Mexican army under General Santa Ana on February 24–March 6, 1836. There, 187 defenders, including Jim Bowie and Davy Crockett, died in combat. REMEMBER THE ALAMO (at bottom) became a battle cry when General Sam Houston routed Santa Ana at San Jacinto on April 21, spelling victory and independence for the Republic of Texas.) Above Miss Victory's wings are the six flags which have flown over Texas: those of Spain, France, Mexico, the Republic, the United States and the Confederacy. Their folds show, though not enough details of devices to enable any one flag to be identified. Behind and below the flags are clouds; within the clouds, below wings, are two medallions representing General Sam Houston (at observer's left) and Stephen F. Austin, with their microscopic names. Below the model of the Alamo are the centennial dates. As the Mint Act of April 1792 still requires the word LIBERTY to appear on all U.S. coins, this word is placed on a scroll partly obscuring the flags. There is even room for the mintmark D (for Denver) or S (for San Francisco)

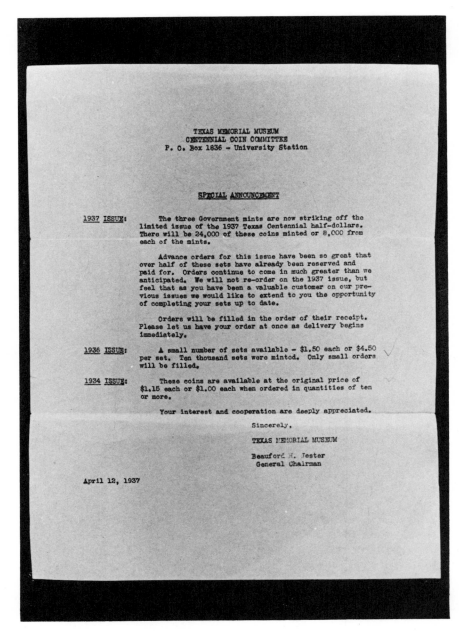

TEXAS MEMORIAL MUSEUM
CENTENNIAL COIN COMMITTEE
P. O. Box 1836 - University Station

SPECIAL ANNOUNCEMENT

1937 ISSUE: The three Government mints are now striking off the
limited issue of the 1937 Texas Centennial half-dollars.
There will be 24,000 of these coins minted or 8,000 from
each of the mints.

Advance orders for this issue have been so great that
over half of these sets have already been reserved and
paid for. Orders continue to come in much greater than we
anticipated. We will not re-order on the 1937 issue, but
feel that as you have been a valuable customer on our previous issues we would like to extend to you the opportunity
of completing your sets up to date.

Orders will be filled in the order of their receipt.
Please let us have your order at once as delivery begins
immediately.

1936 ISSUE: A small number of sets available - $1.50 each or $4.50
per set. Ten thousand sets were minted. Only small orders
will be filled.

1934 ISSUE: These coins are available at the original price of
$1.15 each or $1.00 each when ordered in quantities of ten
or more.

Your interest and cooperation are deeply appreciated.

Sincerely,

TEXAS MEMORIAL MUSEUM

Beauford H. Jester
General Chairman

April 12, 1937

The Committee sent a form letter, order blank, and envelope to future subscribers to inform them that the 1937 Texas set would soon be available.

below Miss Victory's drapery and just above T of THE; there is also room for the designer's initials PC (Pompeo Coppini) at right of the Alamo.

As a monumental relief, perhaps 30 feet in diameter, meant to be viewed from hundreds of feet away, this design might be impressive to people to whom the heroic history of Texas and the Old West still means anything. On a coin, it is impossibly confusing, and the way many of these half dollars were struck, it is often indistinct or even illegible.

Opportunity: The American Legion Texas Centennial Committee planned a Texas-sized Centennial Exposition for 1936, correctly anticipating millions of visitors. (It occupied 186 acres in Dallas, cost $25,000,000, and attracted some 7,000,000 visitors.) For anything this size, advance funding was essential, and one obvious answer was commemorative coinage, preferably on a large scale, after the manner of the Oregon issue, which had already come out in several different date varieties and was expected to

ORDER FOR TEXAS CENTENNIAL COINS

C 1

THE TEXAS MEMORIAL MUSEUM
CENTENNIAL COIN COMMITTEE
AUSTIN, TEXAS

Date_____193____

Please enter my order for the following Texas Centennial Half Dollars:

Number Wanted	Mint	Year	Cost	Total
_____	Philadelphia	1934	$1.15	$_____
_____	San Francisco	1936	1.50	$_____
_____	Denver	1936	1.50	$_____
_____	Philadelphia	1936	1.50	$_____
_____	San Francisco	1937	1.50	$_____
_____	Denver	1937	1.50	$_____
_____	Philadelphia	1937	1.50	$_____

Total - - - $_____

Remittance Record

Amount Enclosed $_____

P. O. Order ☐   Check ☐

Money Order ☐

Name_____

Address (Street)_____

City_____ County_____ State_____

Order blank.

Texas Memorial Museum
Box 1836 University Station
Austin, Texas

Contents - Merchandise
Postmaster: This parcel may
be opened for postal inspection if necessary.
Return Postage Guaranteed

INSURED

No. U2-1536

Mr. E. D. King
37 Bull Street
Savannah, Georgia

Envelope.

The reverse of many Texas Commemorative half dollars were quite weakly struck. Note the Winged Victory's fingers, her rather flattened breasts, and the flowers she holds in her hand on this example.

A normal striking with better definition.

appear in many more. The Legion Committee's friend in Congress, Rep. William Doddridge McFarlane (D.-Texas), pushed and talked and promised and compromised until the bill was voted into law, becoming the Act of June 15, 1933. For the benefit of officialdom, Rep. McFarlane said that any profits accruing from sale of the coins would go towards constructing a memorial building.

Motive: Preliminary fund raising for the Exposition.

Suspects: Pompeo Coppini, sculptor; the American Legion Texas Centennial Committee. The Committee approved Coppini's preliminary models in May 1934 (quite probably they had specified the design elements). Coppini and Congressman McFarlane took them to the Federal Commission of Fine Arts, which disapproved them. Coppini was a competent designer of portrait statues and monuments, though his compositions tended to be as elaborate as many being made in Italy at the same time. However, between his unfamiliarity with the technical requirements of coin design and the apparent necessity of including so many elements in the composition, rejection was inevitable. The original models are pictured in Taxay, p. 134. One feature that came in for special criticism was the "vulture-like" eagle; nobody seems to have noticed (except probably Coppini himself) that it alludes to the Mexican national emblem and thus would have represented Texas' old Mexican heritage. For all that, it still must have struck many people as sneaky and undignified.

Accessories: Congressman W.J.D. McFarlane; Lee Lawrie. The Congressman put pressure on the Fine Arts Commission to approve the designs in improved form, but with all their multiple elements intact. Lee Lawrie is to be credited with insisting that the eagle be redrawn, and making specific recommendations as to layout; he was in close touch with Coppini, and the finished design would not have met with Commission approval without his work. Comparing the coin as issued with the original models will be very instructive on this point!

Modus Operandi: The Fine Arts Commission approved Coppini's revised models on June 25, the Treasury following suit a few days later, after which the models went to the Medallic Art Company of New York for reduction to half dollar size. The Philadelphia Mint struck the first batches in October and November 1934, and the coins went on sale at $1 apiece through the American Legion Texas Centennial Committee.

Sales lagged during summer and fall 1935, but the Mint would not strike any more until the 1934 issue was completely disposed of. And so the Committee returned some 143,650 for re-melting, after which the 10,000 1935-dated sets were struck in November. Most of them sold, only a dozen of the Philadelphia coins being returned. Thereafter only three-piece sets were made, and sales continued to lag, as the following tabulation shows:

Authorized:	Not over 1,500,000
Coined, total:	304,000
Remelted, total:	154,522
Net mintage, total:	149,478

After the Centennial Exposition closed its gates in 1937, the American Legion Texas Centennial Committee (having no further excuse for existing) turned over its white . . . er, silver . . . elephants to a group calling itself the Texas Memorial Museum Centennial Coin Committee (Beauford H. Jester, General Chairman). This operated out of a post office box in Austin, Texas, as the Museum was to be built there; eventually it was, as it remains on the campus of the University of Texas in Austin, where the phallic tower is lit for every football game and lit red for every Texas victory. There are form letters and announcements from the Committee indicating that the 1937 issue was momentarily expected from the mints, and that some of the 1934 coins and 1936 sets were still available at what were supposedly the original issue prices. We are unable to reconcile Mr. Jester's "original price of $1.15 each" for the 1934 coins with their announced (1934–35) cost of $1 apiece. We doubt that the Committee either knew or cared that most of the coins were going to "damyankee" speculators.

Collateral Evidence: About 60 percent, possibly more, of all dates and mints of the Texas issue come weakly struck in centers, the parts most affected being Miss Victory's breasts (which then look unequally flat), hand, parts of branch and drapery at thigh and knee. Collectors unfamiliar with this problem are apt to reject these coins as less than full mint state. The illustrations show plainly where the local weaknesses are found (they are directly opposite the eagle's breast, a detail of maximal relief on this coin). As many of the 1934 issue went to the general public, they have been recovered in recent years in less than full mint state, though they are apt to show nicks and scratches, or poor cleaning, or both, rather than ordinary circulation. Naturally, most will be offered sooner or later as mint state, but in view of this peculiarity of striking, collectors are urged to check the surfaces. A true mint state coin will have much the same kind of mint frost on the weakly struck areas as elsewhere, and there will be no signs of scrubbing, even under a strong glass.

Hoards are known. An original mint-sealed sack of the 1934 issue survives in Texas.

Individual coins in small lots of the 1934 issue were shipped in unprinted Dennison holders like that pictured for the Maryland. These in general are of no importance as it would be fairly simple to locate that type of holder and insert the coins. However, any original envelopes or accompanying literature would definitely increase historical interest and value.

Specimens of the 1935 D are known from brilliantly polished dies—proof-like presentation strikings. (That illustrated at the head of this chapter is one of these.) The entire field of the eagle side is mirror-like; smaller peripheral areas of the other side (mostly around and near inscription) likewise, but much less so. These coins are sharply enough struck so that all fingers of the branch hand are visible. They are very rare, and two have been located in gold foil presentation boxes of issue, each with a slot for the one coin. Another silver foil case housed a 1935 set. This set, like one of the gold foil cases, bore the inscription "Compliments of E.H.R. Green." (Col. Green was the son of Hetty Green, the "Witch of Wall Street," and best known for his vast collections of coins, pornography and railroad cars.)

The Texas Centennial or "Alamo" issue—Scott 776, Type A253.

No holders have been located for the later three-piece sets; in all likelihood the Committee continued to use those highly expendable, unprinted Dennison holders.

An interesting philatelic tie-in, probably inspired by the coin, is Alvin R. Meissner's Texas Centennial or "Alamo" 3¢ purple, Scott 776, Type A253. This shows the inevitable motifs of the Alamo and General Houston and Stephen F. Austin with the Lone Star between them; we suspect that the coin design of 1934 was in Meissner's mind when he created this one, because (among other things) Houston's and Austin's portraits are on vignettes labeled with their names, full face. Beginning March 2, 1936, these stamps were issued in Texas-size quantity, in all some 124,324,500 being distributed.

DATE	MINT	STRUCK	RESERVED FOR ASSAY	RE-MELTED	NET MINTAGE	SALE PRICE
1934	(P)	205,000	113	143,650	61,350	$1.00
1935	(P)	10,000	8	12	9,988	1.50
1935	D	10,000	7	—	10,000	1.50
1935	S	10,000	8	—	10,000	1.50
1936	(P)	10,000	8	1,097	8,903	1.50
1936	D	10,000	7	968	9,032	1.50
1936	S	10,000	8	943	9,057	1.50
1937	(P)	8,000	5	1,434	6,566	1.50
1937	D	8,000	6	1,401	6,599	1.50
1937	S	8,000	7	1,370	6,630	1.50
1938	(P)	5,000	5	1,225	3,775	2.00
1938	D	5,000	5	1,230	3,770	2.00
1938	S	5,000	6	1,192	3,808	2.00

THE FORT VANCOUVER CENTENNIAL HALF DOLLAR

Obverse

Reverse

The Corpus Delicti: Alias *The Vancouver.*

Clues: Dr. John McLoughlin (1784–1857), whose bust dominates the obverse, was a Canadian who gave up medical practice for the fur trade, becoming in 1821 one of the negotiators in the merger of Hudson's Bay Company and the North West Company; he built not only Ft. Vancouver (now Vancouver, Washington) but Oregon City, and from 1824 to 1846 he was the Hudson's Bay Company's top man in the Oregon Territory, during the entire period of U.S./British dispute over ownership of the land. George Pipes (*The Numismatist,* October 1925, p. 543) has characterized him as "an absolute monarch, a benevolent despot, Haroun al-Rashid reincarnated . . . over about 1,000 white men (mostly trappers and traders working with Hudson's Bay Company) and possibly 100,000 Indians." Ft. Vancouver was the only effective seat of government in the entire territory, which made up most of what are the present states of Oregon and Washington; and Dr. McLoughlin was perhaps the main reason why there were no wars between the whites and the Indians.

The reverse inscription is to be read in this order: FORT VANCOUVER CENTENNIAL; VANCOUVER, WASHINGTON, FOUNDED 1825 BY HUDSON'S BAY COMPANY. That will explain in part the device of a frontiersman, dressed in skins, musket at the ready, defending the stockaded settlement. In the background is Mt. Hood, one of the area's most famous landmarks; between it and the fort is the Columbia River. The initials LGF are those of Laura Gardin Fraser, illustrious sculptor whose work we encountered earlier on the Grant coins. Ft. Vancouver (like Vancouver Island, and Vancouver City in Canada) is named for George Vancouver (1758?–98), who had sailed with Capt. Cook in the 1770s (see Hawaii Sesquicentennial), but who is better remembered for commanding the British exploration of the northwestern Pacific Coast in the 1790s.

Mintmark s for San Francisco was unaccountably omitted.

Opportunity: The Ft. Vancouver Centennial Corporation, preparing for local celebration, had Rep. Albert Johnson (R.-Wash.) attempt to push a bill through Congress to authorize a commemorative coin. Rep. Vestal of the House Coinage Committee persuaded him to accept a commemorative medal instead; but when Vestal reported out the bill for the Vermont coins (see p. 245), February 16, 1925, Rep. Raker (D.-Cal.) offered an amendment to authorize the California Jubilee issue (see p. 35), and Johnson moved to add his Vancouver coinage. The amended bill passed, much to Rep. Vestal's chagrin, becoming the Act of February 24, 1925.

Motives: Fund raising for the local celebration.

Suspects: Unidentified local sculptor known only by initials S.B., who in May 1925 furnished the original rejected plaster models (Taxay, p. 108) on behalf of the Centennial Corporation; Laura Gardin Fraser.

Accessories: Unknown. Devices were apparently prescribed by the Corporation. Mrs. Fraser took the liberty of showing Dr. McLoughlin at a later age, though she expressed doubt as to the likeness. (That on the 1948 Oregon Territory stamp (see p. 188) is still more apocryphal.) She also took the greater liberty of adding the frontiersman. The Federal Fine Arts Commission had originally recommended Chester Beach for the work, but as he was out of town, they named Mrs. Fraser—a happy circumstance, as her design was better than anything Beach could have come up with. She obtained the commission on June 15, and completed the accepted models before July 1.

Modus Operandi: The authorizing act specified not over 300,000 pieces. The San Francisco Mint received the dies from Philadelphia in July, and on August 1 it completed the first batch of 50,000 coins, plus 28 reserved for assay. On the same day, the consignment went by plane to Vancouver; Lt. Oakley G. Kelly, flight commander of the Vancouver Barracks, made the round trip from Vancouver to San Francisco in the one day, returning with 1,462 pounds of cargo from the mint, of which some 1,378 pounds must have been half dollars, the rest packing. (*The Numismatist*, September 1925, pp. 444–445.) The Centennial Corporation began selling the coins at $1 apiece through August and September; their Exposition opened August 17 and lasted one week. (*The Numismatist*, October 1925, p. 543.) Several hundred pieces were gilt at the time, ruining any future numismatic value; many others were mishandled, kept as pocket pieces, or spent. Considering the remoteness and exclusively local nature of

the celebration, it is surprising that as many as fourteen thousand coins were sold. In tabular form:

Authorized:	Not over 300,000
Coined:	50,000 + 28 assay pieces
Returned for melting	
as unsold:	35,034
Net mintage:	14,966

Survivors are extremely difficult to locate in choice mint state; one of us (A.S.) estimates that fewer than 300 survive, the remaining thousands being barely mint state or sliders or worse, many poorly cleaned. Dr. McLoughlin's hair and shoulder, and the frontiersman's right knee, should show mint frost to qualify as fully uncirculated.

Collateral Evidence: One matte proof has been seen (by W.B.), two others reported, one of these said to have been from the J.R. Sinnock estate. Aside from the matte surface, the proof has much more detail sharpness than even on the coin pictured above, particularly on Dr. McLoughlin's hair, frontiersman's garment, and the piles of the stockade, because of the extra blows from the dies required to bring up these details for making proofs. There are, however, several others which were given matte surfaces by private parties long after striking; as these were fabricated from ordinary business strikes, they do not have the extra sharpness of details, and should not be deceptive.

There were no original holders or literature.

There has been dispute over whether omission of the s mint mark was intentional or accidental. At this period it would doubtless have been accidental, and may have been a feature of the single pair of dies. (Its logical position would have been near one of the frontiersman's feet.) We need not postulate that more than one pair of dies was used for the first (and, as it proved, only) batch of Vancouver half dollars. Mint marks have normally been placed on working dies at the time of their completion by the Philadelphia mint, before shipment to the branch mints; this procedure has been standard since the first branch mints began operation in 1838, and it remains standard today even though the Philadelphia mint is no longer the largest coining facility.

Accidental omission of mint marks is nothing new. The first time it came to official attention was in 1870, when the gold dollar and $3 dies reached the San Francisco branch without the s, and some 2,000 gold dollars coined from them had to be melted. The Coiner, J.B. Harmstead, later cut an s onto the three-dollar die, and struck at least two pieces from it, one of which went into the cornerstone of the new mint building on Fifth and Mint Streets (between Mission and Market), where it remains; the other coin was looped, went onto his watch fob, and is today in the Smithsonian Institution as part of the Louis Eliasberg estate exhibit. More recently, proof sets made at San Francisco have occasionally shown up with one coin lacking the s—the dime in 1968 and 1970, the nickel in 1971, and reportedly others. However, the Ft. Vancouver commemorative half dollar is the only coin whose entire issue came from a branch mint without a mint mark.

THE VERMONT OR BATTLE OF BENNINGTON SESQUICENTENNIAL HALF DOLLAR

Obverse

Reverse

The Corpus Delicti: Alias *Vermont.*

Clues: The periwigged idealized bust of Ira Allen (1751–1814), labeled FOUNDER OF VERMONT, alludes to the man who took a dominant role in the Provincial Conventions of 1775–77 leading to the Vermonters' declaring the area an independent Republic in 1778. Originally, Ira Allen's aim was not so much to rid the area of British redcoats as to rid it of land grabbers from New York. When Benning Wentworth (royal governor of New Hampshire from 1741 to 1775) originally came into office, the Green Mountain lands were in dispute. Wentworth decreed that the boundary between New Hampshire and New York lay along a north-south line 20 miles east of the Hudson River, and at once began—to his own profit—making extensive land grants in the area, these grants including most of what is now the State of Vermont (they were then known as New Hampshire Grants). New York's own charter of 1664 was vague about its eastern boundary, and successive governors claimed the Connecticut River as the actual boundary. This would have given New York the entirety of the New Hampshire Grants. After an Order in Council of 1764 ruled that the New York claims were valid, Ira Allen and his more famous brother Ethan Allen organized the Green Mountain Boys to drive off land claimants from New York. But after the Revolutionary War broke out, the Green Mountain Boys left off fighting New Yorkers and began instead aiming their muskets at British redcoats, capturing Ft. Ticonderoga on May 10, 1775—the very day that Continental Congress began its first session as governing body of the "United Colonies." Ira Allen is not well known outside of Vermont, but within the state he is recognized as one of the founders of the Republic.

On reverse, the symbolism went from obvious to obscure to effectively irrelevant. Sherry Fry's original designs, selected by the Vermont Sesquicentennial

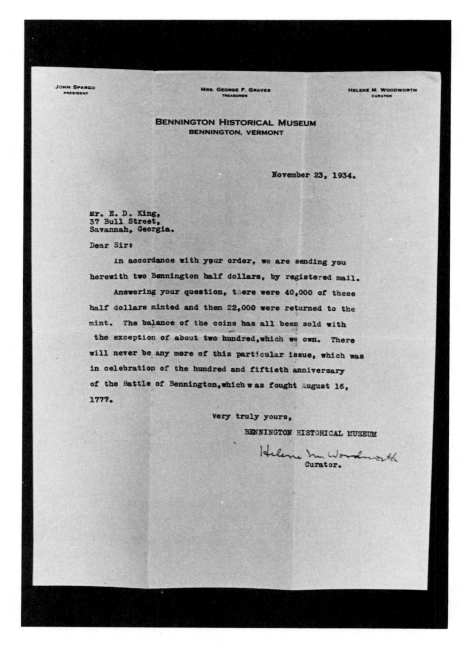

JOHN SPARGO
PRESIDENT

MRS. GEORGE F. GRAVES
TREASURER

HELENE M. WOODWORTH
CURATOR

BENNINGTON HISTORICAL MUSEUM
BENNINGTON, VERMONT

November 23, 1934.

Mr. E. D. King,
37 Bull Street,
Savannah, Georgia.

Dear Sir:

In accordance with your order, we are sending you
herewith two Bennington half dollars, by registered mail.

Answering your question, there were 40,000 of these
half dollars minted and then 22,000 were returned to the
mint. The balance of the coins has all been sold with
the exception of about two hundred, which we own. There
will never be any more of this particular issue, which was
in celebration of the hundred and fiftieth anniversary
of the Battle of Bennington, which was fought August 16,
1777.

Very truly yours,
BENNINGTON HISTORICAL MUSEUM

Helene M. Woodworth
Curator.

A letter from the Bennington Historical Museum indicated a discrepancy between their mintage figure and the Mint's.

Commission, showed for obverse an unflattering portrait of Ira Allen, after Fry's statue on the campus of the University of Vermont (which Ira Allen founded), ultimately from a miniature painted from life in London. But its reverse was an obelisk supposed to represent the Battle Monument at Bennington (misspelled "Bennigton" on the model!); these are reproduced in Taxay, p. 91. The Battle Monument was an obvious choice: The Battle of Bennington (named after the above-mentioned

Benning Wentworth), fought on August 16, 1777, was a turning point not only in the Revolution but in Vermont's role; furthermore, President Calvin Coolidge, himself a Vermonter, had admired it and expected to take part at the sesquicentennial ceremonies on "Battle Day" in 1927 (August 16, a legal holiday in Vermont). However, the Fine Arts Commission correctly regarded a building as an inartistic subject for a coin, and when the Vermont people reluctantly awarded the contract to Charles Keck,

244

Note die break on the forehead just above the eyebrow. It slants down and to the right.

the Federal Commission objected to Fay's Tavern, alias "The Catamount Tavern," on reverse, preferring an actual catamount (lynx or puma) to either the building or the "trophy" (the usual conventionalized representation of a battle: crossed swords, stacked muskets, flags and drum). At which point the Vermonters washed their hands of the project in disgust, saying that the wildcat motif was meaningless, and that they would make no further objections or recommendations; "Life is too short to be spent in futile argument with the Commission of Fine Arts," according to a letter from John Spargo, the Vermont commission's president, quoted by Taxay, p. 101. And so the finished coin represents an almost unrecognizably idealized Ira Allen, mated (so to speak) with an equally unrecognizably idealized wildcat. We cannot be sure of the species: cougar? panther? puma? It is a little nearer to the puma (*Felis concolor*) than any other, but not much like any of them. It is certainly *not* the true Vermont catamount, though that claim is often made; the latter is the short-tailed Canada lynx, *Felis lynx canadensis.* Newspaper reports of cougars or pumas appearing in New England, like

the beast on the coin, are apocryphal. The initials CK are for Charles Keck, the sculptor.

Opportunity: Senators Dale and Greene (R.-Vt.) pushed a bill proposing to authorize coinage of a half dollar and a gold dollar commemorating the Battle of Bennington and the Independence of Vermont, January 9, 1925. On January 24, the Senate adopted an amendment to omit the gold dollar, in which form the bill went to the House, where on February 16, Rep. John Raker (D.-Cal.) offered to amend it further to authorize the California Jubilee coinage. Despite protests on the Mint's behalf by Rep. Albert H. Vestal of the House Coinage Committee, the amendment passed, and at once Rep. Albert Johnson (R.-Wash.) offered a third amendment to authorize the Ft. Vancouver issue, which also passed, much to Vestal's chagrin. The bill became law on February 24, 1925. It probably would not have passed Congress except that President Coolidge, a Vermonter, was known to be interested in the Bennington celebration.

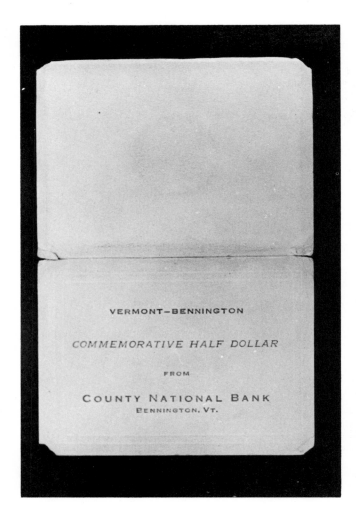

Original holder used to distribute the Vermont Commemoratives.

Motive: Fund raising for the Vermont Historical Trust to promote the study of Vermont and American history, and to aid the Bennington Museum as well as other historical museums and societies within the state.

Suspects: Charles Keck, sculptor.

Accessories: The Vermont Sesquicentennial Commission, John Spargo, president.

Modus Operandi: As soon as Keck's models were approved by the Fine Arts Commission, April 30, they went to the Medallic Art Co. in New York for reduction to half dollar size; the reductions went to

the Philadelphia Mint, which struck the coins during January and February 1927.

A subgroup calling itself the Bennington Battle Monument and Historical Association of Bennington, Vermont arranged for distribution of the coins to local banks, which offered them to the public at $1 apiece. It is a testimony to something or other in Vermont that there was never the faintest breath of suspicion at any time about anything connected with the distribution of the coins. Most went to locals, many of whom did not handle the coins too carefully, so that a considerable proportion of the survivors will be found in less than full mint state.

In tabular form:

Authorized:	Not over 40,000
Struck:	40,000 plus 34 reserved for assay
Returned for re-melting:	11,892, per official records (see below)
Net mintage:	28,108, per official records (see below)

Collateral Evidence: The letter from the Bennington Historical Museum dated November 23, 1934, illustrated above, indicates that "22,000 were returned to the Mint," and that the Museum owned the last couple of hundred unsold specimens. We are unable to account for the discrepancy between the Museum's figure and the Mint's.

The majority of survivors of this issue show weakness in upper central obverse (as illustrated above); specimens with fully sharp curls are very difficult to obtain. As this area is also affected by improper handling or wear, the test of mint state grade for these coins is the presence of mint frost on the weak areas. Some are even flatter on the curl behind the eye than is the piece pictured.

On the other hand, the matte proof from the J.R. Sinnock estate will presumably be much sharper in these details.

The other reason for illustrating this coin is that a tiny minority of Vermonts show a die break on forehead, above the eyebrow, slanting down to right. To date, 150 specimens have been seen with the break as against many hundreds of specimens checked for it since it was discovered.

Some coins were originally distributed in holders of the type illustrated. Only twenty-five of these holders are known at present. Others exist from one of the other banks distributing the issue.

The occasion was also memorialized by a stamp, which makes a good tie-in for exhibit purposes even though the design is very different from the coin.

Centerspread of the holder.

During the correspondence between President Spargo and the Federal Commission of Fine Arts, possible alternative designs discussed for the half dollar had included one of the Green Mountain Boys, but this was rejected on the perfectly sensible grounds that it would "make almost a replica of the Concord-Lexington Minute Man, so lately used" (Taxay, p. 99). This limitation, however, did not deter the Post Office, and accordingly the carmine-rose 2¢ "Vermont Sesqui-centennial" issue, released on August 3, 1927 (in plenty of time for the Battle Day ceremonies), depicts one, clad in skins with fringes (to ease getting rain off the garment) and holding a musket; the word BENNINGTON is there taken as self-explanatory. No designer is credited, but it looks as though it were a collaboration between Charles Aubrey Huston and a couple of the older artists at the Bureau of Engraving and Printing. The stamp is identified as Scott 643, Type A191. In all 39,974,900 were sent to the general public.

An additional tie-in might be found in the "Surrender of General Burgoyne" 2¢ stamp issued in the same color on the same date, Scott 644, Type A192.

The 2¢ Vermont Sesquicentennial issue—Scott 643, Type A191.

Same comment about the designer. This commemorates the battles of Bennington, Oriskany, Ft. Stanwix and Saratoga, all of which are named on its borders. This was distributed to the amount of 25,628,450 specimens.

THE BOOKER T. WASHINGTON HALF DOLLARS

Obverse

Reverse

The Corpus Delicti: Alias *BTW* and a variety of racist nicknames.

Clues: A most unflattering bust of the illustrious educator/polymath/administrator, based loosely on a life mask, dominates obverse; the two buildings on reverse are meant (emblematically at least) for the New York University Hall of Fame with its colonnade of portrait busts, and the slave cabin where Booker Taliaferro Washington was born ca. 1858, in the Hales Ford (Franklin County), Virginia, area. Mint mark D or S will be found, if at all, below the slave cabin.

Opportunity: When it became apparent that the Iowa Centennial commemorative half dollar had a chance of being authorized by Congress, S.J. Phillips, president of the Booker T. Washington Birthplace Memorial Commission, exerted political pressure, and Congress, possibly fearing that voting against the proposal would bring accusations of racism, rushed it into President Truman's hands, where it became law on August 7, 1946, the same day as the Iowa coin.

Motive: Allegedly "to perpetuate the ideals and teachings of Booker T. Washington, and to purchase, construct and maintain memorials to his memory," specifically to buy and restore the 300+ -acre farm with various buildings and the original log cabin. This ostensible purpose was beyond doubt mere political rhetoric. Booker T. Washington's legendary achievements are detailed in *Up from Slavery*; and his real memorial is not that would-be tourist attraction in the Virginia boondocks (which failed of its intended purpose, enriching S.J. Phillips), but Tuskegee Institute, Alabama, which he founded and built from the ground up "with a little help from his friends."

Suspects: S.J. Phillips, defaulting president of the Booker T. Washington Birthplace Memorial Commission.

Accessories: Charles Keck was originally commissioned to design the coin; his design was originally solicited by Dr. Washington's secretary, Dr. Emmett Scott. Keck worked from a photograph provided by Phillips. His models were approved by the Mint, by

Dr. Scott, and by Phillips, who pronounced them "perfect." At this juncture, Isaac Scott Hathaway, a black artist from Lexington, Kentucky, a graduate of the New England Conservatory's Art Department, the Cincinnati Art Academy and the New York College of Ceramics, approached Phillips with a proposition. It seems that Hathaway owned a life mask of Dr. Washington, and that he offered to prepare coin models free, apparently feeling that it would be enough of an honor just to have his designs accepted on a coin to be struck by the mints of the United States. Phillips accepted his offer and submitted both Keck's and Hathaway's models to the Mint and the Federal Commission of Fine Arts. On October 4, 1946, the Commission decided in favor of Hathaway's portrait, but rejected both reverses. Keck had not been informed of these developments, but he learned of them when Phillips gave the commission to Hathaway. The result was furious denunciations by Keck, and extreme embarrassment to the Commission of Fine Arts. Only one honorable option remained: Keck was paid for his work (we have been unable to locate photographs of it), while Hathaway's models were used. Both Hathaway's rejected reverse and accepted models are pictured in Taxay, p. 249; the accepted reverse is based on a sketch by one of the members of the Commission of Fine Arts.

Modus Operandi: As the authorizing act specified that these coins were to be issued from the mints of the United States, to a total of 5,000,000, and that they could be disposed of at par or at a premium by banks or trust companies selected by the Memorial Commission, conditions were set up for a revival of the kind of speculation which had given commemoratives a bad name ten years earlier. Mintage amounts are as specified in the tabulation below.

The Memorial Commission attempted to distribute the 1946 issues on its own, but quickly found that it would be easier to work with coin dealers. Stack's was appointed the authorized agent, according to *The Numismatist* of February 1947. Phillips appears to have quarreled with this firm and appointed A.E. Bebee, then of Chicago, more recently of Nebraska, as his agent for the 1948–51 issues.

We are in a position to make educated guesses about the numbers melted of those dates and mintmarks identified in the above table with a ?. Neither the Mint nor the Memorial Commission kept any record of the numbers melted by date or mint; the corresponding information on the other issues mostly derives from A.E. Bebee. We begin with the information that a total of 1,581,631 pieces went back to the Mint for re-melting, and that some melts

comprised three-piece sets. One of us (A.S.) has made closer estimates based on observed relative frequencies of appearance. The tabulation on page 251 makes everything clear; italicized figures are estimates, but better than ballpark figures.

Quantities of the 1946 and 1946 S issues were thrown into circulation, long before Slabaugh's report (Taxay, p. 153). *The Numismatist,* March 1948:195, reported discoveries of these dates in pocket change.

As early as January 1947 sets were returned to the Memorial Commission because the coins were all nicked up, especially on Dr. Washington's jaw at right. (*The Numismatist* February 1947:172, complaint by F.H. Hisken, who had returned ten sets for that reason.) They appear to have been made at high speed like regular design production coins; gems are scarce.

Issues of 1950 and 1951 were allegedly earmarked for building additional schools and hospitals. There is no evidence any were built; Phillips' grandiose plans all came to nothing. He had originally hoped to sell the entire 5,000,000 authorized mintage at $1 apiece to the 15 million black people in this country—within 90 days, at that!—but by and large blacks ignored them. Slabaugh estimates that less than 3 percent went to blacks, a figure which sounds, if anything, liberal but would be very difficult to document.

Collateral Evidence: Twenty 1946 sets have been seen in black three-piece holders like that illustrated on p. 252.

Ten 1946 sets have been seen in light cardboard holders like that illustrated on p. 253, with the "Gems of Wisdom" quotations. This is because Bebee asked the mint to enclose each individual coin in them, a service for which the charge was 50¢ per coin—accounting for higher issue prices per set. At least two 1948 sets, but no later ones, exist with Bebee's imprint on envelopes.

Before the 1951 issue was exhausted, charges of broken contracts and misappropriated funds were already in the air, and there was much talk of lawsuits. Phillips, desperate but still optimistic, exerted political pressure to have Congress pass an act in his favor which would enable unsold BTWs to be recoined into halves with a new design; the following chapter covers this abortive effort. Even this subterfuge did not work; in 1955 it was reported that the Birthplace Memorial site was to be sold to the State of Virginia, to be presented in turn to the federal government, in order to pay off about $140,000 owed by the Memorial Commission (ill.). Even after

DATE	MONTH MINTED	STRUCK	RESERVED FOR ASSAY	MELTED	NET MINTAGE
1946	Dec.	1,000,000	546	?	?
1946 S	Dec.	200,000	113	?	?
1946 D	Dec.	500,000	279	?	?
1947	Nov.	100,000	17	?	?
1947 S	Dec.	100,000	17	?	?
1947 D	Dec.	100,000	17	?	?
1948	May	20,000	5	12,000	8,000
1948 S	May	20,000	5	12,000	8,000
1948 D	May	20,000	5	12,000	8,000
1949	Jan.	12,000	4	6,000	6,000
1949 S	Jan.	12,000	4	6,000	6,000
1949 D	Jan.	12,000	4	6,000	6,000
1950	Jan.	12,000	4	6,000	6,000
1950 S	Jan.	410,000	74	?	?
	Feb.	102,000	17		
1950 D	Jan.	12,000	4	6,000	6,000
1951	Jan.	60,000	13	?	?
	Aug. 1–6	450,000	69		
1951 S	Jan.	12,000	4	5,000	7,000
1951 D	Jan.	12,000	4	5,000	7,000

TOTALS: 1,654,000 Philadelphia, 856,000 S, 656,000 D.

DATE	STRUCK	MELTED	NET MINTAGE	ISSUE PRICE
1946	1,000,000	500,000	500,000	1.00
1946 S	200,000	100,000	100,000	1.50
1946 D	500,000	300,000	200,000	1.50[1]
1947	100,000	50,000	50,000 ⎫	set
1947 S	100,000	50,000	50,000 ⎬	6.00[2]
1947 D	100,000	50,000	50,000 ⎭	
1948	20,000	12,000	8,000 ⎫	set
1948 S	20,000	12,000	8,000 ⎬	7.50
1948 D	20,000	12,000	8,000 ⎭	
1949	12,000	6,000	6,000 ⎫	
1949 S	12,000	6,000	6,000 ⎬	set
1949 D	12,000	6,000	6,000 ⎭	8.50
1950	12,000	6,000	6,000 ⎫	
1950 S	512,000	235,000	277,000 ⎬	set
1950 D	12,000	6,000	6,000 ⎭	8.50[3]
1951	510,000	230,631	279,369 ⎫	
1951 S	12,000	5,000	7,000 ⎬	set
1951 D	12,000	5,000	7,000 ⎭	10.00[4]
TOTAL	3,166,000	1,581,631	1,574,369	

Notes: (1) In *The Numismatist* 12/47:878, these were announced at $6 + 30¢ postage. In *The Numismatist* 1/47:103 these were announced as 1946 coins at $1 each for P and S plus 10¢ postage, D $1.50 plus 10¢ postage; cheques to BTW Birthplace Memorial, Inc., Rocky Mount, Virginia.

(2) In *The Numismatist* 12/47:878, these were announced at $6 + 30¢ postage.

(3) No price quotation is available for individual type coins of 1950 s. Judging by the price named for 1951, these were probably peddled at $3 apiece. Bebee already advertised them in *The Numismatist* 2/50:98.

(4) Individual 1951 type coins were offered at $3 each. The August delivery was intended to meet the August 7 deadline.

Original holder for the 1946 Booker T. Washington set.

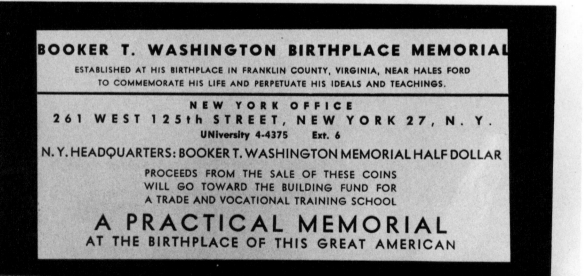

Back of holder.

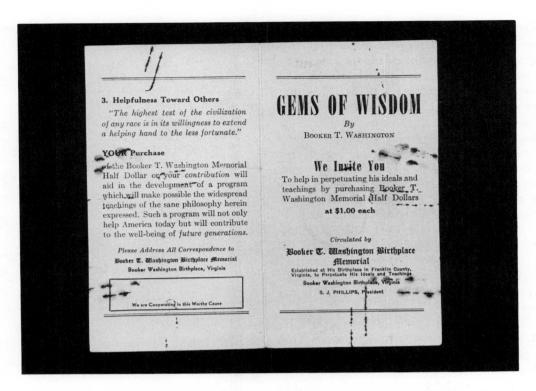

Original mailing card used to mail a single Booker T. Washington commemorative half dollar. The coin travelled in a cellophane envelope inside the folder.

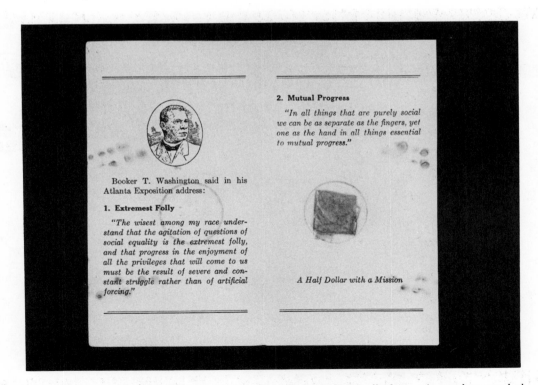

This is the centerspread of the mailing card. The coin was mounted in a cellophane coin envelope attached to the right side of the card.

that, in 1956 Phillips tried to get Congress to pass a third bill in his favor, which would require recall of 100,000 unsold BTW coins for recoinage into a new BTW Centennial issue (taking his birth year as 1856 rather than the usually accepted 1858). This plan was foredoomed to failure. Congress had no more trust in Phillips than did his creditors. After Phillips died, no more was heard about the projects from his heirs. Hathaway also is dead, but we have been unable to learn when he died.

No proofs were made, although a few brilliant 1951 s coins are known (ill.). These have been claimed as presentation coins. However that may be, it is certain that they are from drastically repolished obverse and reverse dies; irregularities in some letters testify to the fact.

Gem specimens of any date or mintmark in this series are very seldom available; expect more or less conspicuous bag marks.

Philatelic tie-ins exist. The first of these is the dark brown 10¢, Scott 873 (Type A332), first issued April 7, 1940 as part of the Educators series, to a total of 14,125,580 pieces.

The other one is the 3¢ deep blue "Centennial of Booker T. Washington" (portraying that same slave

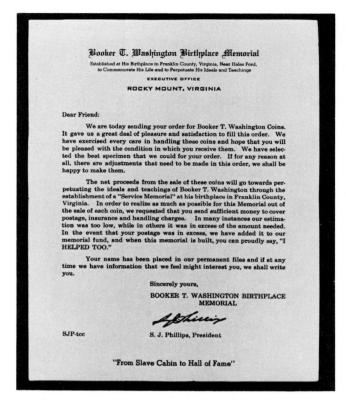

Letter for the Booker T. Washington Birthplace Memorial.

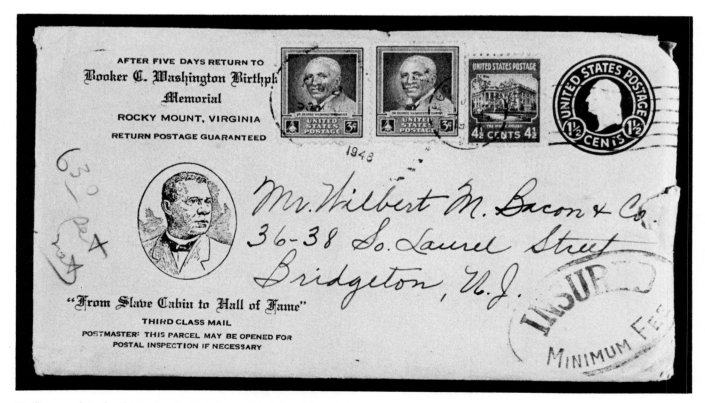

Mailing envelope for the Booker T. Washington Birthplace Memorial.

Obverse and reverse of prooflike Booker T. Washington coin. The irregularities in some of the letters testify to the fact that prooflike specimens were struck from repolished obverse and reverse dies.

The philatelic tie-in with the Booker T. Washington issue—the Scott 873, Type A332.

cabin), Scott 1074 (Type A521), issued April 5, 1956 to a total of 121,184,600 pieces.

This writer (W.B.) recalls seeing BTW half dollars peddled in drugstores at $1 apiece in small cellophane holders during the mid-1950s. They apparently had few takers as the holders were very dusty. Slabaugh adds that after Phillips' 1956 proposal led to nothing, and the commission did not redeem the coins from the banks which had been holding them, these banks threw the remaining coins (largely 1946, 46 s, 47 and 51) into circulation.

THE BOOKER T. WASHINGTON/ GEORGE WASHINGTON CARVER HALF DOLLARS

Obverse

Reverse

The Corpus Delicti: Alias *Washington-Carver*, and a variety of derogatory epithets, some of racist nature.

Clues: The jugate portraits are of George Washington Carver, at observer's left, and Booker T. Washington, on a larger scale. Date behind Carver's neck is that of issue of the individual coins—1951 through 1954. Reverse was originally to show the American Legion badge with the motto UNITED AGAINST THE SPREAD OF COMMUNISM and a reference to some (ad hoc?) McCarthyist group called the National Americanism Commission, whatever that may have been, together with the names of the Booker T. Washington Birthplace Memorial in Virginia and the George W. Carver National Monument Foundation in Missouri. However, after the State Department vetoed this reverse—in an action unprecedented in the history of American coinage—the designer substituted the less blatant design adopted, with a map

of the United States (needlessly labeled U.S.A.) and its platitude mottoes. For the original design, see Taxay, p. 252. Mintmark, if any, will be found above IC of AMERICANISM.

Opportunity: S.J. Phillips, the impresario we have to thank for the original BTW halves (preceding section), found himself unable to sell the remainder of his original authorization by the deadline, August 7, 1951, and managed to push a bill through Congress which became the Act of September 21, 1951. This bill probably would have failed except for a clause specifying that the profits of the new issue were to be used "to oppose the spread of Communism among Negroes in the interest of the national defense." As these were the days when the late and unlamented Senator Joseph R. McCarthy (R.-Wisc.) exercised extraordinary power and was apt to denounce anyone who disagreed with his extreme anti-communist position, Congress, doubtless afraid to seem like a pack of what McCarthy called "com-symps" or "communist dupes," at once approved Phillips' bill, and President Truman signed it in equal haste. This bill authorized all the unsold BTW coins (both those in Treasury vaults and those already in the Booker T. Washington Birthplace Memorial's hands—in all, 1,581,631) to be re-melted for re-coinage into the new design; in addition, the bullion earmarked for the uncoined moiety of the BTW halves—enough to make 1,834,000—could be used for the same purpose. This meant a maximum of 3,415,631 Washington/Carver halves could be coined.

Motive: To help S. J. Phillips get his floundering Birthplace Memorial out of debt, and, to some extent, That Five Finger Word. Only from a speech by Congressman White were we able to learn that Phillips was the prime mover behind both the Booker T. Washington Birthplace Memorial Commission and the George Washington Carver National Monument Foundation: apparently on the *de mortuis nil nisi bonum* "[speak] nothing but good about the dead" principle, almost nothing has been ascertainable about details of Phillips' questionable financial dealings, though evidently Congress heard enough about them privately to reject any further bills introduced in his favor even as late as 1962. We are not certain to what extent Phillips was a cynical opportunist in emphasizing the blatant anti-communist sentiment as a means of insuring passage of his W/C bill, or to what extent he genuinely believed he could sell anywhere near three million of these coins to fellow blacks "united against the spread of communism," even in those paranoid days when millions of people imagined they saw communist bogey-men under every bed and in every gopher hole.

Suspects: S.J. Phillips, for the original concept tying in black heroes and anti-communist hysteria; Isaac Scott Hathaway, designer; Robert Hobday, president of the George Washington Carver Memorial Institute; Rep. Compton Ignatius White, Sr. (D.-Id.), sponsor of both the BTW and the W/C authorizing bills.

Accessories: Felix de Weldon, sculptor member of the Federal Commission of Fine Arts, who approved the original anti-communist design (after consulting with Hathaway, but without making the Mint privy to such consultations), and who—as of November 15, 1951—also approved the revised design. Also, Dean Acheson, Secretary of State, who rejected the original design, lest the Soviet Union deem it grounds for escalating the Cold War. Finally, Gilroy

Roberts, Engraver of the Mint, who at first justly pronounced the designs artistically and technically impossible, but who nevertheless (after the Commission's go-ahead) faced the ungrateful task of rendering them at least marginally coinable. Roberts made a variety of modifications to lettering and portraiture, then lowered the relief of obverse on the Janvier lathe so that specimens could be brought up to full legibility with a single blow in the coining press.

Modus Operandi: Taxay (pp. 251-253) tells the story of the original American Legion design and its replacement.

The table that follows indicates the actual mintages (all previously published figures are either incomplete or inaccurate); the final mintage of August 1–6, 1954, was cut short because the authorizing act specified a deadline of August 7, 1954, or three years to the day after the original authorization had expired. Congress was not about to tolerate a repetition of the Boone, Arkansas, Texas or Oregon abuses, no matter how praiseworthy the cause.

Closer study of the above tabulation indicates that those struck for three-piece sets were the first issued each year, presumably being sold at once, while the extras made for single sales as type coins languished. In ascertaining even ballpark figures for the numbers melted, we can safely assume that those which went back to the Mint were precisely the extras made for type coins, so that the following breakdowns can be taken as reasonable reconstructions. This procedure is necessary because after the authorizing act's expiration a total of 1,091,198 went back to the mint for re-melting, without any accurate accounting of which dates and mint-marks were affected.

Issue price was $10 per three-piece set per year; single type coins were offered originally at $5.50. From the above tabulation, we may deduce that 10,000 sets were made and presumably sold dated 1951, 8,000 for 1952, 8,000 for 1953, and 12,000 for 1954, and that the Denver mint coins (which are rarely seen as singles) were distributed almost completely in sets. Though the 1954 sets were briefly advertised as high as $12, the price sagged during the year and by December 1954 they were being advertised at $6.50 to $7.50—as were the sets of earlier dates. The larger mintages intended for sale as singles—1951, 1952, 1953 S, 1954 S—were eventually dumped by the very banks originally committed to selling them at premiums; some were sold for 60¢ each, others went into circulation at face value, and those that could not be disposed of at once went back to the mint. One of us (A.S.) has made the following reconstruction of meltages and

ISSUE TIME	MINT	QUANTITY	EXTRAS RESERVED FOR ASSAY
December 1951	(P)	110,000	18
December 1951	S	10,000	4
December 1951	D	10,000	4
March 1952	(P)	2,006,000	292
March 1952	S	6,000	3
March 1952	D	6,000	3
December 1952	S	2,000	3
December 1952	D	2,000	3
January 1953	(P)	8,000	3
January 1953	S	8,000	3
January 1953	D	8,000	3
December 1953	S	100,000	17
January 1954	(P)	6,000	3
January 1954	S	6,000	3
January 1954	D	6,000	3
February 1954	(P)	6,000	3
February 1954	S	6,000	3
February 1954	D	6,000	3
August 1–6, 1954	S	110,000	18

TOTALS: (P) 2,136,000   S 248,000   D 38,000
GRAND TOTAL: 2,422,000

DATE	MINT	COINED	REMELTED (est.)	NET MINTAGE (est.)
1951	(P)	110,000	60,000	40,000
1951	S	10,000	0	10,000
1951	D	10,000	0	10,000
1952	(P)	2,006,000	883,000	1,123,000
1952	S	8,000	0	8,000
1952	D	8,000	0	8,000
1953	(P)	8,000	0	8,000
1953	S	108,000	60,000	48,000
1953	D	8,000	0	8,000
1954	(P)	12,000	4,000	8,000
1954	S	122,000	80,198	41,802
1954	D	12,000	4,000	8,000
TOTALS (official):		2,422,000	1,091,198	1,330,802

net mintages based on all available information including relative frequencies of appearance both before and after the rediscovery and dispersal of the hoard discovered in the Kaplan estate.

From the above it is easy to see that the majority of survivors are dated 1952. In our past experience the 1954 set is a little harder to find than any of the others, so it is even possible that a few hundred of these sets might have been melted, though if many had remained unsold into 1955, Phillips would have been unable to convince the mint to deliver coins for the final year. In what may be more than coincidence, the only singles which can be located in pristine gem state well enough struck so that Carver's cheekbone does not appear rubbed will also be dated 1952 Philadelphia. Three-piece sets dated 1951, 1952, and 1954 are of about equal scarcity with each other and a little less scarce than the 1953 set. Singles appear with the frequency indicated by the estimated net mintages.

[PUBLIC LAW 610—79TH CONGRESS]

[CHAPTER 763—2D SESSION]

[H. R. 6528]

AN ACT

To authorize the coinage of 50-cent pieces to commemorate the life and perpetuate the ideals and teachings of Booker T. Washington.

Be it enacted by the Senate and House of Representatives of the United States of America in Congress assembled, That to commemorate the life and perpetuate the ideals and teachings of Booker T. Washington, a great American, there shall be coined by the Director of the Mint not to exceed five million silver 50-cent pieces of standard size, weight, and fineness and of a special appropriate design to be fixed by the Director of the Mint, with the approval of the Secretary of the Treasury; but the United States shall not be subject to the expense of making the models for master dies or other preparations for this coinage.

SEC. 2. The coins herein authorized shall be issued at par, and only upon the request of the Booker T. Washington Birthplace Memorial established at his birthplace in Franklin County, Virginia.

SEC. 3. Such coins may be disposed of at par or at a premium by banks or trust companies selected by the Booker T. Washington Birthplace Memorial of Franklin County, Virginia, and all proceeds therefrom shall be used to purchase, construct, and maintain suitable memorials to the memory of Booker T. Washington, deceased, as may be decided upon by the Booker T. Washington Birthplace Memorial of Virginia.

SEC. 4. That all laws now in force relating to the subsidiary silver coins of the United States and the coining or striking of the same; regulating and guarding the process of coinage; providing for the purchase of material, and for the transportation, distribution, and redemption of the coins; for the prevention of debasement or counterfeiting; for security of the coin; or for any other purposes, whether said laws are penal or otherwise, shall, so far as applicable, apply to the coinage herein directed.

SEC. 5. The coins authorized herein shall be issued in such numbers, and at such times as shall be requested by the Booker T. Washington Birthplace Memorial and upon payment to the United States of the face value of such coins: *Provided,* That none of such coins shall be issued after the expiration of the five-year period immediately following the enactment of this Act.

Approved August 7, 1946.

(289)

(Introduced by Rep. Compton Ignatius White [D., Idaho])

Legislation introduced by Representative Compton Ignatius White (D-Idaho).

Collateral Evidence: Besides the two original issuing agencies, local banks distributed many of these coins; in addition, the late Sol Kaplan had a distributorship, and a hoard turned up in his estate. This hoard has been dispersed during the last year by First Coinvestors, Inc.: 2,211 sets in all—410 of 1951, 227 of 1952, 351 of 1953, 1,223 of 1954.

No proofs or presentation strikings are reported.

The nearest philatelic tie-in is the 3¢ bright red-violet stamp for Dr. Carver, first issued January 5, 1948: Scott 953 (Type A400). This was issued to commemorate the fifth anniversary of his death; his actual birth date is unknown. A total of 121,548,000 were released, of which some 402,179 were on first-day covers postmarked Tuskegee Institute, Alabama, where Carver was buried side by side with Booker T. Washington.

It is to Tuskegee Institute, rather than to Carver's birthplace near Diamond, Missouri, that we must look to find the real memorial to this extraordinary

Laying the Foundation for a Stronger America Through Leadership and Racial Team Work

REMARKS
OF
HON. COMPTON I. WHITE
OF IDAHO
IN THE HOUSE OF REPRESENTATIVES
Saturday, September 23, 1950

Mr. WHITE of Idaho. Mr. Speaker, recently it was my privilege to bring before the House a bill which had for its objective the making possible of funds for the establishment in Diamond, Mo., of a national shrine at the birthplace of the late eminent Negro scientist, George Washington Carver. Four years previous to this, it was also my privilege to assist in the sponsoring of legislation which authorized the coinage of 5,000,-000 Booker T. Washington memorial half-dollars to be sold at a premium to aid in the establishment of a memorial at the birthplace of Booker T. Washington—America's greatest Negro leader. I also cooperated in securing a United States post office known as Booker Washington Birthplace, Virginia, which I understand now has been a second class post office for 3 years. Three Nationwide good will building contests have been conducted with a total of more than 7,000,000 pieces of mail passing through the post office, in addition to the regular mail handled.

AMERICA'S LARGEST MINORITY GROUP

The Negro makes up America's largest minority group. He has grown sufficiently large in numbers to make a definite contribution to national welfare or to serve as a menace to national progress—depending upon the opportunities for development or the lack of it whichever is afforded him.

I have been interested in working with the Booker T. Washington Birthplace Memorial idea and the George Washington Carver National Monument Foundation because it is my opinion that through pride of race and efficient service, the Negro can earn for himself a respected place in the economic life of America, at the same time that he contributes his share to national progress. I further believe that as lawmakers and members of a majority group, it is our duty to seriously consider the needs of these 15,000,000 struggling Americans.

SAFE, SANE LEADERSHIP

Properly helped and intelligently led, the Negro is in position to make large contributions to our American way of life. This has been plainly evidenced in the lives of the large number of Negroes who have measured up in a most commendable way to American standards and ideals—particularly in the case of useful and successful lives like those of George Washington Carver and Booker T. Washington. Just what the Negro can accomplish through safe, constructive leadership is being evidenced too in the very worthwhile program that is being headed by S. J. Phillips, president of the Booker T. Washington.Birthplace Memorial and the George Washington Carver National Monument Foundation. I have cooperated closely with S. J. Phillips and have seen the very telling results of his leadership. Through his efforts and those associated with him, a national program for Negroes in Agricultural Development, Health, Trade, and Industrial Training, and Interracial Goodwill is making itself felt over the Nation in general and in the South in particular. Dr. Phillips is well educated, trained and efficient, an untiring worker, and an ardent apostle of the ideals and teachings of Booker T. Washington—but above all this, he has sufficient courtesy and humility to appeal to men of all races and creeds. He is definitely laying a foundation upon which whites and Negroes can work together for the welfare of the Nation.

EXAMPLES IN PULLING TOGETHER

Through the efforts of S. J. Phillips, the makers of Royal Crown Cola, the Nehi Corp. of Columbus, Ga., has spent a large sum of money to help develop the birthplace of Booker T. Washington, in Franklin County, Va., as an incentive to greater racial pride for the Negro and to help to make possible trade and industrial training to Negroes below high school level. This is an outstanding example of what can be accomplished through understanding and friendship. Because these qualities were injected by S. J. Phillips, this corporation was sold on Booker T. Washington's idea of "helpfulness toward others"—and not only has the Negro benefited materially by this cooperation, but so has the South and the Nation in general.

Hundreds of Negro families in Roanoke and Franklin County in Virginia are being benefited by programs of trade and industrial training which have been set up by Dr. S. J. Phillips, in trade schools established at Roanoke and at Booker Washington Birthplace, Virginia. These schools are efficiently staffed, meet State educational requirements, and are helping to fill what is possibly one of the greatest needs among Negroes today—the need for training adult Negroes of low educational status.

Recently Dr. Phillips has caused to be set into motion in the State of Georgia, a campaign for the establishment of a Negro agricultural service center at Camp John Hope near Fort Valley, Ga.; the object of which is to give help to the thousands of Negro farmers and farm families in the State of Georgia. It is significant to note that the Department of Education of the State of Georgia has set aside a tract of land on which the Agricultural Service Center will be erected and that some of Georgia's most eminent southern leaders are working side by side with Negro leaders of the State and with the Booker T. Washington Birthplace Memorial to initiate the help which this agricultural service center can give to the Negroes of Georgia.

At Diamond, Mo., the birthplace of George Washington Carver, Dr. Phillips is working with the banks of the State and many outstanding Missourians to get under way the program of the George Washington Carver National Monument Foundation, which has the following objectives:

First. To promote racial understanding and harmony.

Second. To help underprivileged youth through opportunity scholarships.

Third. To establish community service clubs which will work toward the higher development of Negro community life.

Fourth. To aid Negroes in the field of agriculture and rural leadership.

Fifth. To secure funds to financially assist nonprofit educational institutions.

BUILDING AN INVINCIBLE AMERICA

Ours is a land of many races and creeds. We must pull together if we would build an invincible nation. To make a strong team, each man must be in position to do his share of the pulling. The Negro can, in the words of Booker T. Washington, offer 30,000,000 hands in our forward pull—or use the same number of hands to retard our progress—depending upon the opportunities which America gives him for development.

The type of race-building program being carried out by the Booker T. Washington Birthplace Memorial under the guidance of Dr. S. J. Phillips, is an example of the type of program that will help in the building of a stronger America. This is the type of program that definitely deserves the help and cooperation of Americans of all races and creeds. The Negro has made wonderfully rapid strides during the 85 years of his freedom. If he is willing to accept the fundamental teachings of men like Booker T. Washington and George Washington Carver, under the type of leadership offered by Dr. S. J. Phillips—his future will be secure.

Anyone interested can receive more detailed information about these projects by writing Dr. S. J. Phillips, president of the Booker T. Washington Birthplace Memorial, Booker Washington Birthplace, Virginia; and Dr. Phillips, as president of the George Washington Carver National Monument Foundation, at Diamond, Mo.

Legislation introduced by Representative Compton Ignatius White (D-Idaho).

This appeared in newspapers nationwide January 19–20, 1955.

polymath, the "Plant Doctor," artist (one of his paintings was exhibited at the Columbian Exposition, winning an honorable mention), mycologist, botanist, agronomist, educator, etc. It is to Carver, rather than to Carter, that the peanut owes its real popularity; Dr. Carver discovered hundreds of industrial uses for peanuts as well as for sweet potatoes and soybeans—everything from fabrics to industrial chemicals to artificial marble.

As for Carver's birthplace, this was made a national memorial as of July 14, 1953, with a bronze bust being dedicated there; after Phillips' failure to make it self-supporting, the site found its way into the hands of the National Park Service, which still maintains it (see the form letter signed by Gentry Davis as Superintendent).

Whether or not Phillips genuinely believed that his coinage project would help oppose the spread of communism among fellow blacks, the record is clear enough: very few blacks bought the coins. And, in fact, research done by one of us (A.S.) at City College of New York in this specific area of inquiry has indicated that the whole problem of communist infiltration among blacks was a chimera. During the early 1950s, very few radical black youth groups existed and even these were not communist-oriented. Most blacks were as distrustful of communism as were Senator McCarthy's cohorts, and with better reason, as the Soviet Union's racist policies were even then becoming notorious.

After the coinage enterprise failed, Phillips' BTW Birthplace Memorial—the 300-acre farm, its outbuildings and restored log cabin—was put up for sale to pay off some $140,000 owed on it. Friendly legislators induced the State of Virginia to buy the site for presentation to the federal government.

Among outcries of broken contracts, misappropriated funds, abuses connected with distribution of the coins, and of various other kinds of corruption, misfeasance, nonfeasance and malfeasance, Phillips

262

United States Department of the Interior

NATIONAL PARK SERVICE

George Washington Carver National Monument
P.O. Box 38
Diamond, Missouri   64840

IN REPLY REFER TO:

Mr. Marc Katz
200 I.U. Willets Road
Albertson, New York   11507

Dear Mr. Katz:

Thank you for your interest in visiting George Washington Carver
National Monument. Please excuse the "form letter," but we
receive many inquiries such as yours and this is the most
efficient means of handling them.

The monument was established to preserve the birthplace site
of one of America's most prominent Black scientists and educators.
Here he spent his formative early years and developed a deep
interest in nature.

The Visitor Center, which is open daily from 8:30 a.m. to 5:00 p.m.,
contains a museum, restroom facilities, and a small sales counter.
A 3/4 mile self-guided trail passes the birthplace site, a statue
of Carver, the restored Moses Carver house, and the Carver family
cemetery. During the summer months guided walks, craft demonstra-
tions, and other activities are scheduled periodically on weekends.
Picnic tables and soft drinks are available, and the grounds are
open from 8:00 a.m. to dusk.

The monument is most easily reached from Interstate 44. Signs will
direct you to take the Alternate 71 exit south to Diamond, Missouri,
then right on Road V.

We hope you will enjoy your visit with us.

Sincerely yours,

Gentry Davis

Gentry Davis
Superintendent

Enclosures:
Brochures
Information

Letter used to explain and publicize the actual birthplace memorial.

Public Law 151 - 82d Congress
Chapter 408 - 1st Session
H. R. 3176

AN ACT

To amend the Act entitled "An Act to authorize the coinage of 50-cent pieces to commemorate the life and perpetuate the ideals and teachings of Booker T. Washington", approved August 7, 1946.

Be it enacted by the Senate and House of Representatives of the United States of America in Congress assembled, That the Act entitled "An Act to authorize the coinage of 50-cent pieces to commemorate the life and perpetuate the ideals and teachings of Booker T. Washington", approved August 7, 1946, is amended to read as follows: "That in order to commemorate the lives and perpetuate the ideals and teachings of Booker T. Washington and George Washington Carver, two great Americans, there shall be coined by the Director of the Mint (1) a number of silver 50-cent pieces equal to the number of 50-cent pieces authorized by the Act of August 7, 1946 (60 Stat. 863), but not yet coined on the date of the enactment of this Act, plus (2) an additional number of silver 50-cent pieces equal to the number of 50-cent pieces coined under such Act of August 7, 1946, and returned to the Treasury in accordance with section 5 of this Act. The silver 50-cent pieces authorized by this section shall be of standard size, weight, and fineness, and of a special appropriate design to be fixed by the Director of the Mint with the approval of the Secretary of the Treasury; but the United States shall not be subject to the expense of making the models for master dies or other preparations for the coinage authorized by this section, or to the expense of making any changes in design which may be necessitated by reason of the enactment of this Act.

"Sec. 2. The coins authorized by the first section of this Act shall be issued at par, and only upon the request of the Booker T. Washington Birthplace Memorial (established at the birthplace of Booker T. Washington in Franklin County, Virginia) and the George Washington Carver National Monument Foundation (established at the birthplace of George Washington Carver in Diamond, Missouri).

"Sec. 3. The coins authorized by the first section of this Act shall be issued in such numbers, and at such times, as shall be requested by the Booker T. Washington Birthplace Memorial and the George Washington Carver National Monument Foundation, and upon payment to the United States of the face value of such coins, except that none of such coins shall be issued after August 7, 1954.

"Sec. 4. The coins authorized by the first section of this Act may be disposed of at par or at a premium by banks or trust companies selected by the Booker T. Washington Birthplace Memorial and the George Washingon Carver National Monument Foundation, and all proceeds therefrom shall be used, in the manner decided upon by the Booker T. Washington Birthplace Memorial and the George Washington Carver National Monument Foundation to oppose the spread of communism among Negroes in the interest of the national defense.

"Sec. 5. (a) From and after the date of the enactment of this Act, no 50-cent pieces shall be coined under the Act of August 7, 1946.

nevertheless tried to persuade Congress in 1956 to pass a bill authorizing withdrawal of unsold coins, re-melting, and re-coinage into still another type of commemoratives, these to number 100,000 specimens, to honor the guessed-at centenary of Booker T. Washington's birth in 1956. This bill did not pass.

After it failed, the banks which had been handling type coins for Phillips began disposing of them at whatever prices they could get, eventually wholesaling them to dealers and spending those the dealers would not take (summer 1956). We have already seen, as well, how as late as 1962, Phillips attempted "(b) At the request of the Booker T. Washington Birthplace Memorial and the George Washington Carver National Monument Foundation, any of the 50-cent pieces coined under the Act of August 7, 1946, but on the date of the enactment of this Act not yet disposed of in accordance with such Act, shall be returned to or retained in the Treasury, and the Director of the Mint shall melt down such 50-cent pieces and use the resulting metal and material for the coinage of silver 50-cent pieces under the first section of this Act.

"Sec. 6. All laws in force on the date of the enactment of this Act, whether penal or otherwise, relating to the subsidiary silver coins of the United States and the coining or striking thereof, regulating and guarding the process of coinage, providing for the purchase of material and for the transportation, distribution, and redemption of coins, providing for the prevention of debasement and counterfeiting and for the security of the coin, or otherwise relating to coinage, shall, insofar as they are applicable, apply to the coinage authorized by this Act."

Approved September 21, 1951.

(Introduced by Rep. Compton Ignatius White [D., Idaho])

Public Law 455 - 83d Congress
Chapter 427 - 2d Session
S. 2845

in vain to push other bills through Congress in aid of his floundering projects.

What may well be our last commemorative coins (aside from the Bicentennial issues dated 1776–1976, which were distributed as regular issues), though intended to honor a couple of the greatest men in our national history, nevertheless failed their intended purpose, and gave rise only to more scandal than their predecessors. Beyond doubt, the dismal record of S.J. Phillips as promoter of these coins has contributed much to the continuing Congressional and Treasury aversion to any resumption of commemorative coinage.

Locating specimens where George Washington Carver's cheekbone *does not* appear rubbed or worn will be quite a job, for due to stacking and striking most coins have this characteristic. The exception to the aforementioned will be the 1952 Philadelphia issue which can be located in gem condition (MS-65+) with some effort at present.

We have always found the 1954 set more difficult to obtain than the '53, though the '53 has always been touted as the key, the biggest obstacle to completeness. We believe there were more coins of the '54 issue melted than people are aware of because there was little public interest in them.

As a numismatic first, we'll present the story as to why the '53 set is considered the key set. Sol Kaplan, a Cincinnati coin dealer, owned over 500 sets, promoting them as the date one had to have for completeness. For a while they were off the market, while Sol bought all he could under the counter; prices rose under this demand and Sol sold out his original 500 sets at double his cost and still had plenty left over.

THE WISCONSIN TERRITORIAL CENTENNIAL HALF DOLLAR

Obverse

Reverse

The Corpus Delicti: Alias *Wisconsin.*

Clues: It isn't clear which side was meant to be the obverse; we assume it is that with the pickaxe and the pile of lead ore and soil, alluding to the lead mines in the southeastern region that attracted numerous immigrants in the 1820s, and copying the Territorial Seal. The date "4th day of July Anno Domini 1836" was that on which Henry Dodge took office as the first Territorial Governor, inaugurating Wisconsin's new status as a Territory (it had formerly been part of Michigan Territory).

On the other side, with a crowd of statutory legends and mottoes, is an American badger *(Taxidea taxus),* the state animal, chosen because it is a heraldic supporter in the Great Seal of the State. Behind the badger are three arrows, said to represent the Black Hawk War of the 1830s, and an olive branch (stylized in Art Deco manner almost to the point of unrecognizability), supposed to represent the peace (i.e., the massacre and expulsion of the Indians) that made the area safe for white settlers. Below the ground on which the badger stands is the initial H, for Benjamin Hawkins, designer of the coin.

Opportunity: Local celebrations statewide sponsored by the Wisconsin Centennial Commission. Enough political pressure was applied that the commemorative coin was one of three authorized by Congress as of May 15, 1936 (the others being the Bridgeport and the Swedish Delaware Tercentenary).

Motive: Local pride, and presumably to help finance the celebrations.

Suspects: The Coinage Committee of the Wisconsin Centennial Commission; Fred W. Harris (a local coin collector) was "Director of Distribution." The Coinage Committee specified the designs.

Accessories: Benjamin Hawkins, a New York City artist recommended by the Federal Commission of Fine Arts, after the Mint and the Commission had rejected the original models by David Parsons (then a University of Wisconsin art student). For no explainable reason other than local chauvinism, the sponsoring committees continued to mention Parsons's name in connection with the coin, though

Parsons's original models (pictured by Taxay, p. 202) show no resemblance to the coin as adopted other than the territorial seal itself (as dictated by the Coinage Committee).

Modus Operandi: In April 1936, while the bill was still pending in Congress, the Centennial Commission chose Parsons to do the original models. After these were rejected by the authorities, the Fine Arts Commission recommended Hawkins, who was awarded the contract sometime in the first or second week of May. Hawkins' own models went to the Mint on June 3, were approved and were forwarded to the Commission of Fine Arts, which followed suit on June 5. The coins were made in the Philadelphia Mint during July. As the authorizing act specified no maximum number, the dies were retained for possible future use after the first (and last) batch of 25,000 went to the Coinage Committee. However, Fred Harris correctly believed that this modest quantity would be plenty at $1.50 each, and no subsequent orders followed. (The total of 25,015 usually quoted includes 15 reserved for assay.)

As late as March 7, 1945, these coins were still available in lots of ten for $1.25 each coin, according to L.M. Hanks, Treasurer of the State Historical Society.

Collateral Evidence: Proofs may have been made for John R. Sinnock, but to date none has shown up. No original holders are known.

THE YORK COUNTY, MAINE, TERCENTENARY HALF DOLLAR

Obverse

Reverse

The Corpus Delicti: Alias *The York.*

Clues: As with some other issues, it is difficult to determine which side was intended as obverse. The side with the stockade is intended to represent Brown's Garrison on the Saco River; the script initials WHR below the Latin motto are for Walter H. Rich, the designer of the coin. York County's seal dominates the other side. Aside from the Fort Vancouver issue, this is probably the most obscure local-pride celebration to be honored by a commemorative coin. York County, Maine, is the oldest and southernmost county in the state, but we know of no event of national significance originating there.

Opportunity: Local celebrations sponsored by the York County Tercentenary Commission; Act of June 26, 1936.

Motive: Probably to finance the celebrations.

Suspects: The Commission, and the York County Tercentenary Commemorative Coin Association (Walter P. Nichols, secretary-treasurer).

Accessories: Walter H. Rich, a Portland, Maine painter of wildlife; anonymous creator of an old woodcut of Brown's Garrison, published in Frank C. Deering, *The Proprietors of Saco,* 1931 (a history of the York National Bank, located on the same spot as the garrison); anonymous designer of the county seal.

Modus Operandi: On July 17, the Federal Commission of Fine Arts conferred with Walter P. Nichols and approved the design of the coin, subject to a minor change (removal of the date 1636 on a scroll above shield). The G.S. Pacetti Co. of Boston made the models—allegedly "carved in solid brass"—from Rich's designs (according to Walter P. Nichols, *The Numismatist,* September 1936, p. 713); these models, on approval, went to Medallic Art Co. for reduction, thence to the Philadelphia Mint, which struck 25,000 (plus 15 reserved for assay) early in August, out of 30,000 authorized by Congress. Of this first (and, as it proved, only) batch, some 10,000 were reserved for residents of York County and the rest of Maine, the remainder for collectors outside the state. But this amount was oversubscribed in Maine, so that locals got well over

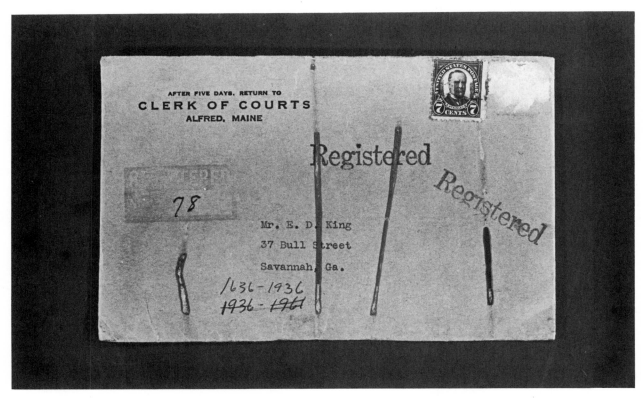

The first delivery of the York Commemorative appears to have been mailed out in unprinted holders by the Clerk of Courts in Alfred, Maine.

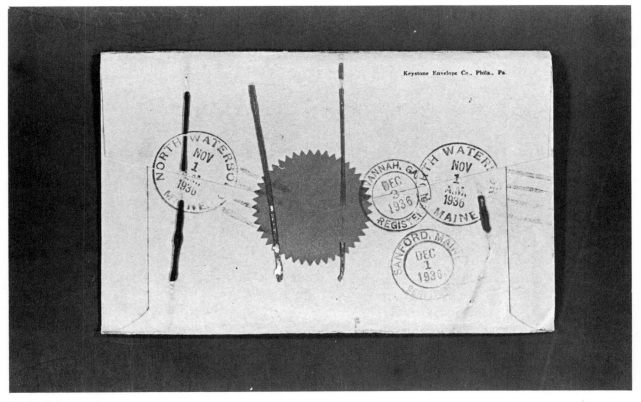

Back of the envelope.

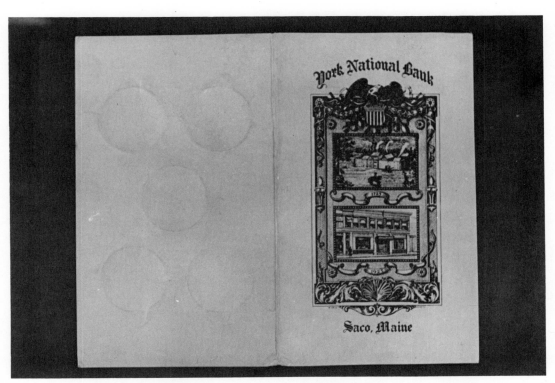

The more elaborate coin mailing holders used by the York County Tercentenary Commission to mail out York Commemorative half dollars.

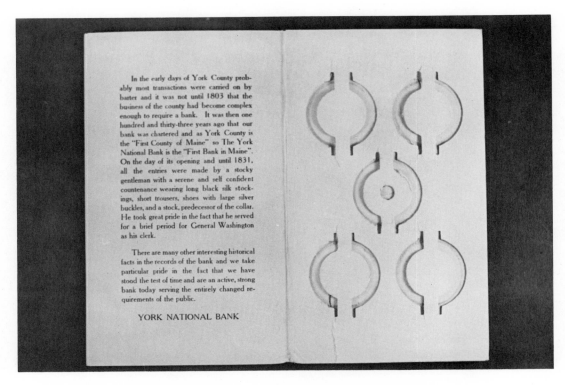

The inside of York mailing holder. It housed a tissue paper insert to protect the coins.

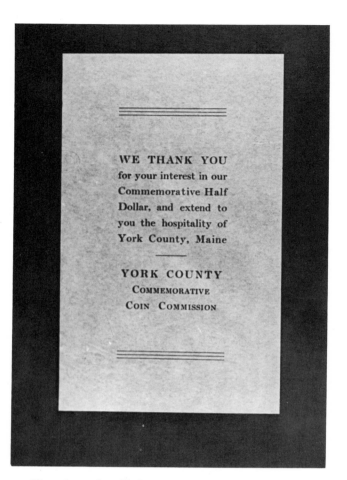

Tissue insert from York Tercentenary Commission.

half the total at the issue price of $1.50. (Out-of-state collectors had to pay $1.65, including shipping.) Issue began August 15.

When the commemorative bubble burst in 1937, the Association still had about 6,000 pieces on hand unsold. Some of these were sold in driblets into the mid-1950s, after which the rest were wholesaled in ten-coin lots at the loss-leader price of 10 for $15.50; they vanished at once.

Collateral Evidence: No proofs are reported, though some may have been made for John R. Sinnock.

The original batch appears to have been mailed out in unprinted holders from the Clerk of Courts in Alfred, Maine (note the illustrated envelope).

Later remainders 1947–57 were in more elaborate five-coin holders, imprinted as illustrated on the preceding page; possibly 65 of these holders have been traced to date.

The purchase of specimens possessing deep bag marks, slide marks, or a lack of mint-given brilliance (luster) is not recommended for your collection or investment holdings at present.

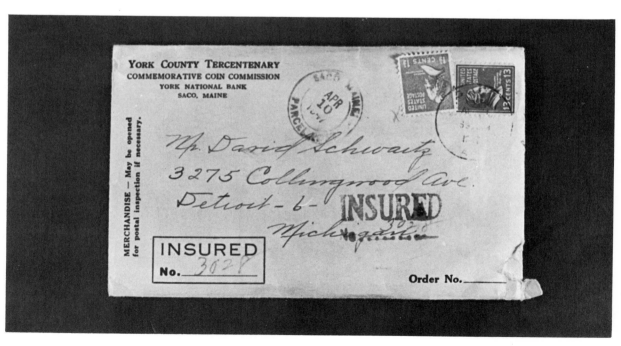

Mailing envelope.

THE EXCESSIVELY RARE PROOF COMMEMORATIVE COINAGE

Some of the rarest items in numismatics are the little known United States commemorative proof coins. In fact, the commemorative series of proof coinage, the father of the sleeping giant is just beginning to make his presence known to many coin collectors and investors.

These excessively rare pieces were struck as brilliant proofs; matte proofs (coins given a uniformly granular or dull surface often by pickling in acid); sandblast proofs (coins whose finish was imparted by sandblasting) and satin finish proofs (coins possessing a light yellow color with satiny patina that is sometimes described as a hybrid between a brilliant and a matte proof).

A good number of the listed commem proofs are seldom seen. Few, such as the Maryland, New Rochelle and Connecticut, ex-John R. Sinnock estate, were last offered for sale at the A.N.A. auction in 1962. The 1937 Boone matte proof set—which was struck at the Philadelphia Mint by order of Mr. Sinnock—has finally made its appearance, in 1979! One of the most beautiful of commemorative designs made as a matte proof, the Oregon Trail issue (1926–P), was in the collection of Aubrey E. Bebee (1948), owner of the famous 1913 Liberty Nickel: it made its appearance in 1975. This writer (A.S.) can name other examples, but believes the point has been made.

When discussing the lower excessively rare mint-age proof issues—if genuine—we are comparing items that are equally as rare as the 1887 proof $20 gold piece ($50,000); the 1907 $10 Eagle—Rounded Edge—Periods ($50,000) and the 1794 Flowing Hair Dollar in EF–AU condition, to mention but a few. Yes, they are rarer than the 1895 Morgan Proof Dollar! Be aware that the above-mentioned have made more appearances than the commemorative matte proof specimens. Also note the sandblast Hawaiian, of which fifty (50) were struck, recently sold for $15,000+ at auction. The great awakening is just beginning to take place! Expect this special coinage—if genuine—to sell for $100,000 per coin in ten years or less! Their purchase is most highly recommended if you're fortunate enough to have one cross your path.

What is thought of as the "not too difficult to locate" Columbian proof has made over two hundred plus appearances since 1962. Unfortunately for their unknowledgeable owners, only eight of those offered were genuine proofs. The balance is made up of those dangerous and beautiful early single struck pieces exhibiting a mirror field. If a gem Barber proof half dollar which is not really too difficult to obtain has sold for $11,000, what is a true proof Columbian worth?

In a conversation with a past mint employee who worked under John R. Sinnock (appointed Chief Engraver of the U.S. Mint from early 1925 until his death on May 14, 1947), I (A.S.) was informed that "Mr. Sinnock ordered two, sometimes four and, one time, ten double struck U.S. Commemoratives." He would not say that they were made personally for Sinnock, but noted he was told by the chief engraver that his interest developed when he was presented with several matte proof issues (Maine; 1920 Pilgrim and he thought the Grant issue) after his appointment at the mint.

However, one might suspect that Mr. Sinnock had these excessively rare items made for himself and possibly a friend. Simply by looking through Walter Breen's *Encyclopedia of United States and Colonial Proof Coins 1722–1977*, we can note that many of the special proof commemorative coins came from the estate of the man who designed both the Roosevelt dime and Franklin half dollar, John R. Sinnock. Yes, he also designed the reverse of the Illinois Centennial or Lincoln commemorative. Such was the catalytic agent for his secret love—matte proof commemoratives.

If you believe you possess a genuine specimen or are offered one, be sure the coin is double struck, giving the coin sharp relief details on both sides. All matte and sandblast specimens made outside the mint do not possess this most important feature! If in doubt, forward to Anthony Swiatek at P.O. Box 343, Kew Gardens, N.Y. 11415 or Walter Breen at F.C.I., 200 I.U. Willets Road, Albertson, N.Y. 11507. Also, read the chapters dealing with the Connecticut, Maryland, New Rochelle, Boone, etc., which deal with the special coinage in more depth.

PROOF U.S. COMMEMORATIVE SILVER

ISSUE	MINTAGE	SURFACE FINISH
1893 Isabella Quarter	20 known	Brilliant
1892 Columbian Exposition	104 struck	Brilliant
1893 Columbian Exposition	1 struck	Brilliant
1900 Lafayette Dollar	10 struck	Brilliant
1915 (No S) Panama Pacific Dollar	3 struck	Matte
1918 Lincoln	2 reported	Matte
1920 Maine	2 Known	Matte
1920 Pilgrim	2 reported	Matte
1921 Pilgrim	1 reported, unverified	Matte
1921 Alabama 2X2	1 reported, unverified	Matte
1921 Missouri 2 4	1 reported, unverified	Matte
1922 Grant with star	3 to 4 known	Matte
1922 Grant (plain)	2 reported, unlocated	Matte
1923 Monroe	2 reported, unlocated	Matte
1924 Huguenot	1 reported, unlocated	Matte
1925 Lexington	1 reported, unlocated	Matte
1925 Stone Mountain	1 reported, unlocated	Matte
1925 California (no S)	1 reported, unlocated	Matte
1925 Ft. Vancouver	3 reported, unlocated	Matte
1926 Oregon Trail	2 struck	Matte
1926 Sesquicentennial	2 struck	Matte
1927 Vermont	1 reported, unlocated	Matte
1928 Hawaiian	50 struck	Sandblast
1934 Maryland	4 struck	Matte
1935 Arkansas	1 reported, unlocated	Matte
1935 Connecticut	4 struck	Matte
1935 San Diego (with S?)	2 known, unlocated	Matte
1935 Hudson	2 known	Matte
1935 Spanish Trail	2 known	Matte
1936 Arkansas Robinson	8 struck	Satin Fin. or Semi-brilliant
1937 Arkansas	2 known	Satin Fin. or Semi-brilliant
1937 Boone Set	2 struck 1 unlocated	Matte
1938 New Rochelle	*50 struck	Struck on Proof Planchet with One Blow
1938 New Rochelle	10 struck	Matte
1938 Arkansas Set	2 known	Matte

*Special Presentation Piece

PROOF U.S. COMMEMORATIVE GOLD

ISSUE	MINTAGE	SURFACE FINISH
1903 Jefferson Dollar	100 struck	Brilliant
1903 McKinley Dollar	100 struck	Brilliant
1904 Lewis & Clark Dollar	6 to 8 known	Brilliant
1905 Lewis & Clark Dollar	4 to 6 known	Brilliant
1915 (No S) Panama Pacific Dollar	8 struck possessing different weights; plain and reeded edges	Satin Finish
1915 S Panama Pacific Dollar	1 reported, unverified	Matte
1915 S Panama Pacific $2½	1 reported, unverified	Matte
1916 McKinley Dollar	4 to 6 known	Brilliant
1917 McKinley Dollar	4 known	Brilliant
1922 Grant with Star Dollar	2 reported, unlocated	Brilliant
1926 Sesquicentennial $2½	2 struck	Matte

As we went to press, several satin finish proofs Panama–Pacific $1 gold pieces (patterns), struck without the s mintmark on the coin's reverse, were sold for $17,000 per coin. A similar pattern struck in silver was sold for $14,000.

HISTORY, INVESTMENT FORECAST OF SIX PARTICULAR COINS, AND COMMENTS

AN ARTISTIC LOOK AT THE COMMEMORATIVE SILVER COINS OF THE UNITED STATES

by Stanley Apfelbaum

Having been "invented" by the Greeks and then proliferated by the Romans, commemorative coins have served the ego and artistic bent of men and women for thousands of years. The graceful porpoise on some of the earliest coins known to man, and the exciting Quadriga (chariot with four horses) found on Roman coins were expressions of great artistry, no less than that of the renowned painters and poets and writers and singers of our story on earth.

And while the United States is not yet an "old" nation it is approaching maturity, I think you will agree. In the history of our country no one series of coins, with the exception of our commemorative dollars, have artistic merit in such profusion that it brings joy to the eye.

Look at the San Francisco-Oakland Bay Bridge coin of 1936. Only 71,000 coins were minted, and this a legal half dollar of the United States of America! A century earlier, in 1836, the mintage of that half dollar was six and a half million pieces! The comparison of prices is also interesting, because the 1836 coin would fetch about $3,500 in Brilliant Uncirculated grade, while the San Francisco coin brings an insignificant $300 or so.

But let's also *look* at the coin. The great bear on the obverse of the coin was designed by a dedicated San Francisco artist. The power and grandeur of the animal is carried over to the reverse of the coin where the great bridge stretches out across the Bay, depicting the power of mankind in contrast to the power of nature. Both are glorious. Now, move on to the Bridgeport Half Dollar, a strange coin, indeed. The designer of this coin created an eagle, so modern in concept that the eye has probably never seen one like it elsewhere. And on the obverse of the coin is a well-done head of P. T. Barnum. Why Barnum? It turns out that he was Bridgeport, Connecticut's best-known citizen, a philanthropist, an organizer, a diplomat, and of course, the wealthy owner of "The

Greatest Show on Earth". It's history — it's modern art. It's interesting!

And speaking of history, what of the Huguenot-Walloon Half Dollar of 1924? It was to "New" Netherlands that these two religious refugee groups came in 1624. The Dutch colonists are represented by the beautiful sailing vessel, "The Nieuw Nederland" on the reverse. A study of Huguenot-Walloon peoples and their troubles would illuminate a corner of history that is unknown to most persons.

Other strange and wonderful things crop up on our commemorative coin heritage. For instance, of the one and a half million persons who reside on Long Island, in the State of New York, we doubt that one person in 10,000 knows that there is a magnificent coin designed by the fine artist, Howard Kenneth Weinman, son of the sculptor, A.A. Weinman (who designed the Liberty Walking Type Half Dollar issued from 1916 to 1947).

The issue (1936) depicts the 300th anniversary of the first settlement on Long Island at Jamaica by Dutch colonists. Yes, a Long Island Half Dollar of the United States of America! Do you think your neighbor knows that such a coin exists? In fact, would he know that there was a New Rochelle, New York, Half Dollar? Or a Cincinnati Half Dollar? And that these coins have a mystique uniquely their own, and sure as heck are valuable! On the New Rochelle the title to the land which the settlers purchased from the landowner John Pell stipulated that a fattened calf be given away each year, and so the calf and the figure of John Pell appear on the obverse of the coin. Strange? Yes! Not so strange, perhaps, is the fact that only 15,266 of these coins were minted in 1938 — that it is listed at $250 in the 1980 Red Book, but the true price of the coin is about $1,200. Our prediction for this coin to increase in value is at the rate of about 81.2% per year for the next five years! On the Cincinnati coin, the head of Stephen Foster commemorated the

50th anniversary of Cincinnati as a center of music. Also bearing the date of 1936, the design is simple, the cleanness of its lines uninhibited, and the coin strange only in that the devices are well integrated with the design and do not give the appearance of clutter as so many of our "regular" coins do.

My favorite commemorative coin from the point of view of artistic rendering is the Oregon Trail Half Dollar. This piece, designed by James Earle Fraser and his wife Laura Gardin Fraser, is gorgeous. It is! The Indian on the obverse of the coin trying to stop the progress of the white man across the United States of America, is dramatic and compelling, and on the reverse, the loneliness of the Conestoga Wagon as it winds its way across the trails of Oregon is graphic and evocative. When you own and hold this glittering silver piece, you'll appreciate the magnificence of this coin. Both of the Frasers were eminent artists and designers of other United States coinage.

Have I begun to prove a point? If I have, well and good. If I haven't, look at these coins and judge for yourself. I believe that our commemorative coinage is undervalued. But I also believe that they are unappreciated. Imagine, if you will, the marriage of value and art in rare coins, and in rare coins of the United States at that! And there you have it.

A LOOK INTO THE FUTURE

The day is coming. It came in the stock market some sixty years ago. It is dawning in the numismatic market.

The Fifties, Sixties and Seventies were inhabited by rather "odd" persons who acquired rare coins — and made money with them. They were surely pioneers, even leaders to a new Promised Land of Investment. Even the rare coin dealers that served them weren't aware of the revolution-on-the-brink-of-becoming-reality. Some persons had rushed into decorative plates, commemorative ingots and the like, most ending with a sour taste and far short of desired goals. But the rush portended a change in investment strategy. Now, the Eighties, the ownership of fine tangible collectibles, those with a huge secondary market, will come to mean real wealth, meaningful combat against vicious inflation.

The day is coming. There's a base of about eight to ten million rare coin collectors throughout the world, creating constant demand for fine material. Serving these millions of Americans, Europeans, and others in South Africa, Hong Kong, Australia and Israel, are thousands of dealers. Dozens of major auctions are held each year, providing constant monitoring of values. National teletype services have hundreds of dealer/subscribers — and the Xerox Corporation just acquired the largest of these vital communication services! The auction market and the dealer network are international in scope; and the scope of the market lends it ever increasing credibility.

I believe that in the 1980's the key to investment success will be the ownership of fine and rare tangibles — those with great market strength. Instead of being subject to economic vagaries dependent upon world markets, and internal and international political dealings, investors in rare coins spurn the printed promises of corporate and political entities to pay dividends or interest. Instead they quietly reap the satisfaction of increasing demand and increasing value (according to the Wall Street firm of Salomon Brothers, increases of 20% per year have been recorded by rare coins over the last decade.)

Tangibles will become indispensable in the Eighties!

INFLATION

It's our most persistent problem. It began in 1971 when the price of gold was $35 per ounce — reaching $600 or so by the end of 1980. This astronomical rise denotes the *meaning* of inflation...the debasement of our paper currency. And some say it's only shown the tip of what may be coming.

All of us are making more money, but the general level of our standard of living is eroding.

The protection of what we own has become more important than acquiring more. Because more — quickly means less, unless our assets keep ahead of inflation.

I have been a pioneer in the rare coin investment market. It didn't exist 15 years ago. With the assistance of researchers like Walter Breen and Anthony Swiatek, my firm, First Coinvestors, has progressed from a capital base of $500 to $50,000 in sales (1967) to assets of over $5 Million and sales of $20 Million (1980). Despite the heavy tread of inflation and its outright robbery of our resources, facts demonstrate that rare coins consistently foil the robber. As the mongoose exerts domination over the deadly snake, so does a rare coin portfolio avert the poison in our economy, and the erosion of our hard-earned wealth.

And now I will happily try to answer the question put to me — "What specific commemorative coins would you choose for maximum appreciation in this decade?"

THE BIG SIX

It's not a secret any more — for the price of this book we'll let you in on it. When this book was in its early planning stage, as a point of focus, we formed a panel of interested persons to help me choose certain of the coins in the commemorative series as "best" for the 1980's. We — Anthony Swiatek, co-author of this volume; Bill Gay, Vice President, Purchasing, First Coinvestors; Jack Lee and Joe Muraca, Executive Vice President and Vice President of Marketing, First Coinvestors, and myself — decided to choose exactly a half dozen of these beautiful coins for our collective recommendation. Bill, Jack and Joe bear responsibility for buying and selling an enormous quantity of American coinage. Tony is the acknowledged expert in forecasting the great moves in "his" commemorative series. As for me — I'm involved in the "long distance" ideas and moves my company chooses.

The process of choosing the "best" coins was sometimes exhilarating, sometimes downright frustrating. How could Bill favor the York over my Vermont? Didn't Joe and Tony understand Jack's argument in favor of the Spanish Trail? This went on and on. Wow — did we argue!

Out of the many meetings came the following six selections. These coins are *not* the "best" for investment — but they are probably among the very best. Moreover, they are coins that can be acquired — not coins that are so rare that growth of value is assured, but taking part in that growth is virtually impossible. These are our consensus coins, but believe me, if you favor others, you could be just as prescient as we are.

THE BOOKER T. WASHINGTON SETS AND THE WASHINGTON/CARVER SETS. ALL OF THEM! (BUT ESPECIALLY THE 1954 W/C SET).

Want to see your investment triple within a decade? I believe that might be a conservative prediction! As rare as the Grant With Star Half Dollar is, the 1954 W/C Set is harder to obtain! That's right! The same amount of effort given to obtain the Grant With Star coin and the 1954 W/C Set will obtain about an equal amount, with the possibility of obtaining more Grants With Stars than the set. Ironically, about 2½ years ago when the commemorative coins were totally languishing in the depths of numismatic disrespect, First Coinvestors launched a campaign to purchase every Booker T. Washington and Washington/Carver set it could acquire. In those days, in the Spring of 1978, we obtained about $135,000 worth of these sets at wholesale costs. By the time we distributed them to our customers, the wholesale cost had risen almost 100% and at this point, after only a 30 month holding, our customers can obtain a very strong profit on every set they bought. But that's not the whole story... the whole story is that included in our acquisition were a number of roll sets (20 coins of every one of the Booker T. Washington and Washington/Carver issues). Somewhere around 100

to 125 1954 W/C sets were sold in those groups, and some of our customers received multiple sets! The acquisition and distribution of those sets launched the Commemorative Coin Society which my Company has maintained successfully since then, but from that time on, we have not been successful in buying any quantity of any of the sets — and very few of the 1954 sets. Yet, they're out there!

The hysteria inherent in the aftermath of the World War II period was illustrated by the reasoning behind the issuance of these two coin sets — to combat Communism within the Black communities of our nation. What idiocy! The honors bestowed on these titanic scientists, Booker T. Washington, and George Washington Carver were more than deserved. And when our nation wakes to the fact that these two fine Americans were honored on legitimate Half Dollars bearing their likenesses, the price of the sets will explode.

A very close second to the Isabella Quarter dollar are all of the B.T.W. and W./C. sets, with a special emphasis on the 1954 W/C Set.

THE GRANT MEMORIAL ISSUE — WITH STAR

Yes, it is the "King" — the stick-out of all Commemorative Half Dollars. Its mintage, in case you've missed it, was 4256!!! And most of the coins were used, cleaned or abraded. In fact, true Uncirculated coins, as noted by Tony Swiatek, will usually be dull in appearance or bright — from cleaning!

The acquisition of this coin in MS-65 or MS-67 is most highly recommended. It would be the equal of purchasing a Rolls Royce, as compared to darting in and out of the automobile market and buying the tin that Detroit sells on an ever-obsoleting basis. You pay for what you get — and this coin, although "expensive" in relationship to other Commemorative coins, is worth every penny you pay for it. Tony Swiatek says that in MS-65 or MS-67 there may be only 75 specimens extant. And that rates an exclamation point — ! There are a few available — keep alert. You'll get one.

THE ISABELLA QUARTER DOLLAR

As our authors relate in the first part of the investment section, this coin is absolutely protected against promotion (as are so many others in the series). The promotions of years ago are like bad dreams that fade away — they won't happen again. Distribution of this entire series almost guarantees that hoards of the better coins will never again be seen, and the "hype" job simply can't happen. Today, should ten of these gorgeous Isabella Quarter Dollar coins come on the market (unheard of) there would be 70 to 100 customers of my Company alone who would instantly be ready to snap them up. This coin typifies the kind of material *we* want our customers to own. The astoundingly low mintage (24,214 pieces) is "just not readily available", and I'm quoting Bill Gay, our Vice President, Purchasing. Yes, you can acquire one or two of these coins — but it won't be easy. In the months between the close of the American Numismatic Association Convention in late August, 1980, and just prior to the publication of this book, with great effort, he was able to purchase seven pieces in MS-65. Now, when you bear in mind that our firm must stock enough coins to supply almost 14,000 customers, our buying staff must come up with the material for our monthly needs. Yet, nothing availed when we attempted to corral a roll or so within the time period stated. We're still looking.

Tony Swiatek believes that there are no more than 250 pieces which truly fall into the Gem class (MS-65)! And in superb condition (MS-67) he believes there are as few as 75 pieces! And that tells the story of why Bill Gay finds these coins "just not readily available".

This coin is our first choice for great price increases over the next five to ten years.

THE ALABAMA CENTENNIAL HALF DOLLAR

We note that although the Eagle on the reverse is generally weakly struck, and although much of the issue is found in AU grade, (that's *Almost* Uncirculated), and although there are excessive facial abrasions to be found on the face of Governor Kilby, in MS-65 or MS-67 we most highly recommend the acquisition of this coin. Heed Tony Swiatek's advice and beware! He states that there are probably no more than 250 coins of each variety in existence in the two grades recommended — but yet most dealers think that the coin is readily available in "nice lustrous appearance". At least that's what the ads say. Don't believe them! Get one of these coins as soon as you can.

THE YORK COUNTY, MAINE HALF DOLLAR

Third on our list is a coin that is readily available in all Uncirculated states, MS-60 to MS-67. For the moment! The increasing demand for these coins is evidenced by the desire of those who are trying to put together the entire set of type coins, and this is about to wipe out the last vestiges of "easy" availability of any commemorative coin, let alone one that is so desirable as this one. Although it's marked third on our "Big Six" List, don't let it slip by — obtain it soon — and count it as dear as the others on the list. It should be as well.

THE FORT VANCOUVER HALF DOLLAR

14,994 specimens in total! And of that infinitesimal amount, many were used as "lucky" coins, or pocket pieces. If one were to believe the advertisements in the coin journals, many seem available — almost more than the amount minted! It just is not true. Many of the AU coins are polished pieces — and the MS-60's are not much better (probably buffed). Once again — beware! Bill Gay notes that this is a very tough coin to find without slight rubs on the highest surfaces — and so we very highly recommend a true MS-60, MS-63, MS-65 and (oh where can we find one?) MS-67.

Since Tony Swiatek is going out on the limb and projecting prices over the next ten years for all Commemorative coins, why shouldn't I? Especially since I am focusing on only six of them. All of the coins are assumed to be in MS-65 grade:

VALUES ARE FOR COINS THAT ARE
CHOICE BRILLIANT UNCIRCULATED MS 65 GRADE

	1968 Price	1975 Price	1980 Price	1985 Prediction
1954 Washington/Carver Philadelphia, Denver San Francisco Set	$ 12	$ 59	$ 170	$ 650
Grant (With Star)	160	910	5200	20,000 +
Isabella Quarter	105	298	1430	10,000
Alabama (2X2)	70	545	1700	4,000
York	30	122	935	2,500
Fort Vancouver	110	425	2100	7,500

A PERIODIC TABLE OF U.S. COMMEMORATIVE COINAGE VALUES

YEAR OF ISSUE	ISSUE	ISSUE PRICE	1948 UNC. VALUE	1958 UNC. VALUE	1968 UNC. VALUE	1980 UNC. MS-60 ADVERTISED VALUE	1980 GEM-BU MS-65 ADVERTISED VALUE
1893	Isabella 25¢	$1.00	$10.00	$30.00	$105.00	$805.00	$1300.00+
1900	Lafayette $1	2.00	13.00	43.00	175.00	2550.00	7000.00+
1921	Alabama	1.00	7.50	30.00	60.00	595.00	1200.00+
1921	Alabama 2×2	1.00	18.00	35.00	70.00	722.00	1700.00+
1936	Albany	2.00	3.50	20.00	60.00	467.00	600.00+
1937	Antietam	1.65	6.00	32.00	105.00	595.00	1190.00+
Type	Arkansas	—	2.50	5.00	14.00	110.00	230.00+
1935	Arkansas Set	3.00	8.00	14.00	40.00	382.00	680.00+
1936	Arkansas Set	4.50	9.00	13.00	40.00	382.00	680.00+
1937	Arkansas Set	8.75	14.00	17.00	41.00	425.00	710.00+
1938	Arkansas Set	8.75	18.00	44.00	85.00	807.00	1700.00+
1939	Arkansas Set	10.00	65.00	140.00	360.00	2295.00	3400.00+
1936	Bay Ridge	1.50	3.50	11.50	35.00	153.00	340.00+
Type	Boone	—	2.50	4.50	14.00	175.00	298.00+
1934	Boone	1.60	2.50	5.00	14.00	178.00	298.00+
1935	Boone Set	4.30	11.00	15.00	40.00	442.00	935.00+
1935/34	Boone Set	8.50	135.00	160.00	340.00	2080.00	2300.00+
1936	Boone Set	4.30	11.00	17.00	40.00	442.00	935.00+
1937	Boone Set	12.40	60.00	125.00	240.00	1062.00	2040.00+
1938	Boone Set	6.50	65.00	160.00	330.00	2125.00	3400.00+
1936	Bridgeport	2.00	2.50	10.00	35.00	238.00	500.00+
1926	California	1.00	5.00	12.00	30.00	255.00	980.00+
Type	Cincinnati	—	8.50	25.00	160.00	722.00	1000.00+
1936	Cincinnati Set	7.50	28.50	68.00	40.00	2210.00	3000.00+
1936	Cleveland	1.50	1.50	3.50	25.00	119.00	248.00+

Type							
1936	Columbia	—	3.50	16.00	38.00	468.00	$ 935.00+
	Columbia Set	6.45	8.50	45.00	110.00	1530.00	2550.00+
1892	Columbian	1.00	1.00	3.00	5.00	38.00	240.00+
1893	Columbian	1.00	1.00	3.00	5.00	38.00	240.00+
1936	Connecticut	1.00	6.00	28.00	60.00	374.00	850.00+
1936	Delaware	1.75	3.00	13.00	50.00	375.00	750.00+
1936	Elgin	1.50	2.50	15.00	50.00	323.00	930.00+
1936	Gettysburg	1.65	4.50	15.00	55.00	467.00	1080.00+
1922	Grant	1.00	3.00	11.00	28.00	162.00	595.00+
1922	Grant Star	1.00	65.00	105.00	160.00	1190.00	5200.00+
1928	Hawaiian	2.00	30.00	125.00	625.00	2380.00	5100.00+
1935	Hudson	1.00	15.00	80.00	300.00	1190.00	2500.00+
1924	Huguenot	1.00	4.00	11.00	28.00	162.00	510.00+
1946	Iowa	2.75	3.00	8.50	23.00	128.00	298.00+
1925	Lexington	1.00	3.00	8.00	14.00	119.00	340.00+
1918	Lincoln	1.00	3.00	11.00	28.00	136.00	425.00+
1936	Long Island	1.00	1.70	6.00	20.00	112.00	240.00+
1936	Lynchburg	1.00	3.50	15.00	52.00	315.00	815.00+
1920	Maine	1.00	6.00	11.00	30.00	170.00	805.00+
1934	Maryland	1.00	2.25	14.00	50.00	272.00	595.00+

YEAR OF ISSUE	ISSUE	ISSUE PRICE	1948 UNC. VALUE	1958 UNC. VALUE	1968 UNC. VALUE	1980 UNC. MS-60 ADVERTISED VALUE	1980 GEM-BU MS-65 ADVERTISED VALUE
1921	Missouri	$1.00	$25.00	$70.00	$160.00	$1317.00	$3400.00+
1921	Missouri 2×4	1.00	35.00	73.00	180.00	1360.00	3650.00+
1923	Monroe	1.00	3.00	8.50	18.00	85.00	275.00+
1938	New Rochelle	2.00	4.00	25.00	80.00	595.00	1265.00+
1936	Norfolk	1.50	4.50	20.00	75.00	595.00	1500.00+
1926	Oregon	1.00	2.50	4.50	13.00	195.00	340.00+
1926s	Oregon	1.00	2.50	4.50	13.00	195.00	340.00+
1928	Oregon	2.00	5.50	5.00	25.00	425.00	850.00+
1933D	Oregon	2.00	7.00	7.00	25.00	468.00	1020.00+
1934D	Oregon	2.00	3.50	4.50	17.00	357.00	850.00+
1936P	Oregon	1.60	2.50	4.50	50.00	221.00	510.00+
1936s	Oregon	1.60	7.00	8.00	60.00	340.00	850.00+
1937D	Oregon	1.60	2.50	4.50	42.00	215.00	420.00+
1938	Oregon Set	6.25	14.00	15.00	116.00	850.00	1700.00+
1939	Oregon Set	7.50	32.00	55.00	250.00	1402.00	2500.00+
Type	Oregon					195.00	290.00+
1915	Pan-Pacific 50¢	1.00	18.00	45.00	100.00	1360.00	5500.00+
1920	Pilgrim	1.00	2.50	5.00	14.00	102.00	340.00+
1921	Pilgrim	1.00	3.00	6.00	17.00	284.00	670.00+
Type	Rhode Island	1.00	3.50	8.50	20.00	255.00	475.00+
1936	Rhode Island Set	3.00	10.00	25.00	60.00	850.00	1530.00+
1937	Roanoke	1.65	3.00	12.00	30.00	255.00	835.00+
1936	Robinson	1.85	2.00	11.00	28.00	215.00	500.00+
1935s	San Diego	1.00	2.50	7.00	20.00	112.00	255.00+
1936D	San Diego	1.50	2.50	8.00	22.00	185.00	440.00+
1926	Sesqui	1.00	2.50	10.00	23.00	85.00	255.00+
1935	Spanish Trail	2.00	12.50	60.00	280.00	1445.00	3460.00+
1925	Stone Mountain	1.00	1.25	4.00	8.00	52.00	250.00+
Type	Texas	—	2.25	6.00	18.00	136.00	250.00+

1934	Texas	1.00	2.25	6.00	18.00	136.00	$ 250.00+
1935	Texas Set	4.50	6.50	11.00	45.00	408.00	250.00+
1936	Texas Set	4.50	7.50	11.50	45.00	408.00	680.00+
1937	Texas Set	4.50	8.00	12.00	46.00	510.00	850.00+
1938	Texas Set	6.00	35.00	45.00	130.00	978.00	1650.00+
1925	Vancouver	1.00	15.00	60.00	110.00	893.00	2100.00+
1927	Vermont	1.00	4.50	20.00	50.00	425.00	1350.00+
Type	B.T.W.	—	—	1.60	3.25	24.00	29.00+
1946	B.T.W. Set	3.50	3.50	4.50	8.00	77.00	85.00+
1947	B.T.W. Set	6.00	6.00	7.00	12.00	94.00	165.00+
1948	B.T.W. Set	7.50	—	10.00	20.00	153.00	340.00+
1949	B.T.W. Set	8.50	—	11.00	36.00	298.00	675.00+
1950	B.T.W. Set	8.50	—	10.50	34.00	230.00	510.00+
1951	B.T.W. Set	10.00	—	10.00	26.00	187.00	425.00+

YEAR OF ISSUE	ISSUE	ISSUE PRICE	1948 UNC. VALUE	1958 UNC. VALUE	1968 UNC. VALUE	1980 UNC. MS-60 ADVERTISED VALUE	1980 GEM-BU MS-65 ADVERTISED VALUE
Type	W.C.	—	—	$2.00	$3.00	$24.00	$ 25.00+
1951	W.C. Set	$10.00	—	8.00	12.00	102.00	170.00+
1952	W.C. Set	10.00	—	8.00	16.00	155.00	340.00+
1953	W.C. Set	10.00	—	8.00	17.00	238.00	425.00+
1954	W.C. Set	10.00	—	8.00	12.00	110.00	175.00+
1936	Wisconsin	1.50	$2.50	14.00	37.00	255.00	880.00+
1936	York	1.50	2.50	10.00	30.00	255.00	935.00+

GOLD COMMEMORATIVES

YEAR OF ISSUE	ISSUE	ISSUE PRICE	1948 UNC. VALUE	1958 UNC. VALUE	1968 UNC. VALUE	1980 UNC. MS-60 ADVERTISED VALUE	1980 GEM-BU MS-65 ADVERTISED VALUE
1903	La. Purchase/ Jefferson	$3.00	$13.00	$25.00	$115.00	$1487.00+	$3230.00+
1903	La. Purchase/ McKinley	3.00	13.00	25.00	115.00	1487.00+	3230.00+
1904	Lewis & Clark	2.00	45.00	125.00	400.00	3825.00+	8500.00+
1905	Lewis & Clark	2.00	45.00	115.00	400.00	3825.00+	8500.00+
1915s	Pan Pacific $1.00	2.00	10.00	18.00	80.00	1912.00+	6800.00+
1915s	Pan-Pacific $2.50	4.00	35.00	80.00	400.00	6035.00+	18,750.00+
1916	McKinley	3.00	12.00	20.00	110.00	1530.00+	3102.00+
1917	McKinley	3.00	13.00	25.00	175.00	1615.00+	3400.00+
1922	Grant	3.00	32.00	70.00	335.00	3188.00+	7055.00+
1922	Grant (with star)	3.50	30.00	60.00	365.00	3188.00+	7055.00+
1926	Sesquicentennial $2.50	4.00	11.00	17.00	.00	1105.00+	1998.00+
1915	Pan-Pacific $50.00 (R)	100.00	575.00	2,000.00	6,000.00	76,500.00+	108,800.00+
1915	Pan-Pacific $50.00 (O)	100.00	475.00	1,500.00	4,750.00	63,750.00	86,000.00

THE INVESTMENT SECTION

The following are the writer's (A.S.) five- and ten-year price projections for the entire U.S. Commemorative series. They are based on inflation continuing at its existing pace, and only a small continuous demand for the series. Keeping this in mind, the projected prices should not be so startling, especially since the 50-piece type set more than tripled in value during the years 1968–1979 and more than doubled in price since 1973!

This was a period where the series advanced mostly on its own strength—with little dealer assistance. Why? People bought into the series because these low mintage pieces offered historical interest as well as aesthetically beautiful designs. They, possibly 300 collectors, saw a very bright investment future for the series then and in the next couple of decades to come. They were proven correct to date and will be proven correct again in the future.

At times in the recent past, the dealer buying prices showed minus signs on many issues that could not be located—properly graded. This was the calm before today's price storm. Now dealers try to put away as many true gem commems as can be located at lower prices. Naturally, some collectors and investors will panic and sell, taking their profits instead of holding for even more unbelievable gains! When the next commemorative advance begins, the ground ungenuinely lost will be rapidly recaptured and all new highs will be attained. However, minus signs on true gem MS-65 specimens should not instinctively follow the minus signs on the more available MS-60 category for two-thirds or so of the issues. After all, why should this be? Those true gem MS-65 issues are not so easily located—especially the superb coins. What storehouse made them available?

As you know, such coins cannot be replaced like other vendables whose constant added supply will decrease their price, particularly with a decline in interest. This is not the case with correctly graded commemoratives, for the aforementioned decreases will hold true only for those issues that are in very abundant supply in all grades for the present time.

The given 1980 values listed in the Periodic Table are dealers' advertised prices. Unfortunately, many do not have in stock those hard-to-get issues they publicize and the unscrupulous will forward an overgraded specimen for a "reasonable" price. Should the coin be accurately graded, the correct price most likely will accompany such. Therefore, I have added a plus sign (+) to the right of the 1980 pricing, indicating the value of that coin should sell for much more than the advertised price listed. Within the next two to five years (or less), collectors and investors will see the "trees from the forest," involving true quality commems.

Grading standards are as follows:

MS-60   A mint state coin with no luster or traces of luster, or fully lusterous with excessive bag marks or heavily cleaned, or mark free with no luster.

MS-63   A coin that possesses half of its original luster along with a few bag marks.

MS-63+   A coin possessing half its original luster and almost mark free.

MS-65   A gem coin possessing full mint luster with no obvious detracting features such as heavy slide marks on the cheekbone of an individual, deep bag marks on the faces or devices and no visible hairlines from cleaning or whizzing.

MS-67   A gem (superb) virtually flawless coin possessing full original mint luster.

MS-70   An absolute flawless specimen.

Natural toning, which has taken many years to develop, be it golden, light brown, sea green, electric blue or an angelic display of rainbow colors will make the coin more desirable in the eyes of many investors and collectors. Should you be offered the above-mentioned, look for natural luster under the toning, as well as excessive negatives on the coin's surface. Grade accordingly. Remember, coins can be artificially toned. However, they cannot come close to resembling the real thing.

In closing, be aware of the following:

(A) There were only several hundred individuals who were interested in commems in the past.

(B) This gave the impression that most issues were around in great quantities and in gem condition. True, most issues could be located without much fuss.

(C) Commems were not part of numismatics' main event—they were an insignificant sideshow. Most numismatists knew only of the seated Liberty series, the Barber series, etc.

(D) At present (1980), the steady inflow of collectors and investors—numbering over 20,000—interested in this rare and scarce low mintage series of sixty different designs is constantly increasing.

(E) There are many sleepers in the series which will bring fantastic monetary gains to their owners.

(F) Large amounts of collector and investor cash will be directed into this area for many years to come.

(G) The possibility that our government will soon issue a new commemorative half dollar with the discontinuance of the Kennedy half—just for collectors!

I'm sure that there will be many people who view my 1985 and 1990 projections as *very* overoptimistic. However, when I first prepared my projections in early 1979, they looked unreal. Many friends looked at them, then at me—then smiled. Would you believe that all those projections were reached—and passed—before the end of 1979! What you see before you are my latest and best projections for the next decade—most of which I expect to become reality and many of which I expect to see exceeded!

In summary, the owners of U.S. Commemorative coinage have a very bright monetary future to look forward to. Compared to the prices that other areas of United States coinage have attained lately, commemorative coinage is tremendously *underpriced*!

A.S.

THE ALABAMA CENTENNIAL HALF DOLLARS

Here is an issue that finds almost 80 percent of both its varieties—the 2×2 and the plain—in almost uncirculated conditions. Beware! They can *all* look good to the unknowledgeable! Most of the remaining specimens fall into the just uncirculated (MS-60) category. In fact, five original rolls of the plain variety which were recently offered for sale (to A.S.) fall into the MS-60 state because all of the coins possessed too much facial abrasion on Governor Kilby, as well as heavy bag marks.

Locating specimens of the true MS-65 and MS-67 class will be very difficult. In this grade, both coins are equally as rare, aside from the fact that the plain variety is offered, at present, for $300 less in price! This situation arises because there exist many more MS-63 specimens than the 2×2 variety. Since they are offered as MS-65 coins, lacking much of their original luster, etc., the "mask of false availability" is created. However, let a true gem original specimen appear on the scene, either at auction or in a dealer's showcase, and watch this price differential vanish! The purchase of both issues in MS-65 and MS-67 is most recommended. We believe there doesn't exist more than 250 coins of each variety in the true gem states.

In summary:
MS-60; MS-63—Purchase of the 2×2 recommended.
MS-65—Most recommended (Both varieties).
MS-67—Most highly recommended (Both varieties).

PRICE PROJECTIONS

	1985				1990		
Issue	MS-60	MS-65	MS-67		MS-60	MS-65	MS-67
2×2	$1800.	$5200.+	$8000.+		$3600.	$9500.+	$13,000.+
Plain	$900.	$5400.+	$8000.+		$1300.	$9500.+	$13,000.+

THE ALBANY CHARTER HALF DOLLAR

Here is an issue that appears to be none too difficult to locate in all uncirculated grades. However, due to a quiet and steady demand for this low mintage issue (17,671), it seems most obvious that true gem specimens are making increasingly infrequent appearances. It is quietly being absorbed.

The purchase of this issue in gem condition MS-65 and superb gem (MS-67) condition is highly recommended.

In summary:
MS-60; MS-63—Recommended.
MS-65; MS-67—Highly recommended.

PRICE PROJECTIONS

	1985				1990		
MS-60	MS-65	MS-67			MS-60	MS-65	MS-67
$600.	$1200.+	$1500.+			$1000.	$2000.+	$2600.+

THE ANTIETAM HALF DOLLAR

Most of this issue can be located in all uncirculated states. However, with its low mintage (18,028), I find the gem BU (MS-65) specimens becoming somewhat difficult to locate. The superb or gem (MS-67) coin, which made its appearance rather often in the past, has not been showing itself much these days, for the supply is starting to dry up. The purchase of this issue in the choice and gem categories is recommended for immediate acquisition.

In summary:
MS-60—Recommended.
MS-63—Recommended.
MS-65—Most recommended.
MS-67—Most highly recommended.

PRICE PROJECTIONS

	1985				1990		
MS-60	MS-65	MS-67			MS-60	MS-65	MS-67
$800.	$1900.+	$2300.+			$1020.	$3100.+	$4000.+

THE ARKANSAS CENTENNIAL HALF DOLLARS

Most of this entire issue, which was not made with much tender loving care, falls into the MS-60 and MS-60+ category at best because of exceptionally poor luster, detracting marks and field abrasions. This will become obvious when trying to locate equal quality specimens of 1935, 1936 and 1937 sets and especially obvious with the "super sleeper" 1938 set and the very tough 1939 set. Should you be that lucky, the purchase of any of the above-mentioned sets in true gem MS-65 condition is highly recommended—especially the latter two dates.

In summary:
MS-60—Except for the 1939 and 1938 sets, don't purchase in quantity at present.
MS-63—Entire issue is recommended except the 1936 issue.
MS-65—Entire issue is highly recommended.
MS-67—Entire issue is most highly recommended.

PRICE PROJECTIONS

		1985				1990	
Issue	MS-60	MS-65	MS-67		MS-60	MS-65	MS-67
1935 Set	$ 550.	$1150.+	$ 1500.+		$ 800.	$ 2000.+	$ 2400.+
1936 Set	$ 550.	$1250.+	$ 1600.+		$ 800.	$ 2100.+	$ 2500.+
1937 Set	$ 600.	$1450.+	$ 1800.+		$ 850.	$ 2300.+	$ 2700.+
1938 Set	$1000.+	$4100.+	$ 5000.+		$1500.+	$ 6500.+	$ 8000.+
1939 Set	$4200.+	$8800.+	$12,000.+		$5900.+	$13,000.+	$25,000.+
Type Coin	$ 150.	$ 275.+	$ 375.+		$ 280.	$ 525.	$ 700.+

THE BAY BRIDGE HALF DOLLAR

The majority of this issue exists in the uncirculated state. However, due to numismatic abuse, much of the aforementioned lacks original luster. This will be most obvious when comparing the coin's obverse with a true gem (MS-65). The abused coin will usually be dull or just look bright from an obvious cleaning. The gem coins do make the appearance and their purchase is recommended.

In summary:
MS-60; MS-63—Don't purchase in quantity at present.
MS-65; MS-67—Most recommended.

PRICE PROJECTIONS

1985				1990		
MS-60	MS-65	MS-67		MS-60	MS-65	MS-67
$200.	$600.+	$875.+		$350.	$950.+	$1500.+

THE DANIEL BOONE BICENTENNIAL HALF DOLLARS

Since the 1934 issue was widely distributed and numismatically abused, it is very underrated in gem condition. Most of its mintage—due to detracting obverse marks and cleaning—falls into the MS-60 and MS-63 category.

The same fate appears to be overtaking the 1935 and 1936 Boone coins. Nice sets will require some effort to locate—as is true with the rest of this series—because the heavy cardboard holders contained sulphur that tarnished the coins. Later, these were cleaned or placed in a silver cleaning solution which could not remove the thick layer of tone, so baking soda was applied and it removed nearly all of the coin's natural surface, making it look falsely new or bright.

There exist only 2003 sets dated 1935 with the added 1934 on the reverse. This is a very rare set and its purchase is highly recommended in all uncirculated states, especially in gem condition. Again, the D and S coins are the rare specimens. They possess a natural semi-matte finish on the obverse because of the die state.

The real sleeper or dark horse of this series is the 1937 set. Again, the branch mint coins are the rare ones (2506). Its purchase is highly recommended in choice and gem condition because the available supply has been overlooked due to its scarcity; also, it's been overlooked because the 1935 with 1934 added and the 1938 coins are always first noted.

The 1938 set where each coin has a mintage of 2100 specimens should be purchased in all uncirculated grades, especially in gem condition. When purchasing a single type coin, make it a gem specimen.

There exist two genuine—double struck—matte proof 1937 Boone sets. The D and S mint marks seem to jump right out of the coin. Other so-called matte proof sets that I have seen of different issues are not double struck and therefore can be classified as fakes. If individual genuine matte proofs have sold for between $15,000 and $17,500, what is the value of this set?

In summary:
MS-60–1934; 1935; 1936 set—Don't purchase in quantity at present.
MS-63—Entire issue is recommended.
MS-65—Entire issue is highly recommended.
MS-67—Entire issue is most highly recommended.

PRICE PROJECTIONS

Issue	1985				1990		
	MS-60	MS-65	MS-67		MS-60	MS-65	MS-67
1934-P	$ 198.	$ 480.+	$ 575.+		$ 345.	$ 850.+	$ 1100.+
1935 Set	$ 540.	$1850.+	$ 2700.+		$ 780.	$ 3000.+	$ 2400.+
1935 Set w/1934 Added	$3350.+	$5800.+	$ 6500.+		$5600.+	$12,000.+	$ 14,000.+
1936 Set	$ 540.	$1850.+	$ 2700.+		$ 780.	$ 3000.+	$ 3400+
1937 Set	$2800.	$4800.+	$ 5800.+		$4600.	$ 9500.+	$ 12,000.+
1938 Set	$3300.	$6200.+	$ 6800.+		$5200.	$11,400.	$ 14,000.+
Type Coin	$ 230.	$ 450.+	$ 550.+		$ 350.	$ 850.+	$ 900.+
1937 Matte Proof Set			$175,000.				$300,000.+

THE BRIDGEPORT CENTENNIAL HALF DOLLAR

The great majority of this issue can easily be located in choice (MS-63) condition. However, locating gem specimens, especially those free of facial nicks or slide marks on P.T.B. or "eagle nicks" on the coin reverse will be a find. The purchase of such is most recommended, as well as a gem BU (MS-65) specimen. Hoards of this issue do exist at present, especially in MS-60 and MS-63 condition.

In summary:
MS-60; MS-63—Don't purchase in quantity at present.
MS-65—Recommended.
MS-67—Most recommended.

PRICE PROJECTION

1985				1990		
MS-60	MS-65	MS-67		MS-60	MS-65	MS-67
$350.	$950.+	$1200.+		$600.	$1400.+	$2500.+

THE CALIFORNIA JUBILEE HALF DOLLAR

Here is another issue which is also most abundant in grades up to MS-63. True Gem MS-65 specimens are now starting to become somewhat difficult to locate because the existing supply is rapidly drying up. This is a coin which exhibits original luster and a minimum of detracting marks. The superb or gem MS-67 piece with semi-proof-like fields and lightly frosted figures (devices) will be a nice find.

Purchase this coin in choice uncirculated and gem condition.

In summary:
MS-60; MS-63—Don't purchase in quantity.
MS-65—Highly recommended.
MS-67—Most highly recommended.

PRICE PROJECTIONS

1985				1990		
MS-60	MS-65	MS-67		MS-60	MS-65	MS-67
$475.	$1800.+	$2000.+		$750.	$2400.+	$3000.+

THE CINCINNATI HALF DOLLARS

The majority of this issue rests in the uncirculated (MS-60) and to a lesser extent in the choice uncirculated (MS-63) state on account of heavy cleaning, abrasions and deep bag marks present on Stephen Foster's portrait, and/or the female figure seen on the coin's reverse. As far as strike is concerned, the way the coin weakly appears is the way it was struck. Due to rapid die wear, only the very early strikings possess—upon a side-by-side comparison—some more detail on Mr. Foster's hair and ear. The reverse's female displays more depth on the horizontal part of her right arm, face and head.

Should you locate a true single coin or gem set containing three uniform coins, make the immediate purchase. I find the D minted coins received more tender loving care than did the s and especially the P mint productions. Why? No one knows! The price of this issue in top condition has been held down because of the constant advertising that has made many believe this set is readily available. I don't think there exist more than 150 sets today which can be truly graded MS-65.

In summary:
MS-60—Don't purchase in quantity at present.
MS-63—Recommended.
MS-65; MS-67—Most highly recommended.

PRICE PROJECTIONS

Issue	1985				1990		
	MS-60	MS-65	MS-67		MS-60	MS-65	MS-67
Set	$1600.	$6000.+	$10,000.+		$2600.	$12,000.+	$20,000.+
Type Coin	$ 950.	$2200.+	$ 4300.+		$1000.	$ 4200.+	$10,000.+

THE CLEVELAND HALF DOLLAR

Here is one of the easiest coins to locate in gem condition, the only category to purchase such, on account of the large existing supply which overhangs the market.

This issue existed in bag quantity for many years after the Exposition closed! They were not abused for the most part; thus, we have a large existing supply available to us today!

In summary:
MS-60; MS-63—Don't purchase in quantity.
MS-65; MS-67—Recommended. (475 pieces exist in two hoards.)

PRICE PROJECTIONS

1985				1990		
MS-60	MS-65	MS-67		MS-60	MS-65	MS-67
$180.	$495.+	$500.+		$225.	$675.+	$900.+

THE COLUMBIA HALF DOLLAR

This issue is not difficult to locate in all uncirculated grades. Superb (MS-67) sets are becoming difficult to locate because of the increased demand for quality. The reverse on a large number of coins possesses dull luster, mostly because they rested against cardboard holders that contained much sulphur. Thus, the surfaces of the reverses were affected. Adding to this is also the fact that the reverse has a different die surface than the obverse!

Purchase the aforementioned in gem 65 and 67 states, should you be purchasing an individual coin or a set. Also remember, all coins in a set must grade MS-65 for the set to be labeled such. A hoard of 20 sets overhangs the market at present!

In summary:
MS-60—Don't buy in quantity.
MS-65; MS-63—Recommended.
MS-67—Highly recommended.

PRICE PROJECTIONS

Issue	1985				1990		
	MS-60	MS-65	MS-67		MS-60	MS-65	MS-67
1936 Set	$2000.	$4800.+	$5200.+		$2500.	$6200.+	$10,000.+
Type Coin	$ 660.	$1850.+	$2800.+		$ 875.	$2100.+	$ 3300.+

THE COLUMBIAN EXHIBITION HALF DOLLAR

Due to heavy numismatic abuse and existing economic conditions at the time, most of the 2,500,000 + specimens produced survive today in worn condition. Approximately 200,000 of these pieces exist in the uncirculated state (MS-60), as well as the Choice B.U. state (MS-63).

Choice B.U. coins are often classified as Gem B.U. (MS-65) because they have been obtained from original rolls—this often says nothing about the condition of the coin!

I have opened several hundred original rolls in the last twelve years, only to discover that the uncirculated coins were dogs, possessing many bag marks, plus unattractive rubbing on Columbus' cheekbone. In fact, many of these rolls were put together from coins extracted from circulation, over seventy years ago.

Although some possessed a beautiful colored toning, they could not be graded uncirculated. These are the kind—both toned and bright in appearance from cleaning—that you see advertised for $18.00 to $125.00 and labeled choice and gem uncirculated. Don't be fooled!

The MS-63 coin is commonly offered as Gem B.U. (MS-65), which unfortunately creates the illusion that quality specimens are easily located. True gem (MS-65) and gem or superb (MS-67) coins will not be easy to find, since they received much numismatic abuse.

Proof-like MS-65 specimens have sold as high as $2,000. True proof specimens, of which only 104 pieces were made for presentation, are rare. In fact, only eight *true* proof specimens have been offered for sale since 1962! Most coins offered as proofs in the past are proof-like coins—again creating the false picture that this issue is not too difficult to locate.

See the Columbian chapter which explains how to distinguish between proofs and proof-like coins—as well as the Isabella Proof specimen.

In summary:

MS-60; MS-63—Do not purchase in any quantity.

MS-65—Highly recommended.

MS-67—Most highly recommended.

Proof-like MS-65—Most highly recommended.

Proof Columbians—Most highly recommended.

Existing Hoards—Bags of 1892 (2) and 1893 (1) existed in 1973.

PRICE PROJECTIONS

Issue	1985				1990		
	MS-60	MS-65	MS-67		MS-60	MS-65	MS-67
1892	$ 55.	$ 700.+	$ 1700.+		$ 75.	$ 1400.+	$ 3000.+
1893	$ 55.	$ 700.+	$ 1700.+		$ 75.	$ 1400.+	$ 3000.+
Full P/L	$ 200.	$ 4000.+	$ 7000.+		$ 400.	$ 8000.+	$13,000.+
Proof	$10,000.+	$30,000.+	$60,000.		$20,000.+	$60,000.+	$100,000.+

THE CONNECTICUT TERCENTENARY HALF DOLLAR

Most of this issue is available in almost all uncirculated grades. Its purchase is recommended in the gem (65) state and especially in superb (MS-67) condition possessing a full strike and full mint bloom. The latter appears to be drying up. There also exist four to six matte proofs of the Connecticut, whose last recorded sales—of these double struck rarities—were made in 1962 and 1975. Needless to say, here we have a very rare coin for the "super collector."

In summary:
MS-60—Don't purchase in quantity at present.
MS-63—Recommended.
MS-65—Highly recommended.
MS-67—Most highly recommended.
Matte Proof—Most highly recommended.

PRICE PROJECTIONS

Issue	1985				1990		
	MS-60	MS-65	MS-67		MS-60	MS-65	MS-67
1935	$495.	$1600.+	$ 2000.+		$775.	$2300.+	$ 2900.+
Matte Proof			$75,000.+				$125,000.+

THE DELAWARE SWEDISH TERCENTENARY HALF DOLLAR

Here is an issue which appears to have experienced little tender loving care at the mint. As a result, a good part of the total mintage falls into the uncirculated and choice uncirculated state because of deep ugly nicks and abrasions located on the *Key of Kalmar's* sails on the reverse—especially on the central sail.

Locating true gem (MS-65) specimens will be difficult, while superb or gem (MS-67) pieces will be a find.

In summary:
MS-60—Don't purchase in quantity at present.
MS-63—Recommended.
MS-65—Most recommended.
MS-67—Most highly recommended.

PRICE PROJECTIONS

1985				1990		
MS-60	MS-65	MS-67		MS-60	MS-65	MS-67
$450.	$1575.+	$1700.+		$750.	$2050.+	$3400.+

THE ELGIN CENTENNIAL HALF DOLLAR

At present, this issue is available in all uncirculated grades. I expect that situation to also change shortly, simply because most who make gem purchases will dry up the available supply. However, those coins possessing heavy bag marks, especially on the pioneer's face (obverse), should be labeled only choice BU (MS-63).

There will be little definition on the reverse pioneers because there was little to begin with on the new dies. As such wore due to striking, some blank faces resulted. There exists at present day a hoard of 425 pieces, mostly original—but possessing unattractive bag marks on the coins' obverses and excessive scratches on the lower section of the pioneer woman's garb.

In summary:
MS-60; MS-63—Don't purchase in quantity.
MS-65—Recommended.
MS-67—Most recommended.

PRICE PROJECTIONS

1985				1990		
MS-60	MS-65	MS-67		MS-60	MS-65	MS-67
$480.	$1800.+	$2000.+		$900.	$2500.+	$3100.+

THE GETTYSBURG HALF DOLLAR

This issue is believed easily located in gem MS-65 condition. However, I find the existing supply drying up rapidly and what seems to be available most of the times are coins with deep ugly bag marks, especially on the coin's reverse shields. These should be placed in the choice uncirculated class. The acquisition of true superb (MS-67) specimens, those frosty gems, can prove to be a difficult task.

In summary:
MS-60—Don't purchase in quantity at present.
MS-63—Recommended.
MS-65—Most recommended.
MS-67—Most highly recommended.

PRICE PROJECTIONS

1985				1990		
MS-60	MS-65	MS-67		MS-60	MS-65	MS-67
$595.	$1900.+	$2300.+		$950.	$2900.+	$3800.+

THE GRANT MEMORIAL ISSUES

The Grant plain variety with its 67,405 mintage has received much numismatic abuse to the point where 80 percent of its total mintage must be placed in the circulated state. There are many slider coins (almost uncirculated specimens) floating around that are worth about "2½ times" less in value than an uncirculated (MS-60) specimen. So beware! Most of the existing MS-60 and MS-63 pieces will grade such because they lack the natural or true coin surface, especially on the coin's obverse. Original surfaces must be present on both sides of the coin—not just on one side! Additionally, these coins possess enough detracting marks to place them forever in the 60 and 63 states.

The gem category (MS-65 and MS-67), possessing full mint luster, possibly some frost on Grant's face and no ugly nicks or marks, will be a find, since it is conceivable that just 500 coins of this nature exist today. Naturally, they are highly recommended! One such specimen sold at a NERCG auction for $2650!

The flatness on Grant's hair in the area diagonally to the right and left above his ear will always appear flat on both silver issues because there was no design in the dies in this area to begin with except for a few strands of hair which rapidly wore away! The opposite is true for the gold issues! Also, you may note what appears to be small scratches below Grant's full name on the obverse. These are die striations or scratches that existed on the die which transferred to the coin blank or planchet during the striking of the coin. On the reverse, the trunk of the second tree from the left is struck flat on both issues.

The Grant with star, the true king of the commemorative half dollars with its "big" mintage of 4256 is mostly found in the circulated state, heavily cleaned and with facial abrasions because it was fully treated as a souvenir. Definite uncirculated specimens almost always will be dull in appearance or bright from cleaning!

Some uncleaned MS-63 specimens can possess luster, but seem to have too many ugly bag marks or nicks. Usually, when these coins are seen with real luster, they are immediately pronounced gem BU. In fact, the bright AU pieces which look good to the uneducated are often advertised as choice BU (MS-63) or gem BU (MS-65) at so-called wholesale or "in line with the market prices." Needless to say, the purchase of this issue in true MS-65 and especially MS-67 condition—an almost impossible task—is recommended in the highest sense of the word! But, I don't believe there exist more than 75 such star specimens that can truly be classified in the gem category. This is an exceptionally rare coin, especially with its original mint bloom, or luster or brilliance. See the Grant chapter dealing with counterfeit star specimens that do not possess the die break at the chin and heavy die striations in back of and in front of Grant's portrait on the obverse. These characteristics are a must on all genuine specimens in any condition!

As far as the genuine issue that does not possess the die break at the chin and "die scratches" on the obverse field is concerned, there might exist less than thirty pieces! I believe these are the few coins that were struck before the obverse and reverse dies clashed. In other words, no coin blank or planchet was in the press when the dies came together to produce a coin. Thus, the dies had to worked on by the mint in order to make them useable as quickly as possible.

One of the above-mentioned specimens sold for (1979) $4200 between dealers. Recently (1980), the same MS-65 coin changed hands at $9500!

In summary:
MS-60—Recommended.
MS-63—Most recommended.
MS-65; MS-67—Most highly recommended.

PRICE PROJECTIONS

Issue	1985 MS-60	1985 MS-65	1985 MS-67	Silver	1990 MS-60	1990 MS-65	1990 MS-67
★	$ 3000.+	$20,000.+	$35,000.+		$ 6000.+	$40,000.+	$ 55,000.+
Plain	$ 265.	$ 1100.+	$ 3000.+		$ 400.	$ 1700.+	$ 4800.+
★ -No Clash Mark	$10,000.+	$27,000.+	$45,000.+		$18,000.	$47,000.+	$65,000.+

There were also 10,016 Grant gold dollars produced with the first 5000 coins bearing an incused star. In the past (1978), despite their low mintage, one had little difficulty in locating these specimens in choice BU (MS-63) and gem BU (MS-65) condition. At present, the small supply available has completely dried up due to demand, which proved these coins were not as abundant as believed. (As yours truly (A.S.) had constantly declared!)

In summary:
MS-60—Recommended.
MS-63—Recommended.
MS-65; MS-67—Highly recommended.

PRICE PROJECTIONS

Issue	1985			Gold	1990		
	MS-60	MS-65	MS-67		MS-60	MS-65	MS-67
★	$4000.+	$14,000.+	$19,000.+		$6000.+	$22,000.+	$26,000.+
Plain	$4000.+	$14,000.+	$19,000.+		$6000.+	$22,000.+	$26,000.+

THE HAWAIIAN SESQUICENTENNIAL HALF DOLLAR

This issue became king of the U.S. Commemorative Coinage (pricewise) in 1957. However, in 1978, the Lafayette dollar has taken its rightful place on the throne. Nevertheless, this is still the king of the half dollar series. I expect the Grant with star in true gem condition to take its place within the next decade, followed by the Panama Pacific half dollar. Most of this Hawaiian issue finds itself in the circulated state, for many were used as pocket pieces in Hawaii. They were later cleaned to look bright for resale—especially in 1957—both here and on the islands. Hence, most MS-60 and MS-63 specimens will exhibit poor luster, handling marks, and most likely fine hairline scratches from improper cleaning. The true gem (MS-65) coin will be very difficult to locate. Its purchase is most highly recommended, as well as desirable true MS-63 specimens; one hoard of some fifty pieces exist. They would be most welcome in today's market!

At times, there is offered for sale the rare sandblast Hawaiian proof. One genuine piece—which must be double struck—was sold for $17,500. Beware, there are fakes around, but they are not *double struck!*

In summary:
MS-60—Recommended.
MS-63—Most recommended.
MS-65; MS-67—Most highly recommended.
Matte proof—Most highly recommended.

PRICE PROJECTIONS

Issue	1985				1990		
	MS-60	MS-65	MS-67		MS-60	MS-65	MS-67
	$3200.+	$12,000.+	$14,000.		$4500.+	$19,000.+	$ 27,000.+
Sandblast Proof			$60,000.				$110,000.

THE HUDSON, NEW YORK, HALF DOLLAR

Most of this issue resides in the MS-60 and MS-63 states because of deep bag marks, nicks, dull luster and a weak strike. Locating true gem (MS-65) coins will take some doing. Superb (MS-67) pieces will not arise too often.

There exists a hoard of 143 pieces in a New York estate. Upon examining a number of these specimens, I concluded that they would also reside with the mass of this issue.

In summary:
MS-60—Don't purchase in quantity at present.
MS-63—Recommended.
MS-65—Highly recommended.
MS-67—Most highly recommended.

PRICE PROJECTIONS

1985				1990		
MS-60	MS-65	MS-67		MS-60	MS-65	MS-67
$2500.	$4900.+	$5800.+		$3200.	$7500.+	$9800.+

THE HUGUENOT–WALLOON TERCENTENARY HALF DOLLAR

Here is a coin which is not difficult to locate in Gem BU (MS-65) condition. The MS-67 specimen will prove to be very elusive to purchase. Acquire the gem specimens only.

In summary:
MS-60; MS-63—Don't purchase in quantity.
MS-65—Recommended.
MS-67—Most highly recommended.
Large hoards exist today, especially in MS-60 and MS-63 condition.

PRICE PROJECTIONS

1985				1990		
MS-60	MS-65	MS-67		MS-60	MS-65	MS-67
$220.	$1150.+	$1350.+		$300.	$1700.+	$2100.+

THE ILLINOIS–LINCOLN HALF DOLLAR

Due to much numismatic abuse, this issue is very difficult to locate in the Gem BU (MS-65) state with true original luster. Should such be present, one usually finds the obverse field exhibiting a little too much of abrasion and too many nicks unfortunately placing the specimen right into the Choice BU (MS-63) category. About 80 percent of this issue has seen some circulation, with most of the remaining 20 percent falling into MS-60 and MS-63 states.

Thus, the possession of true gem quality specimens of this sleeper is highly recommended!

In summary:
MS-60—Do not purchase in quantity.
MS-63—Recommended.
MS-65—Highly recommended.
MS-67—Most highly recommended.

PRICE PROJECTIONS

1985				1990		
MS-60	MS-65	MS-67		MS-60	MS-65	MS-67
$225.	$850.+	$1075.+		$325.	$1200.+	$1600.+

THE IOWA STATEHOOD HALF DOLLAR

Virtually all of this issue exists in the uncirculated states. Purchase the above-mentioned only in gem condition.

In summary:
MS-60; MS-63—Don't purchase in quantity at present.
MS-65; MS-67—Recommended.

PRICE PROJECTIONS

1985				1990		
MS-60	MS-65	MS-67		MS-60	MS-65	MS-67
$200.	$525.+	$650.+		$320.	$800.+	$950.+

THE ISABELLA QUARTER DOLLAR

Most of this issue, a mere 24,214 pieces, can be placed in the worn uncirculated (MS-60) and choice uncirculated (MS-63) category due to numismatic abuse and bad economic times. Unfortunately, many of the available MS-63 coins are usually offered as gem BU (MS-65) because the latter is very difficult to locate even with the recent price increases! I believe there are no more than 250 pieces which truly fall into the gem class. In superb condition (MS-67), some 75 pieces might exist—if that many!

As with her Columbian "brothers," proof-like coins almost always have been sold as proofs—which are most difficult to locate. With exception of two coins, all of the genuine sixteen (16) pieces examined by myself have possessed hairlines due to improper cleaning. Naturally, they were not too impressive.

In summary:
MS-60—Do not purchase in quantity.
MS-63—Recommended, since it appears that this in between grade can bring good future gains.
MS-65—Offers excellent investment potential. Highly recommended.
MS-67—Most highly recommended.
Proof-like MS-65; MS-67—Most highly recommended.
Proof MS-63; MS-65; MS-67—Most highly recommended.

PRICE PROJECTIONS

	1985				1990		
	MS-60	MS-65	MS-67		MS-60	MS-65	MS-67
	$ 875.	$ 8000.+	$11,000.+		$ 1300.	$16,000.+	$ 20,000.+
P/L	$ 1000.	$10,000.+	$13,000.+		$ 1500.	$20,000.+	$ 23,000.+
Proof	$13,000.	$45,000.+	$65,000.+		$22,000.+	$60,000.+	$100,000.+

THE LAFAYETTE SILVER DOLLAR

The high sulphur content of the envelope that housed these coins caused most to become heavily toned. Many, therefore, were improperly cleaned to look like new again. Those that were housed in the envelope for many years developed such a heavy toning that a "liquid dip" could not remove the tarnish and actually destroyed the surface. Baking soda was then briskly applied to get many of these coins looking, yes, like new!

Hard economic times caused many people to spend this souvenir dollar; thus we find most of the 36,000 specimens in the circulated state. However, the Lafayette Dollar is not at present (1980) difficult to locate in true uncirculated condition (MS-60). One in choice uncirculated condition (MS-63) is becoming more and more difficult to locate, while a true MS-65 Dollar possessing beautiful blazing original luster, a good strike and few marks will be a great find. Should the coin be toned, make sure you can see that true original luster with full cartwheel under the veil. If you cannot, the specimen you are looking at is most likely a retoned circulated, uncirculated or choice uncirculated specimen. Beware!

A superb coin (MS-67) with blazing original luster, never cleaned, and possessing full original frost and a good strike will be a tremendous find since there exist three dozen or less of these pieces today!

In summary:
MS-60—Recommended.
MS-63—Highly recommended. Excellent investment potential.
MS-65; MS-67—Most highly recommended. Excellent investment potential.

PRICE PROJECTIONS

1985				1990		
MS-60	MS-65	MS-67		MS-60	MS-65	MS-67
$3800.+	$40,000.+	$50,000.+		$6000.+	$75,000.+	$100,000.+

THE LEWIS AND CLARK EXPOSITION GOLD DOLLARS

Destructive cleaning of these coins, as well as the use of such in coin jewelry casts 85 percent of this issue in the almost uncirculated state. Beware of bargain prices! Most of the coins that truly grade uncirculated (MS-60) lack most, if not all, original luster because their past owners—whoever they might have been—cleaned them to create the illusion of an original surface.

The available supply of this issue—either date—in true gem (MS-65) condition is thin. An appearance of not too difficult to locate is created by those choice (MS-63) coins which are constantly offered for gem BU (MS-65) by the unscrupulous. Needless to say, true superb (MS-67) pieces are very, very elusive.

In summary:
MS-60—Recommended.
MS-63—Highly recommended.
MS-65; MS-67—Most highly recommended.
Genuine Proof Issue—Most highly recommended.

PRICE PROJECTIONS

Issue	1985				1990		
	MS-60	MS-65	MS-67		MS-60	MS-65	MS-67
1904	$5000. +	$25,000.+	$35,000.+		$8500. +	$50,000.+	$ 70,000.+
1905	$5000. +	$25,000.+	$35,000.+		$8500. +	$50,000.+	$ 70,000.+
Proofs			$60,000.				$100,000.

THE LEXINGTON–CONCORD HALF DOLLAR

This issue is most abundant in grades up to choice BU (MS-63). However, it is not easily located today in true gem MS-65 condition—possessing a full strike, no obverse and reverse field abrasion and ugly nicks—as is believed. Superb or gem MS-67 specimens can be quite difficult to locate and are very underrated. The purchase of this issue is highly recommended in gem grades.

In summary:
MS-60; MS-63—Do not purchase in quantity.
MS-65—Recommended.
MS-67—Most recommended.
Hoards of this issue exist, especially in MS-60 and MS-63.

PRICE PROJECTIONS

1985				1990		
MS-60	MS-65	MS-67		MS-60	MS-65	MS-67
$175.	$650. +	$850. +		$195.	$1100. +	$1350. +

THE LONG ISLAND TERCENTENARY HALF DOLLAR

This is another issue that was greatly abused numismatically. Many coins exhibit signs of wear because they were treated as souvenir pieces. They are available in gem BU MS-65 because little interest had been given the issue. Recently, due to demand, the Long Island picture is changing! Watch this issue's price rise dramatically, in the very near future! Frosty and fully struck specimens in the superb or gems MS-67 category can be very elusive.

In summary:
MS-60—Recommended
MS-63—Recommended.
MS-65; MS-67—Most highly recommended.

PRICE PROJECTIONS

	1985				1990		
MS-60	MS-65	MS-67			MS-60	MS-65	MS-67
$130.	$575.+	$750.+			$210.	$775.+	$1100.+

THE JEFFERSON AND McKINLEY LOUISIANA PURCHASE GOLD DOLLARS

A combination of low mintage and numismatic abuse places about 80 percent of this issue in the almost uncirculated state. So beware of the unscrupulous dealer who will attempt to offer one of the aforementioned at a *good* price.

A great deal of the remaining uncirculated offerings fall into the MS-60 and to a lesser degree, the MS-63 state. True gem (MS-65) pieces—and not an over-graded MS-63 specimen offered as a gem—are becoming difficult to locate. The same fate befalls the superb (MS-67) category.

When comparing rarity, I feel this issue in gem condition is actually rarer than the Pan Pacific and McKinley dollars which sell for much more at present.

Genuine proofs (100 of each design) in cardboard pages issued by the mint were recently being offered at $22,000.

In summary:
MS-60—Recommended.
MS-63—Recommended.
MS-65; MS-67—Highly recommended.
Proof issue in *mint frame**—Highly recommended.

PRICE PROJECTION

		1985				1990		
Issue	MS-60	MS-65	MS-67			MS-60	MS-65	MS-67
	$ 2500.	$ 6500.+	$ 7500.+			$ 5000.	$11,000.	$13,000.
*Proof	$22,000.	$32,000.+	$40,000.+			$55,000.+	$70,000.+	$80,000.

THE LYNCHBURG, VIRGINIA, HALF DOLLAR

Most of this issue can be located in all uncirculated grades. However, this situation is rapidly changing. Gem (MS-65) specimens do make their appearance and should immediately be purchased. Small hoards of this issue do exist, but they would be most welcome, since the existing supply cannot withstand a moderate demand much longer. Due to improper handling, fine scratches can be seen on the Carter Glass portrait and also on Ms. Liberty's thigh on the reverse. If these scratches are excessive or too detracting, pass the coin for a true MS-65.

In summary:
MS-60—Don't purchase in quantity at present.
MS-63; MS-65—Recommended.
MS-67—Most recommended.

PRICE PROJECTIONS

1985				1990		
MS-60	MS-65	MS-67		MS-60	MS-65	MS-67
$450.	$1475.+	$1900.+		$900.	$2100.+	$3400.+

THE MAINE CENTENNIAL HALF DOLLAR

Most of the entire mintage was used as pocket pieces. Thus, wear on the coin's high points, surface abuse and a loss of luster drops most of this issue into the almost uncirculated category (AU). Those pieces that grade true uncirculated (MS-60 or MS-63) usually possess little or no natural luster or original brilliance given the coin when the metal flowed as it was struck. Some specimens that have this original luster have excessive bag marks or nicks, classifying the coin only MS-63. What looks like horizontal scratches below the word LIBERTY on the reverse, on some specimens exist in the die (which was worked on by a mint employee) and are transferred to the coin. Upon inspection with a magnifying glass, you will note they are raised lines and not scratches in the coin's surface.

True gem specimens (MS-65) are very difficult to locate, while MS-67 specimens are truly scarce. Their purchase is highly recommended!

In summary:
MS-60; MS-63—Do not purchase in quantity at present.
MS-65; MS-67—Most highly recommended.

PRICE PROJECTION

1985				1990		
MS-60	MS-65	MS-67		MS-60	MS-65	MS-67
$275.	$1500.+	$2700.+		$400.	$2350.+	$4100.+

THE MARYLAND TERCENTENARY HALF DOLLAR

Due to a very poor obverse striking (due to die conditions) on Cecil Calvert's cheekbone, eyebrows and nose, plus some field abrasions and, at times, ugly bag marks on this issue, makes a true gem (MS-65) specimen very difficult to locate. They simply are not around in the quantity believed. Thus, the majority of this issue falls into the uncirculated and choice uncirculated state. The reverse is almost always struck well because of the way the dies were designed.

There exist four known matte proofs, one of which was sold in 1976 for $14,500. The last genuine double struck specimen was sold back in 1975. Naturally, this is a special treasure for the special collector.

In summary:
MS-60—Don't purchase in quantity at present.
MS-63—Recommended.
MS-65—Highly recommended.
MS-67—Most highly recommended.
Matte proof—Most highly recommended
Small hoards exist today of regular issue.

PRICE PROJECTIONS

	1985				1990		
	MS-60	MS-65	MS-67		MS-60	MS-65	MS-67
	$375.	$1200.+	$ 1500.+		$600.	$1900.+	$ 2300.+
Matte Proof			$60,000.+				$120,000.+

THE McKINLEY MEMORIAL GOLD DOLLARS

As with the Panama–Pacific gold dollar, here is another issue where few pieces saw considerable numismatic abuse. Thus, most available specimens of each date will grade Choice BU (MS-63) and Gem BU (MS-65).

Select the finest quality specimens when purchasing this issue. However, the supply of this issue is beginning to dry up. Be quick or purchase next grade (MS-63).

Genuine proofs which are rarely offered do exist. Their purchase—if genuine—is highly recommended. The last sale of a 1916 proof brought $14,000; the last sale of a 1917 proof, $16,500.

In summary:
MS-60; MS-63—Recommended.
MS-65; MS-67—Recommended.

PRICE PROJECTIONS

	1985				1990		
	MS-60	MS-65	MS-67		MS-60	MS-65	MS-67
1916	$1800.+	$3900.+	$ 4800.+		$2500.+	$6800.+	$ 7500.+
1917	$1875.+	$4100.+	$ 4900.+		$2650.+	$7000.+	$ 7900.+
Proof			$35,000.				$70,000.

THE MISSOURI CENTENNIAL HALF DOLLARS

Between the heavy treatment of this issue as a souvenir pocket piece and much improper cleaning, we possibly have no more than 250 combined pieces of the two varieties which fall into the gem MS-65 and MS-67 category. Should there exist 1000 true uncirculated specimens, these MS-60 and MS-63 specimens usually possess obverse facial abrasion and little or no original luster. They might look bright, due to a dip or two or because they have been cleaned with baking soda. When you place an original specimen next to this bright, shiny coin, you will immediately see "the day and the night." The 2★4 variety does possess a somewhat stronger strike than the plain issue because the dies were used first. Upon completion, the 2★4 was polished off. This permitted the striking of the plain issue without having to prepare new hubs. Thus, the aforementioned was struck with equipment that had already produced 5000 coins! Also, the left strap supporting the area above the frontiersman's powder horn seems to vanish, while going upward to his left wing bone. This is the way die was prepared. What is not present on the die cannot be transferred to the coin!

The purchase of this issue in all true uncirculated grades is highly recommended—especially in top condition. Beware of these almost uncirculated specimens offered for sale as choice BU, etc. Also note the entire facial area on the frontiersman. I have seen a number of pieces ever so lightly whizzed to do away with obvious wear and facial abrasions, thus creating an impressive looking coin to many. A five power glass will reveal this, especially when tilting the coin at different angles. Look for a phoney dull aluminum looking luster.

In summary:
MS-60—Recommended.
MS-63—Highly recommended.
MS-65; MS-67—Most highly recommended.

PRICE PROJECTIONS

	1985				1990		
	MS-60	MS-65	MS-67		MS-60	MS-65	MS-67
2★4	$1700.	$7500.+	$10,500.+		$2300.	$13,500.+	$20,000.+
Plain	$1500.	$7500.+	$10,500.+		$1900.	$13,500.+	$20,000.+

THE MONROE DOCTRINE CENTENNIAL HALF DOLLAR

Most of this issue's 274,077 pieces had been numismatically abused because it was placed into circulation at face value. As a result, the greater majority have been cleaned and possess wear.

True uncirculated specimens (MS-60) display field abrasions, nicks and little or no original luster on both sides of the coin. Most choice BU (MS-63) specimens can possess some luster, but exhibit ugly abrasions and nicks. They cannot honestly grade MS-65, but are often offered as such. Beware!

A true frosty gem (MS-65) with original luster and a desirable surface will be difficult to locate. They do manage to make an appearance, so make the immediate purchase. However, the MS-67 specimen, the superb coin, will be most elusive.

In summary:
MS-60; MS-63—Don't purchase in quantity.
MS-65; MS-67—Most highly recommended.
Large hoards exist, especially in MS-60 and MS-63 condition.

PRICE PROJECTIONS

1985				1990		
MS-60	MS-65	MS-67		MS-60	MS-65	MS-67
$125.	$550.	$2200.+		$190.	$900.+	$4000.+

THE NEW ROCHELLE HALF DOLLAR

About 90 percent of this low mintage (15,250) issue resides in choice uncirculated condition (MS-63), mostly because of detracting bag marks, especially on the coin's field. Finding true gem (MS-65) specimens possessing almost no marks will be rather difficult, for the existing supply is beginning to dry up. Superb specimens (MS-67) should be purchased immediately. They too are becoming quite elusive. However, this underrated low mintage issue is recommended for purchase in all uncirculated grades.

There exist 10 double-struck matte proofs of this issue. The last known sale took place in 1975 at $14,000. Again, a great treasure for the super collector. Fifty brilliant specimens struck on proof planchets with one strike of the press were used as presentation pieces. These are proof-like and are not semi-proof-like as were the coins struck for general purposes after the special coins were made. One of those semi-proof-like coins recently sold for $3500.

In summary:
MS-60; MS-63—Recommended.
MS-65—Most recommended.
MS-67—Most highly recommended.
Proofs—Most highly recommended.

PRICE PROJECTIONS

	1985				1990		
	MS-60	MS-65	MS-67		MS-60	MS-65	MS-67
	$ 850.+	$2200.+	$ 2700.+		$1500.+	$ 3600.+	$ 4800.+
Matte Proof			$60,000.				$120,000.
Presentation Specimen	$4500.+	$8500.+	$12,000.+		$8000.+	$16,500.+	$ 20,000.+

THE NORFOLK BICENTENNIAL HALF DOLLAR

This low mintage (16,936) issue exists in all uncirculated grades. It's purchase is most recommended in both gem states while they can be obtained. Beware of those pieces that look bright. You must compare a mint state coin with them to see the difference. They've had their natural luster or mint bloom dipped out of existance and should be honestly graded no higher than the MS-63. On account of the tender loving care given this issue by the mint, many Norfolks will display nick-free surfaces. Remember, it is that original luster you want to see.

In summary:
MS-60; MS-63—Recommended.
MS-65; MS-67—Most recommended.

PRICE PROJECTIONS

	1985				1990		
MS-60	MS-65	MS-67			MS-60	MS-65	MS-67
$675.	$2600.+	$4200.+			$1150.	$4500.	$7000.+

THE OREGON TRAIL MEMORIAL HALF DOLLARS

The 1926 p and 1926 s issues used as type coins were most available in all uncirculated states. However, with a steady demand, this situation is now changing, especially for the gem category. Why the current change? Simply because the supply was there and the demand not large enough in the past. Now, the once thought-of huge available supply is rapidly becoming thin. This is one reason why the price has doubled in less than eight months (1979)! Thus, its purchase is most recommended. It is also most attractive and considered beautiful by most who encounter it. The same situation holds true for the low mintage 1928 p, 1933 d, 1934 d and 1936 s issues. They also have shown greater price gains and are recommended in gem condition, for here is where the most profit is to be made. Two other dates, the 1936 p and 1937 d are more difficult to locate than the type coins and should be purchased in gem conditions at present.

With a steady demand for the 1938 and 1939 sets, the existing supply is also proving itself to be thin, especially in gem condition. Those cardboard holders which housed these sets contained sulphur which heavily toned the aforementioned, resulting in the cleaning of the coins and, in a good number of cases, the loss of much luster. These sets, especially the 1939 issue, are highly recommended for purchase in the choice and gem states.

In the case of the 1926 p matte proof, there exists just two pieces, one of which sold for $15,000 in 1976! Again, a treasure for the super collector.

In summary:
MS-60: MS-63—Purchase of all issues recommended.
MS-65—Purchase of all issues most recommended.
MS-67—Purchase of all issues most highly recommended.
Small hoards of all issues exist—with the exception of the 1938 and 1939 sets—at present.

PRICE PROJECTIONS

Issue	1985 MS-60	1985 MS-65	1985 MS-67		1990 MS-60	1990 MS-65	1990 MS-67
1926P+S	$ 275.	$ 600.+	$ 700.+		$ 500.	$1100.+	$ 1200.+
1928-P	$ 550.	$2,400.+	$ 3,400.+		$ 850.	$2800.+	$ 3200.+
1933-D	$ 600.	$1600.+	$ 2100.+		$ 850.	$3100.+	$ 4100.+
1934-D	$ 475.	$1400.+	$ 1800.+		$ 825.	$2800.+	$ 3400.+
1936-P	$ 275.	$ 850.+	$ 950.+		$ 500.	$1500.+	$ 1800.+
1936-S	$ 500.	$1400.+	$ 1800.+		$ 850.	$1400.+	$ 3400.+
1937-D	$ 300.	$ 675.+	$ 775.+		$ 500.	$1250.+	$ 1350.+
1938 Set	$1100.	$2700.+	$ 3500.+		$1850.	$4600.+	$ 5000.+
1939 Set	$1800.	$4000.+	$ 4,900.+		$3000.	$6000.+	$ 7000.+
Matte Proof			$70,000.+				$140,000.+

THE PANAMA–PACIFIC ISSUES

Out of 27,134 half dollars produced, there possibly exist no more than eighty specimens that can be truly graded superb or gem MS-67. In fact, locating a true MS-65 specimen (Gem BU) with a fully struck Columbia, child and reverse eagle, as well as no detracting marks and true original luster, must be considered a real find, for I believe no more than 150 specimens exist!

Unfortunately, when combining three numismatic villians (circulation, improper cleaning and bad handling), we are left with an issue where almost all of its mintage should be classified Almost Uncirculated (AU). There most likely exist some 300 additional coins which fall into the MS-60 and MS-60+ class. They will possess little or no original luster, some abrasion and at times a weak strike.

Many people have asked me "why was this coin as well as many other issues heavily cleaned?" The answer to this is that the envelopes and holders that housed these coins contained sulphur which chemically reacted in a negative way in most cases with the coins. When the specimen or specimens tarnished, they were cleaned like silverware is today—to look new and bright! One improper cleaning can ruin a coin's surface, taking away most, if not all, of its natural luster which is acquired due to the flow of metal when it was struck. Thus, we are left with a shiny surface, but not a natural one!

The possession of sure quality specimens of this issue is highly recommended. Beware, there are many AU specimens, both bright and toned, that are offered as gem coins!

In summary:
MS-60—Recommended.
MS-63—Recommended.
MS-65; MS-67— Most highly recommended.

PRICE PROJECTIONS

1985				1990		
MS-60	MS-65	MS-67		MS-60	MS-65	MS-67
$2000.+	$13,000.+	$20,000.+		$4000.	$19,000.+	$40,000.+

Most of the Pan Pacific $1 issue remains in the uncirculated state. Many available specimens will grade gem BU (MS-65) because this gold coin was not heavily abused. Since it did not sell as well as expected, large purchases were later made by a number of individuals, thus accounting for their availability today. Be quick, because the gem supply is rapidly drying up.

In summary:
MS-60; MS-63—Recommended.
MS-65; MS-67—Highly recommended.

PRICE PROJECTIONS

1985				1990		
MS-60	MS-65	MS-67		MS-60	MS-65	MS-67
$2500.+	$8500.+	$10,000.+		$5000.+	$13,000.	$16,000.+

The combination of numismatic abuse, plus a mintage of only 6749 specimens equals a very rare coin in all uncirculated grades, especially in MS-65 and MS-67. In fact, it is considered the rarest of the gold issues! However, I consider the Lewis and Clark 1904 and 1905 issues to be equally as rare in MS-67. Its purchase is highly recommended in all uncirculated states. Just beware when purchasing this issue, for I have seen many complete gold sets that contained circulated specimens which were purchased as uncirculated!

In summary:
MS-60; MS-63—Recommended.
MS-65; MS-67—Most highly recommended.

PRICE PROJECTIONS

	1985				1990		
MS-60	MS-65	MS-67			MS-60	MS-65	MS-67
$7500.	$20,000.+	$25,000.			$9500.	$30,000.+	$45,000.+

The 50-dollar gold pieces, the only such denomination made for the public, had some numismatic abuse. Most can be located in AU to Choice BU condition, with gem specimens seldom offered.

In summary:
MS-60; MS-63—All recommended.
MS-65; MS-67—Recommended for a long term investment.

PRICE PROJECTIONS

	1985				1990		
Issue	MS-60	MS-65	MS-67		MS-60	MS-65	MS-67
Round	$80,000.+	$110,000.+	$150,000.+		$88,000.+	$140,000.+	$170,000.+
Octagonal	$68,000.+	$95,000.+	$105,000.+		$72,000.+	$130,000.+	$150,000.+

THE PILGRIM ISSUES

This 1920 issue—which attracted national attention—was believed to be most abundant by many because it would always be seen at coin shows during times when there was little genuine interest in the commemorative field.

With a steady demand for this issue, what I have preached is rapidly becoming a reality. The purchase of truly graded MS-63 specimens is getting difficult because many are being offered as gem BU (MS-65)! These true frosty gems with original luster and no field abrasion are making less frequent appearances. Such is also true for the rarer 1921 issue. As with the 1920 date, many of these coins have seen circulation and heavy numismatic abuse, both in cleaning and mishandling.

Concerning the 1921 die variety noted in the Pilgrim chapter, I believe that there are no more than 40 pieces in existance! They must be considered very rare and offer the collector about the only major mint-caused mistake that can be seen with the naked eye! Some exist in circulated condition as well as in the gem state. Check the melt figure for this date.

The investment in MS-63 through MS-67 specimens of both underrated dates is highly recommended! Should you be fortunate to see the error or die clashed variety, purchase it without hesitation!

In summary:
MS-60; MS-63—Recommended.
MS-65—Most recommended.
MS-67—Most highly recommended.
Variety (1921)—Most highly recommended.

PRICE PROJECTIONS

Issue	1985				1990		
	MS-60	MS-65	MS-67		MS-60	MS-65	MS-67
1920	$ 120.	$ 650.+	$ 800.+		$ 200.	$1000.+	$1300.+
1921	$ 350.	$1200.+	$1500.+		$ 425.	$1800.+	$2200.+
Variety	$1500.+	$3000.+	$4200.+		$2600.+	$4400.+	$8000.+

THE PROVIDENCE, RHODE ISLAND, HALF DOLLARS

In the past most of this issue existed in all uncirculated states. However, locating coins (MS-65 or better) that are almost flawless and possessing no scratches (especially on the reverse Anchor of Hope) will be a somewhat elusive task. Their purchase is most highly recommended. Small hoards of full sets exist at present. Remember that when buying a set of these coins, *all* must be the grade indicated by the seller. A.S. has seen MS-67 sets with MS-60 coins in them. Know your grading!

In summary:
MS-60; MS-63—Don't buy in quantity at present.
MS-65—Recommended.
MS-67—Most highly recommended.

PRICE PROJECTIONS

Issue	1985				1990		
	MS-60	MS-65	MS-67		MS-60	MS-65	MS-67
1936 Set	$975.	$2200.+	$2400.+		$1250.	$3300.+	$3900.+
Type Coin	$290.	$ 700.+	$ 800.+		$ 400.	$1350.+	$1550.+

THE ROANOKE, NORTH CAROLINA, HALF DOLLAR

Virtually all of this issue exists in the uncirculated state. The purchase of gem coins is only recommended. Proof-like presentation pieces—like the New Rochelle issue—exist. Those semi-proof-like coins, which make an occasional appearance, are those coins produced after the special coins made for presentation purposes.

In summary:
MS-60; MS-63—Don't purchase in quantity at present.
MS-65—Recommended.
MS-67—Most recommended.

PRICE PROJECTIONS

1985				1990		
MS-60	MS-65	MS-67		MS-60	MS-65	MS-67
$350.	$1400.+	$1700.+		$550.	$2200.+	$3200.+

THE ROBINSON-ARKANSAS HALF DOLLAR

Here is an issue where practically the total mintage exists in the uncirculated state. Unfortunately, many blazing lustrous pieces exhibit some bag marks, hairline scratches, slide marks, and facial abrasions on Senator Robinson which take away from the coin's appearance. This exists because of improper handling during shipment, placing the pieces in coin holders, plus the abuse the coins undertook when twenty of them were made into a roll. The reverse is almost always struck well. It is best to search for the gem (MS-65) specimen, possessing a pleasing and acceptable obverse. Or, wait until you can locate a superb or gem MS-67 coin.

In summary:
MS-60; MS-63—Don't purchase in quantity.
MS-65—Recommended.
MS-67—Highly recommended.
Satin finish proof—Most highly recommended. (Recent sale—1979—$8900.)
Large hoards of this issue exist today (490 pieces).

PRICE PROJECTIONS

	1985				1990		
	MS-60	MS-65	MS-67		MS-60	MS-65	MS-67
	$350.	$1150.+	$ 1500.+		$600.	$2300.+	$ 2900.+
Satin Finish Proof			$55,000.+				$100,000.+

THE SAN DIEGO HALF DOLLARS

Most of both issues reside in the uncirculated states MS-60 and MS-63. However, only those pieces that exhibit no abrasion on Minerva's knees and breasts should be labeled gem BU (MS-65).

Many coins of both dates display excessive obverse friction in the aforementioned areas. This is the result of improper handling at the mint, and magnified by the abuse the coin encountered when stored, shipped and made into rolls.

As far as strike is concerned, the 35 s issue will possess the better strike of both dates. The s mintmark always appears as a blob of metal. The 36 D issue has a loss of detail on the upper right side of the California Tower or observation building, presenting a worn appearance. Yes, you can read the mintmark D, though I have never seen a fully struck 36 D. See the chapter concerning this issue for additional information.

The purchase of the San Diego issue in gem condition is recommended. There exists a bag of each date in each of two California estates today (1980).

In summary:
MS-60; MS-63—Don't purchase in quantity at present.
MS-65—Recommended.
MS-67—Most recommended.

PRICE PROJECTIONS

Issue	1985				1990		
	MS-60	MS-65	MS-67		MS-60	MS-65	MS-67
1935-S	$175.	$425.+	$575.+		$275.	$ 850.+	$ 975.+
1936-D	$225.	$775.+	$900.+		$375.	$1375.+	$1500.+

THE "SESQUI" HALF DOLLARS

For investment purposes the silver half dollar should be purchased with true original luster in gem condition (MS-65) when available. I have seen some early strikings that have full strikes and full mint bloom. These are simply beautiful MS-67 pieces, but make their appearance most infrequently. Unfortunately, many coins of this issue have been improperly cleaned and/or have seen some circulation. These AU specimens—even if they have been cleaned—can be detected from MS-60 specimens by looking for a rub or a dull whitish area on the cheekbone and jaw of George Washington and in the central area of the inscription on the Bell. The MS-63 specimen, which is most available, exhibits poor dull grey luster and unattractive marks. Due to the abundance of the aforementioned, such are usually offered as gem BU in advertisements, thus keeping the price low, and creating the illusion that this issue is readily available.

In summary:
MS-60; MS-63—Don't purchase in quantity.
MS-65—Highly recommended.
MS-67—Most highly recommended.
Matte proof—Most highly recommended.

PRICE PROJECTIONS

1985				1990		
MS-60	MS-65	MS-67		MS-60	MS-65	MS-67
$115.	$500.+	$3000.+		$140.	$1000.+	$6000.+

The $2½ gold issue saw little circulation, but true MS-65 and MS-67 specimens are now becoming difficult to locate. This is the recommended area of purchase.

In summary:
MS-60: MS-63—Recommended.
MS-65; MS-67—Most recommended.
Matte Proof—Most highly recommended.

PRICE PROJECTIONS

	1985				1990		
	MS-60	MS-65	MS-67		MS-60	MS-65	MS-67
	$1300.	$2400.+	$ 2750.+		$1600.	$3100.+	$ 4000.+
Matte Proof			$50,000.				$100,000.

THE OLD SPANISH TRAIL HALF DOLLAR

Here is an issue which was well distributed. Unfortunately, many were cleaned and possess ugly nicks and field abrasions. These are the pieces—as with a number of difficult to obtain issues in gem condition—that are constantly advertised as gem BU and at "today's going price." I have discovered that the availability of true MS-65 specimens is rapidly decreasing. Superb or gem (MS-67) coins with full original luster or mint bloom, with frosty and virtually nick-free surfaces are doing a disappearing act. Both underrated grades are certainly recommended for purchase. Of the two hoards that exist, one which contained 100 pieces has been sold in New York City (1978) and is now widely absorbed by the field. The issue didn't drop in value, but in fact has risen!

In summary:
MS-60—Don't purchase in quantity at present.
MS-63—Recommended.
MS-65—Most recommended.
MS-67—Most highly recommended.

PRICE PROJECTIONS

	1985				1990	
MS-60	MS-65	MS-67		MS-60	MS-65	MS-67
$1600.	$5400.+	$7000.+		$2700.	$8200.+	$11,000.+

THE STONE MOUNTAIN HALF DOLLAR

This issue is one of the easiest to locate in all grades. Look for only true MS-65 and MS-67 pieces when making a purchase. Many original rolls rest in many vaults in the deep south.

Here is one issue which offers little future investment potential below gem quality. The available supply is just too great.

In summary:
MS-60; MS-63—Don't purchase in quantity.
MS-65—Recommended.
MS-67—Most recommended.

PRICE PROJECTIONS

	1985				1990	
MS-60	MS-65	MS-67		MS-60	MS-65	MS-67
$65.	$225.	$300.+		$100.	$400.	$475.

THE TEXAS CENTENNIAL HALF DOLLARS

The 1934 issue is one of the easiest to locate in gem condition. In fact, there exists one entire bag of this issue in Austin, Texas (1980). Those sets which were struck in 1935 and 1936 are not too difficult to locate in choice and gem condition, at present. I would suggest making a purchase in the true gem state. Such will be most worthwhile. The 1937 set is becoming difficult to locate in true gem condition. Be alert!

The purchase of the 1938 issue in true choice and gem condition will bring a pleasant reward, due to its mintage, thin supply and lack of original luster—due to improper cleaning and die state. On account of the latter, many mint state coins will look like they were improperly cleaned. Original lustrous coins are rare, so obtain expert help when buying this set.

In summary:

MS-60—Don't purchase sets in quantity, especially the single 1934 issue at present.

MS-63—All issues are recommended, except the 1934 issue.

MS-65—All sets are most recommended. Don't purchase the 1934 issue in quantity.

MS-67—The entire issue is highly recommended.

PRICE PROJECTIONS

Issue	1985				1990		
	MS-60	MS-65	MS-67		MS-60	MS-65	MS-67
1934-P	$200.	$ 450.+	$ 500.+		$ 350.	$ 800.+	$ 900.+
1935 Set	$600.	$1200.+	$1400.+		$1100.	$2000.+	$2800.+
1936 Set	$600.	$1200.+	$1400.+		$1100.	$2000.+	$2800.+
1937 Set	$675.	$1400.+	$1700.+		$1200.	$2400.+	$3300.+
1938 Set	$1075.	$2150.+	$2400.+		$1450.	$2900.+	$4500.+
Type Coin	$200.	$ 450.+	$ 500.+		$ 375.	$ 800.+	$1400.+

THE FORT VANCOUVER HALF DOLLAR

Due to exceptionally heavy numismatic abuse, many of the mere 14,994 specimens of this issue fall into the almost uncirculated category because they were badly cleaned, used as "pocket pieces," were gold plated or simply badly mishandled as souvenirs in general! The existing several hundred uncirculated (MS-60) pieces have no original luster and will appear unpleasing because most only look bright, with obverse field abrasion possibly present. When comparing this specimen to a choice specimen which possesses most of the original luster, the difference will immediately be observed. True MS-65 coins are very elusive. They are constantly advertised, making one believe they are readily available. However, I have seen many polished AU and MS-60 coins offered as gem BU specimens. Beware! A true gem specimen should possess a semi-proof-like field, full mint bloom, little to no field abrasion and some frost.

A superb (MS-67) Vancouver is most highly recommended in the true gem state when and where such can be acquired. This coin is so underrated and scarce that most have not seen the "trees" for the "forest!" No hoards exist. It is most conceivable that fewer than 250 pieces exist of this quality.

In summary:
MS-60—Recommended.
MS-63—Recommended.
MS-65—Most recommended.
MS-67—Most highly recommended.

PRICE PROJECTIONS

	1985				1990		
MS-60	MS-65	MS-67		MS-60	MS-65	MS-67
$1000.	$8500.+	$11,000.+		$1700.	$17,000.+	$20,000.+

THE VERMONT HALF DOLLAR

Most of this issue resides in the choice uncirculated state. Nice gem specimens with no detracting marks or abrasions should be purchased. These are not as easily located as is believed. A number of later struck coins possess a die break on Ira Allen's forehead, just above his eye. From what specimens I have examined, all fell into choice uncirculated state, exhibiting slidemarks, excessive abrasion and bag marks on the obverse portraits.

Small hoards of this issue exist (200 pieces in total).

In summary:
MS-60—Don't purchase in quantity at present.
MS-63—Recommended.
MS-65; MS-67—Highly recommended.

PRICE PROJECTIONS

	1985				1990		
MS-60	MS-65	MS-67		MS-60	MS-65	MS-67
$775.	$2400.+	$2800.+		$1200.	$3600.+	$5400.+

321

THE BOOKER T. WASHINGTON HALF DOLLARS

Most of the entire series will reside in the uncirculated and choice uncirculated states because of the coin's obverse design which was so susceptible to many nicks and scratches and possibly the lack of tender loving care by the mints. The 1946 and 1947 sets are the easiest of the series to acquire, followed by the 1948 and 1951 issues. However, not so easily located are the 1949 and 1950 sets for this underrated series. With a steady demand, don't be surprised to see most of these sets double and triple in price within this decade. Thus, their purchase is most recommended. True gem coins do make their appearance on the market and should be purchased immediately, especially in the superb category where they are most difficult to locate. Pass on coins where B.T.W.'s portrait is marred.

In summary:

MS-60; MS-63—All sets are recommended for purchase—except for the 1946 and 1947 issues in large quantity. The same holds true for the purchase of the 1950s and 1951p type coins.

MS-65; MS-67—All sets and single type coins are most highly recommended in these true gem states.

PRICE PROJECTIONS

	1985				1990		
Issue	MS-60	MS-65	MS-67		MS-60	MS-65	MS-67
1946 Set	$105.	$ 175. +	$ 225. +		$195.	$ 325. +	$ 400. +
1947 Set	$145.	$ 320. +	$ 375. +		$230.	$ 550. +	$ 625. +
1948 Set	$205.	$ 600. +	$ 750. +		$360.	$ 950. +	$1150. +
1949 Set	$350.	$1050. +	$1450. +		$575.	$1800. +	$2250. +
1950 Set	$350.	$ 875. +	$1050. +		$550.	$1350. +	$1900. +
1951 Set	$275.	$ 775. +	$ 850. +		$360.	$1050. +	$1125. +
Type Coin	$ 50.	$ 75. +	$ 200. +		$ 50.	$ 125. +	$ 375. +

THE GEORGE WASHINGTON CARVER—BOOKER T. WASHINGTON HALF DOLLARS

As with the B.T.W. coinage, most of this issue resides in the uncirculated and choice uncirculated state for identical reasons—bag marks, gouges, numismatic abuse and especially poor strikes on G.W.C. cheekbones.

The 1951 and 1952 sets are not too difficult to locate at present, while the 1953 set has been labeled the king of the series. However, the 1954 set is rarer than the 1953 set (see the G.W.C. chapter) and at present (1980) sells for less than twice the price. In the very near future, the 1954 set will take over the title "king of the series." Naturally, the purchase of this set is highly recommended as well as the other years of issue, for a slow but steady demand will have these sets double and triple in value within the coming decade. True gem specimens, with full strikes (especially the 1952 P) do make their occasional appearance and should be immediately purchased. They are not as available as believed, for even upon inspecting original sets, that cheekbone on G.W.C. looks worn. Should you locate any issue aside from the '52-P where the cheekbone is covered with mint frost, lacking gouges and bag marks, then jump for joy!

In summary:
MS-60; MS-63—All sets are recommended for purchase. However, the purchase of 1951 P; 1952 P; 1953 S and 1954 S (type coins) in quantity is not recommended.
MS-65; MS-67—All sets and single type coins are most highly recommended in these true gem states.

PRICE PROJECTIONS

	1985				1990		
Issue	MS-60	MS-65	MS-67		MS-60	MS-65	MS-67
1951 Set	$120.	$350.+	$800.+		$260.	$ 600.+	$1300.+
1952 Set	$175.	$675.+	$800.+		$310.	$ 850.+	$1300.+
1953 Set	$310.	$700.+	$850.		$440.	$ 950.+	$1300.+
1954 Set	$290.	$925.+	$1100.+		$440.	$1400.+	$1800.+
Type Coin	$ 35.	$ 60.+	$200.+		$ 85.	$ 120.+	$ 350.+

THE WISCONSIN TERRITORIAL CENTENNIAL HALF DOLLAR

Virtually all of this issue exists in the uncirculated state. With determination, superb or gem (MS-67) specimens can be obtained. Its purchase is recommended especially since they are rapidly being absorbed by collectors and investors. There exists a present-day hoard of 92 pieces.

In summary:
MS-60; MS-63—Don't purchase in quantity at present.
MS-63—Recommended.
MS-65—Most recommended.
MS-67—Most highly recommended.

PRICE PROJECTIONS

	1985				1990	
MS-60	MS-65	MS-67		MS-60	MS-65	MS-67
$410.	$1450.+	$1750.+		$800.	$2200.+	$3300.+

THE YORK COUNTY, MAINE, HALF DOLLAR

The great majority of this issue exists in all uncirculated states, experiencing not a great deal of numismatic abuse. Its purchase is recommended at present only in the gem states. True gem specimens (MS-65) can be located with a little effort, but the demand for quality coins is rapidly changing this situation. Buy now, while the coin is still available in top condition.

In summary:
MS-60; MS-63—Don't purchase in quantity at present.
MS-65; MS-67—Recommended.

PRICE PROJECTIONS

1985				1990		
MS-60	MS-65	MS-67		MS-60	MS-65	MS-67
$410.	$3075.+	$3600.+		$800.	$4500.+	$5400.+

A GRADING GUIDE FOR THE COMMEMORATIVE COINAGE OF THE UNITED STATES OF AMERICA

Since more than 90 percent of those individuals who are interested in the U.S. Commemorative series want to purchase only uncirculated specimens—and not the almost uncirculated kind—I felt it necessary to point out those areas on the coin's surface that we in the numismatic field refer to as the coin's high points, or the coin's high spots, which upon inspection will reveal any initial indications of wear should such be present.

As many educated collectors and investors know, there is a big monetary difference between an A.U. specimen (almost new), that possesses criss-crossing friction lines on the high points that can be seen with the aid of some magnification (10X), and a new or uncirculated specimen.

Should you observe wear on a coin you are inspecting in the areas noted by arrows in the following grading section, I would say you most likely have an almost uncirculated coin. It is true that a coin can be flatly struck; however, such will be noted and you will be further advised on how to determine if the specimen is flatly struck, or if it is almost uncirculated.

Remember, an almost uncirculated coin is a coin that looks just like a new or uncirculated coin at first glance, but shows the smallest trace of wear from any cause upon closer examination. A loss of luster and a difference in the texture of the metal on the coin's one or more high spots, or high points, will be apparent due to the coin's loss of some metal from wear (friction).

My grading system—now adopted by the A.N.A. Grading Board and appearing in the *Official A.N.A. Grading Standards for United States Coins*—was developed over the past five years with the aid of a micrometer, as well as the visual inspection of many coins of each commemorative issue. Should any difference of opinion arise concerning this sytem, your inquiry will be most welcome. However, presented here is a new improved version of the above-mentioned system.

A.S.

THE ALABAMA CENTENNIAL HALF DOLLAR

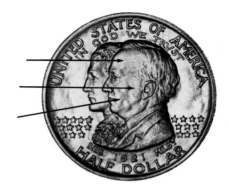

Obverse

Reverse

Obverse: Look for wear on the forehead of Governor Kilby and in the area to the left of his earlobe. The flatness on the curve of his upper ear is due to striking on a mint state specimen. Criss-cross scratches should be noted in the field and especially on Kilby's face.

Reverse: Wear will first be noted on the lower neck of the eagle and especially on the top of his wings. Do not be concerned about the flatness seen on the eagle's right leg. Die wear was responsible for such especially on the "plain" issue.

THE ALBANY CHARTER HALF DOLLAR

Obverse

Reverse

Obverse: Look for wear on the hip of the beaver. Visible will be a difference in the texture of the metal on the high point, caused by the loss of some metal from friction.

Reverse: Wear will first be noticed on Governor Dongan's sleeve.

THE ANTIETAM HALF DOLLAR

Obverse

Reverse

Obverse: Look for wear on the cheek bone of General Robert E. Lee.

Reverse: Wear will first be noticed on the leaves of the tree in the area indicated, as well as on the coin's rim.

THE ARKANSAS CENTENNIAL HALF DOLLARS

Obverse

Reverse

Obverse: Look for wear on the band of Liberty's cap in back of her eye, as well as criss-cross scratches on her cheek.

Reverse: Wear will first be noticed on the head of the eagle and on the top of his left wing. Please refer to the Arkansas section for the photograph showing a poorly struck uncirculated specimen.

327

THE ARKANSAS-ROBINSON HALF DOLLAR

Obverse

Reverse

Obverse: Wear will first be apparent on Senator Robinson's cheek bone.

Reverse: Wear will be observed on the eagle's head and on the top of his left wing.

THE BAY BRIDGE HALF DOLLAR

Obverse

Reverse

Obverse: Wear will be apparent on Monarch's left shoulder.

Reverse: The clouds above the San Francisco–Oakland Bay Bridge will show wear.

THE DANIEL BOONE BICENTENNIAL HALF DOLLARS

Obverse

Reverse

Obverse: Look for wear on the hair in back of and directly above Daniel Boone's ear and on the cheek bone.

Reverse: Wear will first be observed on the shoulder of Chief Black Fish.

THE BRIDGEPORT CENTENNIAL HALF DOLLAR

Obverse

Reverse

Obverse: Look for wear on the cheek bone of P. T. Barnum.

Reverse: Wear will be apparent on the eagle's wing in the area noted.

THE CALIFORNIA DIAMOND JUBILEE HALF DOLLAR

Obverse   *Reverse*

Obverse: Look for wear on the folds of the miner's shirt sleeve and shoulder.

Reverse: Wear will be apparent on the grizzly bear's shoulder, and in the area noted on his leg.

THE CINCINNATI HALF DOLLARS

Obverse   *Reverse*

Obverse: Look for wear on the hair in the area of Stephen Foster's temple and on the cheek bone.

Reverse: Wear will be apparent on the female's left bust.

THE CLEVELAND CENTENNIAL/GREAT LAKES EXPOSITION HALF DOLLAR

Obverse

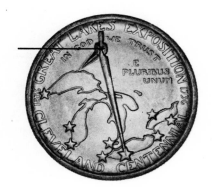

Reverse

Obverse: Look for wear on the hair in back of Moses Cleaveland's ear, as well as criss-cross scratches on his cheekbone, indicating friction and a loss of metal.

Reverse: Wear will be apparent on the compass top.

THE COLUMBIA, SOUTH CAROLINA, SESQUICENTENNIAL HALF DOLLAR

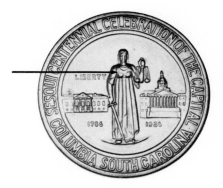

Obverse

Reverse

Obverse: Look for wear on the right breast of Justice.

Reverse: Wear will be apparent at the top of the palmetto tree.

THE COLUMBIAN EXPOSITION HALF DOLLAR

Obverse   *Reverse*

Obverse: Look for wear on the hair just below Columbus' forehead. Please note that this area can be flatly struck, showing little hair detail and showing what appears to be wear or a rub mark due to striking. Should this be the case, refer to the "high spots" on the reverse to determine if the coin in question possesses wear. Should criss-cross scratches be present on Columbus' cheekbone, grade the coin as almost uncirculated, provided wear is present on the reverse.

Reverse: Wear will be apparent on the top of the Santa Maria's rear sail and on the noted area of the Eastern Hemisphere.

THE COLUMBIAN EXPOSITION ISABELLA QUARTER DOLLAR

Obverse   *Reverse*

Obverse: Look for wear in the areas noted. However, due to die wear and/or striking, these areas may appear flat. Fortunately, such was not the case with the coin's reverse . However, should criss-cross scratches be present on the queen's cheek, grade the coin as almost uncirculated, provided wear is present on the reverse.

Reverse: Wear will be apparent on the strand of wool which appears to rest on the lower left thigh of the kneeling spinner. You will see a break in such, as if you had six inches of wool and cut two inches from the central portion, leaving a gap. The gap represents the worn strand of wool on the spinner's thigh.

THE CONNECTICUT TERCENTENARY HALF DOLLAR

Obverse

Reverse

Obverse: Look for wear on the base of the Charter Oak as noted.

Reverse: Wear will be apparent on the top section of the eagle's wing in the area indicated.

THE DELAWARE SWEDISH TERCENTENARY HALF DOLLAR

Obverse

Reverse

Obverse: Wear will be apparent in the center of the lower middle sail of the *Kalmar Nyckel*. However, this area may possess some fine scratches due to handling and cannot be considered wear! Should the discontinuity or difference in texture of the surface's high points of wear worry you, place a magnifying glass there. If you see many fine scratches here and on the coin's other high area of wear, you have an almost uncirculated coin.

Reverse: Look for wear on the section of The Old Swedes Church roof, as noted. The triangular top piece above the church's entrance will appear worn on many specimens, but such is due to striking by the mint.

THE ELGIN CENTENNIAL HALF DOLLAR

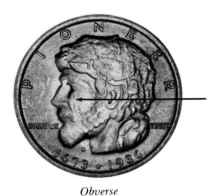

Obverse

Reverse

Obverse: Look for wear on the cheek bone of the bearded pioneer.

Reverse: Wear will be apparent on the pioneer's left shoulder. That's the one holding a rifle in his hands. Please note that the facial features on the pioneers will appear as a smear or blank on many specimens. Naturally, such is no indication of wear, but rather due to the way the coin was made or struck.

THE GETTYSBURG HALF DOLLAR

Obverse

Reverse

Obverse: Look for wear on the cheek bones of the Union and Confederate soldiers. Criss-cross scratches here will tell you your coin is almost uncirculated, provided such appears on the coin's reverse high points.

Reverse: Wear will be apparent on the three ribbons which bind the fasces. Again use a glass and look for criss-cross scratches in the aforementioned areas.

334

THE GRANT MEMORIAL ISSUES—GOLD AND SILVER

Obverse

Reverse

Obverse: Look for wear on the cheek bone and indicated areas of General Grant. Criss-cross scratches in the above-mentioned area will make your evaluation easier.

Reverse: Wear will occur on the leaves of the trees in the areas indicated. Should you have difficulty in making your evaluation—which most likely will be the case—refer to the obverse to be certain wear is present. If such is the case, grade the coin almost uncirculated.

THE HAWAIIAN OR CAPTAIN COOK SESQUICENTENNIAL HALF DOLLAR

Obverse

Reverse

Obverse: Look for wear on the cheek bone of Captain Cook and the roll of hair over his ear.

Reverse: Wear will be apparent on the left hand and fingers of the left hand of the Hawaiian warrior chief holding an erect spear. Also inspect the thighs and knees for slight friction.

THE HUDSON, NEW YORK, SESQUICENTENNIAL HALF DOLLAR

Obverse   *Reverse*

Obverse: Look for wear in the center of the lower middle sail of the *Half Moon*. Some fine scratches, due to handling, may be present in this area and such should not be considered wear. If also present on the reverse, your coin is almost uncirculated.

Reverse: Wear will be apparent on the letters of the city's motto ED DECUS ET PRETIUM RECTI which can be weakly struck. Be alert!

THE HUGUENOT–WALLOON TERCENTENARY HALF DOLLAR

Obverse   *Reverse*

Obverse: Look for wear on the cheek bone of Admiral Coligny.

Reverse: Wear will be apparent in the areas of the ships stern, the center of the main mast and the crow's nest.

THE ILLINOIS–LINCOLN CENTENNIAL HALF DOLLAR

Obverse

Reverse

Obverse: Look for wear on the hair above Lincoln's ear first. Then examine his cheek bone for criss-cross scratches that indicate wear. These marks occur in striking or stacking.

Reverse: Wear will be present on the breast of the eagle. However, due to striking, this area on many coins will be struck flat! Simply look for a difference in the texture of the metal with the aid of a magnifying glass to determine if actual wear is present.

THE IOWA STATEHOOD CENTENNIAL HALF DOLLAR

Obverse

Reverse

Obverse: Look for wear on the back of the head and neck of the eagle. However, due to striking, the back head area can be flatly struck.

Reverse: Wear will be present on the shafts of the Old Stone Capitol building.

THE LAFAYETTE SILVER DOLLAR

Obverse

Reverse

Obverse: Look for wear on the cheek bone of George Washington and on Lafayette's curl of hair in the area indicated.

Reverse: Wear will first be apparent on the fringe of the epaulet covering Lafayette's left shoulder, the horse's blinder and leg in the area indicated. The latter can exhibit a worn look even on true uncirculated due to striking or stacking.

THE LEWIS AND CLARK EXPOSITION GOLD DOLLARS

Obverse

Obverse

Reverse

Obverse: Look for wear in the temple area of Meriwether Lewis.

Reverse: Wear will be apparent in the temple area of William Clark. Due to die wear, a flatness of strike will appear on the gentlemen's heads—especially the hair—on some coins of each date. Look for the tell-tale criss-cross scratches, especially on the coin's portraits.

THE LEXINGTON–CONCORD SESQUICENTENNIAL
HALF DOLLAR

Obverse

Reverse

Obverse: Look for wear on the thighs of the Minute Man.

Reverse: Wear will be apparent on the edge of the Old Belfry.

THE LONG ISLAND TERCENTENARY HALF DOLLAR

Obverse

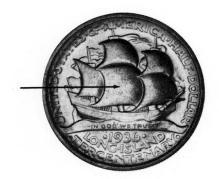

Reverse

Obverse: Look for wear on the cheek bone of the Dutch settler.

Reverse: Wear will be apparent on the center of the middle lower sail of the Dutch sailing ship. However, fine scratches may be present in this area which were caused by handling and cannot be considered wear! Check your obverse.

THE LOUISIANA PURCHASE GOLD DOLLARS

Obverse

Obverse

Reverse

Obverse: Look for wear on the cheek bone of Thomas Jefferson on the Jefferson variety and on the cheek bone of President McKinley on the McKinley variety. Due to die wear, a flatness of strike can be noted on each issue around the ear and in the hair above it. This is particularly noticeable on the Jefferson issue.

Reverse: Wear will be apparent on the words ONE DOLLAR and on the anniversary dates, 1803–1903.

THE LYNCHBURG, VIRGINIA, SESQUICENTENNIAL HALF DOLLAR

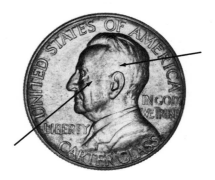

Obverse

Reverse

Obverse: Look for wear on the hair above the Senator's ear and then his cheek bone.

Reverse: Wear will be first apparent on the head of the standing figure Liberty and to a lesser degree on her breasts. Fine scratches may be noted on the obverse portrait and on Ms. Liberty's thigh. These are due to numismatic abuse or improper handling.

THE MAINE CENTENNIAL HALF DOLLAR

Obverse

Reverse

Obverse: Look for wear on the left hand of the male figure holding the scythe and on the right hand of the male figure who is resting on the anchor. The pine tree with a countersunk moose will appear worn. However, on true uncirculated pieces this was due to striking and should not be considered wear!

Reverse: Wear will be most apparent on the ribbon which forms a bow around the wreath of pine needles and cones. This area was not weakly struck! BEWARE!

THE MARYLAND TERCENTENARY HALF DOLLAR

Obverse

Reverse

Obverse: Look for wear on the nose of Cecil Calvert. Unfortunately, however, most of this issue possesses a nose that appears flatly struck, or worn. This condition was due to the striking and the stacking of these coins. Revert to the reverse to see if wear is present to determine if your coin is almost uncirculated.

Reverse: Wear will be apparent on the top of the smaller crown and on the drapery as indicated.

THE McKINLEY MEMORIAL GOLD DOLLARS

Obverse

Reverse

Obverse: Look for wear in the temple area of William McKinley.

Reverse: Wear will be observed in the areas indicated.

THE MISSOURI CENTENNIAL HALF DOLLARS

Obverse

Reverse

Obverse: Look for wear on the hair in back of the ear of the frontiersman. Beware of lightly whizzed specimens. Observe the frontiersman's face—which looks unbelievably gem perfect—for many fine scratches and that phoney aluminum luster.

Reverse: Wear will be apparent on the frontiersman's arm and shoulder.

THE MONROE DOCTRINE CENTENNIAL HALF DOLLAR

Obverse

Reverse

Obverse: Look for wear on the cheek of Quincy Adams.

Reverse: Wear will be most apparent for this issue on the arm of the female figure representing North America.

THE NEW ROCHELLE, NEW YORK, HALF DOLLAR

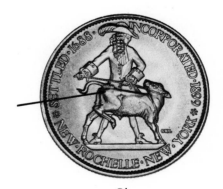

Obverse

Reverse

Obverse: Look for wear on the hip of the "fatte calfe."

Reverse: Wear will be apparent on the fleur de lis in the area indicated. However, on the center petal there appears a main vein, or midrib, which looks worn. This area is almost always struck flat and should not be looked upon as a worn specimen.

THE NORFOLK, VIRGINIA, BICENTENNIAL HALF DOLLAR

Obverse

Reverse

Obverse: Look for wear on the lower rear sail of the sailing ship.

Reverse: Wear will be apparent in the indicated area of the Royal Mace.

THE OREGON TRAIL MEMORIAL HALF DOLLARS

Obverse

Reverse

Obverse: First look for wear on the thumb and fingers of the Indian's left hand. Specimens exist of different dates within this issue which show his right hand (holding the bow) as a blob of metal, and thus we have no definition of a thumb or first finger. Such was due to striking as the coin was produced. Wear may next be observed on the Indian's knee and thigh.

Reverse: Wear will be apparent on the hip of the ox.

THE PANAMA–PACIFIC EXPOSITION ISSUES

HALF DOLLAR

Obverse   *Reverse*

Obverse: Look for wear on Columbia's left shoulder.

Reverse: Wear will be apparent on the eagle's breast. Due to striking, the eagle's claws can be flatly struck.

GOLD $1 ISSUE

Obverse   *Reverse*

Obverse: Look for wear on the peak of the laborer's cap and his cheek bone.

Reverse: Wear will be apparent on the letters ONE DOLLAR and on the heads of the two dolphins.

GOLD $2½ ISSUE

Obverse

Reverse

Obverse: Look for wear on Columbia's head, breast, knee and other indicated areas.

Reverse: Wear will be apparent below the base of the classical standard and the eagle's left leg. All high points—if worn—will display friction lines or criss-cross scratches.

GOLD $50 ISSUE

Obverse

Reverse

Obverse: Look for wear on the cheek of Minerva.

Reverse: Wear will be apparent on the owl's upper breast.

THE PILGRIM TERCENTENARY HALF DOLLARS

Obverse

Reverse

Obverse: Look for wear on the hair in the area covering Governor Bradford's ear, and on his cheek bone.

Reverse: Wear will be apparent on the crow's nest, on the stern (rear of the ship) and on the rim.

THE PROVIDENCE, RHODE ISLAND, TERCENTENARY HALF DOLLARS

Obverse

Reverse

Obverse: Look for wear on the right shoulder of the Indian.

Reverse: Wear will be apparent in the center of the anchor of Hope. Mishandling marks will be plentiful in this area on many specimens. Should such be present on the obverse high point of wear, your coin is almost uncirculated.

THE ROANOKE SIR WALTER RALEIGH—VIRGINIA DARE HALF DOLLAR

Obverse

Reverse

Obverse: Look for wear on the brim of Sir Walter Raleigh's hat.

Reverse: Wear will first be apparent on Virginia Dare's head and upper left arm.

THE SAN DIEGO (CALIFORNIA–PACIFIC INTERNATIONAL EXPOSITION) HALF DOLLARS

Obverse

Reverse

Obverse: Look for wear on Minerva's knees. However, this area may possess some fine scratches due to handling and cannot be considered wear. Full mint luster, if present, will make your evaluation easier.

Reverse: Wear will be apparent on the top right edge of the California Tower. Unfortunately, most of the 1936-Denver issue was flatly struck in this area, as well as the area one-third the way downwards with the design beginning to appear just slightly above and to the left of the "1" in the date 1936. Simply make sure there is no difference in the texture of the surface in this area when examining the coin. Should these criss-cross friction lines be present on this issue's high points of wear—even if flatly struck—the coin is almost uncirculated.

348

THE SESQUICENTENNIAL (PHILADELPHIA) ISSUES

HALF DOLLAR

Obverse

Reverse

Obverse: Look for wear on the cheek bone of George Washington. With practice, one will be able to observe the difference between an almost uncirculated and uncirculated coin.

Reverse: Wear will be apparent just below the lower inscription on the Liberty Bell.

THE 2½ GOLD ISSUE

Obverse

Reverse

Obverse: Look for wear on the bottom part of the scroll held by Liberty and upper left thigh.

Reverse: Wear will be apparent in the areas indicated on Independence Hall.

THE OLD SPANISH TRAIL HALF DOLLAR

Obverse

Reverse

Obverse: Look for wear on the top of the cow's head.

Reverse: Wear will be first apparent on the inscription OLD SPANISH TRAIL. Additional wear can be observed on the lower central portion of the yucca tree.

THE STONE MOUNTAIN HALF DOLLAR

Obverse

Reverse

Obverse: Look for wear on the elbow of General Lee.

Reverse: Wear will be apparent on the eagle's breast.

THE TEXAS CENTENNIAL HALF DOLLARS

Obverse

Reverse

Obverse: Look for wear on the eagle's upper leg and upper breast.

Reverse: Wear will be first apparent on the forehead of Victory, followed by wear on her knee—which can be flatly struck.

THE FORT VANCOUVER CENTENNIAL HALF DOLLAR

Obverse

Reverse

Obverse: Look for wear in the temple area of Dr. John McLoughlin.

Reverse: Wear will be apparent on the pioneer's right knee, which will exhibit a definite difference in the texture of the metal or surface in this area.

THE VERMONT SESQUICENTENNIAL HALF DOLLAR

Obverse

Reverse

Obverse: Look for wear on the hair in the temple area of Ira Allen, as well as his cheek.

Reverse: Wear will be apparent on the upper shoulder of the wildcat.

THE BOOKER T. WASHINGTON HALF DOLLARS

Obverse

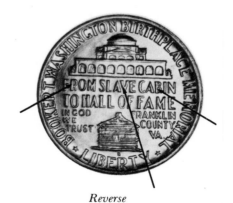

Reverse

Obverse: Look for wear on the cheek bone of Booker T. Washington.

Reverse: Wear will be apparent on the inscription: FROM SLAVE CABIN TO HALL OF FAME.

THE BOOKER T. WASHINGTON—GEORGE WASHINGTON CARVER HALF DOLLAR

Obverse

Reverse

Obverse: Look for wear on the cheek bone of George Washington Carver, but remember this area was very poorly struck except for the 1952–Philadelphia issue.

Reverse: Wear will be apparent on the letters U.S.A. Look for criss-cross friction lines in the aforementioned areas.

THE WISCONSIN TERRITORIAL CENTENNIAL HALF DOLLAR

Obverse

Reverse

Obverse: Wear will be apparent on the miner's hand seen holding a pickaxe.

Reverse: Look for wear on the shoulder of the badger.

THE YORK COUNTY, MAINE, TERCENTENARY HALF DOLLAR

Obverse

Reverse

Obverse: Wear will be apparent on the mounted sentry and on the coin's rim.

Reverse: Look for wear on the pine tree in the upper quarter of the shield and on the coin's rim.

BIBLIOGRAPHY

American Numismatic Association. *Official ANA Grading Standards for U.S. Coins.* Racine, Wisconsin: Western Publishing Co., 1978.

Becker, Thomas W. *Pageant of World Commemorative Coins.* Racine, Wisconsin: Whitman Publishing, 1962.

Biographical Directory of American Congress, 1774–1971. Senate Document 92–8, 92nd Congress, 1st Session. Washington: Government Printing Office, 1971.

Breen, Walter. *Encyclopedia of U.S. and Colonial Proof Coins, 1722–1977.* Albertson, N.Y.: FCI Press, 1977.

Bullowa, David M. *The Commemorative Coinage of the United States.* New York: The American Numismatic Society, 1938.

Deering, Frank C. *The Proprietors of Saco.* Saco, Maine: York National Bank, 1931.

Gettys, Loyd B., and Catich, Edward M. "AU or BU." *Numismatist,* Aug. 1958:899–915, reprinted by ANA (var. eds.) and in Bagg, Richard, and Jelinski, James J., *Grading Coins: A Collection of Readings.* Portsmouth, New Hampshire: Essex Publications, 1977.

Hessler, Gene. *Standard Catalogue of U.S. Paper Money.* Chicago: Regnery, var. eds.

Judd, Dr. J. Hewitt, Breen, Walter, and Kosoff, Abe. *U.S. Pattern, Experimental and Trial Pieces.* 6th ed. Racine, Wisconsin: Western Publishing Co., 1978.

Núñez Cabeza de Vaca, Alvar. *Los Naufragios.* var. eds., originally 1542.

Raymond, Wayte, compiler. *Standard Catalogue of U.S. Coins.* N.Y.: Wayte Raymond, Inc., 1957.

Scott's Specialized U.S. Stamp Catalogue. New York: Scott Publications, var. eds.

Skipton, Amy C. "One Fatt Calfe." New Rochelle, N.Y.: New Rochelle Commemorative Coin Commission, 1939.

Slabaugh, Arlie R. *United States Commemorative Coinage.* Racine, Wisconsin: Whitman Publishing, 1963; rev. ed., 1976.

Taxay, Don. *An Illustrated History of U.S. Commemorative Coinage.* New York: Arco Publishing, 1967.

Vermeule, Cornelius. *Numismatic Art in America: Aesthetics of U.S. Coinage.* Cambridge: Harvard University Press, 1971.

Wood, Howland. *The Commemorative Coinage of the United States of America.* New York: The American Numismatic Society, 1922.

Also used in preparing this book were numerous U.S. government reports, texts of laws, contemporaneous newspapers, coin auction catalogues, *World Almanac* and similar compilations, *The Congressional Record,* and many issues of the following publications: *American Journal of Numismatics, Mehl's Numismatic Monthly, The Coin Collector's Journal, The Numismatist, The Numismatic Scrapbook Magazine, Coins,* and *CoinAge.*

INDEX